D0991480

3995
9-88
u

KF

Corporatism and the Rule of Law

CORPORATISM AND
THE RULE OF LAW

A Study of the
National Recovery Administration

Donald R. Brand

Cornell University Press

ITHACA AND LONDON

353.0082
B81c

Copyright © 1988 by Cornell University

All rights reserved. Except for brief quotations in a review, this book, or parts thereof, must not be reproduced in any form without permission in writing from the publisher. For information, address Cornell University Press, 124 Roberts Place, Ithaca, New York 14850.

First published 1988 by Cornell University Press.

International Standard Book Number 0-8014-2169-1 (cloth)
International Standard Book Number 0-8014-9495-8 (paper)
Library of Congress Catalog Card Number 88-7167
Printed in the United States of America
Librarians: Library of Congress cataloging information
appears on the last page of the book.

mR.

The paper in this book is acid-free and meets the guidelines for
permanence and durability of the Committee on Production Guidelines
for Book Longevity of the Council on Library Resources.

To my wife, Jacqueline

University Libraries
Carnegie Mellon University
Pittsburgh, Pennsylvania 15213

Contents

Acknowledgments

First and foremost, I want to thank Paul Peterson for his encouragement of this project and his guidance and useful comments at almost every stage. In addition, Theodore Lowi graciously agreed to read the manuscript and offered helpful suggestions for revisions; my criticisms of his theories do not detract from my respect for him as a scholar. Kenneth Finegold, David Greenstone, Ed Haefele, Paul Quirk, Lloyd Rudolph, Philippe Schmitter, Fred Siegel, Karol Soltan, and an anonymous reviewer all made contributions even when they disagreed with me. The manuscript would undoubtedly have been stronger if the advice of the late Herbert Storing had been available. His influence on my thinking will be apparent to everyone who had him as a teacher or who is familiar with his work.

Without the generous financial support of the Brookings Institution and the American Council of Learned Societies, this project would never have been completed. Archivists Jerry Clark and Jerry Hess helped me sort through the voluminous NRA materials in the National Archives, and the staff of the Franklin Delano Roosevelt Presidential Library in Hyde Park, New York, was equally helpful on a number of occasions. Blair Berman and David Feltenstal, able student assistants, saved me many hours of work.

I owe a special debt of gratitude to my parents, to my wife, Jacqueline, and to Wilbur and Josephine Curd for sustained support during difficult years. John Cook, Ester Fuchs, Joanne Gowa, Ruth and Steve Grant, David Mayers, Sidney Milkis, David Schaefer, Leonard Sorenson, Paul Stern, Peter Swenson, and Doris Wolin provided friendship and intellectual companionship for many years. Finally, I owe my interest in political science to the influence of Craig Brown and the late Robert Gaudino during my undergraduate days.

DONALD R. BRAND

Mt. Laurel, New Jersey

Corporatism and the Rule of Law

Introduction: Theodore Lowi
and American Corporatism

One of the distinctive characteristics of governments in modern industrial societies is the important role that bureaucracies play in the policy process. Because many of the critical governmental decisions affecting the rights of individuals and the distribution of resources in modern society are now made by bureaucracies, many scholars characterize our times as the era of the administrative state. In the United States the foundations for this administrative state were laid in the late nineteenth century, when Congress became increasingly unwilling to mediate or incapable of mediating the conflicts and addressing the problems of a modern industrial economy through relatively specific statutes.[1] To cope with the problems of governance arising during this period, Congress delegated its responsibilities to administrative agencies staffed by experts through broad and vague authorizing statutes that in some cases provided little more guidance to administrators than the exhortation that the powers be exercised to secure the public interest. These broad delegations of power vastly expanded the scope of discretionary decision making in the bureaucracy.

The problem posed by broad discretion has been a major preoccupation of lawyers, judges, and legal scholars. From the vantage point of the legal profession, excessive discretion is objectionable because it jeopardizes individual rights. Of even more direct concern, unbounded, unstructured, and unchecked discretion is the antithesis of the Rule of Law, one of the constitutive norms of the legal profession. It is hardly surprising, therefore, that the rise of the administrative state has frequently evoked concern from those in this profession.[2]

1. Peter Woll, *American Bureaucracy*, 2d ed. (New York, 1977), pp. 35–75; Lawrence C. Dodd and Richard L. Schott, *Congress and the Administrative State* (New York, 1979), pp. 1–3, 16–34; Stephen Skowronek, *Building a New American State: The Expansion of National Administrative Capacities, 1877–1920* (Cambridge, 1982), pp. 11–14, 34–35, 285–288.
2. The classic expression of this concern remains A. V. Dicey, *Introduction to the Study of the Law of the Constitution* (New York, 1885).

To a considerable extent, administrative law has developed in response to the threat that administrative discretion poses to rights and to the rule of law. Comprised of such statutes as the 1946 Administrative Procedure Act (APA), of constitutional and common law cases, and of agency-made law, administrative law has attempted to confine discretion within the boundaries established by the U.S. Constitution and by statutes, to structure the exercise of discretion by formalizing the procedures through which decisions are made, and to check discretion by providing for review of decisions by administrative appeals boards, the political branches, and the courts. As impressive as the achievements of administrative law have been, however, many administrative law scholars still believe that much of the administrative process has eluded administrative law constraints on discretion. It has been estimated, for instance, that as much as 90 percent of the business of administrative agencies is carried out informally, unregulated by the Administrative Procedure Act and often beyond the reach of judicial review.[3] This has led one of our most prominent administrative law scholars, Kenneth Culp Davis, to conclude: "Government at all levels in the United States is shot through with excessive discretionary power. Such power far exceeds what is necessary for an industrialized society, as is conclusively shown by the relative success of the countries of Western Europe in limiting such power."[4] Davis recommended a number of reforms that addressed the problem of excessive discretion, but he is most noted for his advocacy of a more extensive use of rules and of the rulemaking procedures of the APA in the administrative process.[5]

Despite Davis's concerns regarding administrative discretion and its potential abuses, he was still sensitive to the need for flexibility if government was to fulfill its responsibilities. For this reason, Davis rejected the possibility that excessive discretion could be substantially eliminated if Congress would simply refuse to delegate power unless the delegations were accompanied by clear standards to guide administrators. This "nondelegation doctrine," immortalized in American constitutional law in *A.L.A. Schechter Poultry Co. v. U.S.,*[6] would in Davis's view not only eliminate unnecessary discretion but also deprive administrators of the discretion they need in order to govern effectively. As an alternative to the nondelegation doctrine, Davis recommended a less rigid and more multifaceted approach to the problem of administrative discretion, which focused on the character of the administrative process rather than on the initial congressional delegation.

Similarly, for Davis the marked preference that regulatory agencies have

3. Kenneth Culp Davis, *Administrative Law Text*, 3d ed. (St. Paul, Minn., 1972), p. 88.
4. Ibid., p. 92.
5. Kenneth Culp Davis, *Discretionary Justice: A Preliminary Inquiry* (Urbana, Ill., 1971), pp. 219–226.
6. 295 U.S. 495 (1935).

shown for using adjudication procedures and proceeding on a case-by-case basis rather than relying on rulemaking procedures is not per se a criticism of regulatory agencies. In some cases, Davis argues, regulatory agencies have indeed overused adjudication where rulemaking would be more appropriate. In settled areas of administration where problems are standardized and recurrent and where a ruling in a case will be tacitly used as a rule in resolving other conflicts, formal rulemaking is preferable because it confines the discretion of administrators in a salutary fashion and allows all the interests that may be affected to be represented more effectively than in adjudication, where only the immediate parties to the case are fully represented. But in areas where administration faces new problems, where the consequences of potential rules are uncertain and misconceived rules could be harmful, or in areas where the problems administrators face tend to be more idiosyncratic and where a reliance on rules would hinder the achievement of government goals or work injustices, the greater flexibility of adjudication is valuable. The greater discretion that adjudication permits can be adequately controlled by an appropriate degree of deference to precedents, the time-honored technique of the common law. Davis rejects what he considers an "extravagant" version of the rule of law that simply identifies the rule of law with an exclusive reliance on rules in governance.[7]

In the 1960s and 1970s the moderation that characterized much of Kenneth Culp Davis's approach to administrative law was largely abandoned by a new generation of scholars who were more committed to legal formalism. Advocating a more rigid conception of the rule of law which identified law with rules and principles, these scholars were intensely suspicious of discretionary authority. John Rawls, the preeminent theorist of this era, exemplified the spirit of the times when he defined a legal system as "a coercive order *of public rules* addressed to rational persons for the purpose of regulating their conduct and providing the framework for social cooperation."[8] Rawls's discussions of the rule of law were relatively limited, for a political theorist he was most interested in the rule of law as an application of his theory of formal justice. But the broader jurisprudential implications of his theory were soon developed by others, such as Ronald Dworkin, who propounded a theory of legal decision making that emphasized its principled and rule-bound character.[9]

Among political scientists this trend was both fostered and epitomized in the work of Theodore Lowi. Like other legal formalists of the 1970s, Lowi identifies justice and the rule of law with governance by general rules. "Considerations of the justice in, or achieved by, an action cannot be made unless a deliberate and conscious attempt was made to derive the

---

7. Davis, *Administrative Law Text*, pp. 15–23, 43–46, 51–52, 99–102, 352–354; Davis, *Discretionary Justice*, pp. 15–21, 65–68.

8. John Rawls, *A Theory of Justice* (Cambridge, Mass., 1971), p. 235. Emphasis added.

9. Ronald Dworkin, *Taking Rights Seriously* (Cambridge, Mass., 1978).

action from a preexisting general rule or moral principle governing such a class of actions.''[10] Examining the American administrative state from this perspective, he is distressed far more than Kenneth Culp Davis by its heavy reliance on discretionary authority. Broad delegations of power without standards and case-by-case administration have been the norm rather than the exception for important regulatory programs since the New Deal. Lowi, in contrast to Davis, argues that broad delegations of power without clear standards are inconsistent with the rule of law and that any discretion beyond the minimal amount necessary to apply the standards to particular cases is unnecessary discretion.[11] He appeals for a return to the *Schechter* decision's restrictive version of the nondelegation doctrine. Lowi is also more unrestrained than Davis in advocating ''a requirement for early and frequent administrative rule-making'' because he believes the ''ideal of case-by-case administration [i.e., adjudication] is in most instances a myth.''[12] He equates adjudication with ad hoc decision making and unprincipled bargaining, largely ignoring the fact that adjudication that relies on precedents is neither totally ad hoc nor totally unprincipled. Lowi refers to his ensemble of proposed reforms as juridical democracy.

Lowi is concerned with discretionary administration because he believes it allows interest groups to capture public authority and use it to further their private interests at the expense of the public good. This assertion elaborates a well-established theme in political science. In *Regulating Business by Independent Commission*, Marver Bernstein presented a classic version of this argument in the 1950s concerning independent regulatory commissions. In the modern regulatory state, Bernstein argued, many of the critical policy decisions are made in the administrative arena, far removed from public attention but intensely scrutinized by powerful and well-organized private interests that have much to gain and to lose from administrative decisions. When Congress entrusts administrators with a great deal of discretionary authority and provides little ongoing guidance regarding its proper exercise, administrators will look to other sources for cues in decision making. When those administrators are also relatively free from presidential supervision, as independent regulatory commissioners were in the 1950's, the relevant cues are likely to come from the very businessmen whom Congress had established the regulatory commissions to regulate. The public is victimized by this process because captured regulatory agencies generally protect regulated firms from healthy competition and foster economic inefficiency, and it is equally objectionable on the grounds that it enhances the power of oligarchical business

10. Theodore Lowi, *The End of Liberalism*, 2d ed. (New York, 1979), p. 296.
11. Ibid., pp. 92–93.
12. Ibid., pp. 302–303.

elites and undermines the control of policy making by broad democratic majorities.[13]

Lowi's analysis of the relationship between discretionary authority and captured authority is a radicalization of Bernstein's thesis. Bernstein's account of the problems with discretionary administration focused much more narrowly on the problems that broad delegations of power to independent regulatory agencies posed for the policy process.[14] Lowi generalizes this criticism of independent regulatory agencies, for he finds it as applicable to the Department of Commerce, the Department of Labor, the Department of Agriculture, and other government agencies under the direct supervision of the president of the United States as to the independent regulatory agencies, which are distinguished formally from regular departments by their relative autonomy from presidential supervision. Capture is a pervasive characteristic of the American administrative state.[15] Lowi refers to this system of captured authority as "interest group liberalism," although it is more commonly referred to as "corporatism."[16]

This pattern of politics is disturbing, not only because it is pervasive but also because it has become rationalized and legitimated by a new public philosophy and is therefore highly resistant to criticism and to change. In some cases cooperation between interest group elites and public officials has even become formally institutionalized, with groups being delegated legal authority to participate in policy making and policy implementation. Lowi believes that the new public philosophy that legitimates such arrangements was derived from the pluralist theory prominent in political science during the 1950s. He argues that this version of pluralism, exemplified in the work of David Truman and Robert Dahl, legitimated decision making by interest group bargaining, a form of ad hoc decision making that Lowi believes is antithetical to the rule of law. In the 1960s this pluralist theory was popularized—apparently through the works of Arthur Schlesinger, Jr., and John Kenneth Galbraith—and pluralism captured the public mind.[17]

Pluralism could be popularized because it shared with classical liberal

13. Marver Bernstein, *Regulating Business by Independent Commission* (Princeton, 1955), pp. 86–89, 251–260, 291–296.

14. Ibid., pp. 282–284.

15. Lowi, pp. 67–91, 310.

16. The term "interest group liberalism" is misleading. If, as Lowi argues, interest group liberalism is antithetical to the rule of law, then use of the term "liberalism" to describe this system is inappropriate, because a commitment to the rule of law has been one of the defining characteristics of liberalism. Lowi adopts the term because he mistakenly believes that "liberalism is hostile to law." He therefore generally presents himself as a critic of liberalism even though his commitment to individual rights and to the rule of law clearly identifies him as a liberal. We will substitute the term "corporatism" for interest group liberalism, although in discussing Lowi's theory occasional references to interest group liberalism are unavoidable. See ibid., p. 92.

17. Ibid., pp. 37–39, 53–54.

economics a conception of competition as a self-regulating mechanism, an affinity that has presumably facilitated the absorption of pluralist thought by political actors reared on classical liberal economics. At the same time, pluralism differed from classical liberal economics in its capacity to accommodate the activist state that had emerged during the New Deal and had discredited the latter system of thought. Emphasizing the differences between the politics of laissez-faire capitalism rationalized by classical liberal economics, and the New Deal and post-New Deal politics rationalized by pluralism, Lowi argues that the New Deal marked a crucial turning point in American politics, a transformation so profound that it should be referred to as a regime change. However, although a radically new pattern of politics emerged during the New Deal, it was not until the 1960s, when the popularized version of pluralism finally became the dominant public philosophy of the United States, that this corporatist pattern of politics became truly institutionalized.

Lowi is a relentless critic of corporatism because he sees it both as undemocratic and unjust and as inimical to rational and efficient government. We will examine each of these charges briefly.

First corporatism undermines democracy because it permits an oligarchical elite to control the political process. Corporatism institutionalizes interest group bargaining as a mode of decision making, and this heavily favors well-organized, established groups at the expense of poorly organized groups. Lowi's assertion should not be confused with the claim advanced by Marxists, among others, that the political process is controlled by a business elite or by the capitalist class. Lowi believes that "the Marxist critique of capitalism is overwhelming" when it comes to describing nineteenth-century laissez-faire America, but he also believes that the pluralizing tendencies of modern industrial life, combined with the political consequences of the New Deal, have shattered the hegemony of the capitalist class and compelled them to share their power with union, agricultural, and professional elites. What is crucial for Lowi, however, is that twentieth-century reform movements have succeeded in doing no more than compelling oligarchy to broaden its base; they have not brought about genuine democracy or made significant progress toward achieving social justice.[18]

Second, according to Lowi, corporatism is irrational and inefficient. Lowi asserts that rationality and efficiency in government depend on planning, an activity that only centralized, sovereign states can carry out successfully. In a corporatist system, policy making and policy implementation are either delegated directly to private groups or delegated to administrators who take their bearings from the decentralized network of organized interest groups that scrutinize their decisions. As policies

18. Ibid., pp. 31–32, 58–60, 81–82, 273, 295, 298.

become divorced from one another in quasi-feudal fiefdoms, it becomes impossible to coordinate and integrate policies in a coherent fashion. Furthermore, because only the well organized are represented in these decentralized policy networks, many important but diffuse interests are ignored. Finally, planning entails a willingness to coerce, for any rational plan will disadvantage some interests and advantage others. Corporatism, however, is characterized by a preference for consensual decision making and bargaining among interest group elites. Rationality is sacrificed to short-term political considerations.[19]

Lowi's generalization of capture theory has significant implications for a program of political reform. Earlier critics of capture had generally argued that the phenomena reflected the incapacity of independent agencies to sustain a regulatory program that would antagonize well-organized interests. While broad delegations of power were one of the conditions that allowed capture, it was primarily the concept of an independent regulatory commission that they attacked. Discretion in the hands of the U.S. president, who had the ability to mobilize democratic coalitions that independent agencies lacked, was presumed to have more salutary political consequences. Hence, these early critics of capture generally proposed the abolition of independent agencies and the vesting of regulatory responsibilities in departments subject to presidential control.[20] Lowi's proposed reforms, which collectively would come close to abolishing discretionary governance altogether, are more radical because he believes the problem of capture is more widespread. Legal formalist perspectives like Lowi's played a prominent role in the reform movement of the 1960s and 1970s.

Juridical Democracy?

The 1960s and 1970s was a period of sweeping change in the American political system. Many of the reforms of these decades sought to confine administrative discretion by introducing greater legal formalism into the administrative process. A "due process revolution" imposed a variety of new procedural restrictions on the administrative process, including expanded requirements for administrative hearings, greater freedom of information, and a much wider scope for judicial review of administrative action—all of which significantly curtailed the discretion that administrators had enjoyed while the New Deal legacy prevailed.[21] Regulatory agencies demonstrated a new willingness to use rulemaking procedures in place of adjudicatory procedures.[22] Even Lowi's criticism of vague dele-

19. Ibid., pp. 58–61, 67, 296.
20. M. Bernstein, pp. 101, 284–287.
21. Jerry L. Mashaw, *Due Process in the Administrative State* (New Haven, 1985), pp. 1–49.
22. Antonin Scalia, "Back to Basics: Making Law without Making Rules," *Regulation*, July–August 1981, p. 25.

gations of powers appears to have been influential, especially in the drafting of extraordinarily specific environmental protection laws during the 1970s.[23] By 1980 the Supreme Court had even tentatively hinted that it might revive the nondelegation doctrine.[24]

The reforms inspired by legal formalist concerns, however, often had unintended consequences that raised serious questions regarding the viability of the legal formalist ideal. One of the more notable examples of this concerned the rulemaking procedures of the Consumer Product Safety Commission (CPSC), which was created during the height of the reform movement during the 1970s. To prevent the commission from becoming captured by the business interests it was responsible for regulating, reformers drastically curtailed its discretionary powers in rulemaking. The authorizing statute of the commission permitted any private citizen to petition the agency for establishment of a rule setting product safety standards and compelled the agency to respond to these petitions within 120 days. If the commission rejected the petition for a rule, it had to publish its reasons for doing so in the *Federal Register* and the decision was subject to judicial review. Rulemaking proceedings initiated by this procedure were bound by statutory time limits and had to include an oral hearing. These procedures proved disastrous for the agency. Overwhelmed with petitions, many concerning trivial or useless subjects, it could not establish its own regulatory agenda. By 1981, Congress recognized the inefficiency of these procedures and repealed the provisions for them in the authorizing statute of the CPSC.[25]

Critics of the 1960s and 1970s reformers cited examples like the history of rulemaking at the CPSC to question the impact of legal formalist reforms on effective governance. Is rulemaking, especially when circumscribed by extensive due process protections, an excessively conflictual and time-consuming affair with little to show for great effort? Under many conditions, would not negotiation and bargaining between private parties and between government and private parties be a more productive form of conflict resolution? Is there not a danger that a legalistically oriented administration can become blinded to its overriding goal or purpose in its quest for a legally correct solution? A growing number of studies indicate that in many cases an affirmative answer can be given to each of these questions.[26]

A second set of questions focuses on the relationship of legal formalism

23. Alfred Marcus, "Environmental Protection Agency," in *The Politics of Regulation*, ed. James Q. Wilson (New York, 1980), pp. 269–274.

24. *Industrial Union Department, AFL-CIO v. American Petroleum Institute*, 448 U.S. 607 (1980).

25. Mashaw, pp. 261–263.

26. Donald Horowitz, *The Courts and Social Policy* (Washington D.C., 1977); R. Shep Melnick, *Regulation and the Courts* (Washington D.C., 1983); Peter H. Schuck, "Litigation, Bargaining, and Regulation," *Regulation*, July–August 1979, pp. 26–34.

to the spirit of American political institutions. Legal formalism implies a faith in the capacity of law to establish boundaries that confine the exercise of power. Law confines discretion, and discretion is an indispensable precondition for the exercise of power. A legal formalist strategy can therefore be characterized as an attempt to prevent abuses of power by limiting executive and administrative power altogether.

James Madison, the chief architect of the U.S. Constitution, doubted that law alone (including the fundamental law of the Constitution) would suffice to constrain power. It was because he rejected this premise that he argued against a strict separation of government powers and in favor of a more flexible separation of powers modified by a system of checks and balances.

> Will it be sufficient to mark, with precision, the boundaries of these departments in the constitution of the government, and to trust to *these parchment barriers* against the encroaching spirit of power? This is the security which appears to have been principally relied on by the compilers of most of the American constitutions. But experience assures us that the efficacy of the provision has been greatly overrated; and that some more adequate defense is indispensably necessary for the more feeble against the more powerful members of the government.[27]

The institutional strategy of the American Framers generally rejected the possibility of preventing abuses of administrative power by legalistically precluding its exercise in the first place. Emphasizing that it was necessary to grant power to secure the proper ends of government, their strategy favored granting powers and checking those who exercised them by fortifying other centers' of power that could oppose potential abuses.

Questioning whether legal formalism is compatible with effective governance and consistent with the spirit of American political institutions can cast doubt on the normative framework that informs Lowi's work (and thereby implicitly cast doubt on the normative framework of other legal formalists of the 1960s and 1970s), but without further analysis challenging the empirical foundations of Lowi's theory, neither of these lines of questioning is sufficient. Demonstrating that legal formalism impaired effective governance in the 1960s and 1970s does not undermine Lowi's assertions that discretionary administration subverts democracy, effective governance, and the achievement of justice. It may well suggest that we are confronted with an unhappy choice between the defects associated with legal formalism and the defects associated with discretionary administration. If Lowi has correctly assessed the costs of the latter, critics of legal formalism will be hard-pressed to demonstrate that the costs of the former are even more onerous.

27. Alexander Hamilton, James Madison, and John Jay, *The Federalist Papers* (reprint; New York, 1961), pp. 308–309. Emphasis added.

Moreover, Lowi, with some justification, argues that the decades of the 1960s and 1970s were not an era of juridical democracy and that the consequences associated with the era cannot be attributed to the particular brand of legal formalism he advocated in his proposals for reform. A different mixture of reforms promoting legal formalism, particularly a mix that placed greater emphasis on the nondelegation doctrine than reformers in the 1960s and 1970s did, might have had more salutary consequences. Similarly, Lowi argues that the reforms of those two decades did not go far enough and that the problems of this era are still attributable to the failure to constrain discretionary administration adequately rather than to the "modest" reforms favoring legal formalism.[28]

The argument that juridical democracy is inconsistent with the Constitution and the spirit of American political institutions is no more conclusive against Lowi than the argument that legal formalism impedes government efficiency. While it is true that the framers relied more heavily on a proper structuring of the political process than they did on legal formalism to check the abuses of discretionary authority, the efficacy of their institutional strategy presupposed certain conclusions regarding the character of interest group politics. The institutional mechanisms of separation of powers and checks and balances were only "auxiliary precautions" against abuses of government power, in part because such institutional devices could do no more than retard the victory of a determined factious majority, the danger most feared by the framers. The framers ultimately relied on the salutary characteristics of pluralist politics in an "enlarged republic" to assure good government and respect for individual rights. If the framers' more fundamental arguments concerning the salutary effects of pluralist politics were to prove erroneous, the logic of their separation of powers and checks and balances perspective would be vulnerable as well.

Lowi's criticisms of interest group politics are a repudiation of the American framers' defense of pluralism, although the repudiation is not self-evident. Lowi confines his criticisms of pluralism to the normative defense of a pluralist polity developed by 1950s pluralists, such as David Truman and Robert Dahl. Madison's argument for pluralism in Federalist Paper No. 10 is seemingly treated with greater respect.[29] Lowi even stresses that his concern is with pluralist politics invading the administrative sphere, not with pluralist politics in the legislative sphere. If groups are bargaining over rules—which is to say if groups are bargaining over clearly defined statutes in the legislature and to a lesser extent over administratively fashioned rules in the bureaucracy—then, Lowi argues, pluralist politics is acceptable. Despite this concession to pluralism, Lowi is imposing constraints on pluralist politics (primarily in the legislature

28. Lowi, pp. 274–280.
29. Ibid., pp. 32–36, 55, 58.

and resulting only in clearly defined rules) that are not found in the framers' defense of pluralism and that were inconsistent with their commitment to flexible, discretionary administration.[30] Lowi imposes these constraints because he believes that pluralist politics in the context of discretionary administration advances the interests of well-organized private interests, whereas the framers had argued that pluralism under these conditions would facilitate the emergence of the public good.

To confront the challenge that Lowi's thesis poses to the American political tradition, we must examine the character of interest group politics in the modern American administrative state.

The National Recovery Administration

Scholars have unanimously referred to the National Recovery Administration (NRA), an early New Deal program that governed the U.S. economy from 1933 to 1935, as America's foremost experiment with corporatism.[31] The National Industrial Recovery Act (NIRA), the statute that authorized the NRA, was simultaneously an attempt to promote industrial recovery from the depression and an attempt to reform the American economy. Based on the belief that the hardship of the depression would have been more tolerable if the available work had been distributed more widely among workers, the NIRA had provisions for developing restrictions on the maximum number of hours that workers could work in each industry. To compensate those who were already working for the reduced wages that would accompany reduced hours, and to enhance total labor purchasing power, the NIRA also had provisions for developing minimum-wage requirements that would vary from industry to industry. Because business would bear substantially increased costs from these reforms, and because business cooperation was essential to the success of the NIRA, the NIRA compensated business by relaxing antitrust laws to permit trade associations to draft codes of fair trade competition that became a "law merchant" for all members of the relevant industry. If these codes could

30. The commitment of the American framers to flexible and discretionary administration is a logical implication of the treatment of administration in *The Federalist Papers*. There the distinction between policy-making, which is inherently discretionary, and administration is blurred by an expansive use of the term "administration" to encompass activities clearly associated with policy-making. See *The Federalist Papers*, pp. 435–436.

31. The NRA was even described as an attempt to re-create guilds, an analogy that European proponents of corporatism frequently cited. According to Franklin Roosevelt (*On Our Way* [New York, 1934], pp. 99–100), "No employer and no group of less than all employers in a single trade could do this [i.e., reduce the hours labor worked, and raise their wages] alone and continue to live in business competition. But if all employers in each trade now band themselves faithfully in *these modern guilds*—without exception—and agree to act together and at once, none will be hurt and millions of workers, so long deprived of the right to earn their bread in the sweat of their labor, can raise their heads again" (emphasis added).

eliminate unfair competition, it was hoped, then the great majority of fundamentally decent businessmen would not be forced by competitive pressures to exploit their employees. More generally, cooperation between government, trade associations, and trade unions was to replace competition as the basis for economic life. Responsibility for administering the codes of fair trade competition was to have been left primarily in the hands of trade associations reconstituted as code authorities.

The NRA appears to be ideally suited as a case study for investigating the Lowi thesis. Lowi himself cites the NRA as the most significant corporatist period in our history: "But the peak of business and nonbusiness group participation in government came not during war or during reactionary Republican administration. The essential instrument of New Deal industrial planning was the National Industrial Recovery Act of 1933 and its administrative apparatus, the National Recovery Administration (NRA). In good corporatist fashion, the NRA worked through the officially recognized trade organizations."[32] Furthermore, the links between broad delegations of congressional power, administrative discretion, and corporatism are unambiguous in the case of the NRA. The NIRA was one of the most sweeping delegations of congressional power in the history of the United States. Virtually devoid of standards to guide its exercise, the NIRA vested the U.S. president with immense discretionary powers. Indeed, the delegation of powers was so sweeping that in 1935 a unanimous Supreme Court declared the NIRA unconstitutional in the above-mentioned *Schechter* decision. This was the first and only time that the Court had ever declared a major federal program unconstitutional for an excessive delegation of powers. If any case should exemplify the political dynamics identified by Lowi, it should be the NRA.

The quotation above, however, is one of the only references to the NRA in Lowi's *End of Liberalism*, and the reasons for Lowi's neglect of the program must be closely scrutinized before the choice of the NRA as a case study for investigating the Lowi thesis can be adequately justified. The empirical focus of *The End of Liberalism* is the 1960s and 1970s, not the 1930s. Although Lowi finds the origins of interest group liberalism in the 1930s, he does not believe that corporatism became truly institutionalized in the United States until the later period. As we have noted, the institutionalization of corporatism required a public philosophy that could legitimate discretionary administration and interest group participation in policy making, and Lowi believes that such a public philosophy did not become dominant until the 1960s and 1970s. Because ideology plays a crucial role in Lowi's analysis, it is possible that the NRA would not genuinely exemplify all the corporatist characteristics identified by Lowi if, as Lowi asserts, no such ideology existed in the 1930s.

32. Lowi, *The Politics of Disorder* (New York, 1971), p. 75.

A critical analysis of Lowi's discussion of the origins of interest group liberalism as an ideology, however, reveals weaknesses in his account and points to an alternative theory that would place the origins of a new public philosophy legitimating discretionary government and corporatism as early as the dawn of the twentieth century. Lowi argues that the source of interest group liberalism's ideology was 1950s pluralist theory, but he does not do justice to the subtlety of the pluralists' understanding of American political life. David Truman, for instance, had argued that interest group competition would lead to salutary political consequences if it was based on a deeper consensus concerning the "rules of the game" that provided a framework for competition. While Truman does not fully catalog the "rules of the game" in the *The Governmental Process,* he does specify that they "include acceptance of the rule of law." More important, in the concluding chapter of *The Governmental Process* Truman explicitly considers and rejects corporatism as a mode of structuring the relationship between interest groups and the state, arguing that corporatism would rigidify interest group politics and impede the mechanisms that moderated interest group competition. If Truman's pluralism at least limits discretionary government by a rule-of-law norm and rejects corporatism in favor of pluralism, it is difficult to understand how it could be construed as the foundation for a public philosophy legitimating interest group liberalism.[33]

Neither can Lowi provide a plausible account of the transformation of pluralism from an influential model in the social sciences into a public philosophy legitimating interest group liberal politics for a broad spectrum of the population. Lowi cites the popularizing works of Schlesinger and Galbraith because both have at one time defended the idea that government should use its power to shore up groups in society and establish a system of countervailing powers.[34] But Lowi attributes a systematically apologetic character to the work of both these scholars that does not ring true, for both Schlesinger and Galbraith have been deeply concerned with the disproportionate power of well-organized groups like big business in the modern American state. Furthermore, even if one accepts Lowi's characterization of the tendencies inherent in Galbraith's and Schlesinger's defense of countervailing powers, there is a striking disproportion between the magnitude of the cause and the magnitude of the effect. Schlesinger and Galbraith are unlikely candidates for "founders" of a new regime.

No less troublesome are the temporal problems in Lowi's account. Institutionally, a reliance on discretionary administration and its attendant interest group politics dates from the first decades of the twentieth century. For instance, Lowi cites the Transportation Act of 1920 as an important turning point in the history of delegation, marking the transition from a

---

33. David Truman, *The Governmental Process,* 2d ed. (New York, 1971), pp. xxxvii, 525–526.
34. Lowi, *End of Liberalism,* pp. 53–54.

clearly defined mandate of the Interstate Commerce Commission to vague, broadly defined responsibilities.[35] By the time of the New Deal, vague delegations of power had become so common that the American Bar Association, anticipating Lowi's criticism of the administrative state, felt compelled to call on Congress to put a stop to this practice: "Congress is the legislative branch of government . . . and we do not any longer want Congress to set up bureaus and commissions and say to them 'We recognize there is a great problem in this particular field. We have not the time to solve this problem as we did in the early days of this Republic; we are merely going to set up a commission of some kind and give you full powers and you endeavor to solve that problem.' "[36] Ironically in this case it was generally conservatives who were making the case for the nondelegation doctrine, although even progressive members of the Supreme Court had found the sweeping delegation of powers in the NRA unacceptable.

Not only had Congress failed to constrain the discretion of New Deal administrators by limited delegations of power, but it also had been reluctant to impose procedural constraints on administrative decision making in the 1930s. Even by the 1940s, when many in Congress were beginning to have second thoughts about the administrative behemoth they were creating, efforts to curb administrative discretion were generally unsuccessful. Although the American Bar Association found a receptive congressional audience for its proposals for a restrictive administrative procedure act, the president ultimately vetoed its Walter-Logan Bill. Roosevelt's veto message was a classic expression of progressive hostility to legal formalism:

> A large part of the legal profession has never reconciled itself to the existence of the administrative tribunal. Many of them prefer the stately ritual of the courts, in which lawyers play all the speaking parts, to the simple procedure of administrative hearings which a client can understand and even participate in. Many of the lawyers prefer that decision be influenced by a shrewd play upon technical rules of evidence in which the lawyers are the only experts, although they always disagree. Many of the lawyers still prefer to distinguish precedent and to juggle leading cases rather than to get down to the merits of the efforts in which their clients are engaged. For years, such lawyers have led a persistent fight against the administrative tribunal.[37]

In 1946 a significantly watered-down version of the Walter-Logan Bill was finally enacted and became the Administrative Procedure Act, but this new version did "little to hamper or rigidify the administrative process."[38]

---

35. Ibid., pp. 101–102.

36. William F. West, *Administrative Rulemaking: Politics and Process* (Westport, Conn., 1985), p. 74.

37. Cited in Paul Verkuil, "The Emerging Concept of Administrative Procedure," *Columbia Law Review* 78 (1978): 273.

38. Ibid., p. 278; West, pp. 71–77.

Certainly by this time discretionary administration was well institutionalized.

Lowi's own regime chronology, which dates the era of interest group liberalism from the 1930s to the present, acknowledges its historical longevity.[39] Are we then to assume that discretionary administration and corporatism, which Lowi believes have been developing since the turn of the century and have dominated politics since the 1930s, have evolved until the 1960s without any ideological justification? Is it not the case that discretionary administration and corporatist politics were well established before the 1960s, and that the prominence of the 1960s in Lowi's historical scheme is primarily an artifact of his interpretation of the history of American political thought?

Finally, Lowi's characterization of the 1960s and 1970s as the era of discretionary administration and interest group liberalism par excellence is strikingly inappropriate. Lowi failed to note the significance of a growing movement to reform administrative law and curb discretionary administration and interest group power during this era. For instance, the differences between the NRA and Nixon's 1971 wage and price controls—the most ambitious corporatist program of the 1960s and 1970s—are striking. The administration of the latter program was heavily influenced by legal formalist ideals, especially in its initial phase, and it is therefore not a good example of interest group liberalism in action.[40] Lowi was not an isolated critic of discretionary administration; he was one of the foremost standard-bearers of a powerful intellectual and political movement. Lowi should not be faulted for failing to see the potential significance of developments that were still in the formative stages when he was writing the first edition of *The End of Liberalism*, but by now it is clear that his criticisms of discretionary administration were most justifiably directed at the decades that preceded the 1960s and 1970s.[41]

Lowi appropriately focuses our attention on the development of a public philosophy that could legitimate corporatist politics, but there is a more plausible candidate than academic pluralism as the source of such a public philosophy. That source is Pragmatism, the distinctively American philosophy that rose to prominence in the late nineteenth century and that dominated the philosophic scene at least until the 1950s. In the next chapter we shall see that pragmatism can be linked both to the rise of discretionary administration and to the legitimation of corporatist politics.[42]

39. Lowi, *End of Liberalism*, pp. 273–274. For the relationship between the New Deal and discretionary administration, see also Bruce A. Ackerman and William T. Hassler, *Clean Coal / Dirty Air* (New Haven, 1981), pp. 4–7.
40. See Robert Kagan, *Regulatory Justice* (New York, 1978).
41. For a more-extended discussion of the role of legal formalism in the 1970s, see Donald Brand, "Reformers of the Sixties and Seventies: Modern Anti-Federalists?" in *Remaking American Politics*, ed. Richard Harris and Sidney Milkis (Boulder, Colo., forthcoming).
42. For a parallel argument that the fundamental antagonists of the legal formalists were the pragmatists, see Fred Siegel, "Is Archie Bunker Fit to Rule? or, How Immanuel Kant Became

For now it is important to note that a historical explanation that focuses on pragmatism as the source of a new public philosophy rationalizing discretionary administration and corporatist politics would overcome two of the objections to Lowi's account of the rise of a new public philosophy. First, the problem posed for Lowi by the lag between the rise of corporatist institutions and the rise of a public philosophy legitimating them is rendered moot, because pragmatism became influential far earlier in the twentieth century and had become the dominant intellectual framework during the New Deal era, the turning point that Lowi identified as critical in the institutional history of discretionary administration and corporatism.[43]

A second objection to Lowi's thesis regarding the origins of the new public philosophy had to do with the scope of the influence of pluralism, particularly the way it was transformed from an academic doctrine into a public philosophy. Pragmatism is a more credible source for the new public philosophy because its influence was far more pervasive. A number of secondary works have already documented the important role that pragmatism played in the development of most of the modern social sciences, in jurisprudence, and in sundry other disciplines.[44] Among those influenced by pragmatism were Charles Beard and Carl Becker in history, Arthur Bentley in political science, Thorstein Veblen in economics, Vernon Parrington in literary criticism, and Oliver Wendell Holmes, Roscoe Pound, and Benjamin Cardozo in jurisprudence. That pragmatism spawned a jurisprudence accepted by prominent judges in the American legal tradition suffices to demonstrate that its influence extended beyond the halls of academia, but judges were not the only public officials who imbibed elements of pragmatism. Many of the intellectuals who became the spokesmen for progressivism, the dominant public philosophy of both the Progressive Era and the New Deal, were influenced directly by pragmatism, or indirectly by the applications of pragmatism to other academic disciplines.[45]

Actually, the assertion that pragmatism is the source of the new public philosophy does not refute Lowi's thesis concerning the role of pluralism; it alters and subsumes it. If one turns to Arthur Bentley, founder of the

---

One of the Founding Fathers,'' *Telos* 69 (1986). Siegel also provides additional evidence that the 1970s are best viewed as an era of resurgent legal formalism.

Note that in this book the terms, ''pragmatism'' and ''pragmatist'' are used to refer to pragmatism as an intellectual movement and to people and ideas linked to that movement.

43. Morton White, *Social Thought in America: The Revolt Against Formalism* (Boston, 1957), pp. 3–10; Edward A. Purcell, Jr., *The Crisis of Democratic Theory* (Lexington, Ky., 1973), pp. 3–12.

44. White, pp. 47–106; Purcell, pp. 15–30, 74–114; Cushing Strout, *The Pragmatic Revolt in American History: Carl Becker and Charles Beard* (Ithaca, N.Y., 1958); Wilfrid E. Rumble, Jr., *American Legal Realism* (Ithaca, N.Y., 1968), pp. 1–47.

45. Eric F. Goldman, *Rendezvous with Destiny: A History of Modern American Reform* (New York, 1956), pp. 120–124.

pluralist tradition, rather than to David Truman or Robert Dahl, one finds a version of pluralism that is genuinely conducive to corporatism. Attempting to institute industrial democracy, Bentley believed that cooperation between trade unions, trade associations, agricultural and marketing cooperatives, and government provided a viable middle path between the bureaucratic regimentation he associated with socialism and the social exploitation he associated with capitalism.[46] Like many reformers of his day, Bentley had seen in the corporatist War Industries Board that governed industrial life during World War I the possibilities for a permanent new economic order that would be based on the spirit of craftsmanship and community rather than on a selfish quest for profits.[47]

Bentleyan pluralism had strong corporatist overtones, but it was also rooted in the pragmatist philosophical movement. Bentley had been deeply influenced by William James and Charles Sanders Peirce early in his career, and, considerably later, much of his intellectual life revolved around his extended correspondence and collaboration with John Dewey. The basic orientation of Bentley's pluralist theory, which was an attempt to get behind formal institutions and situate them within a dynamic political process, was an application of pragmatic insights to the field of political science.[48] If pragmatism is the source of pluralism, then Lowi's derivation of interest group liberalism from pluralism is not fundamentally mistaken, it is just too narrow. It mistook the part, pluralism, for the whole, pragmatism.[49]

Substituting pragmatism for 1950s pluralism as the source of a new public philosophy legitimating discretionary administration and corporatism removes the only serious obstacle to the use of the NRA as a case study for examining Lowi's thesis. The ideological foundations of interest group liberalism were solidly established by the early New Deal, so the NRA should fully exemplify the characteristics Lowi identified as central to an interest group liberal regime. Indeed, if Lowi is wrong in his assessment of the 1960s and 1970s and they have in fact been an era of

---

46. Arthur Bentley, *Makers, Users, and Masters,* ed. Sidney Ratner (Syracuse, N.Y., 1969), pp. 192, 232, 234–236, 244.

47. Ibid., pp. 223, 228–231.

48. Purcell, pp. 17, 39.

49. In light of this discussion, we must soften one of the criticisms leveled at Lowi earlier. Rather than argue that 1950s pluralism did not provide an ideological justification for interest group liberalism because it affirmed the rule of law and rejected corporatism (see above), it would be more accurate to say that these elements of 1950s pluralist theory demonstrate that its defense of interest group politics was more limited than Lowi suggests. The more fundamental argument of this section is that pragmatism (including Bentleyan pluralism) is the original source of the new public philosophy that Lowi describes. Pluralist theory in the 1950s is derived in part from Bentleyan pluralism, but it has been leavened by more-traditional liberal elements that make it less suitable than its Bentleyan predecessor as a source for the new public philosophy. See Donald Brand, "Three Generations of Pluralism: Continuity and Change," *Political Science Reviewer* 15 (1985): 109–141.

resurgent legal formalism, as has been argued above, then the NRA should prove to be a better example of interest group liberalism than the programs on which Lowi focused in *The End of Liberalism*. Before we can examine the existing historical literature on the NRA and its bearing on the Lowi thesis, however, we must first devote some attention to the use of the term "corporatism" in describing the NRA and possibly the post–New Deal state in general.

Administrative and Societal Corporatism

The most widely accepted definition of corporatism is that offered by Philippe Schmitter in his seminal article entitled "Still the Century of Corporatism": "Corporatism can be defined as a system of interest representation in which the constituent units are organized into a limited number of singular, compulsory, noncompetitive, hierarchically ordered and functionally differentiated categories, recognized or licensed (if not created) by the state and granted a deliberate representational monopoly within their respective categories in exchange for observing certain controls on their selection of leaders and articulation of demands and supports."[50] This definition focuses on the compulsory character of groups and their hierarchically structured relationships culminating in peak associations of labor and capital, a structure that facilitates tripartite bargaining between labor, capital, and government. Schmitter's definition of pluralism inverts these characteristics, emphasizing the weakness of peak associations, the voluntary character of groups, and their competitive relationships.

Schmitter further refines his definition of corporatism by distinguishing between state and societal corporatism. Historically, corporatist theory was developed to describe the relationship between interest groups and the state in authoritarian regimes, and pluralist theory was developed to describe this relationship in liberal democratic regimes. As dissatisfaction with the empirical adequacy of pluralist theory developed, however, social scientists like Schmitter began to note that institutional practices previously noted only in authoritarian regimes were also found in some Western European liberal democracies. To preserve a distinction between corporatism in a liberal democratic context and corporatism in an authoritarian context, Schmitter introduced the term "societal corporatism" to refer to the former and the term "state corporatism" to refer to the latter.[51]

The use of the term "societal corporatism" to describe the United

50. Philippe Schmitter, "Still the Century of Corporatism," in *Trends toward Corporatist Intermediation*, ed. Philippe Schmitter and Gerhard Lehmbruch (Beverly Hills, Calif., 1979), p. 13.
51. Ibid., pp. 8, 12, 20.

States would generally be inappropriate, and scholars who accepted Schmitter's definition of societal corporatism have focused on explaining "Why No Corporatism in America?" These scholars have noted that the weakness of American peak associations, the anemic levels of American union membership, and the inability of trade associations to develop authority vis-à-vis their individual members do not correspond to the ideal type of societal corporatism.[52] But if post–New Deal politics in the United States does not fit the societal corporatist mold as Schmitter described it, the same cannot be said of the NRA. Schmitter himself refers to the NRA as an "abortive attempt to encourage corporatist forms of policy-making during the early New Deal."[53]

Even the NRA does not meet the rigorous requirements of Schmitter's definition of corporatism, but it does at least approximate them. Although business membership in trade associations was not legally compulsory, the fact that trade associations were drafting and administering legally enforceable codes of fair trade competition provided compelling incentives for firms to join trade associations to assure that their interests were represented. Peak associations did not play nearly as prominent a role in the NRA as would be expected based on Schmitter's definition of societal corporatism, but the NRA did establish a Labor Advisory Board and a Business Advisory Board, which in conjunction with broadly based labor and business organizations—like the American Federation of Labor (AFL), the U.S. Chamber of Commerce, and the Business Advisory Council—did attempt to speak broadly for the interests of business and labor.[54] It at least seems appropriate to describe the NRA as an example of emergent societal corporatism.

In describing the NRA as an "abortive" corporatist experiment, however, Schmitter is emphasizing that the NRA is an exception within the generally more pluralistic pattern of American politics. Lowi views the NRA in a different light. He dismisses the fact that the NRA was disbanded after only two years with the assertion that the corporatist principles of the NRA continue to shape American politics to this day: "The NRA was eventually declared unconstitutional as an excessive delegation of law-making power to private groups and government agencies. However, the practice of government controls in cooperation with trade associations did not end; it simply became somewhat less formal and explicit."[55] Lowi and Schmitter view the place of the NRA within the

52. See esp. Robert Salisbury, "Why No Corporatism in America," in *Trends toward Corporatist Intermediation*, pp. 213–218. For additional evidence that American trade associations have been comparatively weak, see James Q. Wilson, *Political Organizations* (New York, 1973), pp. 149, 165, 167; and Louis Galambos, *Competition and Cooperation* (Baltimore, 1966).

53. Schmitter, p. 30; Salisbury, p. 220.

54. Leverett S. Lyon et al., *The National Recovery Administration* (Washington D.C., 1935), pp. 104–105, 118–123, 427–429, 435.

55. Theodore Lowi, *The Politics of Disorder*, p. 75.

broader context of American politics differently because there are important differences in their understandings of corporatism, differences that led Lowi to characterize American politics since the New Deal as corporatist, whereas Schmitter characterized the same politics as pluralist.

Although Lowi does not provide a concise definition of corporatism that would clarify the differences between his and Schmitter's understandings of that phenomenon, his emphasis on administrative discretion indicates that he is more interested in the characteristics of the administrative process in a state than in the formal interest group structure of society. Lowi appears to identify corporatism with an institutionalized pattern of interest group participation in administration. Since this pattern of interaction between interest groups and the state could logically occur in a context where interest groups were overlapping and competing—an interest group structure closely identified with pluralism—we will add the further stipulation that the groups granted recognition by such arrangements are accepted by state actors as the exclusive spokesmen for the interests they represent. This restriction would exclude few, if any, of the patterns of state–interest group interaction that Lowi has in mind when he refers to interest group liberalism, and it is more in line with the general use of the term "corporatism" in political science. It is important to note that this use of the term corporatism still differs from Schmitter's use of the term in that it does not require that groups be hierarchically organized under powerful peak associations. Confusion can be avoided if we retain Schmitter's definition of societal corporatism but distinguish it from "administrative corporatism," which will be formally defined as an *institutionalized* pattern of administration in which groups monopolistically represent interests and where they play a significant role (formal or informal) in policy making and policy implementation.

Referring to the administrative arrangements that were of concern to Lowi as corporatist rather than as pluralist is justifiable. Although Schmitter's definitions of corporatism and pluralism focused on structural characteristics of interest group systems, those definitions also respectively distinguished cases where interest groups were "recognized or licensed (if not created) by the state" from cases where interest groups were "not specially licensed, recognized, subsidized, created or otherwise controlled in leadership selection or interest articulation by the state." Furthermore, as interest groups become more closely intertwined with the state, power within these groups increasingly gravitates into the hands of the organizational elites responsible for the day-to-day activities of the group. Organizational elites will sometimes be able to use the state's coercive powers to enforce their decisions directly, and at other times they will be able to compel compliance with their preferences indirectly through their access to important resources. Whether or not Lowi's use of Robert Michel's term "the iron law of oligarchy" to describe the transformation of voluntary associations into private governments is appropriate, at the very least interest groups are no longer the strictly voluntary associations the 1950s pluralists presumed them to be. In addition, Lowi would assert that the institutionalized inclusion of groups in the administrative process transforms the interest group system from the highly fluid network of shifting coalitions described by the pluralists into a more rigid system that is highly resistant to changes that might threaten the status quo.[56]

Administrative corporatism and societal corporatism refer to different phenomena, but they are not mutually exclusive. Societal corporatism emphasizes the role of peak associations. It is classically exemplified in countries like Sweden and Austria, where there have been ambitious attempts to fashion social peace treaties between labor and capital. Societal corporatism will generally entail administrative corporatism, for it would be difficult, if not impossible, to institutionalize societal corporatist arrangements unless the legislature explicitly delegated significant decision making powers to private groups or at least tacitly recognized their right to participate in the formulation and administration of public policy. On the other hand, administrative corporatism occurs in many contexts divorced from societal corporatist schemes. Lowi correctly notes that administrative corporatism has occurred extensively in the United States since the New Deal, even though attempts to build public policy around social peace treaties between labor and capital have been the exception rather than the rule in the United States.

New Deal corporatists and their Progressive Era predecessors did not distinguish between administrative and societal corporatism. Their political thought can be construed as compatible with either variety, and in the discussions that follow we will generically characterize that thought as "corporatist" where that is appropriate. This is not to say, however, that the distinction between societal and administrative corporatism is unimportant for understanding these periods. Indeed, it will be impossible to understand the fate of the NRA without this distinction. The NRA exemplified both administrative and societal corporatism. On the one hand, the formal incorporation of business groups into the NRA's administrative apparatus epitomizes the administrative corporatism that is the focus of Lowi's analysis; on the other hand, the NRA's ambitious attempt to fashion a social peace treaty between business and labor and its partial reliance on peak associations of business and labor to facilitate the implementation of that social peace treaty at least approximates societal corporatism.[57] But

56. Ibid., pp. 3–31; Lowi, *End of Liberalism*, pp. 60–61. See also Grant McConnell, *Private Power and American Democracy* (New York, 1966), pp. 119–127.

57. The NRA does not exemplify administrative corporatism, as defined above, in its relationship with labor. The NRA promoted collective bargaining pluralism for labor (described in Chapters 9 and 10) and therefore did not satisfy the requirement that administrative corporatism recognize groups as exclusive spokesmen for the interests they represented. Howev-

the consequences that flowed from its administrative corporatism are at least partially distinguishable from the consequences that flowed from its societal corporatism. Unless the distinction is kept clear, one risks attributing consequences to the wrong cause.

Pluralist, Progressive, and Revisionist Interpretations of the NRA

At first glance the NRA would appear to confound Lowi's thesis about the character of administrative corporatist politics in the United States. The NIRA was proposed by one of the most progressive U.S. presidents in the twentieth century and enacted by one of the more progressive Congresses in this century. Far from being conservative legislation that shored up the status quo, it was a sweeping reform program. The federal government was taking an important step toward assuring workers a humane work week and a decent living wage. Child labor was to be abolished. Because the NIRA sought to increase the purchasing power of labor, Section 7a of the NIRA recognized the right of labor to organize and to bargain collectively. Codes of fair trade competition were ostensibly to protect businessmen from unfair competition, particularly small businessmen from unfair competition from large corporations.[58] If the NRA had lived up to the promise of the NIRA, it would have been the most significant reform introduced by the New Deal and perhaps the most significant reform achievement of the twentieth century.

But the NRA did not live up to its promise. It is the consensus of a wide range of political scientists and historians who have approached this period with different concerns and different interpretations of the broader significance of the New Deal as a whole that the NRA basically served established groups at the expense of both the public good and the organizationally disadvantaged. The one aspect of the NRA that held out the clearest promise of progressive reform—Section 7a, guaranteeing to labor the right to organize and bargain collectively—was jeopardized, many would even say gutted, by an administrative interpretation of the clause partially legitimating company unions.[59] There is compelling evidence that the relaxation of antitrust statutes during the NRA facilitated cartelization and benefited a few businessmen while hindering economic

er, there is evidence that this was viewed as an interim solution and that NRA officials anticipated the eventual emergence of unions that would monopolistically represent workers in particular industries. See Chapter 9, footnote 60. Thus, even with regard to labor policy the NRA might appropriately be described as emergent administrative corporatism.

58. Ellis Hawley, *The New Deal and the Problem of Monopoly: A Study in Economic Ambivalence* (Princeton, 1969), pp. 19–20, 29.

59. Bernard Bellush, *The Failure of the NRA* (New York, 1975), pp. 176–177; William E. Leuchtenburg, *Franklin D. Roosevelt and the New Deal* (New York, 1963), pp. 88, 107–108.

recovery.[60] Scholars studying this era have generally concluded that Franklin Roosevelt's progressive reputation is undeserved as far as the NRA is concerned.

Most of the existing interpretations of the NRA can be roughly divided into three categories. Pluralist interpretations of the NRA have argued that the NRA can be explained in terms of the conflicting interest group pressures on political officials during the early New Deal era. A second interpretive framework has been provided by progressive historians.[61] Arthur Schlesinger, Jr., has succinctly stated the central premise of progressive historiography: "Liberalism in America has been ordinarily the movement on the part of other sections of society [i.e., the people] to restrain the power of the business community."[62] Progressive historians have been somewhat more inclined to see emergent progressive characteristics in the NRA than have the pluralists, but they viewed the NRA as an anomalous program within the history of reform and therefore an exception to their general thesis. Finally, a third general category of interpretations of the NRA was advanced during the 1960s by revisionist historians who rejected the normative orientation of both the pluralists and the progressive historians and their assumptions that groups and/or "the people," rather than classes, were the fundamental units of political analysis. Revisionists have argued that the NRA served the interests of the capitalist class by rationalizing and stabilizing competitive markets.

James MacGregor Burns's interpretation of the NRA exemplifies the first school of thought. Burns concluded that the NRA was basically an institutionalization of what he calls the broker politician's style of leadership, a style of leadership antithetical to the exemplary party leadership of presidents like Thomas Jefferson and Andrew Jackson. "The NRA was essentially an expression of the broker state—that is, of the government acting for, and mediating among, the major interest groups. The NRA was an institutional expression of Roosevelt's plan for a partnership of all groups, achieved through friendly cooperation between the government and group leaders."[63] According to Burns, the president "virtually lost control of the NRA" after it was launched, and Hugh Johnson [NRA administrator] could not provide adequate leadership for the NRA either, at least in part because he "had to delegate huge policy making powers to hastily summoned businessmen who might or might not be representative of the myriad

60. Michael Weinstein, *Recovery and Redistribution Under the NIRA* (Amsterdam, 1980), pp. 29–31, 146.

61. The best overview of progressive historiography is Richard Hofstadter, *The Progressive Historians* (New York, 1968).

62. Arthur M. Schlesinger, Jr., *The Age of Jackson* (Boston, 1946), p. 505.

63. James MacGregor Burns, *Roosevelt: The Lion and the Fox* (New York, 1956), pp. 192–193. Although Burns provides a systematic pluralist interpretation of the NRA, his interpretation of the later New Deal is not pluralist. This issue will be discussed further in Chapter 10.

interests in their industries.''[64] As a political scientist, Burns has focused on the role leadership plays in effective governance, an approach quite different from that taken by Lowi. Yet Burns's description of the NRA as a manifestation of brokered state politics basically supports Lowi's characterization of corporatist politics.

Arthur Schlesinger, the preeminent progressive historian of the contemporary period, has sympathetically portrayed the New Deal in general as a democratic movement to counter the interests of the plutocracy.[65] Despite this general orientation, however, Schlesinger also portrays the NRA as a program fundamentally dominated by powerful interest groups, particularly business interests. Schlesinger accounts for this anomaly by suggesting that an overconfident Franklin Roosevelt was unable to delimit the goals of the program realistically. As progressive New Dealers allowed the NRA to become overextended, it accumulated a ''mass of multifarious administrative responsibilities under which the organization eventually broke down.'' In retrospect it became clear that Roosevelt underestimated the power of private interests.

> So long as the sense of emergency gave the public interest a chance to win out over special interests, NRA worked. With a touch of recovery, the sense of emergency receded, and private interests came to the fore; and the lack of clear economic conceptions in NRA's administration *as well as of clear legal standards in the law* tempted private groups to concentrate on what each could get for itself. In the end, NRA foundered on the problem of asserting a vague public interest against the specific and well-focused demands of self-serving private interests.[66]

Schlesinger's account of the NRA not only provides support for Lowi's conclusion that discretionary administration and corporatism lead to the capture of public authority by private interests, but also at least partly supports the conclusion that well-organized interests benefit from this type of interest group politics. Schlesinger was particularly troubled by Roosevelt's interpretation of Section 7a of the NIRA permitting the formation of company unions. He characterized this policy as ''manifestly anti-union.'' Schlesinger's general conclusions regarding the NRA were that the NRA *to a considerable extent* became captured by well-organized business groups, which used the program to further their interests at the expense of the less well organized consumers and workers. Schlesinger, however, departs from Lowi and James MacGregor Burns's pluralist account of the

64. Ibid., p. 192.
65. Arthur M. Schlesinger, Jr., *The Age of Roosevelt: The Politics of Upheaval* (Boston, 1960), pp. 440–443.
66. Arthur M. Schlesinger, Jr., *The Age of Roosevelt: The Coming of the New Deal* (Boston, 1959), p. 176. Emphasis added.

NRA in asserting that small business did not do so badly under the NRA. Similarly, Schlesinger recognizes the reform aspirations of Roosevelt, and to a lesser extent of Hugh Johnson and Donald Richberg, the two most important administrative officials in the NRA.[67]

Revisionists have criticized not only the NRA but also the New Deal more generally. The more radical among them have even asserted that under capitalism the possibilities for genuine reform enhancing social justice are minimal. Because the New Deal did not socialize the means of production or even dramatically redistribute income, the revisionists concluded that the New Deal was fundamentally a conservative era that shored up capitalism and preserved the status quo. The NRA is portrayed as a program controlled by big business and used to shield major corporations from destructive marketplace competition. While revisionists agree that the consequences of the NRA and the New Deal generally were profoundly conservative, there is disagreement about whether this was the intention of the New Dealers and of Franklin Roosevelt. Some, such as Ronald Radosh, argue that the New Dealers' goal was to protect the interests of the capitalist class. Others, among them Bernard Bellush and Barton Bernstein, portray a less sinister New Deal that was either too inept or too powerless to alter fundamentally the character of American capitalism. When this latter group offers explanations of the New Deal's failure to bring genuine reform through the NRA despite good intentions, their explanations come very close to those offered by Lowi.[68]

Bernard Bellush, for instance, believes that Congress ineffectively dissipated its authority in the NRA by delegating "unlimited decision making power to an unborn bureaucracy" and that this explains the failure of the NRA to fulfill the promise of Section 7a. Roosevelt was vulnerable to the same charge, for he "never seemed to realize that the NRA was a poor use, if not abuse, of this power."[69] Bellush concludes: "Neither Congress nor the President seriously faces up to the task of directing, let alone controlling, the administrative agency created by an irascible Hugh Johnson in Washington, and the individual code authorities that sprouted on all sides."[70]

Ellis Hawley's revisionist classic, *The New Deal and the Problem of Monopoly*, also provides support for Lowi's thesis. Hawley argues that Congress failed to choose between competing and contradictory strategies

67. Ibid., pp. 104, 126, 149, 169–170, 173.
68. Ronald Radosh, "The Myth of the New Deal," in *A New History of Leviathan*, ed. Ronald Radosh and Murray N. Rothbard (New York, 1972), pp. 159–172, 185–187; Barton J. Bernstein, "The Conservative Achievements of Liberal Reform," in *Towards a New Past: Dissenting Essays in American History*, ed. Barton J. Bernstein (New York, 1968), p. 264; Bellush, p. 147.
69. Bellush, pp. 176–178.
70. Ibid., pp. 176–177.

for promoting economic recovery when it enacted the NRA, preferring a vague statute that left administrators with the responsibility for shaping a coherent program. "Within a single piece of legislation, the authors of the measure had made room for the aspirations and programs of a variety of economic and political groups, but in a phraseology that could be used to implement any of several policies, they had laid the basis for future confusion and controversy."[71] This abdication by Congress provided an opportunity for special interests to exert far more control over the program than might otherwise have been the case. Hawley's additional conclusion that "essentially the codes reflected the interests of the larger and more highly organized businessmen" fundamentally supports Lowi's thesis that the well organized are the beneficiaries of interest group liberalism.[72] But Hawley is far more appreciative of the complexities of the NRA than most revisionists are, and he is more willing to qualify his argument.[73]

The pluralist, progressive, and revisionist interpretations are best analyzed separately because the underlying logics of their interpretations differ. Despite these differences, their interpretations of particular historical eras can converge. For instance, revisionists can argue that political actors fundamentally further the interests of capitalists, but they often acknowledge the power of other actors to shape policies of peripheral concern or to reap benefits from programs supposedly designed to co-opt their potential opposition.[74] The pluralists, on the other hand, argue that under conditions of a radically asymmetric distribution of political power a political broker will eschew the conflict associated with attempts to redistribute political power. Characteristically he seeks to placate the powerful, a propensity that reinforces the power of the well organized at the expense of the unorganized.[75] Indeed, these were the conditions prevailing during the early New Deal, when big business was the best-organized economic group. As we noted, progressive historians have viewed the NRA as an exception to the general pattern of reform politics, and at times their explanation of the NRA resembles that of the pluralists. For this reason, pluralist, progressive, and revisionist interpretations of the NRA do not differ as markedly as their respective theoretical frameworks differ.[76] All these interpretations have emphasized that the NRA generally served the interests of big business. They enlist much of the same

71. Hawley, pp. 20–21.

72. Ibid., p. 66.

73. At another point Hawley concludes more tentatively: "By and large, though not completely, the codes reflected the desires of businessmen to erect economic cartels that could check the forces of deflation" (ibid., p. 136).

74. Radosh, p. 185; B. Bernstein, pp. 264, 267.

75. Burns, pp. 192–193, 197.

76. Thus B. Bernstein can cite with approval James MacGregor Burns's brokered state hypothesis, although he pushes it in a more radical direction than Burns did (B. Bernstein, p. 270).

evidence to support their respective positions, and they are often vulnerable to the same criticisms.

All three interpretations have elements that confirm Lowi's analysis of modern American politics. Almost uniformly, New Deal scholars have focused on administrative corporatism as the source of the NRA's problems. It was the vague delegation of powers in the NIRA and the inclusion of private groups in the administrative apparatus of the NRA that allowed the program to become a vehicle for private groups and classes to advance their interests at the expense of the public good. The societal corporatist features of the NRA, characteristics associated with its ambitious attempt to fashion a social peace treaty among conflicting interests, are frequently noted but rarely invoked in explaining the demise of the program.

The NRA Reappraised

Despite the partial convergence of pluralist, progressive, and revisionist accounts of the NRA, unexplained loose ends remain. If the judgments of groups affected by the NRA constitute at least a prima facie case for determining the beneficiaries of the act, then the traditional description of the NRA as a program that served the interests of business—and primarily big business—cannot account for the pattern of support for the extension of the NRA in June 1935 after its two-year trial. Even before the Supreme Court overturned the NRA in the *Schechter* decision, the effective operation of the NRA had been foreclosed by the disenchantment of substantial sections of the business community. Both the Chamber of Commerce and the National Association of Manufacturers, for example, formally repudiated the NRA.[77] Unfortunately, at this level of aggregation the distinctive interests of big business, on the one hand, and small and medium-sized businesses, on the other hand, cannot be clearly distinguished. A critical element in most of the previously cited interpretations of the NRA is the assertion that big business supported the program as a strong form of cartelization that guaranteed monopoly profits. Small and medium-sized businesses, squeezed by the inequitable operation of a cartel controlled by big business, found themselves in the same situation as organized labor, which was struggling to prevent workers from being co-opted by the growth of company unions legitimated by the NRA. Both groups would presumably have opposed an extension of the NRA in 1935.

But the organizational impetus of the NRA alone might suggest that the organizationally deprived small and medium-sized businesses and labor, rather than big business, would be the beneficiaries of the program. The

77. Hawley, pp. 154–157; William Wilson, "How the Chamber of Commerce Viewed the NRA: A Re-examination," *Mid-America* 44 (1962): 95–108.

burst of trade association formation that occurred during the NRA was not organizing firms in oligopolistic markets, for they had organized long before the NRA without the entrepreneurial services of government bureaucrats.[78] Confirming this suggestion, some of the strongest support for an extension of the NRA beyond its initial two-year authorization came from industries like the bituminous coal industry and the cotton textile industry, which were characterized by highly competitive markets and predominantly small and medium-sized firms.[79] On the other hand, many prominent industrialists were already moving to oppose the New Deal and the NRA through such groups as the American Liberty League. Furthermore, organized labor gained 900,000 members during this period, reversing a general decline throughout the 1920s and early 1930s.[80] This was no doubt one of the important considerations that led the American Federation of Labor to support an extension of the NRA.[81] These facts alone do not do justice to the complexity of group forces that shaped the NRA and led to its demise, but they do reveal the inadequacies of accepted interpretations. A reexamination of the NRA is clearly justified.

Part I of this book (Chapters 1–3) outlines the intellectual and political origins of the NRA. Chapter 1 looks at the relationship of pragmatism to both the rule of law and to corporatism. Pragmatism is shown to be a more plausible source than 1950s pluralism for the new public philosophy that encouraged discretionary government and both administrative and societal corporatism. Chapter 1 also includes a review of the differences between pragmatism and classical American liberalism. Chapter 2 examines progressivism and the relationship between pragmatism and progressivism, exploring the ways in which progressivism popularized the pragmatists' critique of the rule of law and their tentative defense of corporatism. Chapter 3 covers the political origins of the NRA and its relationship to progressivism.

Part II (Chapters 4–8) examines relations between government and

78. Almost one-fourth of the trade associations in existence in 1938 were formed during the NRA. More than 500 associations subsequently disbanded, but this could not erase the organizational legacy of the NRA. J. Q. Wilson, *Political Organizations*, p. 151.

79. James P. Johnson, *The Politics of Soft Coal: The Bituminous Industry from World War I through the New Deal* (Urbana, Ill., 1979), pp. 213–216; Galambos, pp. 276–283; *Business Week*, 30 March 1935, p. 36.

80. U.S. Bureau of the Census, *Historical Statistics of the U.S., Colonial Times to 1957* (Washington, D.C., 1960), pp. 97–98.

81. The AFL opposed a ten-month extension of the NRA—a proposal pushed by those who actually wanted to see the program die—and supported a two-year extension of the NRA, as Roosevelt was calling for. The AFL characterized the proposal merely to extend the NRA for ten months as "the end of the definite economic policy inaugurated under the New Deal and a return to the old industrial, social and economic policies administered by the reactionary forces of the nation" (AFL to FDR, 3 May 1935, Roosevelt Papers, OF 466, No. 10, NRA Codes, Misc., May 1935).

business during the NRA and the operation of codes of fair trade practices. Chapter 4 looks at the administration of the NRA's codes of fair trade practices, explaining how the attempt to promote fair trade degenerated into an instrument for business cartelization of the economy. Chapter 5 covers the revisionist interpretation of the NRA, demonstrating that its thesis that the NRA rationalized capitalism and served the interests of big business is seriously defective. Chapter 6 focuses on the troubled relationship between small and medium-sized businesses and the NRA and shows how a program that was developed to aid these businesses nevertheless generated hostility toward the NRA from this constituency. The macro-level analysis of government-business relations during the NRA in Chapters 4 through 6 strongly suggests but does not conclusively demonstrate that the fundamental business constituency of the NRA was small and medium-sized businesses, not big business.

Chapters 7 and 8 will substantiate some of the conclusions of the preceding three chapters by analyzing the impact of the NRA on particular industries—the oil industry in Chapter 7 and the steel industry in Chapter 8. These industries were selected because of their importance in the American economy and because each will allow us to explore an aspect of the NRA that cannot be fully understood at a macro-level of analysis. The oil industry is a semi-oligopolistic industry with a core of large modern corporations—the majors—and a periphery, composed of numerous small independents. It is ideally suited to explore the relationship between large and small business in the NRA because these groups have relatively well defined conflicting interests in the oil industry. The steel industry was selected because it poses an anomalous case for the thesis that emerges from the macro-study of the NRA—a case in which large corporations are relatively satisfied with the NRA. We will demonstrate that a unique conjunction of factors accounts for the anomalous response of big steel to the NRA. When the evidence from these case studies in combined with the evidence from several excellent existing case studies, a fairly comprehensive understanding of the relations between government and business during the NRA can be achieved.

Part III of this book examines the relationship of labor to the NRA. Chapter 9 looks at NRA labor policy and its relationship to the labor policy of its two most important subsidiaries, the National Labor Board (NLB) and the National Labor Relations Board (NLRB), the latter being a reconstituted version of the former. Roosevelt's labor policy during this period is described as not simply a series of ad hoc responses to discrete labor crises, but as having an underlying consistency to it and failing to achieve its foremost goal—the integration of labor into a framework of cooperation between government, business, and labor. Chapter 10 examines the pluralist brokered state hypothesis in the light of labor policy during the NRA and argues that the NRA was far more sympathetic to labor than the pluralists have conceded.[82]

The conclusion contrasts Lowi's analysis of the problem of faction with the American framers' analysis of the problem of faction, and it distinguishes their respective proposals for political reform. Both theories are evaluated in light of the findings of this research on the NRA. Our analysis of the NRA demonstrates that the NRA is neither as undemocratic nor as unjust as Lowi would lead us to expect. More in line with Lowi's expectations, the NRA was irrational and ineffective public policy. But even these failings cannot be attributed to administrative corporatism, the form of corporatism that was the focus of Lowi's concern. While administrative weaknesses did exacerbate the problems of the NRA, the failure of the NRA was ultimately intrinsic to the very societal corporatist conception of the program. It was a failure of the legislative process far more fundamentally than it was an administrative failure. The utopian aspiration to fashion a society based on cooperation rather than on competition was doomed to fail in a large and heterogeneous republic like the United States, an outcome the American framers would have anticipated. Because Lowi does not distinguish societal corporatism from administrative corporatism, his framework is inadequate for understanding the problems of the NRA, and his recommendations for reform are misguided. The history of the NRA points back to the wisdom of the American framers rather than forward to a new juridical democratic regime.

82. The pluralist and the revisionist interpretations of the NRA are systematically examined in this work, but the progressive historians' interpretation of the NRA, while frequently discussed in relation to particular issues of interpretation, is not. This is in part because progressive historians like Schlesinger have treated the NRA as at least a partial exception to their general thesis, and its exceptional character is analyzed in a manner reminiscent of the pluralist or even the revisionist interpretation. The interpretation of the NRA developed in this work will demonstrate why Schlesinger would have been much closer to the mark if he had consistently applied his general framework to the NRA instead of viewing it as something of an exception. Ironically, however, extending Schlesinger's general framework to encompass the NRA at the same time raises serious questions about his normative stance. Schlesinger has been the in-house historian of the reform movement, generally providing a partisan defense of the reform movement against its conservative critics. He is at his best in providing a sympathetic assessment of reformers that genuinely captures the spirit of reform. He is at his worst in his denigration of the opponents of reform. See Thomas B. Silver, *Coolidge and the Historians* (Durham, N.C., 1982). Once it is understood that the NRA is quintessentially a progressive program and that its failures are rooted in problematic aspects of progressivism, Schlesinger's apologetic account of the reform movement becomes questionable. However, pursuit of this line of reasoning is tangential to the goals of this work.

PART I

THE ORIGINS OF
THE NRA

CHAPTER I

Pragmatism and the Decline
of the Rule of Law

The Pragmatic Movement in philosophy and in the social sciences has been aptly characterized as "the revolt against formalism."[1] Dewey's contributions to ethics and logic, Veblen's contributions to economics, and Bentley's contributions to political science were all animated by an attempt to transform those disciplines from deductive, formalistic sciences into realistic or naturalistic sciences. The abstract analysis of institutions and systems of thought was to give way to empirical analysis focusing on the relationship between ideas and institutions and the context or environment out of which they arose and in which they lived. Deductions based on *a priori* knowledge of "universals" or "absolutes," which included all speculation about nature and such derivative concepts as human nature or natural rights, were to be eschewed in favor of more-limited generalizations grounded in experience, the pragmatic substitute for nature.[2]

The antiformalist orientation was also decisive in the development of Pragmatic Jurisprudence. The founding father of pragmatic jurisprudence, Justice Oliver Wendell Holmes, expressed his reservations concerning legal formalism in the following terms: "The life of the law has not been logic: it has been experience. The felt necessities of the time, the prevalent moral and political theories, intentions of public policy, avowed or unconscious, even the prejudices which judges share with their fellow men, have had a good deal more to do than the syllogism in determining the rules by which men shall be governed."[3]

Logic was not the life of the law, nor was it the only legitimate concern of judges. "The whole outline of the law is the resultant of a conflict at

---

1. This is the subtitle of Morton White's *Social Thought in America: The Revolt against Formalism*.
2. John Dewey, *Reconstruction in Philosophy* (Boston, 1948), pp. 36, 44; John Dewey, *Experience and Nature* (New York, 1929).
3. In *The Mind and Faith of Justice Holmes*, ed. Max Lerner (New York, 1954), pp. 51–52.

every point between logic and good sense—the one striving to work fiction out to consistent results, the other restraining and at last overcoming that effort when the results become too manifestly unjust."[4] Holmes was pointing to a tension between the end of the law, to achieve justice, and the means it employs to secure that end, the development of a coherent set of rules, concepts, and principles to govern individual behavior. His warning against legalism, the tendency to conceptualize the law merely as an abstract set of rules and principles detached from its ultimate end, became one of the dominant themes of the school of pragmatic jurisprudence he inspired.

From 1900 to roughly 1925, American jurisprudence was reoriented by the rise of Sociological Jurisprudence, the first of the pragmatist schools of legal philosophy.[5] During this period, Roscoe Pound and Benjamin Cardozo, with some support from Morris Cohen, developed a comprehensive critique of legalism or excessive legal formalism, which was derogatorily referred to as "mechanical jurisprudence."[6] Characterizing mechanical jurisprudence as a "jurisprudence of conceptions" because it "exhibits a rigid scheme of deductions from *a priori* conceptions," Pound insisted that "we have to rid ourselves of this sort of legality and to attain a pragmatic, a sociological legal science."[7] When law becomes strictly a logical enterprise deriving a rigid set of rules from first principles concerning human nature that are assumed to be fixed and immutable, it acquires "the sterility of a fully developed system" and fails "to respond to vital needs of present day life."[8] Contrasting growth and life with arid "scientific" abstraction, Pound reminds jurists that "law is not scientific for the sake of science. Being scientific as a means toward an end, it must be judged by the results it achieves, not by the niceties of its internal structure."[9] The law will avoid the pitfalls of excessive formality only if we develop a "jurisprudence of ends" to replace a "jurisprudence of conceptions," and Pound asserts that in every period in which the law has grown and adapted to new social conditions "we have a jurisprudence of ends in fact, even if in form it is a jurisprudence of conceptions."[10]

Pound's opposition to mechanical jurisprudence was primarily directed

4. Oliver Wendell Holmes, *Collected Legal Papers* (New York, 1952), p. 50.

5. Gary J. Jacobsohn, *Pragmatism, Statesmanship, and the Supreme Court* (Ithaca, N.Y., 1977), pp. 65–88.

6. The brief treatment of pragmatic jurisprudence in this chapter must deal with central tendencies of thought in this school of jurisprudence without exploring some significant variations among individuals generally identified with it. Morris Cohen, for instance, has been classified as a sociological jurist because of his contributions to a critique of mechanical jurisprudence and his links to pragmatism, but he was also highly critical of the excessive antiformalism of mainstream pragmatic jurisprudence.

7. Roscoe Pound, "Mechanical Jurisprudence," *Columbia Law Review* 8 (1908): 608–609.

8. Ibid., p. 614.

9. Ibid., p. 605.

10. Ibid., p. 611.

against American laissez-faire jurisprudence of the late nineteenth and early twentieth centuries. The mechanical quality of the legal reasoning in laissez-faire jurisprudence was epitomized by the Supreme Court's reasoning in *Adair v. United States* and *Coppage v. Kansas.*[11] These cases dealt respectively with federal and state legislation that prohibited employers from discharging employees because they joined a union or from using "yellow dog" contracts, which forced an employee to cede his right to join a union as a condition of employment. In both cases the Supreme Court declared the relevant statutes unconstitutional, in part because they were unjustified infringements on the freedom of contract.

In these cases the Supreme Court had dealt a harsh blow to the cause of industrial unionization because they applied the freedom of contract principle to the relationship between an individual employee and the employer. To the pragmatists the extension of the freedom-of-contract concept in this form to modern industrial employment contracts ignored a vast disproportion in the bargaining power of individual employees and their employers. As Holmes was to note in his dissent from the majority opinion in *Coppage,* it was necessary for the law to safeguard the right of an employee to join a union "in order to establish the equality of position between the parties in which liberty of contract begins."[12] Roscoe Pound identified the fallacy in legal reasoning that led the majority astray. "The conception of freedom of contract is made the basis of a logical deduction. The court does not inquire what the effect of such a deduction will be when applied to the actual situation. It does not observe that the result will be to produce a condition precisely the reverse of that which the conception originally contemplated."[13] The exclusive emphasis on formal rules and principles rather than on substantive justice in mechanical jurisprudence makes it all too easy for rules or principles to be overextended to cover cases for which they are inappropriate.

The legal formalism that sociological jurists like Pound found objectionable was also reflected in constitutional law in the laissez-faire interpretive stance that focused on the literal words of the Constitution without reference to such concepts as "the spirit of the document" or the "intention of the framers." In *United States v. E. C. Knight,*[14] for instance, the Court interpreted the federal power to control interstate commerce in a restricted fashion to apply only to commerce as trade and not to the manufacture of goods intended for trade, and hence it refused to grant the federal government the power to regulate a manufacturing monopoly. Here a literal rendition of the interstate commerce clause led to an artificial distinction directly contrary to the purpose of the clause, since

11. 208 U.S. 161 (1908); 236 U.S. 1 (1915).
12. Lerner, p. 155.
13. Pound, p. 616.
14. 156 U.S. 1 (1895).

such an interpretation in fact severely limited the power of the federal government to regulate interstate commerce. Justifiably criticizing such forms of constitutional interpretation, the pragmatists revealed the essentially political character of judicial power used in this manner and exposed the extent to which judges, under the guise of the rule of law, were simply substituting their policy preferences for those of legislative majorities.

Yet rather than simply note that the meanings of the words of the Constitution were not always self-evident and that they might have to be interpreted in light of the purposes of their authors, the pragmatists emphasized the ineradicable ambiguity of the Constitution's "great generalities."[15] Rejecting the moderate correction of literalism implied by references to the "intention of the American framers" because such reforms would still wed the Constitution to a distant historical era, the sociological jurists insisted on the need for a more expansive mode of interpretation that took account of evolving "considerations of policy and social advantage." The theory of the "living constitution" was a product of sociological jurisprudence.[16]

While Pound attacked a mechanical conception of the law that transformed it into a strictly formal system, he did not totally dismiss the virtues of legal formalism. Acknowledging that a legal "science" helped "to eliminate so far as may be the personal equation in judicial administration, to preclude corruption and to limit the dangerous possibilities of magisterial ignorance," Pound sought only to temper an extreme version of mechanical jurisprudence.[17] Furthermore, the law governing aspects of life not undergoing rapid change could often profitably be rationalized into a stable system of rules, and a mechanical form of legal reasoning was an appropriate method for disposing of cases in these areas of law. Citing commercial law dealing with property and contracts as a "field of legal order" in which the mechanical ideal proved to be "a distinct gain for the legal order," Pound's reservations against mechanical jurisprudence were restricted to the extension of this ideal into other areas of law "involving unique situations, calling for standards and for individualized application."[18]

15. Benjamin Cardozo, *The Nature of the Judicial Process* (New Haven, 1921), p. 17.

16. Holmes was one of the first to suggest, in a qualified form, the new theory in *Missouri v. Holland* (252 U.S. 416, 433): "When we are dealing with words that also are a constituent act, like the Constitution of the U.S., we must realize that they have called into life a being the development of which could not have been foreseen completely by the most gifted of its begetters. It was enough for them to realize or to hope that they had created an organism; it has taken a century and has cost their successors much sweat and blood to prove that they created a nation."

17. Pound, p. 605.

18. Cardozo's call for a more-creative role for judges was similarly restricted to exceptional cases in areas where the law was growing. In more settled realms of law, Cardozo accepted the mechanical conception of judicial decision making. Pound and Cardozo could still see the dangers of pushing the pragmatist antiformalist critique too far. According to Pound (*An Introduction to*

By the mid-1920s the moderate attack on mechanical jurisprudence by those identified with sociological jurisprudence was giving way to a more radical attack by a second generation of pragmatists known as Legal Realists. The legal realists—such men as Karl Llewellyn, Jerome Frank, Felix Cohen, Thurman Arnold, and Herman Oliphant—reiterated many of the themes of sociological jurisprudence, notably emphasizing that an excessive emphasis on the logical character of law could lead to injustices in particular cases. Seconding Pound's appeal for a jurisprudence of ends, the legal realists insisted that strict adherence to rules give way to a more flexible and discretionary quest for equity.[19] The legal realists differed from their sociological jurisprudence predecessors primarily in the consistency and comprehensiveness with which they developed their critique of legal formalism, rejecting even Pound's limited defense of mechanical jurisprudence based on a division of the law into realms amenable to standardized treatment and realms requiring individualized treatment of cases.

Given the common intellectual foundations of sociological jurisprudence and legal realism in pragmatism, it is appropriate to categorize them as subtypes of a more general Pragmatic Jurisprudence.[20] In our analysis of the impact of pragmatism on American political thought, however, it will be appropriate to focus primarily on legal realism. Not only were the legal realists more consistent with the antiformalist spirit of pragmatic philosophy than the more moderate sociological jurists had been,[21] they were also more influential in the long run. By 1960 Hassel Yntema, a prominent realist, could boast with little exaggeration that the realist

---

the Philosophy of Law [New Haven, 1954], p. 63), "Much that has been written by advocates of the equitable theory of application of law is extravagant. As usually happens, in reaction from theories going too far in one direction this theory has gone too far in the other. The last century would have eliminated individualization of application. Now, as in the sixteenth- and seventeenth-century reaction from the strict law, come those who would have nothing else; who would turn over the whole field of judicial justice to administrative methods. . . . Only a saint, such as Louis IX under the oak at Vincennes, may be trusted with the wide powers of a judge restrained only by a desire for just results in each case to be reached by taking the law for a general guide." For Pound, a jurisprudence that provided no more guidance for judges than to rely on the intuitive sense of justice in adjudicating each case was a jurisprudence in name only. Thus if pragmatic jurisprudence could not supply a more rational foundation for decision making than this, even Pound would have been forced to concede its failure.

19. Jerome Frank. *Courts on Trial* (Princeton, 1949), p. 383.

20. For a more elaborate justification for dealing with sociological jurisprudence and legal realism collectively as forms of legal pragmatism, and for treating the debates between Roscoe Pound and the legal realists in the early 1930s as an internecine quarrel within the pragmatist camp, see Robert Samuel Summers, *Instrumentalism and American Legal Theory* (Ithaca, N.Y., 1982), pp. 19–38.

21. John Dewey, the only pragmatic philosopher to venture into the field of jurisprudence, wrote several articles in the legal realist vein, and his seminars in jurisprudence at Columbia inspired a number of the younger legal realist scholars. See esp. "Logical Method and Law," *Cornell Law Quarterly* 10 (1924): 17.

"attitude toward legal problems ... has dominated legal thinking in the
United States during the past generation even to the point of becoming
commonplace."[22]

Pragmatic Jurisprudence and Rule Skepticism

Legal formalism identifies law with rules and principles and treats cases
as derivative applications of these. Paradoxically, C. C. Langdell, the
dean of the Harvard Law School who had revolutionized legal education
by introducing the case study approach to law, was the foremost spokesman
for a formalist view of the law during the late nineteenth century. Actually,
Langdell's emphasis on cases was confined to their pedagogical utility.
Cases provided an inductive route through which the logical coherence of
the legal system could be grasped. In the final analysis his approach
devalued individual cases because they became no more than concrete
manifestations of abstract principles. Principles were the heart of the
law.[23] Pushed to the extremes, the formalist view of law implies not only
that laws are rules but also that "the law" is a self-contained logical
system of rules that can be syllogistically applied to particular cases to
produce unique and certain outcomes. In principles, every possible case
has been provided for, and new cases that arise, however difficult they
may be to decide, have a unique and correct solution within the law.
Because there was nothing arbitrary about the subsumption of individual
cases under general rules, judges did not have any discretion in applying
the law.
    When the formalist view is pushed to these extremes—which is rare—
the pragmatic attack on mechanical jurisprudence or excessive legal
formalism is vigorous and compelling. The pragmatists denied the possibility that any abstract system could anticipate every possible case that
could arise and provide for its determinant resolution.[24] Because the law
could not anticipate all future cases that might arise under it, the
pragmatists argued, judges would necessarily have a great deal of discretion when confronted with situations that called for creative solutions. The
legal formalist ideal provided an overly mechanistic description of judicial
decision making.
    In conjunction with this attack on a mechanistic description of judicial
decision making, the pragmatists attacked the idea that rules were the
essence of law and that cases were no more than applications of rules.
Holmes was one of the first to criticize this devaluation of cases. He

22. Rumble, p. 53.
23. H. L. Pohlman, *Justice Oliver Wendell Holmes and Utilitarian Jurisprudence* (Cambridge,
Mass., 1984), pp. 78–79.
24. Jerome Frank, *Law and the Modern Mind* (Gloucester, Mass., 1970), pp. 3–13.

favored a more empirical approach to the law which considered individual cases to be the essential constituent elements of a legal system.[25] In his famed dissent in *Lochner v. New York*, Holmes emphasized the uniqueness of individual cases by insisting, "General propositions do not decide concrete cases."[26] The task of judicial reasoning was to respond creatively to the distinctive problems posed by new cases rather than to escape by ascending into abstract flights of reason divorced from the facts of a case. But while acknowledging that in creatively deciding cases judges were in effect making law, Holmes minimized the significance of this by suggesting they "do so only interstitially; they are confined from molar to molecular motions."[27]

If general propositions could not decide concrete cases, then the judicial opinions that accompanied decisions must be deceptive because they purport to derive the decision from general propositions. Arguing that formal legal reasoning could in fact be manipulated to justify any decision the judge wanted to arrive at, the pragmatists dismissed the formal reasoning in these opinions as post hoc reasoning that served as a mere rationalization concealing the true grounds for judicial decisions.[28] A variety of psychological and sociological explanations were offered to explain the capacity of these rationalizations to persuade and to legitimate the exercise of power, but most of the pragmatists believed that these modes of legitimization were unnecessary and counterproductive and that a demystification of formal legal reasoning held the promise of more rational governance. Rationality would be enhanced by examining the potential consequences of different decisions and making a selection based on the substantive merits of these outcomes.

As the reaction against legal formalism intensified among pragmatists, the argument that law as discrete cases must be distinguished from the rules and principles that systematized the cases was radicalized into the argument that there was no intrinsic or necessary connection between rules and principles and individual cases and that whatever connection existed was imposed by extralegal considerations. Karl Llewellyn identified the legal realists as those who questioned "the theory that traditional prescriptive rule-formulations are *the* heavily operative factor in producing court decisions."[29] Noting that rules were inherently ambiguous because they

25. Pohlman, p. 160.

26. *Lochner v. New York*, 198 U.S. 45, 74 (1905), cited in Lerner, p. 149.

27. *Southern Pacific Co. v. Jensen*, 244 U.S. 205, 221 (1917). Holmes admonished judges not to abuse their discretionary powers, insisting that the proper judicial stance was one of deference to the legislature.

28. Frank, *Law and the Modern Mind*, pp. 27–31. Joseph Bingham went as far as to propose that judges dispense with opinion-writing altogether. See Joseph Bingham, "My Philosophy of Law," in *My Philosophy of Law: Credos of Sixteen American Scholars*, ed. Julius Rosenthal Foundation (Boston, 1941), p. 13.

29. Quoted in Rumble, p. 52.

were expressed in general language whose empirical referent could never be exhaustively specified, and that many rules could be potentially extended to cover any particular case, the more radical pragmatists concluded that the potential scope of a rule was indeterminate and that the decision to subsume a case under a particular rule was fundamentally arbitrary unless one turned from formal to substantive grounds for making a decision.[30] While most of the pragmatists stopped short of embracing a total rule skepticism, which denied that rules played any role in adjudication, even its moderate proponents thoroughly subordinated formal rationality to substantive rationality in legal considerations.

The alternative mode of reasoning about cases that the pragmatists proposed did not totally dispense with rules, but it did relegate them to the status of "rules of thumb," which were merely suggestions as to how to proceed in a case. Rules were to be treated like all other legal fictions, which are " 'intended for the sake of justice' and should 'not be permitted to work any wrong.' "[31] John Dewey illustrated the role that rules would play in his description of a pragmatist mode of legal reasoning: "Premises only gradually emerge from analysis of the total situation. The problem is not to draw a conclusion from given premises; . . . The problem is to *find* statements, of general principle and of particular fact, which are worthy to serve as premises. As a matter of actual fact, we generally begin with some vague anticipation of a conclusion (or at least of alternative conclusions), and then we look around for principles and data which will substantiate it or which will enable us to choose intelligently between rival conclusions."[32] Whether or not Dewey's "rules of thumb" can legitimately be referred to as legal rules is open to serious doubt. These amorphous guides to legal thinking are so flexible that they do not appear to provide much, if any, constraint on discretion.

Could pragmatism have been the source of a public philosophy legitimating the forms of discretionary administration that Lowi finds objectionable? Given Lowi's identification of law with rules, it is axiomatic that the legal realists' proclivities toward rule skepticism would undermine the rule of law. The pragmatists' assertion that formal rationality served as no more than a mask concealing the true grounds of judicial decisions, the policy preferences of judges, would certainly have influenced attitudes toward administrative as well as judicial decision making. Many administrative decisions are quasi-judicial in character. Denigrating legal formalism might well have influenced behavior in the manner of a self-fulfilling prophecy, encouraging judges or administrators to decide cases on ad hoc policy grounds rather than on legal grounds, and this is the very mode of decision making that Lowi objects to.

30. Frank, *Law and the Modern Mind,* pp. 127–159, 283–306.
31. Frank, *Courts on Trial,* p. 383.
32. Dewey, "Logical Method and Law," p. 23.

Pragmatic Jurisprudence and the American Tradition

While the legal formalists of the 1960s and 1970s vigorously rejected the antiformalism of pragmatic jurisprudence, other commentators who have been more willing to concede that excessive formalism or legalism is a serious problem for any legal system that attempts to govern itself by law have generally had a much more sympathetic reaction. Grant Gilmore's judgment that the legal realists "did much to make of law a more useful and flexible instrument for the resolution of social conflicts" typifies this line of thinking.[33] It is not surprising that this movement away from formalism after a legalistic era like the laissez-faire period would have been welcomed as a healthy restoration of legal flexibility.

This assessment of the impact of pragmatic jurisprudence becomes more questionable, however, when pragmatic jurisprudence is contrasted with the liberal jurisprudence of such men as John Marshall, Joseph Story, or Chancellor Kent rather than with the late nineteenth and early twentieth century laissez-faire jurisprudence. A comparison of traditional American natural rights jurisprudence and pragmatic jurisprudence is appropriate because the pragmatic attack on a "jurisprudence of conceptions," although primarily directed at laissez-faire jurisprudence, was in fact no less a repudiation of traditional American natural rights jurisprudence as well.[34] The pragmatists justified their sweeping repudiation of natural rights jurisprudence on the grounds that any jurisprudence founded on such *a priori* conceptions as natural rights was inherently legalistic and that laissez-faire jurisprudence was the natural outcome of such an orientation—an assertion that ignores the fact that Social Darwinism rather than John Locke's natural rights theory was responsible for some of the excessive formalism of laissez-faire jurisprudence. In fact, a comparison of classic natural rights jurisprudence and laissez-faire jurisprudence reveals important differences between the two, which should be acknowledged. Classic natural rights jurisprudence did not suffer in practice from the same mechanical and legalistic excesses of laissez-faire jurisprudence, and the flexibility of the former was well grounded in its theory; it had not been smuggled in sub rosa by practitioners whose practice transcended their inadequate theory.[35]

The emphasis on judicial flexibility in classic natural rights jurisprudence found expression in the U.S. Constitution, which extended the

---

33. Grant Gilmore, "Legal Realism: Its Cause and Cure," *Yale Law Journal* 70 (1961): 1048.

34. The term "natural rights jurisprudence" points to the strong connections between the jurisprudence of such men as John Marshall and the natural rights political philosophy of John Locke. For an analysis of that connection, see Robert K. Faulkner, *The Jurisprudence of John Marshall* (Princeton, 1968).

35. For a discussion of the natural rights foundation of classical American jurisprudence, see Gary J. Jacobsohn, *The Supreme Court and the Decline of Constitutional Aspiration* (Totowa, N.J., 1986).

judicial power to all cases in law and *equity,* and in the development of principles of equity within the U.S. legal system. Ever since Aristotle noted that written laws cannot provide for all cases because lawgivers, "being unable to define for all cases, . . . are obliged to make a universal statement, which is not applicable to all, but only to most cases," and had therefore asserted that "equity is justice that goes beyond the written law," arguments stressing the need for legal flexibility and for the correction of law by equity have had an honorable place in the Western legal tradition.[36] Joseph Story, one of the most able expositors of natural rights jurisprudence and the father of American equity, had acknowledged that "every system of laws must necessarily be defective" and that "cases must occur, to which the antecedent rules cannot be applied without injustice, or to which they cannot be applied at all."[37] Story therefore insisted that equity be considered in the "interpretation and limitation of the words of positive or written laws; by construing them, not according to the letter but according to the reason and spirit of them."[38] This emphasis on the intention of the lawgiver rather than a literalistic interpretation of text hardly exemplifies the kind of legal formalism that the pragmatists found so offensive.

But if the dangers of excessive legal formalism had long been recognized in the American legal systems, the danger that excessive legal flexibility would degenerate into arbitrary authority—the antithesis of the rule of law—had received no less attention. For instance, Joseph Story tempered his defense of judicial flexibility with a concern for its potential abuses:

> If . . . a Court of Equity . . . did possess the unbounded jurisdiction which has been thus generally ascribed to it, of correcting, controlling, moderating, and even superseding the law, and enforcing all the rights, as well as the charities, arising from natural law and justice, and of freeing itself from all regard to former rules and precedents, it would be the most gigantic in its sway, and the most formidable instrument of arbitrary power, that could well be devised. It would literally place the whole rights and property of the community under the arbitrary will of the Judge, acting, if you please, arbitrio et bono, according to his own notions and conscience, but still acting with a despotic and sovereign authority.[39]

Story's defense of judicial powers of equity rested in part on the demonstration that equity did not imply such open-ended discretion and that decisions in equity were constrained by a logical system of rules and

36. Aristotle, *Art of Rhetoric,* trans. J. H. Freese (Cambridge, Mass., 1926), 1374b.
37. Joseph Story, *Commentaries on Equity Jurisprudence,* 3d ed. (Boston, 1842), 1:7.
38. Ibid., p. 8.
39. Quoted in Gary L. McDowell, *Equity and the Constitution* (Chicago, 1982), p. 76.

precedents in much the same way that common law decisions were. Nevertheless, equity jurisdiction did expand the scope of judicial discretion, and Story was therefore careful to preserve the limits on equity implicit in the maxim "Equity follows the law," an acknowledgment that equity could advance the remedies of the law or mitigate its severity, "but, in no case, does it contradict or overturn the grounds or principles thereof."[40] Story's defense of equity thus provided a corrective to the problem of excessive legal formalism, while his subordination of equity to law upheld legal formalism as indispensable to the rule of law.

With this understanding of classic natural rights jurisprudence in mind, it becomes clear that the pragmatists were mistaken when they asserted that any reference to *a priori* principles or to nature in jurisprudence led to mechanical jurisprudence. The pragmatists ignored the distinction between a jurisprudence that defined the *end* or *purpose* of the law as securing natural rights, as traditional American liberal jurisprudence had, and a jurisprudence that incorporated natural rights as the first premises in deductive syllogistic arguments to determine the outcome of specific cases, as laissez-faire jurisprudence at times did.[41] If the pragmatists had distinguished traditional American jurisprudence from laissez-faire jurisprudence more systematically—noting the ways the former discouraged direct appeals to natural rights in favor of appeals to the Constitution, and understanding the Constitution at least in part as an instrument for securing collective welfare and therefore as an instrument to be construed in accord with the demands of prudence—they would have been forced to retract their assertion that natural rights jurisprudence inherently led to sterile legal formalism.

What is distinctive about pragmatic jurisprudence was not its concern with legalism per se, but the extremes to which the pragmatists were willing to go to avoid legalism. Rejecting as inadequate the doctrines within classic natural rights jurisprudence that moderated propensities toward legalism, the pragmatists assumed that nothing short of a "jurisprudence of consequences" would permit flexibility in judicial interpretation. Virtually ignoring the case for legal rigor, the pragmatists developed a one-sided approach that enlarged judicial discretion far beyond the point that classic natural rights jurisprudence had been willing

40. Ibid. This discussion relies heavily on McDowell's work.

41. In criticizing natural rights jurisprudence, the pragmatists condemned its reliance on "universals" or "absolutes." Precisely because the pragmatists failed to distinguish "universals" from "absolutes," they misperceived the character of the natural rights doctrine. While the natural rights doctrine necessarily asserts certain universal or natural claims, it does not entail the conclusion that those universals are in turn "absolutes," if by the term "absolutes" one implies claims that cannot be compromised in practice and hence must function within the law as the first premises of legal arguments. Edward Purcell Jr.'s reconstruction of the debates surrounding the rise of pragmatic jurisprudence highlights the identification of universals and absolutes. See Purcell, pp. 74–94, 159–178.

to tolerate. Such a jurisprudence was not a healthy tonic for the American legal system, reintroducing flexibility into a system that had become unduly mechanical in the laissez-faire era; it was an excessive reaction to excessive formalism, a reaction that veered so far toward flexibility and discretion in the administration of law that it substantially undermined the rule of law as it became an increasingly influential doctrine within the American legal establishment.

That pragmatic jurisprudence is not simply an attack on a rigid, rule-bound conception of the rule of law, but rather has a more broadly corrosive effect on law per se, is suggested by its response to the common law. The common law mode of legal reasoning has generally been regarded as the most flexible in the Western legal tradition. It is not surprising that the pragmatists were therefore generally favorably disposed toward the common law. A mechanical conception of the law as composed solely of a rationalized system of rules and principles in most plausible when the law is a codified set of legislative statutes. Under a common law system of judge-made law based on concrete precedents, the assertions that the essence of law is grasped through abstract rules and principles and that the role of a judge is a mechanical one are far less plausible. The empirical and inductive approach of the common law, and the traditionalism associated with the role of precedents, are less amenable to systematic rationalization. Nevertheless, the common law may no more dispense with rules, concepts, and principles than any other system of law if it is not to become a contradictory and fragmented amalgam of cases, and hence the most notable practitioners of the common law have been those who have advanced our understanding of its underlying coherence, in part by discovering abstract unities underlying its diverse cases and in part by imposing such unities through a selective presentation of governing precedents.

The importance of rules and principles in the common law points to fundamental differences between the common law mode of legal reasoning and the empirical, consequentialist mode of reasoning recommended by pragmatism. Those differences are manifested in their respective treatments of the role of precedent in judicial decision making. Respect for precedents is at the heart of the common law approach, for adherence to precedents prevents judicial discretion from degenerating into an arbitrary power to make ad hoc decisions—the antithesis of the rule of law. Attention to precedents encourages judges to render decisions that are consistent with past decisions, a focus that permits case-by-case adjudication to achieve at least a minimal degree of formal rationality. The pragmatists, skeptical of formal rationality in all its guises, challenged the assertion that the common law possessed this formal rationality by arguing that judges had a multiplicity of precedents to choose from and that they could pick and choose among the available precedents to arrive at any decision they wanted.[42] Furthermore, the pragmatists believed that contradictory precedents were endemic to the common law and could not be removed by attempts to rationalize the common law by identifying its underlying unity and pruning inconsistent precedents. Thus they were generally unsympathetic to the efforts of the American institute of Law to systematize the common law through authoritative restatements of its cases.[43] As was the case with rule skepticism in pragmatism, precedent skepticism was rarely pushed to the extreme of denying the value of following precedents altogether, but the conclusion that there was a wide-ranging latitude in interpreting precedents and that the formal demands of respect for precedent therefore need not conflict with the demands of policy or equity was widely embraced. This imported a dangerously wide latitude for discretion into the common law, forms of discretion that the most prominent common law practitioners had always striven to avoid.

The full scope of the radical challenge that pragmatism posed to American political and legal traditions becomes even more visible when one shifts from a consideration of means, the plane of formalism versus discretion, to a consideration of ends. In repudiating natural rights theory, the pragmatists formulated a more relativistic and consequentialist doctrine of the ends of government that was closely akin to utilitarianism.[44] The debt that pragmatism owed to the utilitarians is readily apparent in William James's description of the task of ethical theory: "Since everything which is demanded is by that fact a good, must not the guiding principle for ethical philosophy (since all demands conjointly cannot be satisfied in this poor world) be simply to satisfy at all times *as many demands as we can*? The act must be the best act, accordingly, which makes for the best whole, in the sense of awakening the least sum of dissatisfactions."[45] James's ethics shares with utilitarianism the identification of the good or desirable with the desired. Refusing to make objective qualitative distinctions between good and bad desires, he distinguishes the moral and the immoral based on a quantitative scale of desire maximization.

Some pragmatists, like John Dewey, did dissent from the hedonistic implications of utilitarianism and attempt to develop a more subtle utilitarian calculus that did not simply equate the desirable with being desired. Dewey distinguished desires that could be affirmed after reflection

42. William O. Douglas, "Stare Decisis," in *Essays in Jurisprudence from the Columbia Law Review* (New York, 1963), p. 19.

43. Rumble, pp. 156–157.

44. This is not to deny that there are also profound differences between utilitarianism and pragmatism. The most immediately relevant difference is that Bentham's unitarianism was relentlessly individualistic, whereas pragmatism, as we shall see, is strongly linked to the development of a pluralistic group theory.

45. Quoted in Summers, p. 43. See also Dewey, *Reconstruction in Philosophy*, p. 180.

on their consequences from unreflective desires, but because reason was ultimately the instrument of desire in Dewey's thought, it could never become an independent arbiter of the validity of desires. To assign such an elevated role to reason would have been too reminiscent of the attempt to determine the desirable by an objective external standard, a possibility that Dewey steadfastly rejected. Dewey's distinction between reflective and unreflective desires was ultimately as untenable in pragmatism as John Stuart Mill's distinction between high and low desires had been in utilitarianism, and both were driven back to a quantitative maximizing criterion of evaluation.[46]

Pragmatic jurisprudence applied the same utilitarian calculus to legal systems by arguing that laws were instruments for maximizing utility. Roscoe Pound asserted:

> For the purpose of understanding the law of today I am content with a picture of satisfying as much of the whole body of human wants as we may with the least sacrifice. . . . For present purposes I am content to see in legal history the record of a continually wider recognizing and satisfying of human wants or claims or desires through social control; a more embracing and more effective securing of social interests; a continually more complete and effective elimination of waste and precluding of friction in human enjoyment of the goods of existence—in short, a continually more efficacious social engineering.[47]

Pound's utilitarianism was bounded—only "social" interests were incorporated into the sum total of desires to be maximized—but such qualifications tended to disappear as legal realism displaced sociological jurisprudence. Herman Oliphant simply claimed that "the Pragmatism of James and the instrumental logic of Dewey" were allowing Americans "to catch up with Bentham."[48]

The pragmatists conceptualized the law as an instrument for social engineering, and they evaluated laws in terms of their capacity to maximize the satisfaction of desires. The proper mode of legal reasoning involved a factually based estimation of the strength of various desires, which were to be balanced against one another. The legal process had essentially become an extension of the policy process, and the distinction between making law and applying law withered away.[49] Confident that the emerging empirical social sciences would provide adequate guidance in constructing a more efficient and just society, the pragmatists demoted formal rationality and the "ineffective" constraints it placed on judicial

46. Summers, pp. 46–47. See Pohlman, *Holmes and Utilitarian Jurisprudence*, for an extended analysis of the links between utilitarian jurisprudence and the thought of Holmes.
47. Pound, *Introduction to the Philosophy of Law*, p. 47.
48. Quoted in Summers, p. 60.
49. Frank, *Law and the Modern Mind*, p. 130.

and administrative discretion and sought to imitate the professionalism of the new technocratic elite. They were not deliberately fostering arbitrary and capricious government, but it is questionable whether their reliance on social science to provide objective and impartial findings provided adequate safeguards against arbitrary power.

Pragmatic skepticism regarding the distinction between making law and applying law had profound implications beyond its denigration of formal rationality, for that distinction lay at the foundation of American constitutional thought. Without it there is no justification for a separation of powers. In *The Federalist Papers,* Madison and Hamilton systematically distinguish the role of legislators from the role of judges. They fundamentally affirm, albeit with some important qualifications, the traditional conception that legislators make law and judges apply it. To a large extent, legislators (including the president in his legislative role) are responsible for a utilitarian balancing of competing interests, although even legislators should reflect on the constitutionality of proposed legislation and this necessarily entails reasoning concerning rights that transcends a strict utilitarianism. In order to carry out their interest-balancing function democratically, they must be accountable, either directly or indirectly, to the people. The balance between competing interests that is struck is a contingent balance that should generally reflect the preferences of the majority, and because there is invariably an element of arbitrariness to this, Hamilton refers to the acts of the political branches as acts of "will."[50]

By contrast, judges exercise "judgment" rather than "will." They apply preexisting law to particular cases, and that is fundamentally a nondiscretionary act that justifies their insulation from public opinion through lifetime appointments. Even judicial review, which Hamilton defends, is portrayed as an act of judgment based on the Constitution rather than on statutes. The nondiscretionary character of judicial review is suggested by Hamilton's reference to the invalidity of "all acts contrary to the *manifest* tenor of the Constitution."[51] The use of the term "manifest" makes it clear that the courts are to exercise the power of judicial review where the Constitution speaks with a clear voice, and that there is consequently little discretion in applying its limitations on the legislature. In cases where there is ambiguity, cases that would therefore entail judicial discretion, the implication would appear to be that the courts should act in a restrained fashion and generally give the benefit of the doubt to the legislature. This portrait of judges exercising at best limited discretion is confirmed by Hamilton's assertion that we will need specially trained judges and a complex system of laws: "To avoid an arbitrary discretion in

50. *Federalist Papers,* pp. 214–217, 465.
51. Ibid., p. 466. Emphasis added.

the courts, it is indispensable that they should be bound down by strict rules and precedents which serve to define and point out their duty in every particular case that comes before them.''[52]

In isolation, this statement suggests that Hamilton is more of a legal formalist than he actually was. Immediately before making this statement Hamilton argued, ''The judicial magistracy is of vast importance in mitigating the severity and confining the operation of such [i.e., unjust] laws,'' and this acknowledgment of the equitable powers of the courts would be inconsistent with a genuinely rigid legal formalist position.[53] As a whole, *The Federalist Papers* steer the same middle course between the extremes of legal formalism and unfettered discretion that we discover in Justice Story's reflections on equity.[54] Consistent with this moderate approach to legal formalism, *The Federalist Papers* never argue for an absolutely rigid separation of powers. The flexibility of the Federalists' scheme was demonstrated by their willingness to compromise it by adding a system of checks and balances that granted some legislative powers to the president and gave the Senate a share in some executive powers. In addition, the Federalists hoped that the American legal system would be based on the common law, even though the common law involves interstitial judicial lawmaking. But as important as these qualifications of the distinction between making law and applying law are for understanding our framework of government, they should not obscure the fundamental truth that the distinction was central to Hamilton's conception of the separation of powers.

Roscoe Pound recognized that the doctrine of separation of powers basically rested on such as assumption. Identifying the distinction between making law and applying law with mechanical jurisprudence, Pound argued that ''in the eighteenth century it was given scientific form in the theory of separation of powers.''[55] By contrast, sociological jurists recognized that ''lawmaking, administration, and adjudication cannot be rigidly fenced off one from the other and turned over each to a separate agency as its exclusive field.''[56] While it may appear as if Pound is only arguing against a rigid conception of the separation of powers, his more fundamental point is that the doctrine of separation of powers inherently gives rise to a rigid separation of powers, just as the distinction between making law and applying law is presumed inherently to give rise to mechanical jurisprudence. Pound was only acknowledging the logical implications of

52. Ibid., p. 471.
53. Ibid., p. 470.
54. For a more extensive argument demonstrating that *The Federalist Papers* steered clear of excessive legal formalism, see Jeremy Rabkin, ''Bureaucratic Idealism and Executive Power: A Perspective on *The Federalist's* View of Public Administration,'' in *Saving the Revolution: The Federalist Papers and the American Founding,* ed. Charles R. Kesler (New York, 1987).
55. Pound, *Introduction to the Philosophy of Law,* p. 49.
56. Ibid., p. 50.

the pragmatist attack on the distinction between making law and applying law when he argued, "We have to combat the political theory and the dogma of separation of powers."[57]

In attacking natural rights philosophy and American constitutionalism, and in their revisionist approach to the common law, the pragmatists were undermining the public philosophy, institutional forms, and modes of legal reasoning that had sustained a commitment to the rule of law in the United States since the eighteenth century. The belief that individuals possessed certain rights by nature that governments were obliged to respect had rendered illegitimate arbitrary or capricious infringements of those right. It was the natural rights philosophy that had guided the American framers in constructing the U.S. Constitution with its separation of powers and checks and balances, and that Constitution had given us, with the exception of the civil war years, 140 years of stable liberal democratic rule by the beginning of the 1930s. By comparison, the safeguards against arbitrary authority that pragmatism erected in place of natural rights appeared pale and insubstantial. It is therefore hardly surprising that critics of pragmatism during the 1930s, when many European democracies were being replaced by authoritarian or totalitarian regimes, were prone to suggest that the growing influence of pragmatism presaged a similar turn in the United States. When those critics were proven wrong, the case against pragmatism appeared considerably weaker. But the conclusion that pragmatism did not pose a threat to liberal democracy was premature. Those early critics of pragmatism had exaggerated its dangers but, as this study of the NRA will demonstrate, their alarm was not totally without foundation.

Pragmatism and Corporatism

If pragmatism led to the decline of the traditional American conception of the rule of law and replaced it with a jurisprudence that legitimated discretionary decision making on an unprecedented scale, does it also provide positive legitimation for the corporatist and quasi-corporatist political process that, Lowi argues, has replaced governance through law? Pragmatism and pragmatic jurisprudence contributed to the development of an American corporatism in two closely related ways. On the one hand, the pragmatists were rejecting the American political tradition, in part because they believed it was excessively individualistic. For instance, Roscoe Pound characterized the tradition as "ultraindividualism," which he defined as "an uncompromising insistence upon individual interests and individual property as the focal point of jurisprudence." While Pound does not deny the need to protect individuals, he believed that American

57. Roscoe Pound, *The Spirit of the Common Law* (Boston, 1921), p. 181.

law had become "so zealous to secure fair play to the individual that often it secures very little fair play to the public."[58]

Alone, this communitarian thrust to pragmatist theory might not have evolved in the direction of corporatism, but when communitarianism was combined with a radical commitment to democracy, corporatism became an increasingly attractive institutional form. The pragmatists had become skeptical of the rule of law in the early part of the twentieth century because it had become associated with laissez-faire capitalism and oligarchy. Resolutely democratic, pragmatists like John Dewey became convinced that only fundamental structural changes in the mode of economic organization, some form of economic or industrial democracy, could guarantee a genuinely democratic regime. Political democracy alone too easily became an empty form masking the rule of an oligarchical elite.[59]

The pragmatist vision of economic democracy took on strong corporatist overtones. Generally rejecting state socialism because it would simply substitute an autocratic civil service for the capitalist class, pragmatists like Dewey believed that corporatism woud decentralize power and encourage broad participation in economic decision making:

> It must be pointed out that in Great Britain and this country . . . the measures taken for enforcing the subordination of private activity to public need and service have been successful only because they have enlisted the voluntary cooperation of associations which have been formed on a non-political, non-governmental basis, large industrial corporations, railway systems, labor unions, universities, scientific societies, banks, etc. . . . Reorganization along these lines would give us in the future a federation of self-governing industries with the government acting as adjuster and arbiter rather than as direct owner and manager.[60]

Dewey's reference to a "*federation* of self-governing industries" would suggest that at this stage in his career his corporatism was the societal corporatist variety.

Later in his career Dewey grew more suspicious of corporatism, especially after it became linked to fascism in Western Europe. In the 1920s he generally emphasized participation in local governments and local communities as the locus of grassroots democracy, rather than participation in functional organizations.[61] But even during this period he continued to view corporatism as a potential industrial counterpart to town meetings. For instance, in a review of Walter Lippmann's *Phantom Public* late in 1925, Dewey argued:

58. Quoted in Gary Jacobsohn, *The Supreme Court and the Decline of Constitutional Aspiration*, p. 17.
59. John Dewey, *The Public and Its Problems* (Denver, 1927), p. 143.
60. John Dewey, *The Independent*, 22 June 1918, pp. 482–483.
61. John Dewey, *The Public and Its Problems*, pp. 212–213.

One is struck, it may be noted in passing, by the fact that Mr. Lippmann makes no reference to the theories which would organize different social activities functionally, by occupational activities and interest.... But it is difficult to see how even occasional intervening action of the general public is to be made effective in the ways which he postulates until the group activities upon which it is to operate are better organized and more open to recognition.... It is at least arguable that Mr. Lippmann's conception cannot be made workable without something that approximates a "guild" or "soviet"—please note I do not say Bolshevist—organization.[62]

Dewey's reference to corporatism here is more vague, potentially implying either administrative or societal corporatism. Both were in fact compatible with the fundamental principles of his social and political philosophy, which had a strong but undifferentiated corporatist thrust.

Dewey has appropriately been categorized as one of the first group theorists because he believed that small groups were the constituent building blocks of society.[63] Rejecting traditional liberalism for its excessively individualist orientation, Dewey argued that man acquired his distinctly human dignity through participation in group life. Groups socialized and educated man, providing him with the habits that allowed him to manipulate his natural and social environment to satisfy his needs. Groups arose out of the perception of primitive shared needs and interests, but participation in groups soon led to the development of new and distinctly social interests, which in turn propelled man to ever more sophisticated forms of social organization. This progressive displacement of biological man by cultural man was the essence of human advancement.

Although the development of complex social organizations like the large nation-state were essential to human progress, these forms of association also posed a threat to man. Organization on this scale became increasingly remote from the individual, diminishing his opportunities for meaningful participation in communal life and attenuating the social bonds that linked him to his fellow man. If large-scale organizations grew at the expense of primary organizations, where man interacted in a direct, face-to-face fashion with others, Dewey concluded, man's social well-being would suffer. Thus, when Dewey assumed the role of social reformer, proposals to enhance and revitalize man's associational life played a central role in his reform agenda. Even though Dewey abandoned his explicit early flirtations with corporatism later in life, his principles of social action bore a strong resemblance to those of other, more explicitly corporatist theorists of his day, notably his friend and intellectual compatriot Harold Laski.

Although Dewey acknowledged the affinities between his own work and

62. *The New Republic*, 2 December 1925, pp. 53–54.
63. R. Jeffrey Lustig, *Corporate Liberalism* (Berkeley and Los Angeles, 1982), p. 120.

that of European and English pluralists (many of whom were in fact advocating corporatism), he did emphasize one distinction that is important for understanding the peculiar character of American corporatism. Whereas European and English pluralists stressed the role of secondary associations in limiting the claims to sovereignty of the state—a not unreasonable concern in the context of powerful European states—Dewey was reluctant to develop these implications in his own thought because he was writing in the altogether different context of a laissez-faire state. "The hypothesis which we have supported has obvious points of contact with what is known as the pluralistic conception of the state. It presents also a marked point of difference. . . . It is not a doctrine which prescribes inherent limits to state action. It does not intimate that the function of the state is limited to settling conflicts among other groups, as if each one of them had a fixed scope of action of its own. . . . Our hypothesis is neutral as to any general, sweeping implications as to how far state activity may extend."[64] For Dewey, powerful private corporations posed a radical threat to the democratic way of life, and he was reluctant to tie the hands of the one organization that could control corporations—the state.

The decline of the traditional American conception of the rule of law was accompanied by an increasing interest in alternative foundations of social order. In Dewey's communalist social philosophy, group socialization was the fundamental mechanism for providing social order, and although the state and its coercive mechanisms were necessary to regulate the externalities of group activities and to resolve group conflicts, the primary purpose of the state was to facilitate group life. Early in his career, Dewey's emphasis on groups had distinctly corporatist overtones. By the mid-1920s Dewey had moderated those overtones, but despite his later refusal to endorse corporatism he had not altered his fundamental principles. Thus Dewey's subsequent reservations concerning corporatism could not alter the fact that his principles were congenial to corporatist ideas, and if he was reluctant to draw corporatist conclusions from them, some of those who were influenced by him were not.[65]

64. Dewey, *The Public and Its Problems*, p. 73.
65. For the relationship between his principles and those of European thinkers associated with corporatism, see William Y. Elliot, *The Pragmatic Revolt in Politics* (New York, 1928); James Kloppenberg, *Uncertain Victory* (Oxford, 1986).

CHAPTER 2

Progressivism and the
New Deal State

In the Introduction and in Chapter 1, we criticized Lowi's thesis regarding pluralism and its transformation into the reigning public philosophy of the post–New Deal era and offered in its place an alternative thesis focusing on pragmatism and its judicial and social science offspring. Lowi had implausibly argued that Arthur Schlesinger, Jr., and John Kenneth Galbraith popularized pluralist ideas and transformed pluralism from an academic model into a reigning public philosophy. Is it possible to provide a more persuasive account of the popularization of pragmatism?

As influential as pragmatism was in intellectual and legal circles, its political influence has not been so clearly established. There was definitely an affinity between John Dewey's "method of experimental intelligence" and the pragmatic, experimental style of New Deal policy making. Furthermore, Dewey's attempt to forge a middle path between state socialism or other forms of bureaucratic absolutism, on the one hand, and a laissez-faire economic order, on the other hand, were also akin to the moderate reformism of the New Deal.[1] Nevertheless Dewey cautioned, probably with the New Deal in mind, that the "experimental method is not just messing around nor doing a little of this and a little of that in the hope that things will improve," and by the 1930s Dewey was considerably to the left of the New Deal.[2] He steadfastly criticized the New Deal for failing to take the radical steps needed to fashion a genuinely democratic polity, and he was particularly critical of the NRA, which he considered a quasi-fascist form of corporatism far removed from the syndicalist corporatism with which he had flirted earlier in life. Could pragmatism have

1. For a good analysis of New Deal thought that demonstrates that Roosevelt's movement away from laissez-faire did not imply he was embracing statism, see James Holt, "The New Deal and the American Anti-Statist Tradition," in *The New Deal: The National Level*, ed. John Braeman, Robert H. Bremner, and David Brody, vol. 1 (Columbus, Ohio, 1975), pp. 27–49.
2. Kenneth S. Davis, *FDR: The New Deal Years, 1933–1937* (New York, 1986), p. 233.

provided the intellectual horizon for the NRA, despite Dewey's disavowal of it? And if pragmatism was not intrinsically hostile to New Deal reformism, how were its ideas translated into a more moderate and readily accessible teaching that could be digested by political elites and the American public?

Historians have frequently noted that there are strong links between pragmatism and the intellectual and political reform movements of the early twentieth century.[3] It is therefore no surprise to discover that criticisms of legal formalism and an affirmation of corporatist institutions have been elements of the progressive tradition, where the term "progressivism" is understood broadly to refer to types of reformers who dominated both the Progressive Era and the New Deal.[4] We shall argue that the political influence of pragmatism was channeled primarily through progressivism. Progressive publicists popularized the ideas the pragmatists were developing with far more theoretical rigor. In the eras in which progressive activists achieved political hegemony, those ideas became the basis for dramatic reforms in the American political system, and those reforms included the NRA. But to understand the importance of these elements in progressivism it will be necessary to understand progressivism and its various types more broadly, for there are other important aspects of progressivism that cannot be derived simply from pragmatism. In particular, we will have to focus on the role of antitrust law in progressivism, an element that would appear to be antithetical to the development of progressive corporatism and to the NRA.

The Rule of Law and Corporatism in Progressivism

The affinities between progressivism as an intellectual movement and pragmatism are striking. Pragmatists and progressive reformers were both critics of laissez-faire capitalism, and both tended to generalize their criticisms of late-nineteenth-century governance into broader criticisms of the fundamental principles of the American political regime. To be more specific, neither group regarded the Constitution as it had been understood by its framers as a suitable foundation for governance in the first decades

---

3. Goldman, pp. 120–124; Charles Forcey, *The Crossroads of Liberalism: Croly, Weyl, Lippmann, and the Progressive Era, 1900–1925* (London, 1961). See also commemorative issues of *The New Republic*, 17 October 1949, and *Saturday Review*, 22 October 1949, honoring Dewey.

4. The use of the term "progressive" to refer to New Dealers is preferable to the term "liberal"—the term Franklin Roosevelt consciously chose to identify New Dealers—because it distinguishes progressivism from traditional American liberalism, a political orientation that differs significantly from progressivism. The use of the term "progressive" is not, however, intended to preclude the possibility that progressives are in fact liberals in the philosophical sense, a question that cannot be adequately addressed within the scope of this work.

of the twentieth century. Furthermore, both groups believed that modern governance required broad discretionary grants of power to governing elites, and each was reluctant to hamstring government with many of the traditional constraints associated with constitutionalism and the rule of law. Finally, this depreciation of law in both pragmatism and progressivism led to a greater emphasis on nonlegal modes of conflict resolution, an emphasis that led the most insightful pragmatists and progressives to view corporatism in a favorable light.

Herbert Croly was one of the most insightful progressives. Over his thirty-eight-year career, Croly elaborated a systematic critique of the American political system and established a normative framework for progressive reforms. A knowledgeable and sympathetic student of pragmatism, Croly provided a crucial bridge linking its philosophical developments to the political world of early-twentieth-century America. Croly had first come in contact with pragmatism as a philosophy student at Harvard, where he studied with Harvard's resident pragmatists—George Santayana and William James—and his ties to pragmatism were later fortified by a long and fruitful intellectual relationship with John Dewey. Charles Forcey, an intellectual historian who studied Croly, noted:

> Pragmatism was Croly's guiding philosophy during his most active years as publicist and editor. . . . Croly's friends testified to the impact of Pragmatism on him. One described him as "adept in the philosophy of William James and John Dewey"; another saw Croly as "en rapport with all the pragmatists . . . had to say about the nature of conduct"; still another spoke of Croly's "apparent dedication to the Pragmatism of John Dewey." "At a time when John Dewey was still struggling with . . . his . . . pragmatic philosophy," wrote John Chamberlain, "Herbert Croly was already a full-fledged instrumentalist."[5]

Croly's views were developed in his two important books, *The Promise of American Life* and *Progressive Democracy*, and in his numerous articles for *The New Republic*, the intellectually sophisticated progressive journal that he helped found and edit.

In *Progressive Democracy*, Croly contrasts legal conservatism with democratic progressivism, denigrating legal conservatism as an attempt to impose a rigid and fixed morality on a people. "Those who would subordinate democracy to the Law must believe in the existence of certain permanent constructive principles of political conduct, to which society must conform and conformity to which is both the evidence of political character and its necessary means of discipline." Progressive democrats, on the other hand, "would subordinate Law to Democracy" and would

5. Forcey, p. 20.

"object to the attribution of permanent authority to any particular formulation of political and legal principle."[6]

For Croly the legalistic approach was epitimozed in the work of the
framers of the U.S. Constitution. Fearful of democratic excesses, they had
sanctified as natural rights the rights that Englishmen had enjoyed under
the common law. The preservation of man's natural rights then became a
justification for establishing limits on democratic legislatures. The framers
thereby deprived "the sovereign of his own ultimate and necessary
discretionary power" and raised a substantial barrier "against the exercise
by the people of any easy and sufficient control over their government."
The framers placed reverence for law above democracy, in part because
they were concerned with protecting property rights, but Croly did not
simply dismiss the framers as crass, self-interested oligarchs, as some
progressives did, because he also found good intentions behind this
reverence for law. Limits on legislative authority were "at least in part
desired for the purpose of rationalizing and moralizing the political
behavior of the state." The more profound failing of the American
framers, and even more so of those who have continued to espouse their
ideals in the twentieth century, was their inability to see how limited law
was as an instrument for moral elevation.[7]

Croly makes an analogy between the moral development of a nation and
that of a man. In its passionate youth the external restraints of law are
sometimes necessary to fortify moral resolve. But unless the law serves the
end of education, preparing a people to exercise political power, attempts to
impose morality on a people are more likely to lead "to national moral relaxation rather than to national moral vigor."[8] As a nation matures, moral
constraints must increasingly replace legal constraints, and the perpetuation
of outmoded legal constraints will only serve to stunt moral development:

> Does not the most effective protection which any man and any nation can
> enjoy consist in faith in the purpose of their own life and freedom to employ
> every method and every instrument required for the realization of their ends?
> In short, does not the exaggerated value which has been attached to
> constitutional limitations, and the apprehensive and reactionary state of mind
> which has in consequence possessed many patriotic Americans, tend to
> undermine the foundations in human nature and human will upon which the
> whole superstructure of a progressive democratic society must admittedly be
> built?[9]

Croly compares this process of national maturation to the evolution of
religious consciousness in the Judeo-Christian tradition from what he sees

6. Herbert Croly, *Progressive Democracy* (New York, 1915), pp. 164–165.
7. Ibid., pp. 39–40, 138.
8. Ibid., p. 164.
9. Ibid., p. 167.

as the more primitive emphasis on law in Judaism to the more mature emphasis on faith in Christianity.

Some aspects of Croly's analysis of the law bear a striking resemblance to the analysis of the judicial pragmatists, whose position Croly had become familiar with through the writings of Roscoe Pound.[10] Croly accused those conservatives who sanctified the rule of law of perpetuating the myth that the law transcended social conflicts and provided an impartial framework for their resolution. The rule of law, Croly asserted, meant the rule of lawyers, an "aristocracy of the robe" whose interests were intimately intertwined with those of the ruling oligarchs of American society. Under the guise of interpreting the ambiguous phrases of the Constitution, for instance, the courts could impose their policy preferences on an unsuspecting nation:

> They [the ambiguous phrases of the Constitution] could be used as an excuse for the exercise of the courts' judgment as to the meaning or the merits of a piece of legislation. In the exercise of this discretionary power, they were, of course, obliged to make their decisions square with precedent, and they were obliged to consider in each case a group of concrete facts; but not even the warmest advocate of the judicial review will claim that the decision was the automatic result of the application of precedent to a concrete case. The concrete case always provided an opportunity for the exercise of a large amount of discretion in construing the rule and the precedents.[11]

Croly concluded that, because policy preferences necessarily shaped the law and because you "cannot obtain a reasonable human government by enclosing reason within a rule," legalism should not impose substantial barriers to the achievement of democratic purposes.[12]

The pragmatic attack on the rule of law had been linked to an increasing interest in nonjudicial modes of conflict resolution, and in some cases specfically linked to corporatism. This interest was even more explicit in progressivism. Croly recognized the importance of functional associations as a locus of man's moral and cultural life, and although he initially stressed reforms intended to develop an efficient centralized state, he also acknowledged that the need for considerable group autonomy imposed limits on the scope of legitimate state activities. Transforming the liberal tension between individual rights and state sovereignty into the progressive tension between the nation and groups, Croly searched for a balance and division of labor that would reduce conflict and allow these essential modes of social organization to complement one another.

In *The Promise of American Life*, Croly's most influential book,

10. Ibid., p. 178.
11. Ibid., p. 179.
12. Ibid., p. 183.

nationalism was clearly the predominant element in the balance. Croly described American political history as a struggle between a nationalist but undemocratic Hamiltonian tradition and a democratic but antinationalist Jeffersonian tradition. Seeking to curb the excessive localism and individualism of the American ethos, Croly proposed a democratic, nationalist synthesis in which Hamilton's vigorous central government would be democratized and used "not merely to maintain the constitution, but to promote the national interests and to consolidate the national organization."[13]

Croly's nationalistic orientation was associated with a strong skepticism of private groups and their divisive politics of economic self-interest. "The vast incoherent mass of the American people is falling into definite social groups, which restrict and define the mental outlook and social experience of their members. . . . The earlier homogeneity of American society has been impaired and no authoritative and edifying, but conscious social ideal has as yet taken its place." Decrying the destructive consequences of this unrestricted pluralism, Croly warned that "the great obstacle of American national fulfillment must always be the danger that the American people will merely succumb to the demands of their local and private interests." This suspicion of "special interests" is a characteristic theme of all forms of progressivism.[14]

Even in *The Promise of American Life*, however, Croly does not argue that nationalism is simply inconsistent with a pluralistic society. Groups and associations have tended to impede the development of a broader social consciousness, but reformed and reconstituted they could become the means by which wider social identities are fostered. Trade unions, for instance, are suspect insofar as they are merely promoting narrow class interests, yet Croly insists that they "need legal recognition" and even "substantial discrimination by the state in their favor." So important are trade unions to the "economic and social amelioration of the laboring classes" that Croly characterizes nonunion laborers as "a species of industrial derelict" and asserts "that the non-union industrial laborer should, in the interest of a genuinely democratic organization of labor, be rejected." Skepticism about private power is conjoined with an emphasis on the potentially creative role of private associations, and this conjunction would lead to considerable progressive ambivalence toward interest groups as progressives attempted to institutionalize the progressive state.[15]

During World War I, Croly's emphasis shifted from nationalism to corporatism as the destructive consequences of nationalism became increasingly apparent. Without denying "all that the secular state had accomplished for civilization during its period of supremacy," Croly

13. Herbert Croly, *The Promise of American Life* (New York, 1918), p. 39.
14. Ibid., pp. 138–139, 277.
15. Ibid., pp. 386–387.

interpreted World War I as a demonstration that the state was "proving to be an unnecessarily powerful and dangerous servant and an unnecessarily jealous master." Croly could not agree with those who saw the war only as a testimony to the inadequacies of the nation-state and looked to the creation of a world state. Characterizing individuals who held this position as "state worshipers" who would remedy the defects of the nation-state "not by limiting the power of the state but by universalizing it," Croly insisted that "states must, as a result of the war, consent to a diminution and a redistribution of authority" because any organization that claimed "unqualified allegiance" was "an invitation to political and moral anarchy." The war had simply exposed "a fatal malady" of the modern state, that "during its long period of domination the state has systematically suppressed any competition with its own power from whatever source" and for that reason was "unable to furnish its citizens with the essential conditions of security and progress."[16]

These reservations against the state applied not only to all contemporary states, democratic or absolutist, but also to the perfected form of democracy that Croly advocated. Even a genuine democratic commonwealth required a rich network of associations "to obtain a secure foundation for its own authority." Asserting the necessity of "supplemental centers of allegiance," such as trade unions and trade associations that could compete with the state for the loyalty of citizens, Croly concluded that a state that failed to grant associations the "clear right to exist" could "never be anything more than the glorified and falsified incarnation of successful force." Indeed, not only must the state tolerate these associations, as pluralists had argued, it also "should seek to strengthen them when they are weak." Croly was proposing a corporatist polity in which associations would "have independent interests and wills of their own," and the state would act "as a correspondingly strong agency of coordination."[17]

In Croly we discover the same conjunction of themes, skepticism of law, and proclivities toward corporatism that we have discovered in pragmatism. Croly's skepticism of law is associated with his rejection of traditional liberal individualism and his search for a more communitarian philosophical framework. This quest for community had corporatist overtones, although the prominence of the corporatist theme varied considerably over his career, ascending as his faith in nationalism declined. As was the case with John Dewey, the corporatist thrust of Croly's thought was potentially compatible with either administrative corporatism or societal corporatism.

16. Herbert Croly, "The Future of the State," *The New Republic,* 15 September 1917, pp. 180–181.

17. Ibid., pp. 182–183.

Whether Herbert Croly played an important role in shaping the character of reform politics during the Progressive Era or whether he simply provided a more sophisticated intellectual justification for an already mature progressivism remains a matter of historical dispute, but it is clear that Croly struck a responsive chord for many progressives. In July 1910, Theodore Roosevelt wrote to Croly soon after reading *The Promise of American Life*: "I do not know when I have read a book which I felt profited me as much as your book on American life." Roosevelt continued, "All I wish is that I were better able to get my advice to my fellow countrymen in practical shape according to the principles which you set forth."[18] Within a month Roosevelt, speaking at Osawatomie, Kansas, proposed the comprehensive agenda for reform that would become the basis for his 1912 presidential campaign. Roosevelt referred to his reform package as "New Nationalism," a term he borrowed from Croly's book.

That Theodore Roosevelt shared Croly's distrust of the rule of law as well as his vision of social and economic reconstruction was demonstrated by Roosevelt's laudatory review of Croly's *Progressive Democracy*. Roosevelt praised Croly for "showing the damage done to justice and to the whole democratic ideal by the saturation of our government with legalism." Accusing those who defended the rule of law of paralyzing administration and sacrificing the public welfare to "this theory of government by litigation," Roosevelt suggested that the law "shielded officials who had gone wrong, but it never helped to make things go right." He concluded, "Observers of vision finally became convinced that democracy and legalism were incompatible." Given the conservative role that the Supreme Court was playing during the first three decades of the twentieth century, it is hardly surprising that hostility to the Court would have been generalized into a broader suspicion of the rule of law during this era.[19]

But if Croly's criticisms of legalism and his appeals for a new nationalism struck a responsive chord in progressives like Theodore Roosevelt, it is not as clear that his later, more corporatist thought

18. Quoted in Forcey, pp. 124–125.

19. Theodore Roosevelt's fulminations against legalism eventually led to an outright attack on judicial independence. Prior to the 1912 elections, progressives in a number of states had succeeded in democratizing the judiciary by altering the mode of judicial selection from appointment with life tenure to election for specified terms. Roosevelt placed this issue on the national agenda in his 1912 campaign and radicalized it by demanding provisions for judicial recall and for a "referendum by the people themselves in a certain class of decisions of constitutional questions in which the courts decide against the power of the people to do elementary justice." Roosevelt's radical proposals jeopardized the institutional foundations of the rule of law because they would have placed judges at the beck and call of public opinion and would have made it all the more difficult for the judiciary to develop the neutrality and impartiality essential to the rule of law. During the New Deal, Franklin Roosevelt's court-packing scheme would raise some of the same issues. See William H. Harbaugh, ed., *The Writings of Theodore Roosevelt* (New York, 1967), pp. 269, 347.

similarly exemplified the emergence of a corporatist strand of progressivism. It did, however, at least resonate with a number of themes that were prevalent during the Progressive Era. The progressives were virtually unanimous in seeking reforms to democratize the American political system, as some of the most noteworthy political reforms of this era—direct election of senators, the introduction of presidential primaries, the use of recall, referendum, and initiative—demonstrate. Many stressed, as Tocqueville had, the importance of local government and grassroots democracy.

Less attention has been devoted to the progressive emphasis on developing the social and cultural prerequisites for democracy. Theodore Roosevelt, for instance, extended the argument for democracy from the political to the economic sphere: "There can be no real political democracy unless there is something approaching an economic democracy. A democracy must consist of men who are intellectually, morally and materially fit to be their own masters."[20] Woodrow Wilson came to similar conclusions by the end of World War I. Calling on labor and capital to develop "cooperation and partnership based upon a real community of interest and participation in control," he asserted that such cooperation would become possible only through a "genuine democratization of industry" that would allow workers to share "in some organic way in every decision" that affected their welfare.[21] This was by no means a full-fledged corporatist ideology, but it did provide fertile ground for the development of a progressive corporatist tradition. As we have already noted with regard to John Dewey, some form of corporatism was often appealing to those who were searching for ways to institutionalize economic democracy.

Croly's flirtations with corporatism were not simply an aberration, but before we can adequately understand the emergence of progressive corporatism and its later influence during the early New Deal, we must examine progressivism somewhat more broadly as a political movement.

The Progressive Tradition?

The very use of the term "progressivism" to refer collectively to the reform movements of the Progressive Era and the New Deal is a matter of considerable controversy. The definitional disputes concerning the term are closely intertwined with more fundamental and substantive disagreements over the proper interpretation of the movement. For this reason, a survey of the definitional landscape will provide a useful overview of the

20. Ibid., p. 350.
21. Arthur M. Schlesinger, Jr., *The Age of Roosevelt: The Crisis of the Old Order, 1919–1933* (Boston, 1957), p. 40.

relationship of the interpretation of progressive corporatism and the NRA developed in this book to some of the competing interpretations of the NRA, or of progressivism more generally, that have been prominent in recent historiography. Using the term "progressive" generically to refer to reformers in both the Progressive Era and the New Deal deliberately emphasizes the commonalities among elites in each of these periods and the continuities between them. It implicitly asserts that the differences that divided progressives were in the final analysis less important than the shared values that united them.

The division of progressives into Democratic and Republican progressives provides a good example of this. Progressivism was never uniquely identified with one of the major parties, and during both the Progressive Era and the New Deal each party had a progressive wing and a conservative wing. Partisan conflict was therefore orthogonal to ideological conflict. In the first years of the New Deal, Franklin Roosevelt struggled with the tensions posed by this situation. From the beginning of his presidency, Roosevelt was attracted by the possibility of creating a progressive Democratic party that could lure away the progressive wing of the Republican party. To accomplish this, he eschewed the role of party leader, even refusing to participate in the traditional Jefferson Day celebrations of the Democratic party (he recommended that they be replaced by "non-partisan Jefferson dinners").[22] Proclaiming himself a "President of all the people," which politically translated into "President of all the progressives," Roosevelt appealed to progressive Republicans for support for New Deal programs.[23] Progressive Republicans, placing progressivism before party, generally responded favorably, and as a result the legislative battles over some of his most important New Deal programs were fundamentally ideological battles that cut across party lines by pitting progressives against conservatives.

There were limits, however, as to how far Roosevelt would go to establish a unified progressive party. He would not actively support progressive candidates in Senate and House electoral contests if the progressive was a Republican. The most notable example of this was his hands-off policy in a Pennsylvania Senate election despite an appeal by Gifford Pinchot, a prominent progressive and friend of Roosevelt, for help. Reluctant to alienate the conservative wing of the Democratic party, Roosevelt at least made this minimal concession to party loyalty.[24] He was willing to manage the tensions between ideology and party as long as progressives predominated in Congress and some Southern conservative Democrats were willing to trade their support for New Deal economic

22. Schlesinger, *The Coming of the New Deal*, pp. 503–505.
23. Burns, *Roosevelt: The Lion and the Fox*, pp. 183–208.
24. Ibid., p. 199.

programs for federal tolerance of racial discrimination in the South. A prudent balancing of the conflicting demands of party and ideology at this time served the end of furthering his reform agenda.

By the late 1930s this pattern began to change. Conservatives were making gains in the legislature, and the tenuous bargain between Roosevelt and Southern conservatives was wearing thin. In 1938, Roosevelt attempted to purge the conservatives who had most consistently opposed his New Deal from the Democratic party and create a thoroughly progressive party, which would then be able to draw Republican progressives into its ranks. This was a bold and politically risky move, for it violated the most sacred rules of the game governing the Democratic party, but it was also no more than a radicalization of a strategy he had pursued from the beginning of his administration. His gamble failed, but it clearly indicated that in the final analysis ideology was more important than partisan affiliation for Roosevelt.[25] Roosevelt was first and foremost a progressive, and his progressivism linked him to others who shared his fundamental values.

Historians have raised two related objections to the claim that ideology has been a unifying force within progressivism. Some, like Richard Hofstadter, have argued that the differences between reformers in the Progressive Era and reformers in the New Deal are more fundamental than the similarities.[26] Others, like Ellis Hawley, have at least implicitly argued that the differences between progressives in either of these eras are so profound that it is a misnomer to refer to them collectively as progressives.[27] Both objections focus on the role of competition and antitrust policy in progressivism. Hofstadter contrasts the individualist orientation of the Progressive Era, whose values were quintessentially embodied in its antitrust policies, with the more collectivist, organization-affirming orientation of the New Deal era. Similarly, Hawley starkly contrasts antitrusters with planners, but he argues that this cannot be the basis for a distinction between the Progressive Era and the New Deal because both types play a role in both periods. Hawley's analysis is the stronger of the two because it can account for organization-affirming reforms like the creation of the Federal Trade Commission in the Progressive Era and the resurgence of a pro-competitive policy in the latter years of the New Deal. His seminal analysis of the New Deal and the NRA must be examined in greater detail.

Hawley's interpretation of the New Deal focuses on the broad shift from an anticompetitive policy in the early New Deal to a pro-competitive policy in the late New Deal. The NRA, with its partial suspension of

25. Ibid., pp. 358–380. See also Sidney Milkis, "Franklin D. Roosevelt and the Transcendence of Partisan Politics," *Political Science Quarterly* 100 (1985): 479–504.

26. Richard Hofstadter, *The Age of Reform: From Bryan to F.D.R.* (New York, 1955), pp. 302–328.

27. Hawley, pp. 7–15.

antitrust laws, exemplifies the former period; both the dramatic expansion in the activities of the antitrust division of the Justice Department and the investigations of economic concentration and collusion by the Temporary National Economic Commission exemplify the latter period. Arguing that the dominant policies of these two periods are fundamentally incompatible, Hawley concludes that New Deal economic policy as a whole was incoherent. Tracing the anticompetitive thrust of the early New Deal in part to the "New Nationalism" of Theodore Roosevelt, and the pro-competitive thrust of the late New Deal to the "New Freedom" of Woodrow Wilson, Hawley argues that the irreconcilable tensions between these two versions of progressivism had not been overcome by the New Deal, even though the New Deal had managed to enlist the support of both Wilsonians and New Nationalists.[28]

This broad thesis is then qualified by the assertion that even though New Nationalist themes were dominant during the early New Deal, New Freedom themes played at least a subordinate role in the period; just as in the latter New Deal, New Freedom overtones were complemented by New Nationalist undertones. In the NRA, Hawley argues, the New Freedom collided head-on with the New Nationalism, and the program became a microcosm of the economic incoherence of the New Deal as a whole. It is crucial that in Hawley's interpretation there is no distinct progressive corporatist tradition, or more precisely no genuinely democratic corporatist tradition of the kind we discovered in Herbert Croly.[29] If Hawley denies the existence of a progressive corporatist tradition, how does he account for the fact that the corporatist NRA is a New Deal program? According to Hawley, the corporatist NRA elicits progressive support because it appears to provide a compromise between the New Nationalists, who really wanted national economic planning by the state, and the Wilsonians,

28. Ibid., pp. 14–16.

29. Hawley does note that some economic planners had corporatist ideas, but he assimilates them with those who believed in central economic planning. The use of the term "planners" to describe progressive corporatists is misleading, because many explicitly rejected noncorporatist modes of economic planning. Hawley's use of the term "progressivism" to refer to a business corporatist tradition is also misleading, as will become apparent later in this work. In more recent work, Hawley suggested that Herbert Hoover had a vision of the associative state that is neo-corporatist. However, any attempt to derive the NRA from Hoover's vision of the associative state (Hawley's term, not Hoover's) would have to explain Hoover's vigorous opposition to the NRA and to business plans for coordination of economic activities through trade associations, such as those put forward by Gerald Swope and Henry Harriman, two prominent business leaders. Hoover argued that the coercive features of the NRA were "fascistic" and that the Swope plan was an attempt "to smuggle fascism into America through the back door." Neither had anything in common with the voluntarist spirit of his associative state. See Ellis Hawley, "Herbert Hoover, The Commerce Secretariat, and the Vision of an 'Associative State,' " in *Men and Organizations*, ed. Edwin J. Perkins (New York, 1977), pp. 131–148; David Burner, *Herbert Hoover: A Public Life* (New York, 1979), pp. 173, 234, 328; Herbert Hoover, *The Challenge to Liberty* (New York, 1934); K. S. Davis, *FDR: The New York Years, 1928–1933* (New York, 1985), p. 481.

who really wanted to restore free market competition. This unprincipled compromise soon collapsed.[30]

There was, however, a truly corporatist tradition that did shape and ultimately dominate the NRA in Hawley's account, but it was not a democratic reform corporatist tradition. The true corporatists were big-business elites who had come to realize that in advanced capitalism competition was often intolerable and who recognized that state regulation could mitigate competition far more effectively than private agreements among competitors. If control over the regulatory instruments of the state were vested in corporatist bodies controlled by business, a more activist state could be fully compatible with business interests.[31] When united business corporatists confronted the divided forces of reform in the NRA, businessmen were able to dominate the program.

The virtue of Hawley's depiction of reformers is that it captures the complexity and heterogeneity of the progressive reform movement. Any plausible interpretation of progressivism must do justice to the bifurcation of the movement that occurred during the 1912 presidential election pitting Woodrow Wilson against Theodore Roosevelt. This election revealed that progressives disagreed about the character of the economy and the best method for regulating it. Wilsonian progressives were more inclined to believe that large corporations were economically inefficient and had achieved dominance in markets through unfair competitive practices. Roosevelt's New Nationalist progressives were more inclined to believe that many large corporations were economically efficient and that only "bad trusts" had achieved market dominance through unfair competitive practices.

These differences affected their respective reform agendas. New Freedom progressives emphasized the need for more vigorous antitrust laws to restore competitive markets, prohibit unfair trade practices, and protect small businesses. Woodrow Wilson hoped to achieve these goals through a new and specific antitrust law rather than through the creation of a regulatory commission with a vague mandate to promote fair competition, fearing that a commission might be captured by business interests. It is interesting however, that Wilson changed his mind after he became president and ultimately supported the idea of a regulatory commission with broad responsibilities for enforcing antitrust laws. New Nationalist progressives emphasized the regulation of large corporations instead of attempts either to break them up or to prevent them from forming. Theodore Roosevelt did not deny the need for a new antitrust law, but he favored a less-restrictive law that could accommodate efficient large

30. Hawley, *The New Deal*, pp. 35–52.
31. Ibid., pp. 35–43.

corporations. This could best be accomplished through a general statute that authorized the creation of a regulatory commission.[32]

While there is some truth in a description of Progressive Era progressivism that contrasts the New Freedom favoring competition and small business and the New Nationalism favoring cooperation and big business, this description is insufficient. We shall restrict our analysis to the New Freedom, but an analysis of New Nationalism would point to similar problems.[33] Wilsonian antitrust policy had always been marred by self-contradictions. Ostensibly it was intended to promote competition by preventing the rise of monopolistic enterprises, but Wilsonians tended to confuse protecting competition with protecting competitors, although the two goals are frequently in conflict with one another.[34] A competitive marketplace drives less-efficient producers out of business. In industries in which there are considerable efficiencies of scale in production, protecting competition will result in most competitors being eliminated as a few large enterprises come to dominate the market. The only way competitors can be protected in such a market is to eliminate, or at least mitigate, competition. Because Wilsonian antitrust policy had attempted to protect competitors as well as competition, it had always implicitly had both competitive and anticompetitive elements. Moreover, Wilson did not reject large corporations per se. He distinguished those that had grown through unfair trade practices and mergers, which he assumed were economically inefficient, from those that had grown through internal expansion because they were economically efficient. Antitrust reform was intended as an attack only on the former.[35]

Hawley's stark contrast between the New Freedom favoring competition and small business and the New Nationalism favoring cooperation and big business is misleading, because each strand of Progressive Era progressivism sought to establish an optimal mix of competition and cooperation and an economy in which big and small firms coexisted. The use of the term "progressivism" to refer to both the New Freedom and the New Nationalism does not deny that there were important differences between these two groups of reformers, nor that the differences between progressives could be more important than the similarities between them in explaining particular historical episodes, it simply acknowledges that the differences were not so fundamental that it is inappropriate to use a single term to

32. Schlesinger, *The Crisis of the Old Order,* pp. 18–22; Hawley, *The New Deal,* pp. 44–49.

33. Even though New Nationalists rejected antitrust attacks on bigness per se, they were often quite solicitous of the interests of small firms. See the discussion on Rexford Tugwell, a 1930s New Nationalist, below.

34. Alan Stone, *Economic Regulation and the Public Interest: The Federal Trade Commission in Theory and Practice* (Ithaca, N.Y., 1977), p. 46.

35. Woodrow Wilson, *A Crossroads of Freedom: The 1912 Campaign Speeches of Woodrow Wilson,* ed. John Wells Davidson (New Haven, 1956), pp. 208, 281–282; Alan Seltzer, "Woodrow Wilson as 'Corporate-Liberal': Toward a Reconsideration of Left Revisionist Historiography," *Western Political Quarterly* 30 (1977): 189–190.

encompass both. Both strands of progressivism argued that the growth of large corporations within a laissez-faire economic order potentially posed a threat to democracy, to the achievement of social justice, and to economic efficiency. Both rejected the laissez-faire premises of their conservative opponents. They disagreed over regulatory strategies, but not over the need for regulation. If the differences that divided them were as fundamental as Hawley assumed they were, it is difficult to understand how Woodrow Wilson could have been converted from his campaign position favoring a specific antitrust statute over the creation of a regulatory commission with a broad mandate to a position favoring the creation of a regulatory commission with a broad mandate—the policy Theodore Roosevelt had advocated in the 1912 electoral campaign.

Hawley's tendency to exaggerate the importance of differences between the New Freedom tradition and the New Nationalist tradition has significant implications for his interpretation of the NRA. For Hawley, the conflicting policy preferences of NRA advisors drawn from both these strands of progressivism became a template for class and interest group conflict within the NRA as a whole. He argues, "Such conflicting counsels were hardly conducive to logically consistent administration, particularly when they were backed by rival economic pressure groups."[36] This description of the NRA blurs the distinction between conflicts among interest groups and conflicts among economic policy makers and places an unjustifiable emphasis on the latter category of conflicts in determining the fate of the NRA. Thus Hawley fundamentally faults the NRA for its failure to define its goals or lay down a consistent policy.[37]

The NRA did pursue conflicting economic policies, but NRA economic policy was at least no more plagued by internal contractions than had been the policies of Wilsonian progressivism, with its failure to distinguish between protecting competition and protecting competitors. The weakness of Hawley's conclusions regarding the NRA is suggested by the fact that the Wilsonian Federal Trade Commission has at least survived, and even occasionally thrived, despite the economic incoherence of its authorizing statute. Furthermore, whereas Hawley assumes that the failure of the NRA to achieve policy coherence allowed code-making "to be determined by economic and political bargaining, an approach that naturally favored the highly organized group with a specific and well-articulated set of demands," the FTC was sometimes unsympathetic to well-organized business interests despite its failure to achieve policy coherence.[38]

---

36. Hawley, *The New Deal*, p. 51.
37. Ibid., p. 136.
38. Hawley, *The New Deal*, p. 136. Even though Robert Himmelberg argues that cooperation between business and government was the dominant motif of government-business relations during the 1920s, he notes important cases where conflict between the FTC and well-organized interests in the business community erupted despite the ambiguities of the legislation the FTC enforced. See Himmelberg, pp. 9, 12, 20, 36–37, 96–99.

Hawley's account of the history of the NRA is excessively rationalistic in its tendency to identify political conflicts with logical contradictions in economic policy. Although Hawley recognized that the New Deal as a whole had a political coherence that transcended its economic contradictions, he failed to preserve the distinction between political conflict and economic contradiction in analyzing the NRA. Had he done so, he might have recognized that the NRA was at least as much a political failure (a judgment one could not so easily apply to the New Deal as a whole) as it was an economic failure, and that these two failings, though related, were by no means identical. The NRA was not politically viable because of the utopianism of the political vision that inspired it, and that vision was nourished by both the New Freedom and the New Nationalism. It is best described by the term "progressivism."

The argument that the term "progressivism" is appropriate because there are affinities that united reform elites in the first three decades of the twentieth century is supported by the progressive and revisionist historians discussed in the introductory chapter of this work, with the exception of Hawley. According to Arthur Schlesinger, Jr.: "But the gap [between Wilsonians and New Nationalists] soon turned out to be less impassable than it had first appeared. Roosevelt did not—as Wilson charged—want to make monopoly universal, any more than Wilson—as Roosevelt replied— wanted to break up every corporation in the country. In abusing each other and misrepresenting each other's views, they obscured the fact that their agreements were actually greater than their differences."[39] This fundamental agreement not only transcended the divisions between the New Freedom and the New Nationalism, it also transcended the differences between the Progressive Era and the New Deal. "Rejecting the battle between the New Nationalism and the New Freedom which had so long divided American liberalism, [Franklin] Roosevelt equably defined the New Deal as the 'satisfactory combination' of both."[40] The combination may not have satisfied intellectual purists, but for Schlesinger it had "a human content" that was practically workable.

Revisionist historians would argue that the preservation of capitalism rather than humanitarianism was at the core of Franklin Roosevelt's synthesis of the New Freedom and the New Nationalism, but they would not dispute the conclusion that these two versions of progressivism were closer together than the partisans of each position often assumed. Nor would they dispute the conclusion that the New Deal was a combination

---

39. Schlesinger, *The Crisis of the Old Order*, p. 33.

40. Schlesinger, *The Politics of Upheaval*, p. 651. This assertion is supported by the fact that many businessmen believed that Franklin Roosevelt was hostile to big business (a characteristic associated with Wilsonianism) even during the early New Deal, a period when Roosevelt was supposedly promoting policies more akin to Theodore Roosevelt's New Nationalism. See *Business Week*, 2 March 1935, p. 10.

of both.[41] Consistent with their efforts to unmask the oligarchical interests that they believe lie behind the humanitarian appearance of New Deal reforms, the revisionists have generally preferred such terms as "corporate liberalism," "the corporate state," or simply "corporatism" to refer to reform ideology.[42] The revisionist interpretation of the NRA will be examined more extensively in Chapter 5, but in the context of this general discussion of progressivism it is important to note that while the revisionist emphasis on reform corporatism is justified in the case of progressives like the later Herbert Croly, it does not accurately describe either the New Freedom or the New Nationalism. These variants of progressivism may well have provided fertile ground for the growth of corporatist ideals, but they were not themselves corporatist. Even in Croly's case it took the shock of World War I to transform him from a New Nationalist into a progressive corporatist. If we are to describe accurately the reform movement that rose to power in the Progressive Era and then again during the New Deal, capturing both its internal diversity and its unifying characteristics, we must resist the temptation to use terminology that artificially identifies reform with one of its several strands and collapses the distinctions between types of progressives, just as much as we must resist the tendency to drive an artificially deep wedge between the types of progressivism. The term "progressivism," which can appropriately be used to refer to each of these strands and yet is uniquely identified with none of them, is preferable to the term "corporatism" when referring to the reform movement in general.

The concept of a largely unified reform elite has received additional support from two distinct but related interpretations of the reform movement that have emerged in recent years: the state-building and the organizational revolution interpretations. To date, neither of these schools has offered a full-blown interpretation of the NRA, and they are therefore not dealt with systematically in the following chapters.[43] Nevertheless, it

41. Barton Bernstein denigrates the distinction between a New Nationalist early New Deal and a New Freedom later New Deal, arguing that continuities are more striking than discontinuities. Radosh finds the same conservative tendencies in the early New Deal's NRA and the later New Deal's Wagner and Social Securities acts. Gabriel Kolko and James Weinstein both downplay the differences between the New Freedom and the New Nationalism in their histories of the Progressive Era. See B. Bernstein, pp. 275–276; Radosh, pp. 154, 185–187; Gabriel Kolko, *The Triumph of Conservatism* (Chicago, 1963), pp. 5, 210; and James Weinstein, *The Corporate Ideal and the Liberal State: 1900–1918* (Boston, 1969), pp. 139–140, 161–162.

42. Kolko argues that the term "progressivism" is misleading because the progressives were in fact conservatives. While he continues to use "progressivism" because it is so well established, he refers to the system they were creating as "political capitalism." James Weinstein refers to the corporate liberal order, and Jeffrey Lustig, a fellow revisionist, refers to corporate liberalism. See Lustig, pp. 1–36.

43. The most ambitious systematic attempts to apply these frameworks to an understanding of progressivism have both focused on the period from 1877 to 1920. See Skowronek's *Building a New American State* and Robert H. Wiebe's *Search for Order, 1877–1920* (New York, 1967). Hawley's interpretation of the NRA has elements that would be relevant to each of these schools, but because he portrays the NRA as predominantly a response to an organizational revolution among capitalists, his theory is addressed in the context of our analysis of revisionism.

will be useful to comment briefly on each interpretation, noting in particular why each school of thought has generally eschewed the use of the term "progressivism" in developing an analytical framework.

The state-building interpretation has focused on the emergence of the administrative state. Recent literature in this field has demonstrated that reform elites in the Progressive Era and the New Deal, and in both the Wilsonian and the New Nationalist traditions, have been united by their shared interest in creating a modern bureaucratic state and their shared rejection of laissez-faire ideology and the political and economic institutions it legitimated, even if they have differed over appropriate economic policies.[44] The state-building literature does, however, pose a challenge to the use of the term "progressivism." That challenge is not rooted in the claim that the term conceals important differences that have divided reform elites, but rather in the implicit claim that terms like "state-builders" or "statists" more accurately convey the significance of the reforms promoted by these elites. Moreover, a term like "state-builder" encourages comparisons of the development of the American state with the development of other states, whereas the term "progressive" is idiosyncratic to the American context.[45]

Without denying that the use of state-building terminology may be appropriate for the study of some of the reforms of the Progressive Era and the New Deal, its use with reference to the NRA would be inappropriate. As our analysis of Herbert Croly has already demonstrated, some of the progressives who turned to corporatism were explicitly repudiating their own previously unabashed state-building projects. Croly had become convinced that state-building had to occur in conjunction with association-building and that the latter project imposed significant limits on the former. Similarly, our analysis of pragmatism revealed that its corporatist proclivities were derived from a group theory orientation. Normatively, pragmatism was struggling to find a middle path between the statist and free market alternatives. As we shall see, the administrative leadership of the NRA had a similar vision. American state-building theories have appropriately distinguished reform elites from conservative elites committed to a laissez-faire ideology, but their own terminology suggests that the reform alternative to laissez-faire was more statist than it actually was.[46]

---

44. Skowronek treats the differences between Woodrow Wilson and Theodore Roosevelt as variations on a common state-building theme. He implies that his argument can be extended to the New Deal as well. See Skowronek, pp. 176, 288–289.

45. The extent to which this is a virtue depends on whether one considers American political development exceptional. The more unique our political development has been, the greater the danger that a term like "state-builder" will encourage misleading comparisons with elites who have fashioned bureaucratic states in other contexts. The importance of antitrust law in progressivism supports an exceptionalism thesis, for until recently antitrust law was an exclusively American innovation.

46. Holt, pp. 27–49.

A second alternative to the use of the term "progressivism" has been proposed by social scientists who view this era in terms of a comprehensive organizational revolution that has been reshaping American society since the 1870s. These social scientists have refused to focus narrowly on either the state or corporatist institutions, arguing instead that the definitive characteristic of reform is a general propensity to promote modern bureaucratic organization in a wide variety of guises. This interpretation, which Louis Galambos has referred to as "the emerging organizational synthesis in modern American history," can incorporate many of the insights of scholars who have focused more narrowly on state-building or corporatism without in addition asserting the dubious claim that either state-building or corporatism is uniquely identified with reform. A term such as "bureaucratic man" or "organizational man" would be more appropriate in this neo-Weberian interpretation than the term "progressive" to describe a typical reformer, because "the focal point of modern history becomes the underlying patterns of social, political and economic organization— as opposed to particular political events or ideologies."[47]

Galambos distinguishes the organizational interpretation of American history from the earlier progressive historiography, which had emphasized the struggle between business and government elites and which had been comfortable with the term "progressivism." He predicts, "With the organizational synthesis should come new attempts at periodization. Historians in this field will doubtless abandon the progressive categories of Populism, Progressivism, the New Deal and After."[48] The progressive interpretation is rejected in part because revisionist historians have demonstrated that business and government elites often share fundamental values and interests, and organizational history is predisposed to accept this conclusion because it emphasizes the shared values and interests generated by the bureaucratization of the firm and the state. But if organizational historiography is more compatible with revisionist historiography than with progressive historiography, it need not be identified with it. Indeed, some organizational historians have linked the twentieth-century organizational revolution more closely to the interests of rising middle-class professionals than to the interests of the capitalist class.[49] What is more fundamental, progressive historiography is rejected because it had focused on epiphenomenal political struggles and had therefore attributed undue importance to the role of individuals (like Franklin Roosevelt) in the historical

47. Galambos notes that Roy Lubove's *Professional Altruist: The Emergence of Social Word as a Career, 1880–1930* (Cambridge, Mass., 1965) made progressivism "a minor subject," and he praises the work for going "one step further in the direction of organizational history." See Louis Galambos, "The Emerging Organizational Synthesis in Modern American History," in *Men and Organizations,* ed. Edwin J. Perkins (New York, 1977), p. 11.
48. Ibid., p. 10.
49. Wiebe, p. 166.

process. "Organizational history will, no doubt, stress the role of environmental forces acting on the individual. Less emphasis will be placed on the individual's efforts to shape his own historical context."[50]

If the intellectual history of pragmatism and progressivism presented thus far proves relevant to an understanding of the NRA, this will pose as much of a challenge to the emerging organizational synthesis historiography as it does to state-building historiography. The version of organizational historiography most closely identified with the revisionist school will be particularly vulnerable, for hostility to capitalist elites has been a distinguishing characteristic of both pragmatism and progressivism. In at least this sense, progressive historiography was closer to the truth than the interpretations that superseded it. More fundamentally, however, it is the tendency of organizational historiography to divert attention from the political and moral dimensions of the reform movement for the sake of focusing on its organizational substratum, which is its fundamental weakness. Organizational historiography not only excludes or deemphasizes aspects of reform that run athwart the bureaucratizing impulse, it also distorts the bureaucratizing aspects of reform by artificially elevating them from means into ends.

The deficiencies of organizational historiography as a comprehensive framework for interpreting the New Deal (or even specific programs within the New Deal, such as the NRA) are particularly clear when one examines the early New Deal. The administrative strategy of the early New Deal can appropriately be described as "ad-hocracy" because it departed from a broad historical trend toward bureaucratization of government. Distrusting the administrative apparatus he had inherited from his Republican predecessors, Roosevelt created a wide variety of ad hoc agencies to administer his reform programs. To assure the political loyalty of his administrators to the New Deal, he deliberately exempted most of these agencies from civil service laws. Those laws are so closely identified with the emergence of a modern bureaucratic state that the decision to exempt agencies from them constituted a fundamental departure from the bureaucratizing norms that are central to organizational historiography. Roosevelt's reliance on ad hoc agencies clearly indicates that Roosevelt put the political goals of the New Deal above the goal of creating a modern bureaucratic state per se. Later in the New Deal, Roosevelt did become more concerned with administrative efficiency and began to restore civil service laws to their former prominence by extending them to include New Deal agencies. Even these bureaucratizing reforms, however, were intended to solidify the political goals of the New Deal by institutionalizing them and tenuring into the civil service loyal New Dealers who could resist an anticipated conservative attempt to dismantle the New Deal state if the Republicans captured the White House.

50. Galambos, "The Emerging Organizational Synthesis," p. 10.

A proper assessment of the strengths and weaknesses of the state-building and organizational revolution theories would require a more sustained analysis than has been provided here. The general reservations concerning these frameworks, discussed above, are not intended to detract from the genuine contribution these literatures have made to our understanding of the Progressive Era and the New Deal. Work done in these traditions has been useful in formulating the interpretation of the NRA which follows, and some of the conclusions of this interpretation, such as the conclusion that the state was far more autonomous from interest group demands in the NRA than has previously been acknowledged, will in turn be relevant to those schools. But even this brief discussion suffices to indicate why the political dimensions of reform should be considered central in a comprehensive interpretation of either the New Deal or its foremost programs. Understanding the political dimensions of reform, however, will entail in addition an analysis of the moral and intellectual dimensions of reform. The term "progressivism" broadly connotes these dimensions of reform, whereas terms like "state building" and "organizational revolution" unjustifiably abstract from those connotations.

This emphasis on the political, moral, and intellectual dimensions of reform implies that progressive thought can illuminate progressive practice, but it does not imply a Hegelian view of history, where the meaning of historical epochs can be understood exclusively as the unfolding of ideas in concrete historical form. Interests, both economic and political, are also important, and in the interpretation of the NRA that follows, the important groups that shaped the history of the NRA—progressive political elites and business and labor elites—will be portrayed as motivated both by ideals and by interests. Progressive political elites, for instance, not only pursued the ideals of their tradition but also were interested in acquiring and retaining political power. This quest for power was in turn channeled by the government institutions in which they assumed roles, and their interests because institutional as well as personal. The fact that they sought power, however, does not undermine their credentials as idealists, any more than the fact that they pursued ideals would imply that they were indifferent to power. The important question is not whether they were motivated by interests or ideals (the answer is both), but whether their ideals and the interests were congruent. Progressive elites, it is asserted, are more like rising elites who want to acquire political power primarily in order to stamp their vision on the world than they are like declining elites who are bent on preserving their privilege and power even after their idealism has been exhausted. The plausibility of this assertion depends on the power of the interpretation that follows from it. With these considerations in mind, we can now return to the question of the link between the Progressive Era and the New Deal.

Progressivism and the New Deal

Was the Progressive Era the crucible in which a progressive corporatist tradition was forged? Did a corporatist progressive tradition eventually find expression in the National Recovery Administration? Consider the careers of Raymond Moley, Donald Richberg, and Rexford Tugwell. Each played an important role in the history of the NRA. Raymond Moley was the unofficial leader of Franklin Roosevelt's "Brain Trust" during the 1932 campaign, and he was delegated the responsibility for sifting through general proposals for promoting economic recovery after Roosevelt took office. In April 1933, Roosevelt asked him to come up with some specific recommendations for what was to become the National Industrial Recovery Act (NIRA). Although other responsibilities prevented him from playing an active role in the final stages of the legislative drafting of the NIRA, Moley put together one of the two teams responsible for the final legislation.[51] Donald Richberg was one of the men recruited to help draft the NIRA, and he became part of the inner core of New Dealers who worked on the final version of the bill. Once the NRA was established, Richberg first became its general counsel and unofficially second-in-command of the program, and then gradually emerged as the new overseer of the NRA as the first NRA administrator—Hugh Johnson—fell from power. Rexford Tugwell was an important member of Roosevelt's brain trust during the 1932 campaign and helped to draft both the NIRA and the NIRA equivalent in agriculture, the Agricultural Adjustment Act (AAA).[52] In each case, even a brief biographical sketch reveals the pragmatic and progressive roots of their interest in corporatism.

Raymond Moley was an outspoken advocate of "a policy of cooperative business-government planning" during the early New Deal. In his version of progressive corporatism, a program like the NRA was ideally suited to institutionalize cooperation between government and business because it relied heavily on trade associations, which for Moley were "the natural means which economic life has sought to find a way out of chaos."[53] In an autobiographical statement, Moley described the origins of his political orientation in the following way:

> Meanwhile I had absorbed the ideas and spirit of the Progressive movement, although I was never an admirer of Theodore Roosevelt. I doubted his sincerity and was repelled by his ham acting. I preferred Wilson's more intelligent approach to reform. And he was a Democrat! As I shall note later, I also preferred the more concise specifications in Charles Van Hise's *Concentration and Control* to the voluminous writings of Herbert Croly.

51. Schlesinger, *The Coming of the New Deal*, pp. 96–97.
52. Tugwell claimed that the NRA "embodied my ideas." See K. S. Davis, *FDR: The New Deal Years*, p. 118; Hawley, *The New Deal*, pp. 28–29.
53. Schlesinger, *The Coming of the New Deal*, pp. 88, 93.

All in all, it was Wilson who determined my occupation, and the Progressive movement my political faith. Maturity came with the years after that, but these early influences were still alive when the exciting events of 1932 began.[54]

This description demonstrates that the foundations of Moley's political beliefs were established during the Progressive Era and that those beliefs continued to shape his reformism during the early New Deal. While it suggests that Wilsonians as well as New Nationalists could evolve in the direction of a progressive corporatist ideology, that conclusion would be premature at this point because Moley's Wilsonianism was more rooted in partisan affiliation and judgments of individual character than it was in ideology.[55]

Moley's relationship to the progressive version of corporatism found in Herbert Croly's work is suggested by the quotation above. His reservations concerning Croly appear to be more stylistic than substantive. Charles Van Hise's *Concentration and Control*, published in 1912, may have been less voluminous than Croly's *Promise of American Life*, but it was just as suitable a foundation for progressive corporatism. Like many progressives of his day, Van Hise artificially distinguished the economic consequences of monopolies, which he ruthlessly criticized, from the economic consequences of cartels of smaller firms, and consequently his recommendations for reform could easily have been cited in defense of the NRA:

It is believed that in business under modern conditions, cooperation not competition should be the controlling word. Sufficient cooperation should be allowed to prevent fierce and unrestrained competition which goes to the extent of reducing prices below a reasonable amount. Only by cooperation can the enormous wastes of competition be avoided. . . . If all restraints of trade are reasonable which do not produce monopoly, then we may accept the common law principle that unreasonable restraint of trade is not to be allowed, and under this principle secure cooperation. But if reasonable restraint is to be narrowly construed, so as to interdict all combinations which divide territories, regulate outputs and make price agreements, then unreasonable restraint of trade must be redefined by statute in order to secure the benefits of cooperation.[56]

Van Hise went on to assert that greater cooperation was as necessary for labor, as it was for capital, and that trade unions should not be subject to

---

54. Raymond Moley, *The First New Deal* (New York, 1966), pp. 13–14.

55. Moley's concession that the trend "toward greater and greater concentration . . . cannot be checked" and his conclusion that antitrust laws had led to a "state of anarchy" are ideologically much closer to Theodore Roosevelt than they are to Woodrow Wilson. See Schlesinger, *The Coming of the New Deal*, p. 182.

56. Charles Van Hise, *Concentration and Control* (New York, 1973), p. 226.

antitrust constraints. Finally, he argued, "Not only should cooperation between capitalists and cooperation of laborers be allowed, but cooperation of the two groups should be permitted."[57]

Donald Richberg first entered politics during the Progressive Era as a supporter of Charles Meriam's reform bid for the mayorship of Chicago. After Meriam's effort failed, Richberg turned his attention to national politics, where he devoted himself to Theodore Roosevelt's campaign to become the presidential nominee of the Republican party. When the Republicans chose William Howard Taft over Roosevelt, Richberg bolted the party and joined the new Progressive party, which Roosevelt established. In 1913, Richberg began working full-time for the Progressive party as director of the Legislative Reference Bureau of the Progressive National Service, an agency that among other activities prepared model legislation for Progressive legislators. Christopher Lasch and Thomas Vadney, Richberg biographers, argued that Richberg's basic political orientation solidified during the Progressive Era and during World War I and that he remained true to those principles not only during the New Deal but even paradoxically during the 1940s and 1950s, when Richberg found himself on the conservative side of the new political spectrum.[58]

As had been the case with Croly, Richberg's political thinking took on corporatist overtones during World War I. Reacting against wartime infringements on civil liberties, Richberg concluded that war had done no more than make manifest the authoritarian tendencies that were latent in the oligarchical character of the American economy. In articles published in Croly's *New Republic*, and particularly in an article entitled "Democratization of Industry," Richberg called for fundamental reforms that would give workers a stake in and some control over modern industrial enterprises.[59] He proposed that workers be given representation on corporate boards of directors, arguing that such a restructuring of industry would be preferable to subjecting industry to political control.

Like Croly, Richberg's nascent progressive corporatism was coupled to a suspicion of the liberal ideal of the rule of law which had many affinities with pragmatic jurisprudence. Arguing that the law had to absorb the teachings of modern social science if it was to keep abreast of the times, Richberg had only contempt for traditional legal thinking: "Against the rising authority of scientific leadership no group will fight longer and harder than the lawyers who have become more and more the chief protectors of the powers that be. . . . The profession of the law, being

57. Ibid., p. 227.

58. Thomas Vadney, *The Wayward Liberal: A Political Biography of Donald Richberg* (Lexington, Ky. 1970), p. ix; Christopher Lasch, "Donald Richberg and the Idea of a National Interest" (Master's thesis, Columbia University, 1955), p. iii.

59. Donald Richberg, "Democratization of Industry," *The New Republic*, 12 May 1917, pp. 49–51.

peculiarly unscientific in origin, growth and practice, will naturally continue to urge and to contrive that final authority in the state shall be reposed in the executors of dead generations instead of their living heirs.''[60] Later, when he was legal counsel for the NRA and had the responsibility for recruiting legal talent to the NRA, Richberg complained that it was difficult to find capable lawyers who were also "sympathetic with . . . 'sociological' jurisprudence.''[61] Thus it is with considerable justification that Christopher Lasch described Richberg's life as "a kind of extension of the lives of Theodore Roosevelt and Herbert Croly.''[62]

Rexford Tugwell's corporatism is derived directly from pragmatism rather than indirectly via progressivism. Tugwell had been a student of Simon Patten at the Wharton School of Finance and Commerce of the University of Pennsylvania. Patten and Thorstein Veblen were the founders of institutionalist or New Era economics, a school that rejected classical liberal economic theory and developed an historical and empirical approach to economic theory in the pragmatist tradition. Emphasizing the technological transformation of the economic world, Patten argued that the "age of surplus" would soon replace the "age of scarcity" and that in the new economic order cooperation would supersede competition as the driving force in economic activity. Absorbing these concepts from Patten, Tugwell also borrowed heavily from Veblen's theory that the age of scarcity was artificially prolonged by the domination of "industry" by "business." His education in the pragmatist tradition was completed by his contacts with John Dewey as a young professor at Columbia University, and he came to view his own work as a further radicalization of the insights of New Era economics, which he described as "the bridge between classicism and instrumentalism in economics.''[63]

Applying his pragmatic framework to the problem of industrial reorganization in the wake of the depression, Tugwell's *Industrial Discipline and the Governmental Arts* anticipated the NRA in many ways.[64] Tugwell insisted that cooperation could not replace competition as long as progressives adhered to an outmoded conception of antitrust law, which was "the dying effort of the small business system to perpetuate itself.''[65] Like Theodore Roosevelt, Tugwell believed that further economic concentration was inevitable and should be encouraged.

60. Donald Richberg, *Tents of the Mighty* (New York, 1930), p. 252.
61. Donald Richberg, *The Rainbow* (New York, 1936), p. 164.
62. Lasch, p. iv.
63. Schlesinger, *The Crisis of the Old Order*, pp. 136–137, 193–195; K. S. Davis, *FDR: The New York Years*, pp. 268–269.
64. Rexford G. Tugwell, *The Industrial Discipline and the Governmental Arts* (New York, 1977). Although this book was not published until the fall of 1933, the manuscript had been completed the previous year. Tugwell delayed publication because he was closely associated with the Roosevelt electoral campaign in 1932 and the radicalism of this book's proposals could have been politically embarrassing. See Schlesinger, *The Crisis of the Old Order*, p. 451.
65. Tugwell, *Industrial Discipline*, p. 135.

Nevertheless, his criticism of the small business *system* did not mean that the fate of small business was of no concern to him. In fact, Tugwell argued that a program of economic reform would protect the interests of "consumers, *weaker businesses,* workers, farmers, and technicians" (emphasis added). The inevitability of the trend toward economic concentration did not mean that small businesses were to be abandoned to suffer an inexorable fate, a deterministic response that would have been incompatible with the progressive faith in the capacity of government to humanize economic life, but rather that the protection accorded small businesses must not unduly interfere with the slow and steady movement toward more-efficient modes of economic organization. Furthermore, the trend toward replacing market relationships with administered economic relationships did not necessarily entail the destruction of small business. Smaller businesses might well survive in the new economic order if they could efficiently coordinate their activities through trade associations.[66]

Tugwell's concern for social justice is evident in his reflections on the need for industrial democracy. Arguing that workers were exploited and inefficiently coerced in a laissez-faire economic order, Tugwell predicted that "genuinely effective discipline" and "superior productivity" would be possible if control over industry was dispersed and if workers gained a greater say in decisions that affected their lives. Fear was the dominant motive in nineteenth-century capitalism, but "under a more democratic regime, other incentives would have to be depended on; greater democracy weakens rather than strengthens the fears of workers. The new incentives would necessarily be of a more positive sort, such as that the withholding of effort would be detrimental not only to one's own interest but to the interests of one's fellows."[67] Workers could become full partners in a new economic order because their genuine interests were not inimical to technological advancement toward economic abundance, and government should take steps to break down the autocratic control of business elites.

Tugwell valued cooperation not only because it provided greater opportunities for people to realize their ethical potential, but because it opened the door for economic planning, the application of instrumentalist rationality to economic life. Sharing some of the technocratic orientation of Thorstein Veblen, Tugwell did not believe that a competitive economy was self-regulating, and he argued that conscious guidance was necessary if the public good was to be secure in an increasingly sophisticated economic environment. Tugwell envisioned even more extensive planning than that attempted by the NRA, including price-fixing and the centralized

66. "And the close articulation of processes which is the best feature of single management may also be achieved by the recognition and organization of permanent relations even among separate firms." Ibid., pp. 123, 218
67. Ibid., p. 99.

allocation of investment capital. His vision of planning, however, was not a vision of centralized planning by government bureaucracies. The coerciveness of the Soviet five-year plans had little attraction for Tugwell. "Throughout the development of highly integrated industrial enterprises, there have been two extreme views of the duties of government. One held that business should be let alone. Another, that government should take over completely all economic functions. We have proceeded in our history on neither of these dogmatic theories." Tugwell argued for a more flexible and experimental approach to developing institutions for planning, seeking to eschew force by enlisting the cooperation of management, labor, and consumers.[68]

Tugwell did provide some guidance for devising new institutions for carrying out economic planning: "We are not entirely without precedent for such a planning organization. The War Industries Board was an instrument of precisely this sort . . . its advantages, which are admitted even by those most committed to the other features of capitalism, for which it was a substitute, were so great." That Tugwell would cite the War Industries Board, the corporatist agency responsible for industrial mobilization during World War I, as a model of the planning institution he had in mind clearly indicates the corporatist tendencies in his own thinking. Planning would be accomplished by transforming trade associations from agencies pursuing narrow economic interests into agencies with a broader social vision. Government representatives would sit on tripartite boards with representatives of business and labor and would, if necessary, "have the final word." The modus operandi, however, would be bargaining between representatives of all three groups as industry plans were reconciled with government plans. The utopianism of Tugwell's claim that institutions like these would allow self-interest to be replaced by production for the sake of the common welfare and economic scarcity to be replaced by economic surplus is unmistakable.[69]

Progressivism and the Lowi Thesis

All three of these brief portraits confirm the existence of a progressive corporatist tradition that emerged during the latter part of the Progressive Era. Herbert Croly's writings, far from being idiosyncratic, provide some of the clearest expressions of that tradition and its links to the pragmatic attack on the rule of law. Progressive corporatists differed somewhat in their attitudes toward business elites. Moley was more inclined to believe that a business community chastened by the depression could be trusted to

68. Ibid., pp. 199, 201, 209, 228.
69. Ibid., pp. 100–101, 212–216.

cooperate in the establishment of a new economic order. He broke with Franklin Roosevelt and the New Deal when cooperation between business and Roosevelt faltered and Roosevelt became more antagonistic to the business community. In contrast, Tugwell was inherently suspicious of businessmen, and his corporatism had always had a more radical tone to it. Richberg was somewhere in between. But all three were developing a version of progressive corporatism that appealed to the rising professional classes and that looked primarily to government, rather than to business, to establish a new economic order in which cooperation would replace competition.[70]

Thus Theodore Lowi's argument that a new public philosophy arose legitimating discretionary government and corporatism is confirmed, even though Lowi misidentified the source and time period in which that ideology arose. But placing greater emphasis on pragmatism and progressivism as movements that contributed to the decline of law and the rise of corporatism also raises fundamental questions concerning Lowi's assertion that the rise of the new public philosophy served to rationalize the interests of powerful, well-established groups and to defend the status quo. Neither pragmatism nor progressivism is well suited to playing such a role, for both provided a basis for radical criticisms of the American political system and its political traditions on behalf of disadvantaged groups. Dewey, for instance, attacked traditional conceptions of the rule of law because they were associated with laissez-faire jurisprudence and a defense of the interests of capitalists, and he was attracted to corporatism because he saw it as a vehicle for instituting economic democracy, just as such left-wing British intellectuals as G. D. C. Cole and the early Harold Laski saw corporatism as a vehicle for promoting socialism. Similarly, aspirations to achieve social justice were generally decisive in progressivism, and it was those aspirations that would shape the most dramatic and ambitious progressive attempt to restructure the American economy—the National Recovery Administration.

---

70. Thus Tugwell could identify his own approach to economic matters with that of Adolph Berle and the Raymond Moley, who participated in the Brain Trust. He distinguished this approach from "those who, like the later Moley, seemed to think that business confidence was all-important," but added, "Moley had had other views in 1932, and they had seemed to be the same as ours." Moley, on the other hand, did not believe he had fundamentally changed his views, but rather that he was forced to break with the New Deal because the New Deal had changed. Both views of what happened to Moley are partially justified, but it would clearly be wrong to attribute excessive conservatism to Moley in 1932. See, Rexford G. Tugwell, *In Search of Roosevelt* (Cambridge, Mass., 1972), p. 95.

CHAPTER 3

Progressivism and the
Origins of the NRA

When Franklin Roosevelt assumed office in March 1933, he ushered into power a new political elite. In his first inaugural address he attributed blame for the depression to the "rulers of the exchange of mankind's goods," those "unscrupulous money changers" who had failed to lead the nation through their own incompetence, selfishness, and lack of vision, and he then went on to proclaim that the money changers had "fled from their high seats in the temple of civilization."[1] The business elites and their political allies who had run the nation in the 1920s had failed, and the 1932 election had provided a mandate for radical changes. The depression attested to the bankruptcy of the old order, but it also presented unique opportunities for sweeping reforms. Rejecting the possibility that economic recovery could be achieved without fundamental reforms, Roosevelt argued that nothing less than a new economic order would suffice.[2]

Although Roosevelt did not have an explicitly formulated agenda for political reform, the general principles that would guide economic reconstruction were clear. The old order had been based upon economic competition and a legal order based on individual rights, with particular sanctity attached to property rights. The progressives rejected the premise that economic competition would suffice to channel individual selfishness along socially beneficent paths. Similarly, they did not believe that our legal system had provided an order in which the rights of all were genuinely protected. The new order that Roosevelt envisioned would rely primarily on cooperation rather than competition and on nonlegal modes of conflict resolution rather than on the rule of law. Disciplined cooperation for the sake of the common good would have to replace undisciplined individualism and the narrow focus on maximizing profits.

1. Franklin D. Roosevelt, *The Public Papers and Addresses of Franklin D. Roosevelt*, ed. Samuel Rosenman, 13 vols. (New York, 1938), 2:11–12.
2. Franklin D. Roosevelt, *Looking Forward* (London, 1933), pp. 32–35.

These overarching principles were fundamentally consistent with John Dewey's pragmatism and Herbert Croly's progressivism, but it is highly unlikely that Roosevelt's intellectual framework was directly shaped by either author. He had no scholarly inclinations and apparently had done little serious reading after he became governor of New York.[3] But if Roosevelt was far more a man of action than a man of thought, he nevertheless forged an unprecedented alliance between the university and the state. The most powerful symbol of that alliance was Roosevelt's Brain Trust, a group of intellectual advisors who joined Roosevelt's entourage during his first campaign for the presidency and who acted as a conduit channeling people and ideas from the university into his adminis- tration. This rapprochement between intellectual and political elites facili- tated the absorption of pragmatist and progressive ideas by political activists, for pragmatism and progressivism were the dominant intellectual currents among those in academia who embraced the New Deal because they were committed to sweeping reforms. As the legislative history of the NIRA makes clear, these intellectual elites played a pivotal role in the creation of the NRA.

Even during his first presidential campaign, Roosevelt indicated the direction and general outlines of his reform agenda. In a speech written by Adolph Berle, one of the charter members of Roosevelt's Brain Trust, which Roosevelt delivered before the Commonwealth Club of San Francisco on 23 September 1932, Roosevelt declared that the foremost task of government in its relation to business was "to assist the development of an economic declaration of rights, an economic constitutional order." Rejecting the uninhibited competition of the previous laissez-faire age, he insisted that businessmen controlled their private empires as a public trust on the condition that they subordinate their self-interest to the common good, and he anticipated an expanded regulatory role for the government to protect the public interest. But government "should assume the func- tion of economic regulation only as a last resort" because businessmen were recognizing their responsibility and sought "a form of organization which will bring the scheme of things into balance, even though it may in some measure qualify the freedom of action of individual units within the business."[4] The NRA institutionalized the cooperative ideal, and the division of labor between public and private authorities prefigured in this speech.

To many New Dealers, industrial mobilization during World War I under the War Industries Board (WIB) provided the appropriate model for a new economic order. The WIB had demonstrated the virtues and flexibility of decentralized planning carried out by committees of volun-

---

3. K. S. Davis, *The New Deal Years*, p. 207.
4. Roosevelt, *Public Papers*, 1:752-755.

teers from industry, and it had carried out its tasks relying largely on the moral discipline created by a shared commitment to the clearly defined end of victory and the pressure of public opinion. Voluntarism alone did not suffice to assure compliance with WIB guidelines, and where necessary the state did use its powers of coercion, but on the whole coercion remained in the background. Persuaded that the depression posed a threat to our national well-being not unlike that posed by foreign enemies during World War I, the New Dealers fashioned the NRA along the lines of the WIB.[5] Unlike the WIB, however, the NRA was not simply an emergency measure. It was to have been the foundation of a new corporatist economic order.

The Drafting of the NIRA

The legislative history of the NIRA clearly identifies the bill as a progressive measure.[6] The bill was proposed by the Roosevelt administration, and the only member of Congress who played a critical role in the drafting of the bill was Senator Wagner, himself a noted progressive. Legislative drafting began in the earliest days of the administration, when Roosevelt asked Raymond Moley to serve as a clearinghouse for general proposals for economic recovery. Moley gathered around himself a talented group of advisors, among whom were Hugh Johnson, a former WIB official and soon to become NRA administrator, Donald Richberg, and Rexford Tugwell. As was often the case with Roosevelt, at the same time that he had entrusted Raymond Moley with responsibility for coming up with a recovery bill, he also encouraged Senator Wagner to work independently on his own draft. Wagner also recruited a number of talented advisors to assist him, among whom were Harold Moulton, president of the Brookings Institution; Jerome Frank, general counsel for the Department of Agriculture; and John Dickinson, assistant secretary of commerce.

The NRA was to be the centerpiece of Franklin Roosevelt's recovery program, and he proceeded cautiously in developing a legislative proposal. His initial uncertainty and hesitancy in developing the NIRA have

---

5. Gerald D. Nash, "Experiments in Industrial Mobilization: W.I.B. and N.R.A.," *Mid-America* 45 (1963): 157–174; Gerald D. Nash, "Franklin D. Roosevelt and Labor: The World War I Origins of Early New Deal Policy," *Labor History* 1 (1960): 39–52; William E. Leuchtenburg, "The New Deal and the Analogue of War," in *Change and Continuity in Twentiety-Century America,* ed. John Braeman, Robert H. Bremner, and David Brody (New York, 1964).

6. Because the story of the drafting of the NIRA has already been told many times, the account below focuses primarily on illuminating aspects of the process that have not received sufficient attention. For a detailed account, see Schlesinger, *The Coming of the New Deal,* pp. 87–102.

suggested to some the absence of self-directed leadership, although in view of the sweeping reforms being contemplated a cautious approach seems clearly justified.[7] At one point, delays in fashioning an administration recovery program even appeared to jeopardize his control over the tempo and direction of reform politics. On 6 April a restless Senate passed a bill introduced by Senator Hugo Black of Alabama to ban from interstate commerce all goods produced in factories employing workers more than six hours a day or more than five days a week. Although Roosevelt did not want to alienate his progressive allies backing the bill, he was convinced that the recovery program he was developing would provide a more viable and flexible approach to recovery. Using his political clout to bottle the Black Bill up in the House, Roosevelt postponed action on it until he was able to introduce the NIRA, a move that then preempted further consideration of the Black bill.

At the time, Roosevelt's opposition to the Black Bill appeared to be a slap in the face of organized labor, which had hinted at the possibility of a general strike unless the measure was passed.[8] Black's thirty-hour bill promised reduced unemployment and had an immediate appeal to organized labor, but Roosevelt believed that labor simply did not understand their own best interests in this regard. The higher costs and inflexibility it would have imposed on industry threatened to retard recovery and prolong unemployment. The bill had made no provisions for establishing minimum wages as well as maximum hours, partly because of the hostility of the AFL to minimum-wage legislation. Black had been optimistic that a shorter work week would have created a labor shortage that would allow organized labor to push wages up and compensate workers for their reduced hours, but Roosevelt was not persuaded that wages would necessarily rise.[9] Furthermore, Roosevelt believed that Black's bill was unconstitutional, having received a memo to that effect from the attorney general.[10]

In retrospect, Roosevelt's confidence in his own judgment of labor's interests was not misplaced. There is substantial evidence to support the

7. Burns, *Roosevelt: The Lion and the Fox,* pp. 191–202; Leuchtenburg, *FDR and the New Deal,* pp. 84, 88–90, 107–108. Questions concerning Roosevelt's leadership during the early New Deal were not confined to academicians. The Roosevelt files contain the following anecdote: "Some time ago where a group of Democrats were comparing Roosevelt to Washington and Lincoln that [*sic*] they were interrupted by a Republican who said he thought Roosevelt could be more aptly compared to Christopher Columbus, because when he started he did not know where he was going, when he got there he did not know where he was, and when he got back he did not know where he had been" (Clarke to FDR, 19 September 1934, Roosevelt Papers, OF 172, Box 1, Business, July–October 1934).

8. Schlesinger, *The Coming of the New Deal,* p. 92; Hawley, *The New Deal,* pp. 22–23; Irving Bernstein, *New Deal Collective Bargaining Policy* (Berkeley and Los Angeles, 1950), p. 30. The AFL continued to push for some version of this bill even after the NRA had been enacted. William Green, *Labor and Democracy* (Princeton, 1939), p. 142.

9. Schlesinger, *The Coming of the New Deal,* pp. 92, 95.

10. Frank Friedel, *FDR: Launching the New Deal* (Boston, 1973), p. 419.

conclusion that a uniform forty-hour work week imposed by the Popular Front in France under similar circumstances hindered recovery by decreasing productivity, and the much more extreme thirty-hour work week of the Black Bill would undoubtedly have hampered American recovery.[11] If the new elites swept into office by the 1932 election were going to establish their superiority over business elites in being entrusted with political power over the economy, one of their first tasks was to control impractical proposals from their left which promoted short-term interests at the expense of longer-term economic growth. Rejection of the Black Bill was consistent with intelligent progressivism.

Until the Black Bill forced his hand, Roosevelt had been waiting until his advisors could either coalesce around a single alternative or, barring that, until the positions jelled sufficiently to allow Roosevelt to make a clear choice. It was important that precipitant action be staved off, for he was unwilling to be pushed into a premature program that might rebound to the discredit of reformers. Now, with a new sense of urgency, Roosevelt brought the leaders of the Wagner group and the Moley group together on 10 May and arranged for them to lock themselves in a room until they ironed out the remaining differences in the respective proposals.[12] The bill that emerged permitted industrial self-government utilizing trade associations to administer codes of fair trade practices regulating business competition, and it included Section 7a, with its proclamation of new rights for labor. The plan required a relaxation of antitrust laws to permit greater cooperation among businessmen, but business agreements were sanctioned only after review by the president to assure government supervision of the codes. If an industry failed to agree on an acceptable code, the president had the power to impose one. If it became necessary in order to enforce the codes, the president could invoke a licensing provision (effective for one year) that would have required businessmen to secure a federal license to engage in interstate commerce, the license being contingent on adherence to the code. The bill also authorized appropriations for public works.

Business and labor leaders were consulted during the drafting of the NIRA, but it is doubtful that either decisively influenced the Act. This is most clearly the case with labor. Although Section 7a of the NIRA, guaranteeing to labor the right to organize and bargain collectively, clearly benefited organized labor, the AFL had little to do with the drafting of this section. Donald Richberg, who had been a prominent labor lawyer during the 1920s and who had been recruited to serve on Moley's NIRA team because of his labor expertise, was the primary author of Section 7a, and

---

11. Paul Warwick, *The French Popular Front: A Legislative Analysis* (Chicago, 1977), pp. 27, 39–42, 153, 159, 163–164.
12. Schlesinger, *The Coming of the New Deal*, p. 98.

he did not consult with labor leaders in drafting this section.[13] Despite frequent assertions to the contrary by historians of the period, business leaders also played a marginal role. James Warburg, a Wall Street banker sympathetic to the New Deal, had played a prominent role in developing an early proposal for government guaranteed loans for business in return for a share in later business profits, but this proposal was rejected by Roosevelt when he realized the potential cost to government. After this, Warburg did not play a prominent role in the drafting of the NIRA.[14] Henry Harriman, president of the U.S. Chamber of Commerce, sat in on some of Senator Wagner's brainstorming sessions but, Wagner insisted, "Mr. Harriman had nothing to do with drafting this legislation."[15] In the later stages of legislative drafting, interest groups even found their official representatives excluded from decision making. Requests by both the AFL and the National Association of Manufacturers (NAM) to send representatives to the final conference to explain their respective positions were turned down with the terse explanation that the meetings were informal. Nor was it an accident that the two members of the administration with the strong ties to labor and business—Secretary of Labor Perkins with the AFL and Assistant Secretary of Commerce Dickinson with business groups—both had subordinate roles in the final drafting process.[16]

Congress and the NIRA

On 17 May, Roosevelt forwarded his National Industrial Recovery Bill to Congress. In the House, which was firmly controlled by Democrats loyal to Roosevelt, the NIRA sailed through smoothly. The House confined its legislative efforts largely to writing a taxation provision to finance the program, a provision that the president had left up to the discretion of Congress. By a lopsided majority of 325 to 76, the House approved the measure only nine days after it was introduced.[17] In the Senate the NIRA met greater opposition, but on 9 June the Senate also passed the measure by a vote of 58 to 24. Progressives generally supported the bill, and conservatives opposed it.[18] After a conference committee reconciled the

13. Richberg, *The Rainbow,* p. 45; James MacGregor Burns, "Congress and the Formation of Economic Policies" (Ph.D. diss., Harvard University, 1947), p. 40, citing a letter from Richberg to Burns.

14. Burns, "Congress," pp. 13–18.

15. *Congressional Record,* 73d Cong., 1st sess., 1933, 77:5164. The NIRA ultimately differed in important ways from Harriman's proposals for industrial recovery. This is dealt with more extensively in Chapter 5.

16. Burns, "Congress," pp. 39–40.

17. Roos, p. 48.

18. After a conference committee reconciled the Senate and House versions and weakened the

Senate and House versions, Roosevelt signed into law the National Industrial Recovery Act on 16 June 1933, noting, "History probably will record the National Industrial Recovery Act as the most important and far-reaching legislation ever enacted by the American Congress."[19]

The most revealing of these latter phases of the NIRA legislative process was the debate in the Senate. A number of senators questioned the constitutionality of the bill, arguing that its broad delegations were a virtual abdication of congressional authority that vested too much discretionary power in the hands of the president. Some argued that the NIRA's licensing and penal provisions smacked of dictatorships. Others were disturbed by the NIRA's expansive understanding of interstate commerce, noting that it would destroy the distinction between interstate and intrastate commerce and thereby infringe upon states rights.[20]

Senator Borah, a Progressive Era holdover from the state of Idaho, expressed concern that the NRA would foster monopoly and harm small businesses. Borah acknowledged that this was not the intention of those who were proposing the NRA, but he argued that in practice the NRA would inevitably allow big business to draft and administer the codes of fair trade competition with minimal supervision from the president. "When the time comes that the large interests in an industry, gathered together for the purpose of making a code, do not dominate the situation, but permit the small independent to write the code for the large industry, the millennium will have been here for many years."[21] The protection against such abuses of the codes provided by presidential review of the codes was minimal, Borah concluded, because the president could not possibly carefully supervise a large number of codes.

Senator Wagner countered Borah by arguing that the restraints on competition permitted by the NIRA were means to "protect the small businessman," by proscribing the use of "rebates, discrimination and selling below the cost of production in order to destroy some little business man." "Large industrialists," Wagner insisted, "will not formulate the codes." Wagner did not attack big business per se. He argued that the task confronting legislators was how to utilize "the wealth-creating

---

Borah Amendment (see below), some progressives who had supported the NRA in its first vote broke away and voted against the final measure, so the final vote in the Senate was less clearly ideological. That the final bill was still fundamentally a progressive measure was made clear by the fact that only two senators who had opposed the initial bill switched in favor of it. See K. S. Davis, *FDR: The New Deal Years*, pp. 143–145.

19. Schlesinger, *The Coming of the New Deal*, p. 102.

20. *Congressional Record*, 73d Cong., 1st sess., 1933, 77:5062, 5166, 5174–5176, 5180, 5237, 5260.

21. Ibid., p. 5165. The limits of Borah's political vision are suggested by the history of the oil code in Chapter 7.

possibilities of large size" so that we could reap its benefits without checking its efficiency. But neither did he assume that large size was a prerequisite for efficiency. The NIRA would allow small businesses to cooperate in ways that only large businesses had been able to cooperate under existing antitrust laws, and this would allow them to achieve new levels of efficiency. "Yet the same law [the Sherman Antitrust Act] prevented smaller business men from cooperating in order to put competition upon a basis of efficiency, and has resulted instead in a destructive, cutthroat competition." Wagner argued that antitrust laws had failed to protect the small businessman and that the NRA was simply a new means to achieve this old goal.[22]

Indeed, the NRA's emphasis on fair trade competition did partially resemble Wilsonian antitrust policy, embodied in the Clayton Act and Federal Trade Commission Act, even though the NRA relaxed the enforcement of those laws in a manner that strict Wilsonian progressives found objectionable. Senator Newlands, a sponsor of Wilson's Federal Trade Commission Act, had described it as an attempt to "civilize competition" and to bring about "fair competition" in accordance with the "moral law," terms frequently also used to describe the intent of the NRA.[23] One of the most prominent Wilsonian progressives, Louis Brandeis, had in fact objected far more strenuously to economic concentration than he did to collusion among smaller producers, especially if such practices tended to prevent smaller units from being driven out of business.[24] While there is a difference between stifling competition in the guise of prohibiting unfair trade practices and directly promoting cooperation among businessmen to achieve fair trade, the differences are not as stark as they appeared to Borah.

Borah's doubts that the new means (the NRA codes) would secure the old end (protection of small business) were not assuaged by Wagner's reassurances that the cooperative thrust of the NRA entailed only a *partial* suspension of the antitrust laws, not their wholesale renunciation. "This is supplemental to the anti-trust laws; it is not destructive of them. We are going to retain competition. We are simply going to put competition on a high standard of efficiency rather than on a low standard of exploitation of labor."[25] Despite these protestations, Borah insisted that the Senate add an amendment prohibiting "combinations in restraint of trade, price fixing, or other monopolistic practices."[26] Wagner, who never had intended the

22. Hawley, *The New Deal*, p. 29; *Congressional Record,* 73d Cong., 1st sess., 1933, 77:5163, 5165.
23. Stone, p. 40; Lyon et al. pp. 19, 670–671.
24. Thomas McCraw, "Rethinking the Trust Question," in *Regulation in Perspective,* ed. Thomas McCraw (Cambridge, Mass., 1981), p. 29.
25. Lyon et al., p. 20.
26. Ibid., p. 46; Hawley, *The New Deal*, p. 30.

NRA to be a vehicle for monopoly or for systematic price-fixing, consented to the amendment.[27]

It soon became clear to NRA proponents, however, that Borah's amendment was so sweeping that it would have substantially undermined the capacity of the NRA to promote industrial cooperation, and administration officials later persuaded the conference committee that met to reconcile the Senate and House versions of the NIRA to water down Borah's amendment to a less-restrictive prohibition on "monopolies and monopolistic practices."[28] Despite protests from Borah, the Senate went along with these changes.

While the conflict between New Deal progressives and more traditional progressives like Borah often occupied center stage in the Senate consideration of the NIRA, the more fundamental conflict was between progressives and conservatives. Despite Borah's tirades, the NRA still was a progressive program. The NIRA proposed an unprecedented peacetime expansion of government economic regulation, granting powers to the federal government that were anathema to conservative senators steeped in the laissez-faire tradition.

Five Senate democrats who were later to lead the Senate opposition to the New Deal typified the conservative response to the NIRA. Carter Glass of Virginia, now a conservative despite a progressive past, opposed the NIRA as a "tyrannical" unconstitutional act that both stifled individual initiative and crippled infant Southern industries through minimum-wage provisions. After the NRA was initiated, he stated his intention to go to jail before he would comply with the act, and he warned General Johnson, "Your blue buzzard [the blue eagle was the symbol of the NRA] will not fly from the mastheads of my two newspapers." Other conservatives in the Senate followed suit in opposition to the NRA. Thomas P. Gore of Oklahoma, Millard Tydings of Maryland, Josiah Bailey of North Carolina, and Harry Byrd of Virginia all split with Roosevelt over the NRA's departure from the conservative tradition of laissez-faire.[29]

The conflict between progressives and conservatives was less visible than the conflicts within progressivism, primarily because conservatives

27. *Congressional Record*, 73d Cong., 1st sess., 1933, 77:5244, 5246.

28. Walker Hines, former president of the Cotton Textile Institute, said, "My acquaintance with the cotton textile industry leaves me convinced that the Borah Amendment would largely if not wholly destroy the wholesome purpose of the bill" (Telegram of W. D. Hines to FDR, 9 June 1933, cited in Galambos, p. 213). An irony that is central to the history of the NRA was that in offering his amendment Borah purported to be defending the interests of smaller firms that were threatened by larger firms, but in the cotton textile industry (and other industries too) the anticompetitive features of the NRA codes that Borah would have disallowed were the means by which smaller firms protected themselves against the competition of larger firms. This theme will be explored more extensively in the next two chapters.

29. James T. Patterson, *Congressional Conservatism and the New Deal* (Lexington, Ky., 1967), pp. 20, 22–31.

were in disarray in the wake of the 1932 election and their opposition was fragmented and ineffective. Furthermore, Roosevelt's popularity and the apparent failure of the free market had disoriented conservative constituencies such as big business, rendering them more open to creative populist leadership. Only the staunchest conservatives were willing to vigorously oppose the program when many in the business community were either embracing the program or at least cautiously tolerating it.

Responses to the NIRA by Business and Labor

The responses of business and labor to the NRA varied considerably. The most favorable response from business came from the U.S. Chamber of Commerce, whose president, Henry Harriman, referred to the bill as "the Magna Charta of Industry and Labor,"[30] a misleading statement because Harriman and the Chamber of Commerce had significant reservations concerning the NRA. The Chamber of Commerce was "cautious and cool" regarding Section 7a.[31] In testimony before the House Ways and Means Committee, Harriman had noted that the Chamber of Commerce "has consistently stood for the real open shop," and he had urged the committee to write that principle into the bill.[32] More generally, Harriman conceded, "There are provisions in the act which I should have been very glad to have seen eliminated or changed."[33] The more conservative National Association of Manufacturers found redeeming features in the bill, particularly in its provisions for industrial self-government and its relaxation of antitrust laws, but it was also highly suspicious of Section 7a and of the provisions for government supervision of industrial self-government, a feature it believed opened the door for possible government regimentation of the economy.[34]

To some extent, business responses to the NRA were a function of the state of the economy. Speculators had induced a brief business "boomlet" from May to July 1933, partly in anticipation of higher prices under the

30. Roos, p. 43.

31. William Wilson, "Chamber of Commerce," p. 98.

32. Ibid., p. 99. Automobile manufacturers, among others, were similarly disposed. See Sidney Fine, *The Automobile under the Blue Eagle: Labor, Management, and the Automobile Manufacturing Code* (Ann Arbor, Mich., 1963), p. 46.

33. William Wilson concluded that "there never was a 'honeymoon' between the Chamber and the NRA" and that "the Chamber, never enthusiastic over the NRA, grew increasingly estranged from the recovery administration" (William Wilson, "Chamber of Commerce," pp. 95, 98–99).

34. The NAM was particularly opposed to the licensing provision in the NIRA. Although they did succeed in limiting the authorization of licensing to one year, Roosevelt's insistence that a "vigorous licensing power" was an "indispensable safeguard" prevented the NAM from eliminating it altogether. K. S. Davis, *FDR: The New Deal Years*, p. 141; Hawley, *The New Deal*, p. 30.

NRA, and this mini-recovery strengthened the argument that a natural recovery would occur without government interference.[35] Business reservations concerning the program became more pronounced, and the NAM even warned that the NRA might "nip in the bud the business recovery already manifesting itself."[36]

This business response to the mini-recovery in the spring of 1933 prefigured a similar tendency for the business community to become increasingly critical of the NRA during the lifetime of the program whenever economic recovery gained momentum. The onerous controls that the NRA imposed on businessmen seemed justified only as a response to dismal economic conditions, and doubts were awakened even in the minds of those who had enthusiastically embraced the NRA when recovery appeared just around the bend. But when the first mini-recovery of the spring of 1933 collapsed, business adopted a more conciliatory posture toward the NRA. Although the NIRA had some provisions that business found offensive, the character of the NRA would ultimately depend on the manner in which it was administered. An administrator sympathetic to business interests could easily steer the program in a direction that business would have found congenial, and business therefore adopted a wait-and-see position.

Labor was generally more enthusiastic about the NRA than business, but even labor had significant reservations. William Green hailed Section 7a of the NIRA as the "Magna Charta of Labor," and he hoped that the NRA would reinvigorate the union movement by safeguarding labor's right to organize and bargain collectively.[37] The AFL was far more suspicious of the minimum-wage provisions of the NIRA, just as it had been suspicious of most previous progressive attempts to enact minimum-wage statutes at the state level because it feared that such statutes would undercut the incentives workers had for joining unions. Furthermore, labor would have preferred more drastic limitations on maximum hours than the limitations that were likely to emerge from the NRA, and they continued to press futilely for the additional enactment of some version of Black's thirty-hour bill.[38] Despite these reservations, however, the AFL decided that the benefits of the proposed NRA so outweighed its costs for labor that they generally suppressed the temptation to seek amendments and confined their legislative role to that of providing support for the bill and beating off business attempts to gut Section 7a.[39]

35. Lyon et al., p. 489; K. S. Davis, *The New Deal Years,* pp. 136–137.
36. James Emery, NAM general counsel, in testimony before Congress; cited in Roos, p. 49.
37. Bellush, p. 27.
38. Green, p. 142.
39. Roos, p. 49.

Cooperation and Compulsion in the NRA

The NRA was the most ambitious attempt to institute societal corporatism in American political history. A new cooperative relationship between government, business, and labor was to have been achieved by transforming cutthroat free market competition into "fair" competition and by transforming the antagonistic relationship between business and labor under laissez-faire capitalism into a cooperative relationship based on collective bargaining. In the proposed structure of industrial self-government, Roosevelt believed he had found a program that was congruent with American progressivism and that promised to unite diverse constituencies in order to stimulate recovery. The NRA promised benefits to each of the interest groups whose cooperation it solicited, but it also demanded self-discipline. To business the NRA promised greater scope for mutual cooperation, but it demanded in return restraint on price increases. Otherwise the attempt by businessmen to recover the business losses of the last few years would end up depriving workers of their increased purchasing power to the detriment of recovery. To labor it promised eventual recognition as a full partner in industrial life, demanding in return restraint in the assertion of its new rights and wage demands lest strikes disrupt the hopes of recovery.

As long as trade associations or trade unions are viewed solely as a locus of private power pursuing private interests diametrically opposed to the public interest, the inclusion of these organizations within the administrative apparatus of the NRA will appear to be a crucial limitation on the progressive intent of the NRA. If the NRA was meant to secure public purposes, why incorporate private interests in the administration of the act? Why not leave the administration to civil servants, where professional norms and formal claims of authority direct officials to carry out the politically determined will of the people? At least civil servants have to be "captured" to deflect them from the public interest; inclusion of the very interests to be regulated in the administrative structure of control seems to preordain capture.

Actually, incorporation of private interests in the administration of the program can be an extremely successful technique of public co-optation of private interests. Social scientists have frequently recognized the possibility that business elites might use corporatist participation to co-opt labor opposition to a capitalist regime, but the possibility that a political elite might use the same technique to co-opt opposition from private interests generally has not been as extensively explored. Trade associations and trade unions were not to be organizations that merely represented the interests of their members. They were incorporated into the administrative apparatus of the NRA (administrative corporatism) with the expectation that they would subordinate their economic self-interest to broader national goals.[40]

40. This was in accord with Herbert Croly's understanding of corporatism. See Croly, *The Promise of American Life*, pp. 404–405.

Trade associations and trade unions were to provide the organizational basis for effectuating a new social ethics. According to the progressives, the domestication of capitalism, the reconciliation of private property and democratic public purposes, required the supersession of the ethics of capitalism, with its extreme concessions to economic self-interest. They shared with many European corporatists the belief that the craftsmanship spirit of pre-capitalist guilds supplied an appropriate alternative, an ethic that was compatible with modern economic organization without undermining man's social nature. Identification with functional role and the ethics of professionalism would replace self-interest as the driving force of economic production. This new economic order would more effectively safeguard the interests of groups that had been victimized under the laissez-faire order, particularly small business and labor, and would impose a new social discipline on big business. No system of government can rely solely on compulsion to advance its purposes, and the progressives were at least in part displaying a sound political realism in focusing considerable effort on moral reforms that could infuse institutional and political changes with sufficient energy to succeed.

Had the New Deal progressives relied solely on moral reform to advance their cause, it would be difficult to persuade skeptics that the naiveté of moralistic attempts to control self-interest did not hide an ulterior motive to promote the very interests that the morality professed to restrict. But the New Dealers were aware that even a successful program of moral uplift would not suffice. Industrial self-government was to occur under government supervision. A federal bureaucracy, and ultimately the president, would have to approve industrial codes before they could become operative. In extreme cases the federal government even had the power to impose a code on an industry without their consent. Finally, the president could cancel or modify specific rules or entire codes of fair trade competition if he deemed it necessary to secure the goals of the NRA.[41]

Once a code was operative, the NRA would work with the code authority to assure that the code was enforced. Even a code that was scrupulously adhered to by the vast majority of businessmen in a particular industry could be imperiled by a recalcitrant minority who violated its provisions and thereby secured a competitive advantage.[42] Recalling the War Industries Board experience, the New Dealers noted that a legal framework for mobilization during World War I had been enacted and was indispensable in controlling the few profiteers who were oblivious to moral appeals. If the morally obtuse had not been compelled to abide by collective decisions, the war mobilization effort would have collapsed, as even those committed to adhering to collective decisions were forced to meet the competition of the more unscrupulous.

41. NIRA Sections 3a, 3d, and 10b; Roos, pp. 478–480, 488.
42. Lyon et al., p. 260; Richberg, *The Rainbow*, pp. 168–169.

Although the NRA included provisions for central bureaucratic supervision of code authorities and a variety of enforcement mechanisms, it is nevertheless the case that the spirit of the program was voluntarist. State coercion alone could never have compelled the sacrifices made by industrial groups during World War I, even if it is true that moral enthusiasm can be sustained only when sacrifice is equally shared, and that may require some coercion. Coercion was a supplement, albeit an essential one, to the spontaneous consensus and civic virtue that disciplined self-interest during the war, and the NRA was supposed to work on the same principle. Thus New Dealers portrayed the NRA as the moral equivalent of war. That the conditions during the NRA were different from those prevailing during World War I would soon become apparent.

Just as public opinion was mobilized during the war to reinforce civic virtue, so the NRA attempted to mobilize public support for its measures during the summer of 1933. General Johnson, the newly appointed NRA administrator, displayed a remarkable talent for symbolic politics in the first few months of the NRA. He selected the Blue Eagle as the NRA symbol and launched a Blue Eagle campaign. Support-the-NRA parades were held in cities across the nation. Opposition to the program became tantamount to disloyalty. Businessmen who enlisted in the NRA program were allowed to display their badge of compliance prominently.[43] Businessmen who refused to cooperate were stigmatized and boycotted by consumers who had been encouraged by Johnson to buy only NRA approved products.[44] Within a few months almost every major industry, and countless minor ones, had enlisted under Johnson's banner.

Moral enthusiasm at least partially carried the day for the NRA during its first few months, but inevitably this high-spirited willingness to sacrifice flagged as time wore on.[45] Even the severity of the depression could not summon the same level of virtuous self-restraint as a nation at war. Granted the authority to draft codes of fair trade competition under the NRA, businessmen frequently succumbed to the temptation to use this opportunity to cartelize their industries. Individual businessmen found the economic incentives to violate codes of fair trade competition just as powerful, and noncompliance became epidemic as moral enthusiasm dwindled. Even labor, placing its organizational self-interest above the cooperative goals of the NRA, went out on strike repeatedly to gain organizational recognition despite adverse consequences for economic recovery.

In a nutshell this is the history of the NRA. It is the history of a program inspired by a lofty moral vision of a new corporatist economic

43. Richberg, *The Rainbow,* p. 161; Hawley, *The New Deal,* pp. 53–54.
44. Schlesinger, *The Coming of the New Deal,* pp. 114–116; Lyon et al., pp. 52–53; Roos, pp. 75–79, 88–93; Hawley, *The New Deal,* pp. 53–55.
45. Hawley, *The New Deal,* p. 68.

order that gradually collapsed as economic self-interest reasserted itself. It is a story of utopian expectations and their inevitable disillusionment. The corporatist structure of the NRA, which had been intended to provide a basis for a new social discipline that would have permitted industrial recovery, instead became a vehicle for business cartelization and an impediment to economic recovery. The attempt to achieve industrial harmony by recognizing labor as an equal partner in a framework of industrial cooperation became the occasion for industrial strife. The gap between the intentions of the NRA and its actual consequences was immense.

PART **II**

BUSINESS AND
THE NRA

CHAPTER 4

The NRA and Codes of
Fair Trade Competition

The National Recovery Administration began auspiciously. President Franklin Roosevelt chose General Hugh Johnson, a former WIB administrator and a key figure in the drafting of the National Industrial Recovery Act, to administer the new recovery program. Johnson had experienced first-hand the problems of economically troubled firms after World War I while working for the Moline Plow Company, first as assistant to the president and general counsel of Moline, while George Peek, another man who was to play a prominent role in the early New Deal, was president, and second, after Peek's resignation, as president of the company.[1] The contrast between his exhilarating experience with WIB planning and the harsh struggle of Moline to survive in the 1920s had already led Johnson to repudiate the laissez-faire ideas of many businessmen of the day but, when the depression struck, Johnson became even more radicalized, arguing that capitalism had brought the nation close "to collapse and revolution."[2]

Johnson was an enthusiastic New Dealer, and he saw the NRA as an opportunity for broad social and economic reconstruction.[3] In his eyes the NRA was nothing less than an attempt to alter fundamentally the individualist, competitive ethic of capitalism. "The very heart of the New Deal is the principle of concerted action in industry and agriculture *under government supervision* looking to a balanced economy as opposed to the

1. Hugh S. Johnson, *The Blue Eagle from Egg to Earth* (New York, 1968), pp. 103–110.
2. Schlesinger, *The Coming of the New Deal*, p. 22.
3. Johnson remained loyal to FDR and to the New Deal for some time after he was eased out of the NRA. He wrote to Roosevelt: "I have seen repeatedly in the Tory press that I, who protest loyalty to you, am attacking you. . . . I shall support you as long as I have a voice. To me the choice is between liberalism and toryism. You are the symbol of the former and I think the latter is ruin. . . . When people tell you that I am leaning to your enemies or omitting any chance to rip their hides off—from Herbert Hoover to the Liberty League—they are lying." (Hugh Johnson to FDR, 27 September 1935, Roosevelt Papers, PPF 702).

99

murderous doctrine of savage and wolfish individualism, looking to dog-eat-dog and devil take the hindmost."[4]

Corporatism provided a comprehensive alternative to capitalism for Johnson, and he could even express admiration for Mussolini's fascist corporatism in excessive moments of exuberance, although in fact he had no sympathy with and little understanding of its authoritarian dynamics.[5] Johnson constructed the NRA based on the WIB example, but at times he envisioned an even more radically societal corporatist program. Taking stock of the NRA one year after it had become effective, he proposed to Roosevelt that his own position as NRA administrator be pared down now that the NRA was launched, and that his policy-making responsibilities be assumed by a "board of directors" drawn from industry, labor, and the professions.[6] Even so, he insisted that the NRA administrator would retain executive responsibilities for the codes, because a board was poorly suited to administer a program vigorously and because this would provide government with a potential veto power over activities of code authorities that were inconsistent with the public interest. "This should be the dead-line beyond which control by industry should *not* go. In other words, it is recommended that there never be any over-head industrial council, composed of or selected by Code Authorities, or otherwise, which shall have any administrative or executive powers derived from N.R.A. That function must be jealously retained by government itself."[7]

Donald Richberg, who was second in command at the NRA as its general counsel and who subsequently replaced Johnson as NRA administrator, shared Johnson's skepticism of laissez-faire capitalism. "The truth is that no man of any political intelligence and economic vision has been able to defend the existing economic order since the World War laid bare its utter inadequacy and its insane consequences." For Richberg the depression was the death knell of the old order, and he demanded a new social order based on the "democratization of industry."[8]

Johnson's business experience led many in the business community to breath a sigh of relief when he was selected to head the NRA. But the hope that someone sympathetic to their interests would administer a program with such extensive regulatory powers proved to be short-lived. While Johnson did not share the hostility toward business that motivated some New Dealers, his subordination of business to the state linked him to

4. Schlesinger, *The Coming of the New Deal*, p. 88. Emphasis added.

5. John P. Diggins, *Mussolini and Fascism: The View from America* (Princeton, 1972), p. 280.

6. Johnson to FDR, 26 June 1934, Roosevelt Papers, OF 466, No. 2, NRA, June–July 1934, p. 2.

7. Ibid., pp. 3–4; *Business Week*, 25 November 1933, p. 9.

8. Schlesinger, *The Crisis of the Old Order*, p. 39.

progressive rather than business elites.[9] Thus Johnson could insist on the NRA provision to license corporations engaged in interstate commerce despite the vigorous opposition of the NAM.[10] Similarly, he could propose an excess profits tax to Roosevelt as a means of socializing the gains attributable to government stabilization of the market and preventing the NRA from becoming a pretext for profiteering.[11] Finally, he could come out in support of the essential features of the Wagner Act during the spring of 1935, despite virtually unanimous business hostility.[12] Johnson was a moderate in New Deal circles, but moderation should not be mistaken for subservience to business interests.

Johnson lost no time in getting the NRA off the ground. Initially, he concentrated on bringing ten important industries under codes of fair trade competition. Personally presiding over the cotton textile code hearings, the first code to be considered, he prodded and cajoled businessmen in that industry to reconcile their differences. His efforts were soon rewarded, and the cotton textile code was approved by Roosevelt on 9 July 1933. When other industries failed to develop codes as expeditiously, Johnson initiated the President's Reemployment Agreement (PRA), an abbreviated code that committed employers to paying a minimum wage of $12 to $13 a week for forty hours of work and eliminated child labor. Employers who signed the agreement were entitled to display the Blue Eagle insignia of the NRA. The response was enthusiastic, and economic prosperity appeared to be just around the corner.

By the fall of 1933, however, problems latent in the very conception of the NRA were beginning to emerge. Although the framers of the NRA had anticipated the need for enforcement powers to compel a minority of inveterate antisocial price chiselers and sweatshop operators to go along with the codes, they had not expected widespread business cheating, and they were not prepared to endorse extensive regimentation as a means to remedy such a situation. Neither were they fully prepared for the possibili-

9. Johnson was a career army officer before he became a businessman, and his attraction to coporatism derived from this period.

10. Roos, pp. 37, 45. Roos described the impact of the licensing provision on code drafting in the following terms: "In all these bargainings the President's thesis that hours had to be shortened and wages raised, and the NRA's threats to invoke the licensing provision hung like guillotine knives over the heads of industry. . . . Fear of the Government was the compelling motive" (ibid., p. 69).

11. Hugh Johnson Memorandum, 10 February 1934, Roosevelt Papers, OF 137a, Box No. 8, Folder: Taxes-Income, 1933–37.

12. Johnson's support for the Wagner Act was never explicit, but Wagner could plausibly claim Johnson's support based on his testimony to the Senate Finance Committee on 17 and 18 April 1935. While this may seem to contradict some of the positions he took while administrator of the NRA, chapters 9 and 10 will demonstrate the affinity between the Wagner Act and the NIRA and make it more plausible that Johnson could have taken such a position. Senate Finance Committee, *Investigation of National Recovery Administration Pursuant to Senate Resolution 79,* 74th Cong., 1st sess., 1935, 3:2451–2452. See also *Saturday Evening Post,* 12 January 1935, p. 77.

ty that entire industries might use the codes to cartelize and raise prices to levels where they would retard economic recovery, especially failing to anticipate the difficulties administrators would confront in attempting to distinguish between socially desirable and illicit cooperation. The NRA had been conceived as a grand experiment with societal corporatism, and when the requisite ethical revolution failed to materialize, it proved impossible to administer the program.

The NRA's Enforcement Dilemma

Codes of fair trade practices were drafted amid widespread moral enthusiasm for the NRA experiment. Progressives had high hopes that business, having been convinced by the depression that the old order had to go, would voluntarily commit itself to the NRA. In his statement inaugurating the NRA on 16 June 1933 President Roosevelt had reassured business that the new controls would be used to "free business, not to shackle it."[13] The assumption of cooperation by all parties was critical if this vast extension of government responsibility over wages, hours, prices, and production was not to collapse in a nightmare of regimentation, and in the first few months of the NRA, appeals for cooperation and self-sacrifice did not go unanswered. A spirit of compromise was visible in the early days of code drafting, and the vast majority of businessmen were voluntarily complying with NRA provisions.[14]

The success of the NRA's moral revolution proved short-lived. As economic self-interest reasserted itself, price chiseling and wage slashing became more common. Some could not resist the temptation to violate the codes because noncompliance granted competitive advantages over rivals who continued to bear the financial burdens associated with adherence to a code. Furthermore, this noncompliance was infectious, for even those committed to the NRA could be forced to violate its codes to compete with rivals who had no compunctions about ignoring the NRA. The initial overreliance of the NRA on voluntary cooperation, and its failure to develop effective methods for enforcing the codes, no doubt contributed to the compliance crisis.[15] But as subsequent efforts to enforce the codes demonstrated, any attempt to alter the character of the NRA from a program based on voluntary cooperation to a program based on compulsion was inherently self-defeating. Even if the NRA had devoted more attention to the problem of enforcement from the beginning, it is unlikely that its efforts would have done anything more than slightly retard the competitive dynamics that were undermining the codes. Without moral

13. Roosevelt, *Public Papers*, 2:253.
14. Schlesinger, *The Coming of the New Deal*, pp. 116–120; Lyon et al., p. 259; *Business Week*, 10 November 1934, p. 24.
15. Lyon et al., pp. 266–267.

enthusiasm to sustain the NRA, the program would fail, just as surely as prohibition had failed in the 1920s when temperance enthusiasm waned.

Moreover, moral enthusiasm was waning. That was clearly visible in the contrast between the successful Blue Eagle campaign during the summer of 1933 and the unsuccessful "Buy Now" campaign in the fall of 1933.[16] In October, General Johnson had used the same mass-propaganda techniques he had used so effectively the previous summer to encourage consumers to embark on a spending spree, hoping that such a spree would trigger industrial recovery. The public had responded to appeals to buy war bonds during World War I, and Johnson was confident that a similar appeal could be effective during economic crisis. But the depression had not evoked the same sustained level of moral enthusiasm that World War I had, and the changing public attitude toward the NRA, which had thus far done little to promote economic recovery, was visible in the widespread public cynicism that this campaign evoked.[17]

Diminishing moral enthusiasm for the sacrifices demanded by the NRA combined with powerful economic incentives for violating the NRA codes to produce a crisis of compliance in the fall of 1933. Code-abiding businessmen were demanding that the NRA take further steps to curb NRA violations, and by late 1933 the NRA had reorganized its compliance machinery, creating an independent Compliance Division, a National Compliance Board, and a field organization of regional offices in every state.[18] The credibility of the administration depended on the ability of the NRA to ensure that those who violated the law would receive swift punishment.

The problems that this "rage for compliance" would pose for the NRA were insurmountable. Oblivious to the organizational prerequisites for the mitigation of competition, the NRA had nonchalantly blanketed American industry with extensive codes of fair trade competition. Yet in highly competitive industries like the service industries, where a multitude of small establishments prevented the industry from developing significant elements of self-discipline prior to the NRA, the level of government intervention necessary to stabilize the industry had not been foreseen. The problems of enforcement in highly decentralized industries were further reinforced in some cases by hastily drafted and overly ambitious codes that had gone far beyond wages and hours provisions to regulate the minute details of sales transactions. Violations of these provisions were often difficult to detect. The participation of business in the drafting process often gave voice to a longing for a gentlemanly world of moderate competition without sufficient attention to problems of implementation.[19]

16. See discussion of Blue Eagle campaign, p. 94.
17. Hawley, *The New Deal*, p. 68.
18. Lyon et al., p. 58.
19. Ibid., pp. 268–269, 395; Schlesinger, *The Coming of the New Deal*, p. 161.

A few timely prosecutions might well have temporarily improved the compliance situation, but this new focus on compliance brought with it a new dilemma. Many in the business community, and the most thoughtful administrators within the NRA itself, argued that the attempt to transform the NRA from societal corporatism into a regulatory state was an ominous development. Reflecting on the NRA experience, Donald Richberg concluded, "The need of promptly creating a national machinery to check and enforce compliance started the NRA on the downward path of compulsion with dangerous speed and without some very necessary brakes."[20] This emphasis on compulsion appeared all the more offensive because the most frequent violators of the codes were small businesses on the verge of bankruptcy, and NRA attempts to penalize these businesses generated a great deal of adverse publicity.[21]

Furthermore, the government could assure compliance only by creating a large bureaucracy, and the growth of an extensive regulatory state evoked the ire of businessmen otherwise sympathetic to the ends of the NRA. "That was the alternative we were facing constantly during the second phase of the NRA. Without more enforcement we would lose the support of those willing to comply. With more enforcement we would increase the number and vigor of our opponents."[22] By the latter half of 1934 it had become clear to Donald Richberg, who by now had become NRA administrator, that the costs of the compliance program were outweighing its benefits:

> It was clearly evident some time before the autumn of 1934 that, in the tremendous speed and spread of the NRA in codifying all major industries, there had developed a huge governmental machinery of lawmaking and enforcement that had gone far beyond the original intentions of those sponsoring the law. It was most important to reestablish, if possible, in the thought of management and labor and in the public mind, the original conception of voluntary cooperation and the ideal of self-government in industry.[23]

By the end of 1934 the NRA had reversed gears under Richberg's leadership. "The NRA was moving definitely at the end of 1934 toward a reorganization and rededication to its original purposes. It was moving away from an undesigned and dangerous drift toward political regimentation, with the definite intention of checking also any trend toward private regimentation."[24] Yet Richberg's perceptiveness regarding the insoluble problems of the NRA operating in a coercive, regulatory mode was not

20. Richberg, *The Rainbow*, p. 161.
21. Lyon et al., pp. 260, 269; Schlesinger, *The Coming of the New Deal*, p. 161.
22. Richberg, *The Rainbow*, p. 170.
23. Ibid., p. 74.
24. Ibid., p. 75.

matched by a corresponding perceptiveness regarding the insoluble problems of the NRA operating in a voluntaristic societal corporatist mode. The NRA had come to emphasize enforcement precisely because voluntary cooperation had not been sufficient to assure compliance with the codes. By then it should have been clear that the social consensus necessary for the NRA to succeed simply did not exist, but Richberg and Roosevelt refused to abandon the NRA.

Cartelization and the NRA

Just as the decline in moral enthusiasm for the NRA was creating a compliance crisis in the program, it was creating, or at least exacerbating, a crisis concerning the character of codes of fair trade competition. Contrary to the intentions of the framers of the NRA, codes of fair trade competition were becoming a vehicle for uncontrolled business cartelization. Although the former crisis involved the problem of individuals undermining collective action by refusing to adhere to codes, and the latter crisis involved the problem of industries acting collectively through the codes to undermine the goals of the NRA, both problems were rooted in the failure of the NRA to sustain its new ethics of social responsibility as economic self-interest reasserted itself. Furthermore, as was the case with the former crisis, the NRA attempted to deal with this problem by shifting from a societal corporatist mode of governance to a regulatory mode of governance, but this response ultimately proved inadequate.

The most critical issue in the relationship between the NRA and cartelization involves NRA price-fixing. Here the intention of those who framed the NRA is mired in considerable obscurity. At Senate hearings on the NIRA, Senator Wagner had been asked by Senator King if the philosophy behind the program was that of the "old German cartel system," to which Wagner replied, "Not at all."[25] However, Wagner then opposed Senator Borah's amendment to explicitly prohibit price-fixing under the NRA, preferring a less-restrictive ban on "monopoly or monopolistic practices" because he believed that under some circumstances price controls might be necessary to protect small enterprises or to halt destructive price wars."[26] As NRA administrator, Hugh Johnson faithfully attempted to carry out the confused mandate of the NRA. On the one hand, he discouraged industries from including price-fixing provisions in their codes of fair trade practices, steering them toward less-restrictive attempts to mitigate competition, such as prohibitions on sales below costs.[27] On the other hand, he admitted the need for price-fixing in

25. Lyon et al., p. 20.
26. Hawley, *The New Deal*, pp. 30–31.
27. H. Johnson, p. 224.

exceptional cases, suggesting that "the purpose of the Act just goes out the window if you don't."[28]

The NRA was to establish a mean between too much competition and too little; it was authorized to redraw the boundaries around behavior proscribed by antitrust legislation. Progressivism was intrinsically hostile to uncontrolled cartelization and unjustified business profits, but the promotion of rational and fair competition was a goal fully consistent with other progressive ends. Unfortunately, the ability of the government to distinguish cartelization and "fair" competition and to use public policy to inhibit the former and foster the latter was considerably less than optimistic New Dealers had imagined. Nor would the NRA be capable of developing rational criteria that distinguished emergency situations when price-fixing would be temporarily justified by NRA guidelines from more normal situations where price-fixing would not be justified by NRA guidelines. In redrawing antitrust lines to permit previously excluded forms of cooperation, the NRA opened the doors for more abuses. While the NRA generally held the line against explicit cartelization in the early days of code drafting, it was not until much later that the NRA developed a more sophisticated analysis of the relationship of weaker forms of price stabilization to price-fixing and began to establish guidelines for them as well.[29] Even then its efforts to prevent cartels from operating were only partially successful.

During the hectic early days of the NRA, the overwhelming task of negotiating codes of fair trade competition for more than 500 industries covering 90 percent of industrial activity left little time for worrying about the mutual consistency of the many parts of the NRA or for carefully weighing the provisions in every code at the outset.[30] Johnson justified his strategy of quickly mobilizing the nation onto the NRA bandwagon at a sacrifice of some central supervision by asserting that the short life-span of many of the codes allowed for later revisions when the effects of certain types of code provisions could be more accurately determined, an assumption that seriously underestimated the political problems that subsequent

28. John Kennedy Ohl, *Hugh S. Johnson and the New Deal* (Dekalb, Ill., 1985), p. 177.
29. Hawley, *The New Deal*, pp. 99–100; Lyon et al., pp. 620–621.
30. Lyon et al., 48–53, 739. The most notable example of haste detracting from adequate review of the codes by NRA officials involved the cleaning and dyeing code, which had one of the most extreme price-fixing provisions approved by the NRA. Johnson signed the cleaning and dyeing code believing that the code had been approved by lower-level NRA officials and advisory bodies. Actually, the division advisor of the Research and Planning Division had approved the proposed code, but the Division Advisory Committee of the Research and Planning Division had disapproved the code by a vote of nine to one. In reviewing the recommendations on the code, the papers recommending approval were on top of the documents forwarded to Johnson, and the critical appraisal was buried in the body of the report. Johnson read only the initial statements and, under the mistaken impression that the Research and Planning Division had approved the code, attached his signature. See Roos, p. 341.

revisions of the codes would pose for the NRA.[31] Many of the code provisions that later provoked storms of controversy for aiding price-fixing were not the product of an intentional government-sponsored plan of cartelization, but rather slipped through the hastily constructed code review process.[32]

This is not to say that private interests had carte blanche even during this initial period. While the NRA sought to mitigate competition, from the beginning a loose form of supervision was exercised over the formulation of fair trade practice provisions lest they eliminate competition altogether. The steel industry code, as one of the earliest codes submitted, did permit the steel code authority broad discretion in setting a minimum price, but the NRA tightened its criteria for price stabilization clauses soon afterward. Only in very exceptional cases were industries actually permitted to fix prices, and these were always fiercely competitive industries with long histories of demoralizing price wars that threatened the existence of smaller firms in the industry and that imposed a constant downward pressure on wages as businesses searched for means to reduce costs.[33] Moreover, even in these exceptional codes the government did not allow uncontrolled private cartelization. The inclusion of price-fixing provisions generally entailed more extensive government supervision. According to Johnson, "In these codes it will be proper for an industry to say that it will not sell below cost of production, but if it uses the code to fix extortionate prices, I would have to step in immediately in conformance with the law."[34]

Nevertheless, as the NRA codes became operational NRA critics argued that business cooperation through the NRA was facilitating cartelization despite these constraints. To substantiate their claims that the codes were being misused, they pointed to rapidly rising prices for many goods. For Johnson and the NRA staff, however, the issue was more complex. The NRA had intended to raise prices *within limits*. Prices had collapsed in the wake of the depression, and Roosevelt believed that a reinflation of prices and wages could induce economic recovery. Furthermore, the NRA had imposed significant new costs on industry in wage increases and hours reductions which would have increased prices even in a competitive market, and to have denied business the right to any price increases would have driven even more financially shaky businesses into bankruptcy. Thus, from Johnson's perspective, the crucial issue was not whether the

31. H. Johnson, pp. 251, 288–289; Schlesinger, *The Coming of the New Deal*, p. 119; Hawley, *The New Deal*, p. 479; Lyon et al., p. 401.

32. Lyon et al., p. 111.

33. Hawley, *The New Deal*, pp. 57–58.

34. Quoted in Roos, p. 86.

NRA had contributed to rising prices, but whether prices were increasing faster than wages.[35]

Johnson, like Roosevelt, believed that the depresion had been brought on by a maldistribution of income, and he saw the NRA as a reform program for redistributing income as well as a recovery measure. As long as the working man had an inadequate share of the national income, the net purchasing power in the economy was not adequate to sustain economic growth. Thus, according to the NRA plan, business was to be allowed to pass on some of the cost increases associated with the NRA, but it would also be expected to absorb *some* of them, although the proportion of costs passed on to costs absorbed had never been precisely determined. Johnson appealed to the long-term self-interest of businessmen in encouraging them to absorb some of the costs associated with the NRA. If price increases commensurate with increased costs were passed on or, even worse, if business cartels increased prices beyond those justified by new costs, enhanced purchasing power would have been negated.[36] But if businessmen absorbed some of the NRA costs, Johnson argued, they would eventually recoup their losses on a higher volume of sales as prosperity returned.

By January 1934, however, there was a growing body of evidence that suggested that Johnson's appeal to business self-restraint was failing and that some businesses were using the new permissiveness toward business cooperation to promote socially irresponsible cartels. Suspiciously large price increases in certain commodities were eating away at the increased purchasing power of labor and undermining the economic rational of the NRA. Johnson convoked public hearings on NRA-related price increases, hearings that led to a "field day of criticism" by groups representing consumers and their agents. But what was also becoming clear was that many of the worst offenders were small businesses. Lumber, textiles, and bituminous coal were heavily criticized at these hearings, yet these industries were highly competitive industries with small and medium-sized firms, many of whom were having difficulty absorbing the additional costs associated with the NRA. Even in some of the more oligopolistic industries that were criticized, like steel, the anticompetitive features of the code generally enjoyed the strong support of smaller firms in the industry. Vigorous pursuit of NRA objectives would compel the government to take action against some of those it was intended to benefit.[37]

Confronting this dilemma, Johnson vacillated. On the one hand, he defended the NRA against its detractors by arguing that some of the anticompetitive provisions in codes of fair trade competition which the

35. Lyon et al., pp. 757–760.
36. Ibid., pp. 6, 772.
37. Hawley, *The New Deal*, pp. 57, 80, 102; Lyon et al., p. 260; See also Chapter 10.

NRA permitted, and some of the price increases which resulted, were in the interest of smaller firms. If employment was to be increased—the primary goal of the NRA—it could occur only through price increases that allowed at least the average producers some profits. Furthermore, while he acknowledged that the NRA had led to abuses, he also noted that it had achieved some of its goals. Two million men had been reemployed, wages had risen, child labor had been prohibited, the right to join a union was being protected, bankruptcies were down, and the economy did show signs of improving. Given these successes, Johnson argued, it made more sense to reform the NRA than to dismantle it altogether. On the other hand, he urged businessmen to exercise restraint in pricing. In his conclusion to an important address to the National Retail Dry Goods Association, Johnson pleaded: "If I had only nine words with which to address you... I would rise here and say: Keep prices down. For God's sake, keep prices down." Going beyond moral appeals, the NRA cautiously began to pare down the codes, attempting to eliminate provisions that facilitated cartelization without upsetting the provisions they believed were having a more beneficial effect.[38]

One of the clearest indications of an increasing concern with the anticompetitive consequences of the NRA was the growing influence of economists and consumer advocates within the NRA. Both the Consumer Advisory Board (CAB) and the Research and Planning Division, manned by economists and sociologists who had little faith in industrial self-government, became centers of opposition to price and production controls under the codes. This was true especially after Leon Henderson, an economist from the Russell Sage Foundation, was promoted to the head of the Research and Planning Division. Neither the CAB nor the Research and Planning Division had an immediate and dramatic impact on NRA policy. Johnson was convinced that many of their policy proposals would have prevented achievement of key NRA goals, but he was willing to make concessions in the details of administration that added some protections against cartel abuses. The Consumer Advisory Board and the Labor Advisory Board insisted that consumer and labor representatives also sit on the code authorities, a move resisted by industry. Johnson at first insisted that the public interest was adequately protected by the administration members, but early in 1934 he compromised by agreeing to provide labor and consumer advisors for the government representatives on each code.[39]

After the January price hearings, the NRA officially began to acknowledge that some industries had improperly used codes of fair trade practice as a device for securing unjustified price increases, but there was consid-

38. Hawley, *The New Deal*, pp. 81, 131.
39. Ibid., pp. 75–77, 89.

erably less certainty about the specific provisions responsible for abuses. Some of the strongest anticompetitive clauses were permitted in only a few industries, yet abuses were not similarly localized. Thirty-eight codes had provisions for minimum price-fixing, and in only twelve of these was "power given to code authority with or without approval of NRA, to establish at any time minimum prices, no cost basis being provided." With the exception of the steel and petroleum codes, these were in highly competitive industries like coal, lumber, and cleaning and dyeing. Even this figure overstates the extent of legal price-fixing under the NRA, for the provisions for minimum price-fixing never became effective in at least half of the latter group of codes. The NRA began to retreat, prohibiting some of the provisions in codes that were clearly linked to cartelization and offering fewer exemptions from antitrust prosecution, but rather than use the shotgun approach toward codes, administrators from the Consumer Advisory Board, the Research and Planning Division, the Legal Division, and other ad hoc groups within the NRA were all trying to pinpoint the objectionable fair trade provisions.[40]

One provision found in many codes had become highly suspect. Some 422 NRA codes sanctioned open price systems that allowed competitors to share information about their selling price, and another twenty-nine had open bid filing systems.[41] Open price systems that permitted the anonymous exchange of information about past selling prices had existed even before the NRA, and the Supreme Court had upheld their legality in the early 1920s.[42] But most of the NRA open price systems went beyond these earlier prototypes by permitting the exchange of information about current and future selling prices, an exchange that would have been illegal under the prevailing interpretation of antitrust statutes without the NRA exemption.[43]

In theory, an open price system increased the information available to competitors and made competition more rational and fair. Deceptive claims by either sellers or buyers concerning prices could be eliminated. Prices would become more uniform and would "truly reflect market conditions" rather than short-term marketing strategies. Demoralizing price wars that encouraged sellers to sell below costs would be less likely, and as markets became more stable, long-term planning would become possible.[44] But NRA open price systems were viewed with suspicion because the exchange of price information not only permitted the rationalization of competition but also facilitated illicit collusion. The identifica-

40. Ibid., pp. 58, 85–90; Lyon et al., p. 579.
41. Lyon et al., p. 610.
42. *Maple Flooring Manufacturers Association et al. v. United States*, 268 U.S. 563; *Cement Manufacturers Protective Association et al. v. United States*, 268 U.S. 588.
43. Hawley, *The New Deal*, p. 59.
44. Roos, pp. 277–278; Lyon et al., pp. 674–678.

tion of price cutters simplified the enforcement tasks of cartels and correspondingly strengthened them.[45] Yet even a comprehensive open price system did not eliminate competitive behavior. An open price system per se left competitors free to each set their own prices. Generally an open price system had to be combined with other cartelistic devices to contribute to the elimination of competition.[46]

When an open price system was supplemented with a provision for a waiting period that required a fixed time lag between filing a new price and selling at the new price, possibilities for cartelization increased markedly. Some 297 of the open price plans approved by the NRA had provision for a waiting period, and those provisions generated more criticism and adverse publicity for the NRA than the more exceptional price-fixing provisions did. Charles Roos cited some of reasons used to justify waiting periods: "(1) that the reporting agency is thereby given time to supply the entire industry with the price list, and (2) that 'surprise moves' designed to secure special contracts, which tend to demoralize the market, are eliminated, and (3) that buyers are protected to the extent (a) of having time to make complaints of price increases and adjust their plans, buying in advance if necessary, and (b) of knowing that competitors will not be able to obtain materials at bargain prices without notice to the industry."[47] In theory, the waiting period would facilitate rational competition, forcing competitors to calculate the response of others to their pricing policy and denying them the advantage of price-cutting based on any factor other than superior efficiency. But waiting periods also allowed cartels to isolate and counteract through peer pressure threats to price agreements before the price cutter could provoke an all-out price war, breeding antagonisms that made a return to the cartel price more difficult.[48]

The NRA had initially approved provisions for open price systems and waiting periods in the hope that they would promote fair and rational competition, but as evidence of the consequences of NRA codes began to accumulate, suspicion began to mount that these provisions were being abused. Thirty of the codes criticized in the January price hearings had open price provisions, and most of these included some form of waiting period. Immediately after the hearings, the Research and Planning Division prepared a report for Johnson on these provisions that stated that the effect of the provisions was unclear and called for further study. Despite this uncertainty, Johnson issued an order announcing that the NRA would not approve any new codes that included waiting period provisions until a study of their effect had been completed. The order was not applied retroactively to codes that had already been approved, nor did it prohibit

45. Lyon et al., p. 611; Hawley, *The New Deal*, p. 59.
46. Roos, pp. 277–282.
47. Ibid., p. 280.
48. Ibid., pp. 279–282; Lyon et al., pp. 611, 676, 682.

new codes from including open price systems without waiting periods. Six weeks after Johnson's order, the Research and Planning Division issued an adverse report concerning waiting period provisions, and the NRA announced that henceforth waiting period provisions could not be included in codes except under exceptional circumstances.[49] This decision was a warning shot fired by the central NRA administration at the code authorities, indicating a tightening of supervisory control. As the screws were tightened, business became increasingly aware of the discrepancy between the NRA and their advocacy of industrial self-government.

The same report, however, concluded that the advantages of open price systems outweighed their disadvantages, and it recommended that NRA approval of simple open price systems be continued. That recommendation was contested by the Consumer Advisory Board, which had issued a report in February 1934 comdemning both open price provisions and waiting period provisions because they facilitated cartelization, but the evidence on which the Consumer Advisory Board based its recommendation was questionable. The CAB had sent out questionnaires to industry members to determine whether they were being pressured by code authorities to keep their prices in line with other prices in the industry. While ninety-seven cases of such pressure were alleged, only forty of the cases were in industries that had actually adopted open price systems, and only three cases could clearly be attributed to the open price provision.[50] The NRA therefore rejected any move against open price systems.[51]

Prohibiting waiting period provisions in codes could not alone satisfy the demands for price restraint by NRA critics. Although the NRA had discouraged industries from including any direct provisions for collective price-setting and had approved relatively few codes with provisions prohibiting sales below costs based on notions such as "the lowest reasonable cost of production" or "fair and reasonable" costs, far more common were code provisions that prohibited sales below individual firm costs, with additional provision for standardized accounting procedures to identify costs. Some 352 industries had adopted codes prohibiting sales below individual costs. These kinds of provisions had been justified, as were most NRA fair trade practices provisions, as means for promoting rational competition, not means of suppressing competition. The promotion of standardized accounting systems encouraged producers to calculate

49. Roos, p. 281.
50. Ibid., p. 288n.
51. We cannot say that the NRA refusal to ban open price systems is evidence of the capture of the NRA by business. The NRA action was based on a recommendation of its Research and Planning Division, which had been outspoken in its criticisms of the use of NRA codes to cartelize. Furthermore, many progressive economists of this era, rightly or wrongly, continued to defend open pricing even if they sought revisions in the specific open price plans adopted by many codes. The Brookings study of the NRA, begun soon after the NRA was launched and published in April 1935, still defended open price systems. Lyon et al., pp. 675–678.

prices rationally in relation to costs, making producers aware of hidden costs and mitigating the competitive tendency to drive prices below production costs. It initially appeared that the legitimation accorded individualized price-setting by such a policy would limit the possibilities for using NRA codes to cartelize.[52]

Furthermore, NRA guidelines for implementation of provisions prohibiting sales below costs provided some additional safeguards that restricted their use as devices for cartelization. Interpreted literally, the prohibition on sales below costs would have shut high-cost producers out of the market. To avoid this, the NRA allowed firms to sell below cost "to meet competition of producers who were not selling below their costs."[53] This qualification introduced so much discretion into individual price determination that it rendered many of these provisions worthless as price stabilization devices.[54] Furthermore, many of the minimum price provisions required additional administrative approval of cost formulas prior to being activated. Only half the codes that had provisions for adopting cost formulas ever submitted specific proposals to the NRA for approval, and of the 175 cost systems that were submitted, only 40 were approved by the NRA—an approval rate of less than 25 percent.[55]

The extent to which these NRA rules, advanced during the early days of the program, limited opportunities for business to use the *formal* NRA codes to cartelize was suggested by the rising level of dissatisfaction with the NRA in the business community. Many opposed these NRA policies on the grounds that competition on that basis tended to reduce the price to the cost of the lowest producer, and at that level no firm could make a profit. Many discontented businessmen demanded that a system based on average industry cost be substituted for the individual cost system, so that at least half the industry would be assured profits.[56] They argued persuasively that code provisions based on individualized costs were unenforceable because it was administratively not feasible to monitor the individual costs of firms to assure compliance.

NRA policy was not altogether unresponsive to these demands because many codes had failed to make any headway toward significantly promoting "fair competition"—the goal of the NRA. To counteract the competitive tendencies that continued to put downward pressure on wages, Colonel Robert H. Montgomery, a professional accountant and friend of Hugh Johnson's, was brought in to take over the Research and Planning

52. Ibid., pp. 585, 587–588, 678–679.
53. Roos, p. 251.
54. Roos notes that business opposed this interpretation because it failed to assure high prices (ibid., p. 254).
55. Hawley, *The New Deal*, p. 58; Herbert Taggart, "Minimum Prices Under the NRA," *Michigan Business Studies*, vol. 3, no. 2 (Ann Arbor, Mich., 1936), p. 257. Lyon et al. (p. 586) note that only 39 were approved, out of 350 codes that provided for their establishment.
5C. Hawley, *The New Deal*, pp. 87–88.

Division of the NRA in January 1934, and he shifted NRA policy toward the acceptance of "lowest reasonable cost" rather than individual cost as a basis for prohibiting sales below cost.[57] Yet even in this case, where the NRA acted to further limit competition, the manner in which it acted revealed the intention of government bureaucrats to keep a firm grip on the operation of the codes.

Johnson did not issue final approval of this change in NRA policy until April 1934, and in the meantime the "lowest reasonable cost" formula had been embedded in a broader model code for recommendation to all industries. According to that model code,

> When the Administrator determines that destructive price cutting has caused an emergency in the trade/industry such as to render ineffective or seriously to endanger the maintenance of the provisions of this code, the code Authority may cause an impartial agency to investigate costs in the trade/industry and to determine the lowest reasonable cost of the service(s)/product(s) affected by such practice. Such determination shall exclude all forms of return on capital investment and shall be in all respects subject to such rules and regulations as may be issued by the Administrator and to his approval or modification after such notice and opportunity to be heard as he may prescribe.[58]

The administrator, a Johnson appointee, had sole responsibility for declaring an emergency, and he could review and modify the lowest reasonable cost established. Furthermore, because the model code allowed the use of minimum price provisions only on an emergency basis, they were subject to periodic review and renewal, even though the "disorganization" that characterized many markets was not the product of transient causes. The periodic review requirement enhanced the capacity of the government to supervise business behavior.[59]

Effective implementation of this new policy did not quickly follow its promulgation. In some cases—the graphic arts industries, for example—exceptions to the new policy were granted because of special conditions prevailing in the industry. In other cases, confusion surrounding the relationship between the new emergency price-fixing provisions and earlier methods of price stabilization led to the subsequent approval of codes and supplements that contained both the emergency provision and some form of a permanent price stabilization clause, a fact that illustrated the incompetence of the NRA to administer so many codes, especially as Johnson's leadership of the agency declined. Furthermore, many of the codes had been approved before the new restrictive attitude toward price

57. Ibid., p. 88.
58. Roos, p. 257.
59. Hawley, *The New Deal*, pp. 87–88.

stabilization became prominent, and the NRA could not afford to undermine all business support for the codes by single-handedly altering their
codes, so the administration did not impose the new policy retroactively.
This decision was less significant than it might at first appear, however.
Most codes were approved for relatively brief periods of time and were
renegotiated to bring them in line with new policies when they lapsed.[60]

The NRA provided ample confirmation that it was moving to a policy
of promoting competition when it released Office Memorandum 228 on 7
June 1934. Encapsulating the piecemeal victories of the economists in the
central administration of the NRA over the business-dominated code
authorities, the memorandum set forth the goal of the NRA as the
establishment of a free and competitive market. Open price provisions
were watered down to prevent price-fixing, and it became more difficult to
substantiate a violation of a fair trade practices code. Selling below costs,
which had been a violation of most codes as initially formulated, became
merely evidence of a violation after Memorandum 228. Additional evidence concerning the impact of small business on labor's conditions was
required to substantiate destructive price-cutting. The memorandum made
it clear that the central administration of the NRA would not be a rubber
stamp for the policies of the code authorities, and the intensity of NRA
administrators' scrutiny of the codes increased as external criticism of the
NRA mounted.[61]

Business opposition to the triumph of economists in Memorandum 228
was swift and vehement. On 8 June, Johnson tried to reconcile the
opposed forces by announcing that the memorandum applied only to
future codes, an interpretation that opened up a potentially wide gulf
between the official NRA policy proclaimed in the memorandum and the
operation of most of the codes.[62] But even if provisions in codes already
approved were not suspended, the ability of code authorities to enforce
provisions on recalcitrant employers depended on the cooperation of the
central administration of the NRA, and such assistance was unlikely
where compliance ran contrary to the intention of the memorandum.[63]

60. Ibid., pp. 101–102.
61. Ibid., p. 100; Schlesinger, *The Coming of the New Deal*, p. 135.
62. Hawley, *The New Deal*, pp. 101–103.
63. Louis Galambos provides an interesting illustration of the importance of the pro-competitive
shift in the NRA in his study of the Cotton Textile Institute. The cotton textile code had been the
first code approved by the NRA, and it contained a variety of anticompetitive provisions that
attempted to deal with the problem of excess capacity in this severely depressed industry. After
the publication of Memorandum 228, the leaders of the Cotton Textile Institute realized that their
code was inconsistent with the new policy guidelines of the NRA and therefore vulnerable in
future negotiations with the NRA to extend the code. To save their code, and possibly even create
conditions under which its anticompetitive features might even be strengthened, the institute
leadership adopted a new tactic in dealing with the NRA. Dropping a line of argument that had
stressed the virtues of fair competition for all industries, the cotton textile leaders began to portray
the industry as a particularly distressed industry that called for exceptional remedies. An appeal

Despite these efforts to introduce more competition into industrial self-government, cartelization remained a problem. The NRA could go only so far along the pro-competitive path before it totally undermined the rational for its own existence. Unable to be an effective instrument for promoting fair competition, and unwilling to be an instrument for promoting industrial cartelization, the NRA floundered in a no-man's-land until it was mercifully put to rest by the Supreme Court in May 1935.

The Failure of the NRA

The relationship between the NRA and business cartelization has done more to discredit the progressive credentials of the NRA—and by association the early New Deal—than any other aspect of the program. How could a program that was conducive to cartelization have been initiated and administered by a genuinely progressive elite? If, as has also been argued, "unlimited relief was accorded most large businessmen from the start"[64] and the anticompetitive aspects of the NRA codes were "used by powerful groups to penalize and suppress small competitors, 'the little fellows,' "[65] then the progressive "pretensions" of the NRA were clearly little more than hypocritical rhetoric.

Many NRA critics, however, have misunderstood cartelization under the NRA and failed to examine seriously the possibility that the intentions behind the NRA were very different from the consequences that actually ensued from the program. Describing cartelization as an unintended consequence of the NRA is plausible, even though the relaxation of antitrust laws and the promotion of business cooperation was the explicit rational of the program. It is also plausible even though the architects of the NRA wanted to raise prices. The fair trade practice provisions of NRA codes intentionally mitigated competition because the New Dealers believed that unregulated market competition had driven businessmen to slash workers' wages and lengthen the work week and that government regulation would put a floor under this downward spiral of immiseration. The New Dealers asserted that small business would also be protected if ruthless and often unfair competition was replaced with a more gentlemanly variety of competition based solely on productivity and efficiency. There is a distinction, *at least in theory,* between, on the one hand, the relaxation of antitrust laws, the promotion of business cooperation, and a desire to raise prices, and, on the other hand, uncontrolled business

---

for "special" consideration would not have been necessary if the trend toward enhancing competition within the NRA had been merely cosmetic. See Galambos, *Competition and Cooperation*, pp. 276–279.

64. Bellush, p. 47.

65. A charge noted by Lyon et al., p. 709.

cartelization. Even though the NRA's attempts to mitigate competition also opened the door for businessmen seeking to dispense with competition altogether, this was clearly not its intention. It was a consequence that the New Dealers had anticipated in part and had taken steps to counteract, although the steps proved to be inadequate.

Ultimately it was the impossibility of the task that the NRA had undertaken—the establishment of fair competition—which proved the undoing of the program. NRA attempts to bring prices within an industry more in line with costs, for instance, presupposed the possibility of arriving at an acceptable, standard system of cost accounting. "Wherever cost determination is necessary," Leverett Lyon observed, "a series of difficult, *indeed practically insurmountable,* administrative difficulties arise." Variations in size of units within an industry, types of products produced, techniques of production, channels of distribution, and age of units "all combine to make the extremely difficult problems of cost-accounting approach the impossible when an attempt is made to apply any single system to an industry as a whole."[66]

Even the more modest efforts of the Federal Trade Commission to prohibit specific unfair competitive practices had often overtaxed the administrative capacities of that agency, and the far more ambitious attempt to fashion a law merchant that would effectively secure fair trade would appear to be beyond the capacities of even the most skillfully administered program. As Lyon sensibly noted:

> There is, in many quarters, an easy-going assumption that it is easy to distinguish between the fair and the unfair; that a mere reference to "unethical" or "dishonorable competition" provides in itself the criteria of judging what is "unethical" or what is "dishonorable." The history of six centuries of common law, the enactment of a large number of federal and state statutes, and the efforts of the Federal Trade Commission have all indicated the fallacy of this view. It has again been demonstrated by the experience of the NRA.[67]

Cartels mushroomed under the NRA, despite the NRA's attempts to distinguish legitimate forms of business cooperation from illegitimate cartelization because the theoretical distinction did not prove viable in practice.

Furthermore, a distinction must be drawn between cartelization that occurred through practices legitimated by the NRA and cartelization that occurred because practices legitimated by the NRA were supplemented with practices that were illegitimate and illegal even by NRA standards. Many of the codes that had contained provisions prohibiting sales below

66. Ibid., p. 612. Emphasis added.
67. Ibid., p. 551.

individual costs, for instance, were not supposed to become operative until a cost accounting system was approved by the NRA. Despite the restrictive NRA policy of granting approval to cost accounting systems, many code authorities apparently exceeded their legal authority and informally implemented such systems, a practice that was not opposed by members of the industry, either because it served their interests or because they were unaware that the code authority had exceeded its legitimate powers.[68] The NRA was often incapable of preventing these abuses because of the difficulties it encountered in detecting abuses.

The NRA was ill-suited to operate in a regulatory mode because it had never been intended to function in that mode. To view the NRA simply as a failure of the American regulatory state would therefore be to judge it by criteria that are foreign to its initial conception. It had been intended as an experiment in societal corporatism, and the weaknesses in the NRA are those inherent in any attempt to establish societal corporatism in a large and diverse nation like the United States. But the intractability of the problems associated with attempts to develop societal corporatist cooperation in large countries can be obscured if the failure of the NRA is attributed to either of two factors that did shape the administrative history of the program but that were not fundamentally responsible for its failure. First, the NRA was a poorly administered program, and its administrative weaknesses exacerbated the problems created by its conceptual weaknesses. Had the program been administered well, it would not have escaped the fundamental problems associated with the NRA's attempt to distinguish fair and unfair competition, but at least some of its adverse consequences could have been avoided or minimized. Second, administrative corporatism was a *necessary* condition for institutionalizing the NRA's societal corporatism, and it can easily appear as if administrative corporatism was a *sufficient* condition for the NRA to become a vehicle for promoting private interests at the expense of public interests. If administrative corporatism per se allowed trade associations to capture the NRA, this conclusion would follow, but if the federal bureaucracy of the NRA demonstrated considerable autonomy from private interests despite administrative corporatism, then the problems of the NRA are more likely to be rooted in the goals the NRA was attempting to accomplish than in the means it was using to accomplish them. Each of these considerations must be examined in more detail.

If many of the problems associated with the NRA were inherent in its very conception, responsibility for the failure of the NRA must be attributed in part to Congress and to the president in his legislative role. These institutions had simply defined for the NRA a task that it could not hope to accomplish. Nevertheless, Hugh Johnson certainly compounded the

68. Ibid., p. 587.

NRA's problems by expanding the program unnecessarily. Despite his business and regulatory experiences, Johnson proved to be a poor choice for NRA administrator. He was a visionary who was incapable of assessing the resources of the agency and realistically setting goals in light of those resources. Naively believing that the NRA would usher in a new era of cooperation among business, labor, and government, and that only relatively limited government supervision of the codes would be necessary,[69] he rejected a modest conception of the program that would have confined it initially to a small number of key industries (thirty to fifty had been the original projection). Instead he encouraged all of American business to enlist under its banner.

Soon after the NRA was launched it was inundated with proposals for codes of fair trade competition—144 in the last half of July and 546 in August.[70] Industries as specialized as "pickle packers and powder puff makers" and manufacturers of everything "from anti–hog cholera serum to wood cased lead pencils" applied for codes.[71] Within a year the NRA was confronted with the task of supervising more than 500 codes of fair trade competition. This task overwhelmed the NRA. Deputy administrators and assistant deputy administrators could not master the complex economic affairs of the many industries for which they were responsible.[72] Hastily approved codes were often administratively infeasible, and the NRA was discredited when they proved unenforceable. In other cases the codes were lax enough to facilitate illegitimate forms of collusion and hinder economic recovery. By the time the NRA was struck down by the Supreme Court on 26 May 1935, it was on the verge of administrative collapse anyway.

Johnson could also be hopelessly naive about the problems that the NRA would face in attempting to promote fair competition. When critics challenged his defense of code provisions prohibiting sales below costs by questioning the objectivity of the concept "costs," Johnson dismissed their weighty objections with the assertion that anyone could determine costs or could hire an accountant to do so.[73]

Compounding these administrative problems, Johnson refused to delegate sufficient administrative responsibility to subordinates to permit him to focus on general concerns. He played an intimate role in specific code negotiations and rushed around the nation intervening in local labor disputes arising under the NRA while the agency as a whole floundered

69. "I look to this new industrial self-government to be self-policing" (NRA Release No. 28, Roosevelt Papers, OF 466, No. 1, NRA, July 1933).
70. Schlesinger, *The Coming of the New Deal*, p. 116.
71. William Wilson, "Chamber of Commerce," p. 99.
72. Lyon et al., pp. 131–137.
73. Ohl, p. 178.

without a coherent overall plan.[74] He was a highly emotional, easily angered man who had difficulty working with others, and as the pressures on him mounted he increasingly found refuge in alcohol.[75] By the summer of 1934 even Roosevelt, who was always reluctant to fire subordinates, had come to the conclusion that Johnson had to go, but by this time many of the decisions that helped derail the NRA had already been made.

Nevertheless, Hugh Johnson's failings as an administrator cannot alone explain the failure of the NRA, especially its failure to restrain business cartelization. The history of the oil code makes this particularly clear. When the NRA was launched, administration of the oil code was placed in the hands of the Interior Department rather than the NRA because that department had a long history of dealing with the oil industry. Harold Ickes, secretary of the interior, was a far more capable and cautious administrator than Johnson,[76] and he could call on the resources of a well-established and respected department of government in carrying out his tasks. Furthermore, Ickes had a long and distinguished political career and unimpeachable progressive credentials. Yet despite his administrative skills and his progressive skepticism of business, the oil code led to the partial cartelization of the oil industry just as codes administered under the NRA led to cartelization in other industries. This would suggest that the tendency of the NRA to give rise to cartels had less to do with the manner in which it was administered than with problems inherent in the task the NRA had undertaken.

The second factor that shaped the program administratively but that was not fundamentally responsible for its failure was its administrative corporatism. Most critics of the NRA have emphasized the importance of code authorities within the larger NRA administrative apparatus, arguing, in a manner reminiscent of Lowi's arguments concerning administrative corporatism, that this administrative structure allowed the program to become a government-imposed rationalization of the market for the sake of business interests. This interpretation of the NRA fails to pay sufficient attention to the NRA central administration, which remained a crucial counterweight to the power of code authorities dominated by businessmen. Between August 1933 and February 1935, the nadir of NRA growth, the paid staff,

74. Ibid., p. 50. Secretary of Labor Perkins advised Roosevelt against delegating additional NRA presidential powers to Johnson because "if past experience is any criterion, those new problems would be disposed of by rules promulgated by General Johnson with a minimum of study, thought and discussion" (Perkins to FDR, 18 June 1934, Roosevelt Papers, OF 466, No. 2, NRA, June–July 1934.

75. Schlesinger, *The Coming of the New Deal*, pp. 105, 152–153.

76. Ickes was also responsible for administering the public works program of the NRA, and the cautious style in which he adminstered that program was as diametrically opposed to Hugh Johnson's administrative style as any. Ickes carefully screened each project to make certain it would not have been a waste of government money. His caution was excessive, for so few projects were approved under his rigorous standards that the primary goal of the program, getting the unemployed to work on public works projects, was being frustrated. See ibid., p. 109.

as distinct from the unpaid businessmen serving on code authorities, grew from 400 to 4,500. Administrative expenses reveal a similar pattern, growing from $393,000 a month in August 1933 to $1,054,000 a month in January 1935. Many of the code authorities, on the other hand, hovered near bankruptcy as business disenchantment with the codes dried up voluntary contributions.[77]

During the two-year life-span of the NRA, the responsibilities of the code authorities were pared down, and they steadily declined in power while the authority of the central administration of the NRA grew.[78] In the first days of the NRA, when Johnson and Richberg still had high hopes that a moral consensus among producers backed by the coercion of informal public opinion would basically suffice to discipline industry, Richberg had sent the following memo to all members of the legal division: "It is not required and it is not proper, *except in special instances,* to grant in a Code any general power to the Administrator to review and modify actions taken by the Code Authority. If anyone insists upon incorporating such a clause, you may refer to this memorandum as a statement of policy to promote self-government of industry, as distinguished from political government of industry, which should guide the legal division."[79] As special interests refused to accept the sacrifices demanded by the NRA, however, the permissive attitude of NRA administrators relying on industries to discipline themselves gradually gave way to a more active regulatory posture. Prices fixed by the retail coal trade were reviewed by the NRA in the summer of 1934 and were lowered despite the vigorous protests of the code authority. The NRA censured the rubber industry code authority and suspended the operation of its price provisions after a Federal Trade Commission investigation revealed a bid-rigging conspiracy.[80] In December 1934 the NRA temporarily decertified the cotton garment code authority and transferred its responsibilities to the general code authority of the National Recovery Administration pending a reorganization of the code authority, despite vigorous opposition from the industry.[81]

These actions were exceptional, but they were taken in pursuit of announced NRA policies, and they suggested that the NRA was moving away from its earlier commitment to industrial self-government. As Marc Rose, editor of *The Business Week,* noted about business anxieties concerning the NRA, "The emphasis is strongly upon the future. Could business be fully reassured that the *trends* it distrusts were not going to be developed further, business would accept what actually has been done up

77. Lyon et al., 30–31, 220–223.
78. Hawley, *The New Deal*, p. 89.
79. Richberg, *The Rainbow*, p. 120.
80. Hawley, *The New Deal*, p. 117.
81. R. B. Paddock (executive director of the Cotton Garment Code Authority) to FDR, 10 December 1934, Roosevelt Papers, OF 466, No. 4, NRA Codes, 1934C.

to now—not with relish, but with reasonable composure and at least the confidence to go ahead.''[82] Even though the NRA never reduced code authorities to strictly subordinate administrative units, many in business nevertheless believed that this was the tendency of the NRA.

The NRA was under direct presidential control, and thus in a very different administrative position than were independent regulatory commissions, which many administrative scholars believed became captured because they were insulated from that control. Presidential control was further enhanced when Congress exempted the NRA from civil service requirements, allowing Roosevelt to staff the agency with New Deal loyalists.[83] Because the NRA was the keystone of Roosevelt's early New Deal, Johnson had a virtually open pipeline into the oval office, and he could frequently enlist presidential prestige and power in advancing his goals.

Roosevelt's decision to entrust direction of the NRA to a single administrator rather than to a committee indicated his commitment to an activist agency that could vigorously defend the public interest.[84] Furthermore, Roosevelt reinforced this concentration of administrative power when the NRA encountered problems. Initially, policy making and coordination for the NRA had been vested in the Special Industrial Recovery Board, which was composed of several cabinet members, the chairman of the FTC, the director of the budget, and the NRA administrator.[85] When the aims of raising agricultural prices through the Agricultural Adjustment Act came into conflict with the goals of the NRA, the Special Industrial Recovery Board became a battleground between Hugh Johnson, on the one hand, and George Peek, Rexford Tugwell, and Henry Wallace, on the other. Unable to reconcile the conflicting factions, Roosevelt diffused the conflict by disbanding the Special Industrial Recovery Board on 18 December 1933. Henceforth, supervision of the NRA would be carried on by the recently created National Emergency Council, a more distant agency that would assure Johnson a freer hand in administering the NRA. Whatever consequences this would have for the coordination of industrial and agricultural policy, it made it less likely that internal policy disputes would sap the vigor of the NRA. Roosevelt chose to follow the maxim of the science of public administration that authority should be made commensurate with responsibility, since he favored an activist administration capable of shaping the problem in accord with New Deal goals.[86]

82. "Address of Marc A. Rose...at the 36th quarterly meeting of the New England Council," Roosevelt Papers, OF 172, No. 1, Business, July–October 1934; *Business Week*, 25 August 1934, p. 10.

83. Roos, p. 59.

84. One reform the NAM had sought in the NIRA was to make the NRA an agency headed by a commission, an administrative form that had proved less threatening to business interests. Ibid., p. 49.

85. Schlesinger, *The Coming of the New Deal*, pp. 113, 123, 126.

86. Ibid., pp. 127–128; Hawley, *The New Deal*, p. 73.

The ability of the NRA to develop relative autonomy from the interests it regulated was contingent on its capacity to transcend the day-to-day administrative tasks of the agency by evaluating these functions in light of broader, long-range policy decisions. By October 1933 the sheer press of administrative detail forced reorganizations that permitted greater delegations of power. A new level of division administrators was placed between the NRA administrator and the deputy administrators responsible for specific codes. Each division was assigned an operating staff to enhance the decision-making capacity of these units. While the diversity of industries lumped under a single division still limited the ability of administration to supervise individual codes, the decentralized structure was a marked improvement over its predecessors. Indeed, as the task of the central administration shifted from drafting codes to establishing code authorities to administer these codes, the central administration played a more active role in scrutinizing bylaws and budgets proposed by industry. The development of such an agency structure was explicitly designed to facilitate an adequate NRA response to the growing data concerning cartel abuses under the NRA.[87]

Johnson tried to further enhance the policy-making capacity of the NRA by refurbishing a Policy Board composed of division administrators and the chairmen of the advisory boards in January 1934, but the other administrative duties of these officials limited its success. This weakness was mitigated by the use of the Legal Division to promote the formulation of a model code and greater uniformity in code practices, an enterprise requiring attention to broader policy issues. Legal advisors for specific codes went beyond a narrowly confined role of determining legality to promoting general policy aims. The Legal Division, adequately funded and well staffed, was a source of independent advice to counter the demands of business groups seeking to advance their own interests through the codes. Later, after the codes were drafted, this supervisory role was increasingly taken on by the Review Division, which was reorganized in February 1934 to facilitate its pursuit of this goal.[88]

The autonomy of a central administrative structure was compromised to some extent by the administration's need to recruit many businessmen to serve on the NRA staff because they needed their technical expertise to help administer the codes. One safeguard instituted to secure the progressive ends of the program against co-optation by the special interests of industry was to prohibit anyone with a direct financial interest in an industry from supervising its code.[89] Moreover, professional economists, statisticians, engineers, and lawyers, whose prior occupational orientations were quite distinct from those of businessmen, were also heavily recruited

87. Lyon et al., pp. 50–51; Hawley, *The New Deal*, p. 98.
88. Hawley, *The New Deal*, pp. 65–66; Lyon et al., pp. 62–66.
89. Hawley, *The New Deal*, p. 65.

for middle-level administrative positions. Academicians secured important posts in the Research and Planning Division and the Code Analysis Division.[90] They collected and analyzed much of the data that was later used to substantiate charges of business abuses under the codes and to justify a more restricted role for code authorities. Because the NRA was not bound by civil service requirements, it was free to recruit people who were most sympathetic to its aims in all occupational strata. As a result, many NRA officials were predisposed to carry out NRA policies by the political values they brought to their jobs.

These factors alone, however, do not explain how the NRA preserved its autonomy from business interests, an autonomy demonstrated by the recurrent discrepancies between NRA policy and the demands of business groups. The NRA did rely heavily on personnel with business backgrounds, and yet this did not guarantee business a sympathetic hearing in the agency. NRA officials generally acted in accord with the expectations attached to their role within the NRA, and they generally defended the institutional interests of the state. In fact, New Dealers were more concerned with the competence of a politicized NRA staff than they were with its political loyalties.[91] This can be explained only if we assume that the socialization process within the NRA was effective enough to inspire a professional commitment to the goals of the agency which overshadowed values acquired during earlier business careers. The NRA was a new agency with a bold mission, and Hugh Johnson had a charismatic appeal for many—characteristics that are conducive to successful socialization. While no socialization process is completely effective, and while the need to rely at least in part on businessmen to staff the NRA undoubtedly moderated the progressive zeal of the NRA, the hypothesis that a probusiness NRA staff corrupted the agency by deflecting it from its progressive goals is simply inconsistent with the history of the NRA.

Neither did administrative corporatism subvert the NRA. Business participation, which was essential if the NRA was to succeed, had been enlisted within a broader organizational framework that included government supervision. In cases where business abuses were clear, the NRA acted forcefully to correct the problem. The NRA was never a captured agency. Even so, the NRA created a regulatory climate that was conducive to cartelization. In promoting its ambitious societal corporatist goals of fair trade and an equitable relationship between large business and small business, it had permitted forms of cooperation between businessmen that could too easily be used to suppress competition altogether. Fair competition was as elusive as a goal for the New Deal as the fair price had been elusive for medieval states and their guilds.

90. Roos, pp. 60–61, 71.
91. Ibid., p. 59.

CHAPTER 5

The Revisionists

and the NRA

Revisionists have portrayed the NRA as a vehicle for the rationalization of the interests of capitalists or big business. One attraction of the revisionist approach to the twentieth-century regulatory state in general is that it can explain an aspect of economic regulation that appears anomalous from the vantage point of progressive historiography. The latter interpretation of the regulatory state portrays it as the product of successive triumphs of democratic movements over the resistance of big business, an interpretation that has difficulty accounting for cooperation between business elites and the political elites who have supposedly led the democratic revolt against corporate capitalism. For instance, in Gabriel Kolko's revisionist classic *The Triumph of Conservatism,* Kolko tried to refute progressive historians' interpretation of American history by demonstrating that business elites were in fact the interests behind and the chief beneficiaries of such Progressive Era regulation as the Pure Food and Drug Act and the Federal Reserve Act. Revisionists like Ellis Hawley and Robert Himmelberg have proposed similar interpretations for the NRA, and Ronald Radosh and Barton Bernstein have been even more radical, suggesting that the entire New Deal can be understood within this framework.

The serious problems with any revisionist interpretation of the New Deal era are clearest in its most radical version. If the New Deal served the interests of capitalists, why did business, and particularly big business, come to loathe Roosevelt more than any other president in the twentieth century?[1] Business elites clearly believed that the New Deal was a radical threat to their interests, and it is diffcult to dismiss that belief when one considers New Deal policies like Roosevelt's response to "the power

---

1. Marquis Childs, "They Hate Roosevelt," in *The New Deal: The Critical Issues,* ed. Otis L. Graham, Jr. (Boston, 1971), pp. 61–67.

trust." Even while he was governor of New York, Roosevelt had created a national reputation for himself by fighting "the power trust" tooth and nail over the issue of hydroelectric development of the St. Lawrence. Chastising the power companies' disregard for the public interest, and overcoming bitter industry opposition, Roosevelt insisted that the power plants on the St. Lawrence remain in public hands to compete with and discipline private companies.[2] He continued his battle with this industry, which had become identified in the public mind with abuses of monopoly power, once he became president. First subjecting the power trust to public discipline through public development of the Tennessee Valley, Roosevelt then proposed and led the battle to enact the Public Utilities Holding Company Act, which eventually broke up power company empires. Furthermore, although Roosevelt's attack on the power companies was one of his most dramatic clashes with the business community, it was by no means his only one. Similar conflicts occurred over securities regulation, monetary policy, labor policy, and federal relief for the unemployed, to name only a few.

If the broader revisionist interpretation of the New Deal does not do justice to intense, relatively pervasive conflict between Roosevelt and business elites, the narrower revisionist interpretation of the NRA has far more initial plausibility. The NRA attempted to institutionalize cooperation between government and business, and many businessmen were willing to enlist under the NRA banner. Even the conservative and combative National Association of Manufacturers was willing to give the president's program a chance.[3] Big business had also demonstrated a strong interest in the relaxation of antitrust laws during the 1920s and had often tried to establish cartels among competing firms to dampen competitive pressures on profits. The NRA relaxed antitrust laws and led to a marked increase in cartelization. If any New Deal program provides evidence supporting the revisionists' thesis, it is the NRA. Indeed, the plausibility of the revisionist thesis with regard to the NRA was probably the reason the more radical revisionist thesis received as much attention as it did.

Despite initial appearances, a more careful analysis of the NRA does not support the revisionist conclusion. We have already noted in the previous chapter that cartelization was not, as the revisionists have assumed, generally the goal of the NRA. Further analysis of relations between government and business during the life-span of the NRA reveals that the attempt to institutionalize a cooperative relationship between business and government failed because of fundamental conflicts between progressive elites and business elites. In the first months of the NRA, that

2. Rexford G. Tugwell, *The Democratic Roosevelt: A Biography of Franklin D. Roosevelt* (Baltimore, 1957), pp. 176–177; Burns, *The Lion and the Fox*, pp. 112–115.
3. Hawley, *The New Deal*, pp. 19, 26–27.

conflict was less overt than it was with regard to many other New Deal programs, but the seeds of conflict had been sown from the very beginning. As the NRA began to take shape, appeals for cooperation became increasingly ineffective and the more characteristic New Deal pattern of mutual hostility between business and progressive elites began to emerge. To the extent that a cooperative relationship between government and business was established, it was primarily with small and medium-sized businesses and their representatives—a conclusion that is inconsistent with the revisionist thesis.

Corporate Liberalism and the NRA

The industrial self-government themes of the NRA struck a responsive chord for some in the business community. Gerald Swope, executive director of the General Electric Company, had proposed a plan for industrial recovery that superficially resembled the NRA. Like the NRA, Swope's plan called for a greatly expanded role for trade associations and sought to mitigate destructive competition. The resemblance between Swope's plan and the NRA, combined with the active advisory role that Swope and other corporate leaders who shared his views played in the NRA administraton, has led revisionist historians to identify the animus behind the NRA with the interests of big business, and more specifically with the interest of "corporate liberals" in new modes of interest coordination.[4]

To the revisionists, Gerald Swope typified a new corporatist attitude emerging among the business leaders of modern industrial corporations. Whereas traditional business leaders had asserted the virtues of the unimpeded market and rejected the distortions in market allocations brought about by either labor unions or government regulation, these new business elites—corporate liberals—acknowledged a legitimate role for unions and accepted the need for cooperation between government and business to provide the infrastructure for a healthy economy.[5] According to the revisionists, corporate liberals saw the state as an invaluable instrument for securing broad class interests and mitigating intraclass and interclass conflicts. A new cooperative ideology legitimated this role for the state.

The revisionists link the emergence of corporate liberalism to transformations in the underlying economic structure of capitalism. The complexity of a modern industrial economy is presumed to have awakened business

4. Ibid., pp. 8–14, 36–43; Robert F. Himmelberg, *The Origins of the National Recovery Administration* (New York, 1976), pp. 1–4.
5. B. Bernstein, pp. 265, 268–269; Radosh, pp. 151, 164.

to the potential role of the state and unions in stabilizing and rationalizing competitive markets. While they concede that not all the leaders of modern corporations shared the "corporate liberal" perspective, the revisionists stress the ascendance of this "modern" view and the decline of a more traditional laissez-faire perspective. Laissez-faire was the business ideology of the nineteenth century, and corporate liberalism was becoming the business ideology of the twentieth century. The most astute and powerful businessmen kept abreast of the times, but the beliefs of some lagged behind transformations in the "real" organizational base of capitalism.

One enduring contribution of revisionist historiography is its discovery of an emergent corporate liberal ideology with corporatist overtones during the first decades of the twentieth century.[6] How pervasive corporate liberal beliefs were remains a matter of historical dispute, but it is clear that corporate liberals were more conciliatory toward both government and unions than their more intransigent laissez-faire business cohorts. Nevertheless, business corporatism differed fundamentally from progressive corporatism. Collective welfare was much more closely identified with the welfare of the business community in business corporatism than in progressive corporatism. Business corporatists believed that the business elite could successfully respond to the social and economic problems of their day, even the problems posed by the depression, and they insisted on business control of corporatist institutions. Government had a supporting role to play in promoting economic recovery, but bureaucratic regimentation was to be avoided.[7] Progressive corporatists believed that corporatist institutions provided a vehicle for promoting cooperation between government and business *on progressive terms*, and they insisted that control of corporatist institutions be vested in the new progressive elite swept into office by the election of 1932.

The history of the NRA reveals the inherent tensions between these alternative conceptions of corporatism. When the NRA was first proposed, corporate liberals provided strong support for the program, believing that the NRA would permit them to promote their interests and realize their business corporatist ideals. Progressive corporatists often cultivated this support, but they were firmly opposed to business control of the NRA. The tensions between progressive corporatism and business corporatism were clearly revealed in Rexford Tugwell's reactions to the Swope plan and to a similar plan put forward by Henry Harriman. Addressing

---

6. Kim McQuaid, "Competition, Cartelization, and the Corporate Ethic," *American Journal of Economics and Sociology* 36 (1977): 418.

7. Theda Skocpol, "Political Responses to Capitalist Crisis: Neo-Marxist Theories of the State and the Cases of the New Deal," *Politics and Society* 10 (1980): 155–201; *Nation's Business*, June 1935, pp. 17, 76. Hawley, *The New Deal*, pp. 30–33, 38–43; William Wilson, "Chamber of Commerce," pp. 97, 99, 101–102.

the American Economic Association in March 1932, Tugwell dismissed both proposals. Characterizing Swope's and Harriman's business corporatist plans as "partial" planning, Tugwell insisted that nothing less than "total" planning would suffice.[8] While Tugwell did not specify at this point what "total" planning entailed, he was at the same time developing a more elaborate prescription for industrial reform, which was subsequently published as *The Industrial Discipline and the Governmental Arts*. This book made it clear that Tugwell did not envision a centralized federal bureaucracy coercively imposing a comprehensive plan on industry. Tugwell's program was no less corporatist than Swope's or Harriman's, but the role of government differed radically.[9] Having no faith in the ability of businessmen to clean their own house, Tugwell insisted that the new institutions that would be designed to facilitate corporatist planning "must be surrounded by entirely adequate safeguards to ensure the full protection of those public interests which are likely to be neglected in business plans."[10]

The NIRA was sufficiently ambiguous to encourage corporate liberal aspirations while at the same time encouraging the progressive belief that the NRA would initiate a new era in which business self-interests were subordinated to national interests. Soon after the program was implemented and it became clear that progressive elites were exercising far more power than business corporatists had anticipated, business corporatists began to demand reforms that would have permitted greater business control over the program. Some were so unhappy with the NRA that they argued for scrapping it and rebuilding a new program from the ground up. Others believed that a revised NRA would suffice. Both were dissatisfied with the existing NRA, and their dissatisfaction indicates how limited their control over the NRA was.

The tensions between business corporatism and progressive corporatism were clearly illustrated in the evolution of Gerald Swope's attitude toward the NRA. Initially enthusiastic about the NRA because of its partial

8. Kenneth S. Davis, *FDR: The New York Years*, p. 270.

9. Ellis Hawley deemphasizes the corporatist dimensions of Tugwell thought by characterizing Tugwell as a planner and suggesting that Tugwell had in mind central planning by a federal bureaucracy. While Tugwell's speech before the American Economic Association lends some credence to this description of Tugwell, Arthur Schlesinger appropriately cautions that this speech "could perhaps be fairly read as an expression of Tugwell's cocky desire to shock an audience with the implications of its too glib slogans." Schlesinger treats *The Industrial Discipline and the Governmental Arts* as Tugwell's more "sober" approach to economic reconstruction and correctly notes that "Tugwell's own program now bore a strange resemblance to the plans of Harriman and Swope which had so recently roused him to such sardonic reflections." Indeed, the plans were similar in form, but they differed fundamentally in spirit, and it was this difference of spirit that inspired Tugwell's attacks on Swope and Harriman in the speech before the American Economic Association. Tugwell's corporatism was described more extensively in Chapter 2. See Schlesinger, *The Crisis of the Old Order*, pp. 195–198.

10. Tugwell, *Industrial Discipline*, p. 211.

resemblance to his own corporatist Swope plan, Swope deemphasized the features of the NRA that did not conform to his proposals. But as the history of the NRA was to demonstrate, the spirit of the NRA differed profoundly from the spirit of the Swope plan. Swope's plan was ultimately a call to the business elite to cooperate and assume responsibility for mitigating market dislocations. According to his plan, trade associations would assume significant new powers vis-à-vis individual firms, and trade associations would be joined in an industrial congress to coordinate their respective programs.[11] Even the Swope plan would have allowed some government supervision of industrial self-government. Because he conceded that greater opportunity for cooperation for recovery also expanded the opportunity for cartel abuses, Swope acknowledged the government's legitimate concern in preventing the use of federal power to enforce agreements contrary to the public interest. But while a government role was not excluded, it would be minimized by confining it largely to the role of vetoing proposals adopted by the private code authorities.

The NRA did not provide for an industrial congress because its own bureaucracy assumed responsibility for coordinating industrial codes, a structure that was more akin to the War Industries Board. Because the National Industrial Recovery Act extended federal government regulation of fair trade practices and regulated such previously unregulated activities as the setting of wages and hours and union recognition, the substitution of federal coordination for business coordination was increasingly viewed by many corporate liberals as a critical departure from a sound scheme of industrial self-government. Furthermore, the NIRA gave the president the authority to impose a code unilaterally on an industry, a provision that was radically different from the voluntarist Swope plan.[12]

Even at the time the NRA had first been proposed, these features of the NRA elicited a far more ambivalent response from the corporate liberals than the Swope plan had. While the NIRA was being considered by Congress, Henry Harriman, president of the U.S. Chamber of Commerce and a noted corporate liberal, hedged his support for the bill with warnings that its provisions for government control could lead to "autocracy and bureaucracy."[13] His position resembled the official posture that the Chamber of Commerce had adopted at its annual meeting in May 1933, where it objected to "endeavors from outside [i.e., of business] to apply arbitrary rules" to commercial life and asserted that both public and private interests would best be served by giving business a freer hand,

---

11. Gerald Swope, *The Swope Plan* (New York, 1931), pp. 25–45; McQuaid, p. 419.

12. Although the president only invoked this power once during the life-span of the NRA, he threatened to use it on other occasions. Businessmen perceived it as a constant threat to their interests, and proposals to eliminate the power figured prominently in the political maneuvering to extend the NRA. See *Business Week*, 12 May 1934, p. 25.

13. William Wilson, "Chamber of Commerce," p. 97.

because "those who are best equipped to solve the problems of industry are those who are themselves engaged in industry."[14] Despite these reservations, corporate liberals were still optimistic that in practice business would control the NRA.

By the beginning of November, the importance of the differences between the NRA and the Swope plan had become clear to most corporate liberals. Discussing the "bedlam" in the NRA, Henry Harriman claimed: "I know of no representative group of businessmen today in which some do not question the whole NRA."[15] Swope was now sufficiently disenchanted with the NRA to call for its replacement and a vesting of its regulatory powers in a National Chamber of Commerce and Industry, an expanded U.S. Chamber of Commerce that would function as a peak association of all trade associations.[16] Swope's proposal to replace the NRA with a genuine program of industrial self-government was simply a reassertion of his original proposals for industrial recovery, but his belief that those proposals entailed a repudiation of the NRA was evidence of growing awareness of the fundamental differences between business and progressive corporatism. Swope's perspective on the NRA was captured by his biographer, David Loth, when he noted that even though Swope "had a hand in its [the NRA's] operation as well as its preparation, he always disclaimed paternity. The fundamental difference between his original proposal and the one that became law on June 16, 1933, was that the emphasis shifted from voluntary cooperation managed by industry under government supervision to Federal edicts accepted by industry under government compulsion."[17]

Swope's disaffection with the NRA clearly reveals the tensions between business corporatism and progressive corporatism, but the differences that distinguish them were not necessarily reflected in their corporatist ideologies. Business and progressive corporatists both spoke of cooperation within business and between business, labor, and government. Both defended industrial self-government under the supervision of the federal government. The differences between them emerge more in practice than in theory. In practice, progressive corporatists assert and defend the interests of the state, whereas business corporatists assert and defend the interests of business firms, and while these institutional interests are not mutually exclusive, they are not identical either. Corporatism as an ideology emphasizes shared interests and cooperation, but the representatives of business and government (and labor representatives as well) who

14. Final Declaration of Annual Meeting of U.S. Chamber of Commerce, May 1933, cited in a letter from George H. Cless, Jr., to Henry Harriman (president of the U.S. Chamber of Commerce), 29 May 1934, Roosevelt Papers, PPF 1615, No. 1.

15. Schlesinger, *The Coming of the New Deal*, p. 121.

16. Ibid.

17. David Loth, *Swope of G.E.* (New York, 1958), p. 223.

actually participate in corporatist institutions soon find themselves in conflict with their institutional counterparts, often despite the best efforts of all parties to repress or work through these conflicts. Cooperation may prevail for short periods of time, especially if reinforced by ideological zeal and propitious circumstances (such as an immediate external threat in wartime), but in a large nation, with diverse and heterogeneous interests, it is unlikely that cooperation will be permanently institutionalized.

Revisionists who assume that the interests of the state and the interests of the firm are fundamentally identical have therefore failed to understand the internal dynamics of the NRA. One could suggest that the revisionists have attributed too much importance to ideas and not enough to objective institutional interests. Noting the ideological similarities between business and progressive corporatism, they have unjustifiably assumed that these similarities reflected common objective interests. But even if business and progressive corporatists feel a kinship with one another based on shared ideas, or, more radical, even if business and progressive corporatists are indistinguishable from one another when removed from their institutional settings and roles, this does not establish common objective interests within those roles.

Laissez-faire and the NRA

The revisionist interpretation of the NRA is flawed not only in its failure to understand the tensions between the business corporatism of corporate liberals and progressive corporatism, but even more fundamentally in its failure to understand the importance of laissez-faire ideas in the 1930s. As important as corporate liberalism was during the New Deal, it was not the dominant business ideology of the period. Many businessmen found corporate liberalism's emphasis on cooperation rather than competition too idealistic. This was particularly true of corporate liberalism's appeal for cooperation with labor. For instance, Gerald Swope's dramatic appeal to the AFL to unionize General Electric was clearly out of step with most of the business community, which bitterly fought any recognition of the AFL. Furthermore, contrary to the revisionist thesis that it was the leaders of the modern mass-production industries who were the backbone of corporate liberalism, it was also the leaders of these industries who figured most prominently in the fight against the AFL. Continuity is more striking than change in comparing late nineteenth-century and early twentieth-century businessmen.[18] The business attitudes that made the late

18. James Prothro's *Dollar Decade: Business Ideas in the 1920s* (New York, 1970) emphasizes traditional business concerns with economic liberty and preservation of private property without a hint of any fundamental reorientation of attitudes concerning government-business relations. While Prothro may have exaggerated the homogeneity and conservatism of businessmen, he clearly was describing a prominent strand of business opinion.

nineteenth century the locus classicus for laissez-faire capitalism were in many cases the same attitudes that fashioned business hostility to the New Deal in the 1930s.

Certainly the organizational forms of a capitalist system had changed between the mid-nineteenth century and the beginning of the New Deal. The single entrepreneur had given way to the corporation, which had grown dramatically in size and complexity. But the corporation itself was perceived by the business community as a complex organization in the service of entrepreneurship. It was simply a mode of cooperation that permitted businessmen to compete more efficiently with others. Organizational change did not lead to a questioning of the fundamental beliefs in the laissez-faire universe. Indeed, the corporation had come into its own during the post–Civil War era, when laissez-faire held undisputed sway.[19] Neither did the waves of national trade associations formation in the thirty years prior to the depression represent a fundamental challenge to capitalists' self-understanding. This cooperative network facilitated entrepreneurial activity, instead of displacing it. Trade associations remained weak organizational entities with few means to discipline their members in the pursuit of collective goals.[20] The theme of the trade association was service delivery, a function that left the association subordinate to the firm.[21] The brisk growth of the U.S. economy throughout the 1920s had for many American businessmen laid to rest any doubts that an economic system based on competition and a laissez-faire belief system could not adapt to the complexity of modern industrial life.

Businessmen could retain the same ideals throughout these organizational transformations because they identified the fundamentals of capitalism with the eternal fundamentals of human nature. Man would pursue his self-interest according to the inexorable dictates of human nature, and only a competitive free market system could channel the energy latent in man's selfishness to maximize economic growth. Government was a necessary evil that always threatened to extend its authority tyrannically over the individual. To guard against this danger, the government should be restricted to limited means, confirmed by an elaborate system of separation of powers, checks and balances, and federalism. American business-

19. Martin Schnitzer, *Contemporary Government and Business Relations* (Boston, 1983), p. 35.

20. J. Q. Wilson, *Political Organizations*, pp. 145–152; Galambos, *Competition and Cooperation*, pp. 35–75.

21. In his history of the Cotton Textile Institute (CTI) Galambos characterizes the period from 1900 through 1925 as an era of service association development, and the period after 1935 as a return to a service association conception. From 1925 to 1935, trade association officials in the CTI hoped to turn the organization into an agency for industrial self-governance, but it is not clear that the membership shared this aspiration, and the failure of the CTI to stabilize the cotton textile market makes it even more unlikely that the period from 1925 to 1935 would have produced a fundamental shift in business ideology.

men have remained some of the staunchest advocates of our traditional liberal constitution precisely because such a government structure could restrain the populist excesses possible under a more activist regulatory state.[22]

The most frequently cited evidence for the assertion of a transformation in business attitudes away from laissez-faire values was the business movement to reform antitrust laws, which culminated in a resolution to that effect sent to Congress by the U.S. Chamber of Commerce in 1930.[23] In fact, the call for antitrust reform was perfectly consistent with traditional laissez-faire views. Laissez-faire had always meant allowing business maximum scope to conduct its own affairs free from the restraints of government, and antitrust was just one more form of government interference with business, even if in the name of preserving the market. The demand for the relaxation of antitrust statutes does in part attest to a powerful drive among businessmen to develop cooperative relationships with competitors to mitigate the rigors of competition in the free market, a drive that frequently influenced nineteenth-century entrepreneurs as well. But such tendencies would have led to a complete breakdown of laissez-faire views only if the desire to escape competition had led businessmen to embrace state regulation as a means to mitigate competition. Yet this was not the case with railroads in the late nineteenth century, which faced one of the most competitive markets in the American economy. Railroads generally preferred to stabilize their markets through mergers and cartels rather than through public regulation, fearing that the latter introduced external control over the railroads that infringed on their managerial autonomy.[24]

Even the depression could not fundamentally undermine the faith in those ideals, although that faith sometimes wavered in darkest days of the depression. Myron Taylor, chairman of U.S. Steel, wrote to Daniel Roper, secretary of commerce:

> I do not believe individualism has failed. I believe thoughtful study of what took place in 1928 and 1929 would develop that we were caught in the aftermath of an economic bulge which naturally came to us after the war. . . .
>
> As I understand individualism, it is the thing that has given promise to the boyhood and manhood of this country—that there was nothing which they might not do in an independent way, if they set about it and worked hard and diligently and observed the old fashioned precepts which through all time have been rewarded.[25]

22. Prothro, pp. 39–42, 179.
23. Himmelberg, pp. 110, 115, 125–146.
24. From his study of the development of modern railroads, Alfred Chandler concluded: "After 1893 very few railroad men considered government regulation a more practical method than system-building for controlling competition" (Alfred Chandler, *The Visible Hand* [Cambridge, Mass., 1977], p. 175).
25. Myron Taylor to Daniel Roper, 13 April 1934, Roosevelt Papers, PPF 423, No. 1.

The revisionist argument has achieved some unwarranted credibility from the general reluctance of most academics to take seriously the commitment of business to laissez-faire ideology. Laissez-faire ideology has been dismissed as little more than pious platitudes, observed more in the breach than in the practice. Businessmen admire the market in principle, but they are motivated by their fear of competition (a behavioral pattern that is rationalized by the claim that they are not attempting to mitigate competition per se, but only excessive competition). Laissez-faire, for instance, has been selectively interpreted by the business community to mean freedom from regulatory controls but not freedom from government subsidies, government secured loans, or protective tariffs. As self-serving as this business interpretation of the meaning of laissez-faire is—a fact economists never fail to point out—it renders twentieth-century businessmen no more and no less hypocritical than their reputedly more entrepreneurial nineteenth-century predecessors. Business in the latter half of the nineteenth century demanded massive government subsidies, especially for the railroads, and high tariffs.[26] Nevertheless, businessmen in the late nineteenth century were in some sense genuinely committed to a laissez-faire ideology, for we could not explain the existence of the laissez-faire state otherwise. In that era, business—including the emerging large corporations—clearly did resist federal regulation, especially when it was demanded by agrarian populists. Dismissing the importance of business laissez-faire beliefs in the twentieth century, and particularly during the New Deal, has obfuscated the extent to which businessmen in this era have attempted to avoid government regulation as well.

Much of the confusion surrounding the genuineness of business commitment to laissez-faire could be diminished if laissez-faire was conceptualized not simply as a business ideal but as a calculation of long-term interest. Laissez-faire was a business ideology; it was ultimately a judgment of the optimal conditions for business' own long-term commercial prosperity and managerial autonomy. Framed in this manner, laissez-faire beliefs should be taken seriously even by those who are reluctant to concede that businessmen could be motivated by anything other than economic interests.

It is therefore not difficult to explain why laissez-faire ideology has survived well into the twentieth century. It reflected a genuine conflict of interest between businessmen and a state. Why else would business forgo a government-imposed stabilization of the market, such as that provided by the NRA? In the absence of any compelling government threat to business interests, a refusal to temper the rigors of the competitive market would appear to be an implausible form of laissez-faire idealism. While

26. Schnitzer, p. 409.

private forms of market rationalization, such as vertical and horizontal integration, or cartelization, can significantly reduce competition, none can offer the potential long-term stabilization that government regulation has provided, particularly in establishing barriers to entry. If regulation can provide benefits and these benefits are voluntarily relinquished, the costs must outweigh the benefits. The most plausible explanation of these costs is that twentieth-century reform movements, which have attained power through successful electoral appeals to the economically disadvantaged, have at least partially institutionalized a centralized bureaucratic state that displayed considerable autonomy to act against major corporate interests. Without denigrating the desire of businessmen to avoid the risks associated with market uncertainties emphasized by contemporary political economy, a more balanced presentation would portray the firm as poised between the dual risks of government control and market competition, seeking to maximize stability and minimize external control.

Given the dominant laissez-faire orientation of the business community, it may appear strange that the majority of businessmen did not reject the NRA outright. Had the NRA been proposed in the more prosperous 1920s, there is every reason to believe this would have occurred. The majority of the business community during this era had strongly supported Calvin Coolidge and his vision of the minimalist state, a vision that even the revisionists would concede was incompatible with the more active role of the state in the NRA.[27] But the length and severity of the depression had shattered the self-confidence of business elites in the United States. Their faith in the self-governing character of free markets wavering, a few businessmen went as far as to call on Roosevelt to assume dictatorial powers over industry or to nationalize them.[28] Others argued that businessmen would have nothing to fear from government price-fixing because a progressive government would still have an interest in keeping up profits, both for the sake of maintaining high tax revenues and for encouraging investment.[29] Often these were not sober calculations of business interests; they were the desperate pleas of a panic-stricken class that saw their world crumbling around them and hoped that Roosevelt would be able to chart a path out of economic ruin.

Roosevelt's strong electoral showing in the 1932 election, combined with the declining prestige of business elites, also weighed heavily in favor of a conciliatory stance toward the New Deal. Conservatives among

27. Contrary to this assertion, Robert Himmelberg has argued (in *The Origins of the National Recovery Administration*) that the origins of the NRA lay in the movement to reform antitrust laws during the 1920s. The problem with Himmelberg's analysis is that he equates the regulated suspension of antitrust laws under the NRA with the unregulated relaxation of antitrust statutes sought by business in the late 1920s and early 1930s.

28. Norman Nordhauser, *The Quest for Stability* (New York, 1979), p. 106; *National Petroleum News*, 10 May 1933, pp. 9–11; J. Johnson, *The Politics of Soft Coal*, p. 140.

29. *The Iron Age*, 20 July 1933, p. 261.

the business elite had not been happy to see Roosevelt win the election. Roosevelt had criticized the business elite during his 1932 campaign, and they feared that the rise of a progressive elite threatened the power, status, and interests of business. Nevertheless, business recognized that some antibusiness rhetoric was good politics and that it did not necessarily follow that Roosevelt would seriously threaten their interests. Both progressives and business had a common interest in economic recovery, and some in the business community hoped that recovery rather than reform would become the focus of the New Deal.

Furthermore, most business leaders agreed that concessions by business were essential if even more radical reforms were to be avoided. The president of Goodyear Tire and Rubber Company, P. W. Litchfield, argued, "If we are to save our traditional freedom for the future, it is probable that we must make substantial concessions to what we have in the past classified as the more radical school of thought." The most politically astute businessmen recognized that progressives generally rejected comprehensive public planning and control of the economy as a form of regimentation that stifled initiative, just as progressives acknowledged the success of the corporation in harnessing entrepreneurial energies and developing efficient techniques of management. The corporation in a progressive state would not be deprived of "reasonable" profits; it would only be denied monopolistic profits, and there could always be bargaining over what constituted "reasonable" profits. The moderation of progressivism vis-à-vis business interests—at least by contrast with either late-nineteenth-century populism or socialism—led many businessmen to conclude that some form of accommodation with Roosevelt was possible.[30]

Economic collapse, Roosevelt's strong electoral showing, and a fear of more radical left-wing movements contributed to an initial business predisposition to cooperate with Roosevelt, even among those who still adhered to the traditional laissez-faire ideology of business. This predisposition was reinforced when Roosevelt made the NRA the centerpiece of his recovery program. The NRA promised relief from antitrust enforcement, a reform that many in the business community had demanded for many years. Other aspects were less savory, but the NIRA was ambiguous, and it could have been administered in a manner compatible with business interests. The remaining suspicions of business were at least partially allayed by the two-year statute of limitations on the legislation. Nevertheless, this willingness to cooperate was short-lived. Once the downward economic spiral had been arrested and even minimal recovery had begun, conservative businessmen returned to traditional values. As it became clear that the NRA was a program for fundamental reform as well as recovery, opposition to the NRA mounted.

30. William Wilson, "Chamber of Commerce," pp. 96–97.

The Extension of the NRA

Roosevelt had always envisioned the NRA as the basis for permanent restructuring of the American economy and not simply a temporary response to depression. Nevertheless, he had initially requested only a two-year authorization for the NRA to placate those who were suspicious of the program. By the spring of 1935, Roosevelt had made it clear that he still viewed the NRA as a viable economic framework and that he intended to seek a two-year reauthorization of the program. As business and labor groups positioned themselves for the battle for the extension of the NRA, a battle that was cut short by the Supreme Court's *Schechter* decision, their final assessments of the NRA and the impact it had had on their interests became clear. Under these circumstances, business and labor groups were reacting no longer to a proposed program with a great many ambiguities, as they had been when the NRA was first proposed, but to a program that had decisively shaped the environment in which they had been operating for the two preceding years. An analysis of the political coalition lobbying for an extension of the NRA in the spring of 1935 reveals more big-business opposition to the program than would be expected based on the revisionist interpretation.

The business organization in which the revisionists have been most interested is the Business Advisory Council (BAC). This council was formed in 1933 as an advisory body to the Department of Commerce, and it rapidly became an important conduit between Roosevelt and the business community. The BAC was traditionally dominated by representatives of big business, and at the time of the NRA many of these big-business representatives were corporate liberals—those in the business community who were most willing to search for some sort of accommodation between Roosevelt's New Deal and business interests.[31] The revisionists have correctly noted that in the spring of 1935 the BAC supported Roosevelt's call for a two-year extension of the NRA, and they concluded that the NRA must therefore have served the interests of the capitalist class. BAC support for a two-year extension of the NRA can then be contrasted with the opposition of both the U.S. Chamber of Comerce and the National Association of Manufacturers to reinforce the revisionist conclusions. The latter two business organizations, some revisionists assert, primarily represented small and medium-sized firms that had been victimized by NRA policies systematically favoring the interests of big, modern corporations.

As was the case with the revisionist analysis of the Swope plan and the origins of the NRA, however, the revisionist analysis of the battle for an extension of the NRA fails to do justice to the difference between the

---

31. Robert Collins, "Positive Business Responses to the New Deal: The Roots of the Committee for Economic Development, 1933–1942," *Business History Review* 52 (1978): 370.

proposals of the BAC and of Franklin Roosevelt for an extension. The BAC was proposing a two-year extension of a modified NRA, whereas Roosevelt was supporting an extension without significant modifications. The BAC modifications were intended to assure that codes of fair trade competition were based on the mutual agreement of business and the president, but with "the primary responsibility for formulating and presenting a code to rest with the industry."[32] They would have stripped the president of the power to impose an unwanted code on an industry or to modify existing codes without the consent of the industry. Furthermore, just as the president could abrogate an agreement that was working to the detriment of the public, likewise business would gain the power to withdraw from code provisions that were working contrary to business interests. The BAC's proposed modifications were an attempt to alter fundamentally the character of the NRA by transforming it into a genuine form of industrial self-government. The proposal was in the spirit of the original Swope plan, although the proposal was more moderate than Swope's earlier attempt to replace the NRA with a National Chamber of Commerce and Industry.

It would be a mistake to interpret BAC support for a two-year extension of the NRA as a sign of big business' satisfaction with the existing program. Prudent businessmen were willing to bury their discontent with the NRA because it represented a lesser evil, particularly when it came to labor policy. The BAC excepted Section 7a from their general advocacy of voluntary codes. Even in their proposal the president could require that Section 7a be included in any approved code, or even imposed on an unwilling industry.[33] No doubt a few corporate liberals sincerely believed that independent unions were necessary to protect the American labor force and that corporations could work out an acceptable modus vivendi with the responsible unions. But most other corporate liberals simply shared the realistic political perception that without Section 7a the political pressure to pass the Wagner Act, which was then before Congress, would be irresistible. With the most radical Congress in American history debating the Wagner Act, Roosevelt's moderation on labor policy was the final defense of business. However offensive some interpretations of Section 7a could be to business interests, at least it offered business the possibility of forming company unions and competing with the AFL for the loyalty of the American worker. The Wagner Act would disallow company unions completely. As long as Roosevelt was persuaded that the NRA provided an environment in which responsible unionism could develop, he might be willing to sidetrack more radical measures.[34]

32. "Resolution Adopted by the Executive Committee of the Business Advisory and Planning Council at Meeting on March Thirteenth, 1935," Roosevelt Papers, OF 3, No. 9, 1933–35.
33. Ibid.
34. Roosevelt, *The Public Papers*, 4:157.

The BAC's proposals for NRA reform were sweeping enough to indicate considerable dissatisfaction with the NRA as presently constituted. The problems this poses for the revisionist interpretation of the NRA are particularly clear when one examines the relationship between these BAC proposals and the stance of other business groups toward the NRA. The U.S. Chamber of Commerce had chosen to support the NIRA in 1933, despite serious misgivings concerning its potential implications for government regulation of business and for the preservation of the open shop. *Nation's Business*, the official voice of the Chamber, made it clear that the Chamber had supported the NRA with the expectation that it would allow "self-government by industry chiefly through its trade associations, with minimum of government regulation."[35]

By November 1933 the board of directors of the Chamber had become sufficiently concerned with the direction the NRA was taking to commission a secret investigation of the program, and by the following September the Chamber's NRA committee had strongly advocated reforms in the program. The committee recommended that NRA codes be developed only for businesses engaged in interstate commerce, and then only with the voluntary consent of the industry. The president would have the right to approve or veto a code, but he could not impose a code, and he could enforce it only against those who signed the code. Any member of an industry or the industry as a whole would have the right to abrogate a code. In addition, the committee recommended a prohibition on the closed shop and a recognition of the right of labor to deal individually or collectively through any group of their choosing with their employers (an attempt to further legitimate company unions).[36]

Roosevelt's electoral victory in the November elections forced the Chamber to tone down its anti–New Deal rhetoric, but the Chamber did not fundamentally alter its position. In December 1934 the Chamber co-sponsored with the National Association of Manufacturers a national business conference to examine the impact of the early New Deal on business. This conference, which met in White Sulphur Springs, West Virginia, from 17 December to 19 December, brought together about eighty-five prominent business leaders under the chairmanship of C. B. Ames of the Texas Company (Texaco) and included top officers from such firms as the American Sugar Refining Corporation, General Foods Corporation, the Baldwin Locomotive Works, Goodyear Tire and Rubber Corporation, Du Pont de Nemours & Company, Westinghouse Electric and Manufacturing Company, and the General Electric Company, as well as many prominent trade association leaders. The final report of the conference thus clearly reflected the views of many prominent big-

---

35. William Wilson, "Chamber of Commerce," pp. 99, 102.
36. Ibid., p. 104.

business leaders as well as the views of small and medium-sized firms. The participants of the conference recognized that the NRA had conferred some benefits on business, and they were not anxious to return to the earlier days of cutthroat competition. But the disturbing trends toward government control of industry—not only in the NRA but also in legislation regulating banking, the securities market, labor relations, and agriculture— all demanded immediate attention.[37]

Their conference report suggested a moratorium on additional banking regulation, a return to the gold standard, easing the requirements for securities registration and shifting the burden of proof in securities cases to the plaintiff, rejection of the Wagner Act or Black's thirty-hour bill, and the extension of a modified NIRA for only one year. Under the revised NIRA, the president would lose the power to impose a code on a recalcitrant industry, and industry gained the right to terminate unilaterally a code working contrary to their interests. Voluntary codes would still include labor provisions regarding child labor, wages, and hours, but collective bargaining provisions would be modified to include recognition of the right of labor to deal either individually or collectively with employers without intimidation or coercion from either party. Collective action under the auspices of fair trade practice codes was exempted from antitrust prosecution.[38]

The conference proposals for reform focused on the need to preserve the voluntary character of the codes. Only in the few cases of blatant noncompliance should the NRA have recourse to coercion, and then only within the limits defined by due process of law in the courts. In the early days of the NRA, business sentiment had shifted back and forth between the demand for swift enforcement, which was crucial to the success of the codes, and a fear of regimentation, depending on which danger seemed more salient at the time. By the end of 1934, the fear of regimentation overshadowed other concerns. The joint conference of the U.S. Chamber of Commerce and the National Association of Manufacturers concluded:

> Violations should, in the first instance, be adjusted, if possible, by the code authority with the aid, on proof of violation, of the administrative agency, with ultimate resort to judicial process. The government in its purchases should not require compliance certificates of any kind nor discriminate against any person not determined by the due process of law to be violating a code. The use, application or possession of NRA labels or other such emblems or devices should not be required as a condition of the right to manufacture or sell commodities.[39]

37. Ibid., p. 105; *Business Week,* 22 December 1934, pp. 5–6.
38. *Business Week,* 22 December 1934, pp. 5–6. "Recommendations for Revision of the NIRA," NRA Records, RG 9, Entry 6, NIRB L.C. Marshall Official Files, Folder: Recommendation for Revision of the NIRA.
39. Ibid.

Persuaded that the rule of law was a mainstay against arbitrary authority of administrators, business generally sought to eliminate the extralegal appeals to public opinion as an enforcement device that Johnson had been so successful in mobilizing in the early days of the NRA.[40] The emphasis on business autonomy implicit in the preference of business for the courts over administrative agencies was asserted, even though the rights being defended were being abused by less-public-spirited competitors at the expense of the majority of code abiding businessmen. If businessmen had seen the regulatory state as a mechanism for rationalizing capitalism, it would have been necessary to concentrate power in flexible administrative agencies that could use informal techniques of bargaining and enforcement to act quickly. The fact that they chose the slow-moving formality of the courts, which was better suited to protect the rights of private parties from arbitrary government than to administer a complex economy, would suggest that they did not trust government to represent their interests.

By May 1935, only one month before the authorization for the NRA was due to lapse, business' dissatisfaction with the NRA had risen to new heights. The more conservative NAM had always been the least sympathetic to the NRA, and it was now openly opposing Roosevelt's plans for reauthorization. More surprising was the decision of the more moderate U.S. Chamber of Commerce to openly break with the Roosevelt administration and to oppose extension of the present NRA. When in the winter of 1934 a chamber referendum on the continuance of the present NRA had rejected the program by an overwhelming 6 to 1 ratio (1,693 local chambers voted against the NRA, and only 251 local Chambers favored it), even the U.S. Chamber was stirred to vigorous action. Yet despite Chamber hostility to the NRA, the Chamber had not forsaken the cause of industrial self-government. The Chamber recommended that the NRA be replaced by a new and more voluntaristic program along the lines of the Sulphur Spring conference report. These recommendations for a new program of industrial self-government had been approved in the same Chamber referendum by a 4 to 1 ratio of local chambers.

There was actually not a great deal of difference between the Business Advisory Council's position on NRA extension and that of the U.S. Chamber of Commerce. Both insisted that an NRA-type program was desirable, but only one that allowed genuine industrial self-government and was not a pretext for government regulation of business. Both wanted to deprive the U.S. president of the power to impose a code on an industry, and both wanted to establish the right of an industry to abrogate a code that had proved unsatisfactory. However, these fundamental similarities between the two organizations were obscured by the events of May 1935.

40. *Nation's Business*, June 1935, pp. 78–79.

As the annual convention of the U.S. Chamber of Commerce met on 2 May and 3 May, "the atmosphere seemed charged with anti–New Deal sentiment."[41] Henry Harriman was deposed as president of the Chamber because he had not been sufficiently vigorous in criticizing the New Deal, and the Chamber chose the more conservative Harper Sibley to take his place. Prominent members of the Chamber were openly critical of the New Deal. As the dispute between the Chamber and Roosevelt flared up, the BAC hurriedly arranged a meeting with Roosevelt, purportedly to assure him of their continuing support despite his split with the Chamber.[42]

Revisionists who have recognized that the opinion of big business was very influential in the Chamber of Commerce can dismiss this episode only if they resort to the sort of explanation that Ellis Hawley offered for the Chamber of Commerce's dissatisfaction with the New Deal during and after the summer of 1935. According to Hawley, "Through most of these attacks [Chamber attacks on Roosevelt] ran a theme of impending catastrophe and shocked moral outrage, a feeling that was probably rooted much more in a sense of psychological loss *than in reasoned self-interest.* Ideologically the New Deal was tampering with some of the most revered dogmas of the business creed; and psychologically, it was striking at the foundations of business prestige and class security."[43] Yet Hawley's interpretation of the early New Deal assumes that the wounded pride and ideology of the business elite had not been an obstacle to business cooperation with the NRA in 1933, even though Roosevelt had argued during the 1932 campaign that the depression attested to the bankruptcy of business leadership, and even though the NRA was as much an affront to the traditional business creed as later New Deal programs. If they had put aside their pride and ideology to pursue their real economic interests in 1933, why were they failing to do so in 1935?

The attempt to explain business hostility to the New Deal in terms of status rather than interests is problematic for other reasons as well. On other occasions the American left, the breeding ground for revisionist historiography, has emphasized that status and interests are closely linked and that those who prosper are those who win respect. Why should it be different in this context? Furthermore, if the revisionist account of the NRA is accurate, the NRA should have opened up new opportunities for businessmen to acquire status. Businessmen were being called on to participate in industrial self-government. Participation in the administration of a federal program, especially a program as important as the NRA, would enhance rather than detract from status, *unless* business influence in the NRA was considerably less significant than the revisionists have

41. Quoted in William Wilson, "Chamber of Commerce," p. 107.
42. Collins, "Positive Business Responses," p. 372; *New York Times,* 3 May 1935.
43. Hawley, *The New Deal,* p. 154. Emphasis added.

asserted it was. Surely it is more plausible to assume that in 1935 the Chamber of Commerce was repudiating Roosevelt because they had discovered that their economic interests were being jeopardized by the NRA and other early New Deal programs.

Barton Bernstein offers an alternative revisionist account of the split between Roosevelt and the U.S. Chamber of Commerce: "Though the smaller businessmen who filled the ranks of the Chamber of Commerce resented the federal bureaucracy and the benefits to labor and thus criticized NRA, representatives of big business found the agency useful and opposed a return to unrestricted competition. In 1935, members of the Business Advisory Council . . . vigorously endorsed a two-year renewal of NRA."[44] Ronald Radosh supplements Bernstein's argument by also describing the National Association of Manufacturers as an organization of smaller businesses rather than corporate elites. According to Radosh, it is a mistake to identify the "business position" with "local anti-labor and small-town mentality NAM business-types."[45]

The preceding account of the evolution of the business community's response to the NRA makes it clear, however, that the U.S. Chamber of Commerce and the NAM were both heavily influenced by big business. This conclusion is partially confirmed by an observation of Charles Roos, an NRA economist. Roos noted, "The sponsorship of the NIRA by the United States Chamber of Commerce . . . branded the organization from its inception as an ally of big business." Even the NAM, which had generally not attracted members from big business during the 1920s because of its strongly ideological posture, began to undergo a transformation during this era. As big business became increasingly alienated from the New Deal, it became more ideological, and many large firms joined the NAM. Historians who have noted this change in the character of the NAM have argued that the turning point came as early as 1933. This explains the growing membership overlap between the American Liberty League, a group clearly identified with big business, and the NAM.[46]

It would be more plausible to argue that although the Business Advisory Council was united with the Chamber of Commerce and the NAM in their opposition to government controls over industry, the BAC differed from these other organizations in its reluctance to forgo the encouraging steps in the direction of industrial self-government and government-business cooperation that had been taken, however hesitantly, during the NRA. The BAC

44. B. Bernstein, p. 275. Bernstein, however, identifies Henry Harriman (president of the Chamber during all but the final days of the NRA) as a corporate liberal and member of the business elite. If the attitudes of the corporate elite differed from the attitudes of small businessmen as much as Bernstein presumes, and if the Chamber was composed primarily of small businessmen, it is difficult to understand how Harriman could have become president of the Chamber in the first place.

45. Radosh, pp. 156–158.

46. Roos, p. 374; Philip H. Burch, Jr., "The NAM as an Interest Group," *Politics and Society*

believed a conciliatory style would ease Roosevelt toward industrial self-government, while the Chamber, disagreeing with the BAC only with regard to means, and not ends, believed confrontation was essential to compel Roosevelt to take industrial self-government seriously.[47]

The extent to which business elites had become concerned with the policies of the New Deal was suggested even more clearly by the formation of the American Liberty League in August 1934, barely one year after the NRA had gone into operation.[48] The prominent business membership of the American Liberty League conclusively demonstrates that laissez-faire ideas were not confined to a fringe of small businessmen clinging to an outmoded nineteenth-century ideal in a world of large organizations that had bypassed them. Formed to protect traditional constitutional rights, especially the economic rights deemed essential to a free enterprise economy, this organization recruited such political leaders as Al Smith and John W. Davis, both former Democratic presidential candidates, and Jouett Shouse, former chairman of the National Democratic Committee. Within the business community the most prominent leaders of the group were Alfred Sloan and William Knudsen of General Motors and the du Ponts. This weighty group was joined by Ernest Weir of the National Steel Company, Edward Hutton and Colby Chester of General Foods, Sewell Avery of Montgomery Ward, J. Howard Pew of Sun Oil, and others.[49] To the American Liberty League, the NRA exemplified the disturbing trend toward bureaucratic regimentation of the economy and had led the nation into a "quicksand of visionary experimentation."[50]

As different as the ideological-based hostility of the American Liberty League to the New Deal appears from the more pragmatic, accommodating response of the BAC, they had many shared goals. Had that not been the case, it would be difficult to explain how Alfred Sloan and Pierre du Pont, both of whom had been original members of the BAC, could have so soon afterward become charter members of the American Liberty League. The American Liberty League condemned programs like the NRA, which were leading to government regimentation of business, and it called for a return to sound traditional principles, yet even the American Liberty League would have been willing to support a temporary one-year extension of the NRA to allow businesses to gradually readjust to a free market environment if the most objectionable features of government control were removed. The BAC was also extremely critical of New Deal

---

4 (1974); Alfred S. Cleveland, "NAM: Spokesman for Industry?" *Harvard Business Review* 26 (1948); Richard W. Gable, "NAM: Influential Lobby or Kiss of Death?" *Journal of Politics* 15 (1953).

47. Schlesinger, *The Politics of Upheaval*, p. 271.

48. Frederick Rudolph, "The American Liberty League, 1934–1940," *American Historical Review* 56 (1950): 19–23.

49. Ibid., pp. 21–22.

50. Schlesinger, *The Politics of Upheaval*, p. 518.

attempts to regiment business, and by the summer of 1935 many prominent BAC members were resigning from the agency in protest over New Deal economic policies.[51]

If there was far more big-business opposition to the NRA than can be explained by the revisionist theory, there was also far more "peripheral" business support for the NRA than the revisionists have led us to expect. The term "peripheral" has been chosen to denote small and medium-sized firms that lack many of the competitive advantages that big businesses have. Peripheral firms are generally labor intensive and "managerially thin."[52] They are typically not vertically integrated firms, and they generally make decisions based on a limited time horizon. They focus on short-term profits rather than long-term growth. Even firms that become fairly large in terms of the number of workers they employ can remain peripheral firms if the character of the firm remains traditional and they fail to develop any oligopolistic power over their market. Bituminous coal and textiles are classic examples of industries in which almost all the firms, including the largest, are peripheral.[53]

Peripheral firms differ markedly from center firms, the firms that have hitherto been referred to as big business.[54] Center firms are capital intensive, technologically advanced, and enjoy significant economies of scale. They have well-developed managerial structures and are more likely to take a long-term perspective regarding growth and profits. They are generally vertically integrated. Finally, center firms have often established at least some oligopolistic control over at least one of the markets in which they compete. Steel and automobiles were industries dominated by large, modern corporations that have developed some oligopolistic control over their respective markets. The larger firms in the petroleum industry are also center firms, for they are vertically integrated, capital intensive firms that have developed significant oligopolistic power in at least refining and pipelines, although production and gasoline retailing remained highly competitive markets with a large number of peripheral independent firms.

51. Collins, "Positive Business Responses," p. 372.

52. McCraw, "Rethinking the Trust Question," p. 18.

53. For the peripheral character of firms in the coal industry, see J. Johnson, p. 13. Textiles was a leading sector in the nineteenth-century industrial revolution, but by the twentieth century it was a relative laggard. The financial and management techniques that firms in this sector relied on well into the twentieth century were traditional, compared with those developed by the twentieth-century center firms. Attempts to produce large, vertically integrated textile firms by merger during the merger wave at the beginning of the twentieth century had failed almost uniformly. For similar reasons the coal industry was an industry of peripheral firms. Referring to the firms in an industry as "peripheral" does not suggest that the industry was marginal in terms of the size of its total market. The textile and coal industries were both among the "big ten" industries targeted by Johnson for early NRA codes because of their importance in the economy. See Chandler, pp. 67–72, 90, 248–249, 340; Galambos, *Competition and Cooperation*, pp. 18–20; J. Johnson, p. 13.

54. McCraw, "Rethinking the Trust Question," pp. 17–18.

The use of the terms "peripheral" and "center" to refer to large and heterogeneous categories of businesses does not imply that firms in those categories are necessarily united by shared economic interests. Small firms have often been pitted against medium-sized firms. Peripheral firms in competitive markets often have very different interests from peripheral firms in oligopolistic markets. Firms in different economic sectors often have conflicting economic interests. Indeed, the most characteristic form of conflict in regulatory politics is probably a coalition of center and peripheral firms opposing another coalition of center and peripheral firms. Nevertheless, peripheral firms have at times perceived a shared interest in restraining the economic and political power of center firms, and this perceived interest has at times shaped political alignments. Because progressive elites have also distinguished the interests of small business and big business (the treatment of medium-sized firms has often depended on whether they are relatively large within their industry or whether they are dwarfed by the yet larger central firms), conflict between peripheral and central businesses has generally been more significant during reform eras.

Peripheral firms were at the forefront of the business lobby that supported an extension of the NRA. The Industry and Business Committee for NRA Extension, a group established to coordinate business lobbying on behalf of the NRA, was spearheaded by peripheral firms in the textile, apparel, and retail sectors.[55] With bankruptcy a real prospect for so many in these industries, even NRA regimentation looked acceptable if it would provide some relief for producers. Strong support for an extension of at least a modified NRA, preferably along the lines recommended by the Business Advisory Council, also came from the Consumer Goods Committee of the NRA. George Sloan, chairman of the committee and executive director of the Cotton Textiles Institute as well, wrote to President Roosevelt on 5 May 1935 to inform him of the support of "the great majority of consumer goods manufacturing industries" based on a survey of more than 200 code authorities by the Consumer Goods Committee. This constituency included some oligopolistic industries (the tobacco and chemical industries were represented on the Consumer Goods

55. In describing a conference held by the Industry and Business Committee for NRA Extension to Senator William King, the group described itself as "made up principally of medium and small businessmen" representing a wide variety of trade associations. This claim is quite plausible because some of this group's most prominent spokesmen, including its president, Ward Cheney, were in the textile industry, where center firms had failed to establish themselves. Moreover, the group's notoriety came from a business march on Washington in support of the NRA on 22 May, 1935. This tactic was more likely to be associated with peripheral businesses than with the leaders of center firms. Some 1,500 businessmen participated in the pilgrimage to Washington, and 400 of them were New York merchants in the men's clothing and apparel trades. See "Telegram to Senator William King," 20 May 1935, Roosevelt Papers, OF 466, Box 10, NRA Misc., May 1935; *Business Week*, 30 March 1935, p. 36; ibid., 25 May 1935, p. 18. *New York Times*, 20 March and 23 May 1935.

Committee), but industries composed primarily if not exclusively of peripheral firms in the consumer goods sector outnumbered industries dominated by center firms during the New Deal, and the fact that a "great majority" of the 200 code authorities surveyed supported the NRA undoubtedly indicates substantial peripheral support for an NRA-type program.[56] That Sloan's "great majority" probably refers primarily to peripheral industries is suggested by Sloan's additional observation concerning the source of industry opposition to the NRA. "That minority objection from my observation," noted Sloan, "usually comes not from those in the highly competitive industries but rather from those engaged in industries which by reason of the large size of the relatively few units comprising the industry or other circumstances are better able to prevent the effects of cut throat competition without the aid of the recovery act."[57]

Further evidence bearing on the constituencies served by the NRA can be gleaned from an examination of the pattern of industrial legislation that was enacted to replace the NRA after the NRA was declared unconstitutional. A number of troubled industries lobbied Congress and state legislatures after the demise of the NRA, requesting special legislation that would recreate "little NRAs" (a reference to the similarity of the anticompetitive devices in the NRA with those in the special legislation) for their industry. Some of these efforts were successful. The outstanding example of this at the federal level was in bituminous coal, where the Guffey coal acts facilitated cartelization of coal industry after the demise of the NRA.[58] The cotton textile industry, the lumber industry, the apparel trades, and anthracite coal all attempted to secure similar legislation and failed.[59] In several cases, states stepped in where the federal government refused to tread. In Wisconsin, a state with a well-developed progressive heritage, a "little NRA" law allowed codes of fair trade competition in the cleaning and dyeing, barber, beauty parlor, shoe repair, and bowling trades.[60] Virtually all these attempts to revive NRA protections occurred in peripheral industries.[61] They were generally "attempts by small businessmen to enlist the power of the state and use it to solve the problems of some particular trade or alleviate conditions in a particularly depressed area."[62]

---

56. George Sloan to Hugh Johnson, 15 March 1934, Roosevelt Papers, OF 466, No. 6, NRA Codes, Misc. 1933.

57. George Sloan to FDR, 5 May 1935, Roosevelt Papers, OF 466, No. 3, NRA, May–June 1935.

58. Hawley, *The New Deal*, pp. 205–212.

59. Ibid., pp. 220–224.

60. Ibid., p. 264.

61. At the national level, cotton textiles, lumber, and apparel were all highly competitive industries, although anthracite coal was more oligopolistic. See J. Johnson, p. 18.

62. Hawley, *The New Deal*, p. 263. Hawley, however, believes that some oligopolistic firms also had an interest in recreating the NRA. Consideration of that issue is beyond the scope of this

Our analysis of the pattern of business support and opposition for the extension of the NRA would appear to support a theory diametrically opposed to the revisionist theory. Big business, composed of center firms, was almost uniformly opposed to the ways in which the NRA had allowed government to regulate business more extensively, and it consistently sought reforms that would have moved the NRA toward industrial self-government, although the means it chose to pursue this goal varied considerably, from organizations like the BAC to organizations like the American Liberty League. On the other hand, peripheral firms provided the strongest support for the NRA, and although they would also have preferred that the NRA evolve more in the direction of industrial self-government, they were often more willing to countenance government regulation than center firms were.

This analysis of the constituencies of the NRA would make sense if the NRA is, as we have suggested, a progressive program. A recurrent strand of progressive thought has been a suspicion of big business and, obversely, a special concern to protect the interests of small businesses. Furthermore, this progressive concern is clearly evident in the administration of the program. The New Dealers worked assiduously to see that small-business interests were represented in the NRA. Fearful that a reliance on trade associations to draft the codes of fair trade competition would grant larger firms an undesirable amount of control, Johnson insisted that proposed codes be submitted to public hearings that included representatives of small firms. On several occasions he used his authority to uphold provisions demanded by those interests.[63] Code authorities were established as administrative bodies distinct from trade associations to supervise the codes, and the NRA generally insisted that these bodies be representative of all business interests, including those of small business, within an industry.[64]

Weighing against this conclusion, however, is the fact that there was considerable peripheral business opposition to the NRA. To cite a single example, locally based cleaners and dyers found their NRA code unworkable, and many came to prefer free market competition to the NRA.[65] Even a theory asserting that peripheral businesses were the intended constituencies of the NRA would require substantial refinement to allow us to account for a host of intervening variables that have sometimes operated to alienate peripheral firms from the NRA despite the best efforts of the New Dealers and that on other occasions have made center firms more receptive to the NRA than would be anticipated.

book, but his account of such an "attempt" in the petroleum industry is rendered questionable by the history of the oil code provided in Chapter 7.

63. Lyon et al., pp. 83–84.
64. Ibid., pp. 100–101, 206.
65. Hawley, *The New Deal*, pp. 97–98.

CHAPTER 6

Peripheral Businesses:
The Dissatisfied Constituency

Searching for the historical events that led up to the creation of the NRA, historians have frequently noted the significance of the vigorous trade association movement that arose during the 1920s.[1] What has less frequently been noted is that this movement was predominantly a response to the needs of peripheral businesses. The impulse to organize competitive markets had never been exclusively associated with major corporations, and the more the economic landscape came to be populated with large corporations and oligopolistic industries, the greater the incentives for peripheral businesses to get organized as well. Thus, for example, one of the most important goals of trade associations in the 1920s was the development of open pricing systems, a device that was more critical in decentralized, competitive markets, where information was inaccessible, than in oligopolistic markets, where informal exchanges of information could suffice to keep firms abreast of the prices of their competitors. Trade associations also became critical when firm size was too small to support such activities as research or data collection and analysis, but the activities could be supported on a collective basis. By the 1920s, large firms in oligopolistic markets had either already organized into associations or had less need for trade associations because many functions performed by trade associations were being handled within the large firm or by informal understandings among a few competitors.[2]

Herbert Hoover's efforts in the 1920s to use the Commerce Department as a catalyst for the organization of trade associations in all sectors of the economy was directed particularly at industries with peripheral firms. Hoover was convinced that the development of an extensive network of trade associations would help rationalize market competition and alleviate

1. Hawley, "Herbert Hoover...," pp. 131–148.
2. J. Q. Wilson, *Political Organizations*, p. 146.

some of the pressures toward more extensive forms of economic integration and more radical attempts to eliminate competition altogether.[3] Hoover's efforts did win the support of many peripheral businesses, but despite that support the trade association movement disappointed those who had hoped it would usher in a new and more humane form of capitalism. Trade associations lacked the organizational resources to rationalize markets significantly or to mitigate the severe competition that plagued some markets. Some trade association activities ran afoul of antitrust laws, and others could do little more than exhort members to observe limits on production levels or on the number of shifts they ran their machines. The economic incentives for members to cheat on such voluntary agreements, especially in markets with many firms, were so great that they rarely stabilized markets for very long.[4] Unhampered market forces continued to take their toll of peripheral businesses, and the appeal of more-radical measures to limit competition persisted.

In the 1920s, trade associations generally lobbied for a revision of antitrust statutes to enhance their organizational power.[5] This was an issue that could unite center firms, who were concerned about antitrust prosecution for monopolistic practices, and peripheral firms, who feared antitrust prosecution for cartelization. Even though the courts had developed a more flexible approach to antitrust enforcement through the use of the "rule of reason" in examining cooperative business behavior, statutory revision was still necessary to allow trade associations to undertake the more extensive stabilizing activities that most believed were necessary to save countless peripheral firms from bankruptcy.

With the advent of the depression, the problems that peripheral firms and their trade associations faced became far more severe, and more radical measures seemed necessary. Although these groups did not abandon the ideal of industrial self-government, they became increasingly receptive to a more-extensive role for government in stabilizing markets, and a program like the NRA, which mixed industrial self-government with government regulation, was an attractive hybrid. The possibility of using the coercive powers of the state to bring uncooperative "price chiselers" into line appealed greatly to the organizationally disadvantaged, who had no other means to effect market stabilization.[6] Ironically, the history of the NRA would demonstrate that government coercion could not bring about market stability where the organizational infrastructure for industrial self-government was missing.

3. Hawley, "Herbert Hoover...," p. 132.
4. Galambos, *Competition and Cooperation*, pp. 126–130, 135.
5. Himmelberg, pp. 76–85.
6. Lyon et al., p. 92; Galambos, *Competition and Cooperation*; J. Johnson's *Politics of Soft Coal* (pp. 197–204) shows the same was true for at least some peripheral bituminous coal operators.

Peripheral businesses were generally enthusiastic about the NRA because progressive political elites were insistent that the NRA provide relief for these businesses. New Dealers took extensive precautions to assure that these firms were represented in the code drafting process and on the code authorities that would administer the codes so that their interests would be protected.[7] When peripheral firms complained that big business was dominating the NRA codes despite these steps, Roosevelt and Johnson redoubled their efforts to protect the interests of peripheral businesses. In January 1934, Roosevelt issued an executive order that allowed a small businessman to appeal to the Federal Trade Commission if he was dissatisfied with the NRA disposition of his case.[8] Appeal to the FTC would add yet another protection for small business, for the FTC had been created to protect peripheral firms from unfair competition of center firms.[9]

In some cases these progressive efforts to protect peripheral firms were successful, and some of the NRA's strongest supporters were from these NRA constituencies. In other cases, attempts to aid these businesses went awry. NRA economist Charles Roos concluded: "It thus appears that the NRA made many earnest special efforts to assist small enterprise through special code provisions. Some of these definitely fulfilled their purpose; others proved to be of uncertain value; and still others actually hurt one group of small businesses while benefiting another."[10] By 1935 many in this business class had also turned against the NRA, joining with their big-business colleagues to vent their anger toward the NRA and the early New Deal through organizations like the U.S. Chamber of Commerce. This attempt to bite the progressive hand that was feeding them is paradoxical, but the paradox can be resolved when the causes of peripheral firm dissatisfaction with the NRA are examined in more detail.

Why Peripheral Firms Turned against the NRA

Revisionist historians have argued that peripheral firms became disillusioned with the NRA because the administration of the program was controlled by center firms.[11] These firms used the NRA to advance their interests at the expense of the smaller and less-well-organized peripheral firms. It is true that some periphery firms objected to the NRA on these grounds, although the instances of this are far less pervasive than the revisionists have assumed. More important, in many cases such objections

7. Lyon et al., pp. 84, 91, 101.
8. Hawley, *The New Deal*, p. 84.
9. Thomas McCraw, *Prophets of Regulation* (Cambridge, Mass., 1984), chap. 3.
10. Roos, p. 408.
11. B. Bernstein, p. 269.

were ill-founded, based on serious misconceptions about the operations of the NRA. Frequently big business was simply a convenient scapegoat for small business confronting problems that had nothing to do with oligarchical power and its oppression of peripheral businesses.

There were many reasons that peripheral businesses did not do as well under the NRA as they had hoped they would. Peripheral firms became hostile to the NRA in part as a reaction to the failure of the NRA to bring about business prosperity. The depression had hit these firms even harder than it had hit their larger competitors, and a return of full economic prosperity was essential to their economic well-being.[12] They judged the NRA based on its consequences, not its intentions, and when the NRA failed to deliver on its promise of economic recovery, the fact that it had attempted structural reforms of the economy that were meant to protect peripheral businesses from the unfair trade practices of center firms could not compensate for sluggish economic conditions.

Furthermore, the NRA had been sold to the public as Roosevelt's most important recovery program, yet it had failed to address one of the most important economic problems confronting peripheral firms—their credit crunch.[13] When Roosevelt's attempt to deal with this problem through the Reconstruction Finance Corporation (RFC) proved totally inadequate, peripheral firms became disenchanted—not just with the RFC but also with the entire early New Deal, and particularly with the most visible symbol of the early New Deal—the NRA.

Even where the NRA genuinely hurt the interests of peripheral businesses, it did not necessarily do so because it favored the interests of center firms. A fundamental goal of the NRA was to increase employment by shortening the work day and to increase purchasing power by putting more money in the hands of workers. The implementation of this policy placed a heavier burden on peripheral firms, whose costs rose disproportionately because they were more labor intensive, putting them at a competitive disadvantage vis-à-vis less-labor-intensive larger firms.[14] Hugh Johnson pointed out that the most frequent request of small businessmen hostile to the operation of the codes were for exemption from the wages and hours provisions of the code, not for exemption from the fair trade practices provisions that many critics of the NRA had pinpointed as the source of monopoly power.[15] Various forms of price stabilization prevented center firms from taking full advantage of their diminishing relative costs, an outcome that was in part justified because the competitive advantage of center firms was intensified as a by-product of government policy, but the

12. Roos, pp. 374–375, 388–394.
13. Charles Roos believes that the failure of the early New Deal to address the credit problem adequately is its most serious failing vis-à-vis small business. Ibid., p. 415.
14. Ibid., pp. 395–402.
15. H. Johnson, p. 274.

NRA would not intervene to save firms that had survived previously only because they paid sweatshop wages.[16] The New Deal constituencies included both labor and peripheral businesses, and when the interests of these two groups diverged, as they frequently did, the New Deal sometimes advanced the interests of the former at the expense of the interests of the latter.

Peripheral firms were being squeezed during the early New Deal. The NRA had imposed heavier costs on them, but also, at least with regard to labor costs, those costs were disproportionately heavier than the costs imposed on more capital intensive larger firms. On the other hand, the NRA had failed to rectify the credit crunch, which bore more heavily on peripheral firms. This squeeze, however, had nothing to do with the way the NRA was administered. The NRA had not been authorized by Congress to deal with the credit situation, and it was just as clearly simply carrying out its congressional mandate in raising wages and limiting the maximum hours labor could work.[17] When this added to the woes of peripheral firms, NRA administrators bore the brunt of peripheral-firm anger, which should have been directed toward Congress and the president.

Just as NRA efforts to help labor sometimes harmed peripheral businesses, so NRA efforts to help some peripheral businesses sometimes rebounded to the disadvantage of other peripheral businesses. Peripheral businesses were not a homogeneous constituency, and policies that limited competition may have kept firms afloat in one sector, but often at the expense of other peripheral businesses, which had to purchase materials from these businesses at artificially inflated prices. Hardest hit were industries facing an extremely elastic consumer demand curve.[18] These were the grounds, for instance, that provoked Representative Henry Luckey of Nebraska to complain to President Roosevelt on behalf of his constituents, "The N.R.A. has retarded rather than aided recovery." As a representative from a farming state, Luckey was no doubt poorly disposed toward the NRA, since farmers resented higher prices for manufactured goods, but he also objected to the NRA because it had been detrimental to the construction industry in his state by raising prices to the point where "it had practically stopped the building of homes." Although Luckey went on in a good

16. Roos, pp. 87, 403.

17. Nor can the congressional failure be attributed to congressional deference to center firms, for many executives of center firms had argued that government-subsidized loans to industry were imperative. Such arguments (e.g., the Warburg proposal; see Chapter 3) had been rejected by a cost-conscious Congress.

18. A concern with the rising prices of raw materials as a result of cartelization in industries appears to have been especially important for some of the peripheral industries that helped organize the Committee for Elimination of Price-Fixing and Production Control in February 1935 to oppose extension of the NRA. The furniture and carpet industries joined because they were affected by the anticompetitive NRA codes in the lumber and textile sectors. These were cases of struggles between peripheral industries, not struggles between peripheral firms and center firms. Hawley, *The New Deal*, p. 122.

populist fashion to argue that the NRA had discriminated against the small businessman "to the advantage of a rapidly growing, monopolistic group of big business concerns," the higher prices he cited could as easily have been due to the cartelization of peripheral businesses as to the growth of monopoly.[19]

Consistent with progressivism, the New Dealers sought to limit only specific abuses of corporate power, without denying center firms the fruits of successful competition on the basis of economic efficiency. Peripheral firms were to be given every chance to prove they could compete efficiently with center firms in a fair contest. But peripheral firms were not always satisfied with such modest goals. Easily persuaded that every center firm advantage was the result of market power rather than efficiency, many peripheral firms wanted the codes to go much further toward protecting even high-cost, inefficient producers.[20] Once government had decided to intervene in the market, its willingness to let some peripheral firms go under provided additional ammunition for NRA opponents, who sought to discredit it by portraying it as the tool of big business.

Ineffective enforcement of many codes contributed significantly to the growing revolt of peripheral firms against the NRA. In the latter days of the NRA, the New England Council conducted a survey of New England businesses and requested suggestions for revisions of the NRA. The most frequently listed suggestion was "improved enforcement."[21] A similar survey by the Southern States Industrial Council concluded, "There seems to be a great deal of disappointment in the way enforcement has been and is now handled."[22] Cautious NRA administrators were hesitant to evoke legal penalties except in clear-cut cases where the government hoped to be sustained by the courts.[23] Because NRA regulation had the best chance of being upheld in a case unambiguously involving interstate commerce, and because some of the most questionable code provisions (i.e., price-fixing provisions) occurred in codes that governed predominantly peripheral firms, the Department of Justice seems to have been more leery of enforcing codes against these firms. Thus the Justice Department withdrew its complaint in the Belcher case, a case involving the lumber code, because of its weaknesses as a test case, an action that incensed many code abiding businessmen in this industry of peripheral firms.[24]

19. Henry Luckey to FDR, 15 February 1935, Roosevelt Papers, PPF 777, No. 1, NRA, 1933–41.

20. The attempt of independent oil producers to institute price-fixing through the oil code, discussed in the next chapter, illustrates this tendency.

21. *New England News Letter*, Supplement, May 1935, Roosevelt Papers, PPF 1820, Box 18, Folder: Speech Material, Schechter, p. 4.

22. Southern States Industrial Council (SSIC), "What Should Be the Future of NRA," NRA Records, RG 9, entry 6, NIRB L.C. Marshall Official Files D, NIRA Continuance File, p. 4.

23. Lyon et al., p. 268; Peter Irons, *The New Deal Lawyers* (Princeton, 1982), pp. 35–41.

24. Hawley, *The New Deal*, pp. 127–128; Irons, pp. 79–82.

A poorly enforced code generally made businesses worse off than they would have been without any code by putting the majority of law abiding firms at a competitive disadvantage with less-scrupulous rivals, who could evade either the higher labor costs of code adherence or win business away from honest competitors through some form of discount that the code disallowed as an unfair trade practice. Codes in such service areas as cleaning and dyeing, restaurants, and hotels provided the worst examples of enforcement breakdown, and these were codes for industries with peripheral firms and highly competitive markets. Ironically, this dissatisfaction was rooted in the absence of an oligarchical industrial structure rather than its presence. In fact, peripheral businesses in an industry dominated by giants may have been generally better off, because the giants provided the organizational infrastructure necessary for stability, while the NRA assured that the giants would not use their strength to the disadvantage of their smaller rivals. In some cases, business dissatisfaction with codes suffering an enforcement breakdown became so strong that NRA administrators were forced to discontinue their fair trade practice codes, although the NRA continued to demand adherence to minimal labor requirements.[25] Businesses in these areas could hardly be sympathetic to a program that had imposed higher labor costs while failing to mitigate competition.

Peripheral industries did not have a structural basis conducive to cooperation, and this competitive reality could not be overcome even by a legally enforceable code. *Nation's Business,* the voice of the Chamber of Commerce, expressed a particularly cynical view. "In industries which have had a high development of the cooperative spirit, the agreements will work fairly well. These are the industries which did not need NRA. In industries which have had poor internal cooperation, the voluntary agreements will not work. These needed the NRA, but had never succeeded in enforcing their codes anyway."[26] The success of a code was often directly related not only to industrial structure but also to previous organizational history. A history of associative activity prepared individualist firms for the cooperative effort of the NRA and supplied industry leadership with the requisite organizational skills to administer a code. In the absence of skilled leadership, some highly competitive industries adopted overly ambitious codes, often including the strongest price stabilization provisions, which proved unenforceable. Nothing short of a huge enforcement division could have coped with the compliance problems posed by these industries, and such regimentation was offensive to business and government alike.[27]

25. Hawley, *The New Deal,* pp. 98, 114–115; *Business Week,* 9 March 1935, p. 7.
26. *Nation's Business,* July 1935, p. 34.
27. Lyon et al., p. 111; *Business Week,* 20 October 1934, p. 22.

Finally, peripheral businesses often found the regulatory apparatus of the NRA oppressive. Code authorities were expensive to run, and peripheral businesses that were financially hard-pressed often found code assessments burdensome.[28] Many peripheral businesses complained that the NRA "tends toward bureaucracy" and that "the small business man has little time to familiarize himself with the complicated rules and regulations which change frequently."[29] Because this frequently observed consequence of government regulation is characteristic even of programs that attempt to aid peripheral firms, the fact that it was a source of peripheral business dissatisfaction with the NRA can hardly be attributed to the dominance of the NRA by center firms.

The "Spokesmen" of Small Business

As the dissatisfaction of peripheral businesses with the NRA grew, their cause was taken up by those progressives in Congress who had never been sympathetic to the anticompetitive thrust of the NRA. Senators Nye and Borah were the most outspoken of the dissident progressives. Nye began Senate discussions of the NRA with the accusation that price-fixing under the NRA was a monopolistic device that benefited big business at the expense of small businessmen, the same charge the revisionists would take up nearly thirty years later.[30] He vastly exaggerated the monopolistic trends that could be attributed to the NRA, in part because he confused monopolies and cartels. Nye failed to note that cartels could and often did save relatively inefficient smaller firms by artificially raising prices to a point where they could make a profit. Ironically, a great deal of the dissatisfaction of peripheral firms with the NRA arose not because the NRA was trying to limit competition but because it was ineffective in enforcing anticompetitive provisions.

Revisionist Ellis Hawley succinctly summarized (and approved of) the economic logic that lay behind Nye's attack on NRA price-fixing provisions:

A study of the codes as a whole could only conclude that most of the price clauses were directed against price cutting by "little fellows." In numerous industries the advantage of large firms lay not so much in the area of price as it did in non-price fields, in such matters as advertising, access to credit, ability to conduct research, control of patents, and attraction of the best managerial talent. Small firms often existed only because they offered lower

28. Some 40 percent of all small-business complaints to the NRA had to do with code assessments. See "The Status of Small Enterprises Under Auspices of the National Recovery Administration," Richberg Papers, Box 45, Memo, 22–25 May 1935, p. 2.

29. Henry Luckey to FDR, 15 February 1935, Roosevelt Papers, PPF 777, No. 1, NRA, 1933–41.

30. Hawley, *The New Deal*, p. 81.

prices to offset consumer preference for advertised brands, prices sometimes made possible by lower wage rates, sometimes by more favorable location, sometimes by other advantages arising out of specialization or recapitalization. It was in the interest of larger firms, therefore, to eliminate price and wage differentials and wipe out the special advantages that made them possible.[31]

Hawley, more even-handed than New Deal critics like Nye, does acknowledge that these conditions did not apply to all industries and that Hugh Johnson could justly claim to have aided smaller producers by raising prices in such highly competitive industries as bituminous coal, cotton textiles, retail trade, and the needle trades.[32] But Hawley justifies his general conclusion by characterizing these industries as exceptions. No evidence is given for this assertion.

Hawley's own description of the advantages of larger corporations in the "nonprice" field suggests factors that would equally convey advantages in price competition. If larger firms enjoyed an advantage in price competition, the anticompetitive provisions of NRA codes would aid small business by artificially raising prices to a point where even relatively inefficient smaller firms could make a profit and by preventing larger firms from exploiting a competitive advantage.[33] Under these circumstances, price-fixing could convey a decisive competitive advantage to peripheral firms. Where center firms had offered lower prices to consumers but peripheral firms had been able to compete by offering more-convenient or extensive services, price-fixing was particularly disadvantageous to center firms. Even if the codes tried to limit competition in services as well as price, which they often did by attempting to standardize services accompanying sales, standardization of services is intrinsically more difficult to achieve than standardization of prices.

In fact, countless peripheral firms were saved from bankruptcy during this period,[34] and this is why the relationship between NRA cartelization

31. Ibid., p. 83.
32. Ibid.
33. One example of this situation was in tobacco retailing. An independent tobacco retailer wrote to Roosevelt: "As a result of price-fixing, you have been established as the greatest man ever known in American history, so far as the retail tobacco industry is concerned." This retailer noted that, prior to the NRA code, large retailers and chains were using cigars and cigarettes as loss leaders and driving retail tobacco dealers out of business. These larger firms had opposed retail price-fixing: "As you know, there has been intensive propaganda, particularly by representatives of R. H. Macy & Company and the A&P, to eliminate price-fixing from the tobacco industry." Howard S. Cullman to FDR, 16 January 1935, Roosevelt Papers, OF 466, No. 6, NRA Codes, 1933–35, T–W.
34. The NRA presented data showing that in 1934 a smaller proportion of small businesses failed than in any year since 1921 and that economic concentration was not increasing under the NRA. See Schlesinger, *The Coming of the New Deal*, p. 170; "Report of Executive Secretary of the Excutive Council to the President," 21 August 1934, Richberg Papers, Box 48, NRA General No. 2.

and NRA progressivism is so difficult to determine. On the one hand, progressives did want to aid peripheral businesses and were reluctant to destroy cooperative business agreements that served this end. On the other hand, they had broader responsibilities to promote economic growth and to protect consumers, goals that were jeopardized by cartelization. Progressives tried to weave a middle path between extremes. They simultaneously tried to prevent cartels and to limit price increases associated with the NRA while trying to allow businessmen to cooperate more effectively so that more peripheral firms could be kept afloat. This proved to be a case where the middle path simply was not a viable option.

Nye's attacks on NRA price-fixing were seconded by Senator Borah, who asserted that his office had received complaints from more than 9,000 small businessmen.[35] As the self-appointed spokesmen for small business, both called for a revival of antitrust enforcement and greater competition. Actually, Hugh Johnson and the NRA could with equal plausibility claim to speak for small businessmen. The NRA files are filled with letters from small businessmen thanking Johnson and President Roosevelt for saving the little man. For example, the Jessop Steel Company wrote to Senator Pat Harrison, chairman of the Senate Finance Committee, favoring an extension of the NRA: "Our company is a very small one. We make only the so-called Jewelry of the steel business—tool steel and stainless steels, and similar grades, but the NRA has been a life saver to us." The company also noted that, although the large manufacturers continued to wield more influence than the small ones, "this has been held in check under the NRA."[36] Nye and Borah did not understand that small-business praise of competition usually meant regulated competition that prevented larger firms from driving out smaller firms, nor did they understand that the NRA fulfilled this demand for some industries.

Nye and Borah tried to buttress their case against the NRA by calling for investigations of the program. Borah introduced a resolution calling on the FTC to investigate price-fixing in the steel and oil industries. Eventually Franklin Roosevelt and Hugh Johnson agreed to authorize an independent investigation of the NRA under the direction of Clarence Darrow.[37] Darrow's investigation confirmed the charges that Nye and Borah had been leveling at the NRA, but his study was slipshod and extremely biased. According to Charles Roos:

35. Hawley, *The New Deal*, p. 81.

36. Jessop Steel Company to Senator Pat Harrison, 22 March 1935, NRA Records, RG 9, Entry 267 Approved Code Histories: Iron and Steel, Box 7574.

37. Johnson later characterized his decision to permit Darrow to head the investigation as a "moment of total aberration," but it was characteristic of his style of administration. Johnson administered the NRA in a "goldfish bowl" of virtually unfettered publicity, confident that the public and even his critics would take a sympathetic view of the NRA once they had all the facts before them. Before the Darrow Commission was established, Senator Nye proposed to Johnson the creation of a board like the National Labor Board to study complaints that the codes "permit

Unfortunately the board made little or no attempt to investigate the justness of charges, failing to call rebuttal witnesses and not even troubling itself to ask deputies for transcripts of hearings on the codes. . . . Although the NRA had a section of over fifty people studying the operation of the coal agreements, the board condemned the retail solid fuel code without even making contact. Despite the fact that an internationally recognized specialist on cartels had spent considerable time studying monopolistic code provisions, the board alleged widespread monopoly without attempting to examine his material. In view of these considerations it is difficult to avoid the conclusion that the board consisted largely of men with preconceived opinions about NRA code operation, determined to make these public at any cost.[38]

Roos's criticisms of the Darrow Commission appear to be well justified. The report was heavily ideological in tone and plagued with internal contradictions. Arthur Schlesinger noted that the report in one place declared, "All competition is savage, wolfish and relentless; and can be nothing else," and yet then went on to call for a restoration of competition through stricter enforcement of antitrust laws.[39] The report charged that small enterprises had been "cruelly oppressed" under the steel and motion picture codes, yet the motion picture code was one of the most notable cases where the NRA had compelled revisions in trade practices that benefited smaller firms.[40] It had asserted that, among the codes it examined, only the cleaning and dyeing code was free from "monopolistic practices," although the NRA was faulted even with regard to this code for failing to enforce it. Ironically, the cleaning and dyeing code had one of the most flagrant price-fixing provisions of any NRA code.

---

monopolies and oppress small enterprises," and he recommended that Johnson "invite such anti-monopolists as Senators Borah and LaFollette to serve on it." Johnson reported himself "100 percent." in favor of the idea, and even Roosevelt noted "Excellent idea—go ahead & put it through" (Memo, 12 December 1933, Roosevelt Papers, OF 466, No. 6, NRA Codes, Misc., 1933). Subsequently an Industrial Appeals Board was created to handle small business complaints.

38. Roos, p. 409. Roos's opinion of the Darrow Commission is particularly weighty because he was the principal economist and director of research on policy matters for the NRA from July 1933 until September 1934 and because he was a strong critic of the anticompetitive tendencies of the NRA. His conclusions are basically seconded by Arthur Schlesinger, who characterized the investigation as "random, slapdash and prejudiced" and the report as "no measured appraisal of the program" (Schlesinger, *The Coming of the New Deal*, p. 133). A similar conclusion emerges from an FTC report on the condition of Southern sawmills. This report was the product of an FTC investigation requested by the NRA after the Darrow Commission cited the plight of these sawmills as evidence for the pro–big business orientation of the NRA. The FTC, which was frequently critical of the anticompetitive effects of NRA codes, concluded that the Darrow Commission was mistaken and that these small mills had benefited greatly from their code. See *Business Week*, 28 July 1934, p. 12.

39. Schlesinger, *The Coming of the New Deal*, p. 133.

40. Hawley, *The New Deal*, p. 96. The NRA code had altered trade practices in the motion picture industry through provisions that allowed the smaller exhibitors to reject some of the films the larger distributors attempted to force on them and by limiting the use of exclusive dealing

One of the six members of the Darrow Commission resigned during its initial investigations, and another issued a minority report that accused the commission of sloppy research and analysis. Clearly ideological bias rather than dispassionate analysis of facts shaped the conclusions of the Darrow Commission's report. To the report had been attached a supplement— signed by Darrow and William O. Thompson, who had been Darrow's former law partner—which asserted that unregulated competition was impossible and that "the choice is between monopoly sustained by government, which is clearly the trend in the NRA; and a planned economy, which demands socialized ownership and control."[41] Thompson subsequently became the second member of the Darrow Commission to resign when the commission was preparing its second report on the NRA, a report that was more favorable than the first because the NRA had begun to support pro-competitive reforms by this point. In resigning, Thompson warned that the trend of the NRA was toward monopoly and fascism. He insisted that the NRA was "an attempt of the capitalists to find a way out of the crisis," and the only alternative to fascism he recognized was "a government by workers and farmers" that "can plan production, produce goods for use and not profit, eliminate profit and raise the standard of living of the entire population."[42]

Despite the weaknesses of the Darrow Commission's report, the findings were extremely damaging to the NRA. The report reinforced both congressional critics of the NRA, such as Nye and Borah, and those within the administration who wanted to see the NRA move toward a more pro-competitive policy.[43] The restoration of a competitive market, critics argued, would allow the small entrepreneur to challenge the dominance of larger corporations. Dismissing the idea that the success of

---

contracts between distributors and chain exhibitors that could prevent small independent exhibitors from acquiring first-class films. Roos characterized the motion picture code as "the NRA's outstanding effort to protect the small operator" (see Roos, p. 404). Sol Rosenblatt, the division administrator responsible for the motion picture code, provides a plausible explanation for Darrow's error. Darrow had given unjustified credence to the testimony of three "Movie Code-wreckers," Messrs. Brandt, Blumenthal, and Samuelson. All three had refused to sign the code and were chronic violators of its provisions, and the former two had "run a racket scab-union fighting the A.F. of L." None was a typical independent, for Brandt and Blumenthal were in the business of buying up independent theaters and then selling the resulting small chains to larger companies at a tidy profit, and the NRA had a "file a mile long" on Samuelson's activities. Yet all three had testified to Darrow that they were being driven out of business by the NRA code. Samuelson had fed the Darrow Commission the line they had wanted to hear—that the code was "against the independents" and that "its Boards are stacked against the independents." In view of the substantial evidence that Darrow's investigation was slipshod, it would be reasonable to presume that Darrow simply accepted the testimony of these three at face value. See Sol Rosenblatt to Marvin McIntyre (secretary to the president), 22 May 1934, Roosevelt Papers, OF 466, No. 5, NRA Codes, 1933–35, N–O.

41. Schlesinger, *The Coming of the New Deal*, p. 133.
42. *New York Times*, 14 June 1934.
43. Hawley, *The New Deal*, pp. 96, 99–100.

the larger corporation was the result of superior efficiency, the antitrusters claimed that monopoly and oligopoly were the fruits of unfair competitive practices that strictly enforced antitrust laws would eliminate. This argument had great appeal to some peripheral businessmen, especially those who sought a scapegoat for their economic woes, but many of the more astute businessmen who owned peripheral firms realized that intensified competition would only increase peripheral firm bankruptcies, and they more realistically continued to look to some form of price stabilization for relief.[44] Thus the leaders of peripheral industries like the retail drug industry, which represented 60,000 small businesses, condemned the Darrow Commission's report as "intemperate, unjust and unfair."[45] The intemperate attacks of Darrow, Nye, and Borah on the NRA entitled them to a place of honor in the long tradition of opponents of economic concentration, but as has frequently been the case in that tradition, the attacks on big business were often more deeply enmeshed in symbol and myth than in fact and rational judgment.

Peripheral Firms: Responses to the NRA

These conclusions are at least partially supported by the only detailed aggregate data on business reactions available to the NRA, although the evidence is inconclusive. This data was collected through surveys of

44. The differences between the pro-competitive reforms that Borah and Nye demanded, ostensibly on behalf of peripheral businesses, and the actual demands and interests of peripheral businesses are especially clear in the case of the cotton textile industry. Production controls in the cotton textile code were attacked by pro-competitive economists within the NRA—in particular, Leon Henderson and Victor von Szeliski of the Research and Planning Division. Henderson and von Szeliski, however, were more realistic concerning the consequences of pro-competitive reform than Borah and Nye were. Henderson and von Szeliski pushed for pro-competitive reforms to aid the consumer, not the marginal producer. Henderson proposed that the machine-hours limitations in the existing cotton textile code be replaced by an inventory control system, a less onerous restriction on production that would have allowed efficient producers to take a larger share of the market. Von Szeliski was even more radical, proposing that production controls be dismantled altogether and that the NRA allow the efficient cotton textile manufacturers to drive the inefficient manufacturers out of the business. According to Von Szeliski, "Preservation of . . . high cost mills is really the sole achievement of the Cotton Textile Industry. The machine-hour restriction works by preventing the low cost manufacturer from manufacturing at low cost—preventing his goods from being put on the market in quantities. This results in a higher price than the consumers would otherwise pay and enables the high cost producers to hobble along." These reforms were vigorously resisted by the Cotton Textile Institute, which in this case was the authentic spokesman for the interests of the marginal producers, and the Cotton Textile Institute proceeded to push for even more extensive production controls. See Galambos, *Competition and Cooperation*, pp. 273–279.

45. *New York Times*, 24 May 1934. Organized labor was even more vociferous in its criticisms of Darrow. Sidney Hillman charged the Darrow group with promoting sweatshops, and John L. Lewis accused the Darrow Commission of having relied on information from "malcontents, sweatshop employers and business interests which had lost special privileges." See *New York Times*, 24 May 1934; Schlesinger, *The Coming of the New Deal* p. 134.

affiliated firms by the New England Council and the Southern States Industrial Council (SSIC) in the latter days of the NRA and by the NRA itself. In the New England Council survey, 42 percent of the respondents believed the codes were harmful rather than helpful, and only 24 percent believed they benefited from the codes. In the breakdowns by industry size that the council provided (see Table 1), small business was more dissatisfied than big business. Some 50 percent of the small businesses surveyed believed the codes had hindered their operations, compared with only 30 percent of the larger firms. Yet even among larger firms, a slightly higher number of respondents believed the codes had been harmful rather than helpful, and the most common attitude was that the codes had had no effect. The most positive response was given by medium-sized firms, which would have been the most likely victims of big-business machinations if the codes promoted monopolies.

Table 1. Attitudes of Firms toward Codes (by Size)

	Large		Medium		Small		Total	
	No.	%	No.	%	No.	%	No.	%
Helpful	39	27	76	29	38	17	153	24
No effect	55	38	70	26	66	29	191	30
Hurtful	44	30	112	42	114	50	270	42
Total	138	95	258	97	218	96	614	96
Not voting	8	5	8	3	10	4	26	4
Grand Total	146	100	266	100	228	100	640	100

Source: Data from *New England News Letter,* Supplement, May 1935, p. 2.

Indeed, it became a common business reflection that "the penalties of NRA regimentation have fallen most heavily on the largest and smallest units of business." Great corporations, which generally belonged to many codes, often bore a large share of the costs of code administration, as well as suffering a drain on personnel who became occupied with code business.[46] Furthermore, large corporations generally had to be assiduous in carrying out the provisions of codes because they were in the limelight, while smaller competitors would reap the benefits of cheating with impunity.[47] On the other hand, some of the smallest units were most hard-hit by the imposition of a minimum wage because they had thrived on sweatshop labor.[48]

46. *Business Week,* 30 March 1935, p. 36.
47. Lyon et al., p. 260; *Business Week,* 9 March 1935, p. 7.
48. Roos, pp. 402–403.

When asked whether the codes should be extended in some form, a similar picture emerges (see Table 2). A slight majority of 53 percent of businesses in general were in favor of some sort of recovery program, undoubtedly along more voluntarist lines, while 40 percent would have abandoned the codes outright. Small firms were most prone to abandon the codes, with 50 percent ready to do so, while only 38 percent of big business was prepared to abandon the codes. Once again, the medium-sized firms were the most positive toward the codes.

Table 2. Attitudes of Firms on Extension of Codes (by Size)

	Large		Medium		Small		Total	
	No.	%	No.	%	No.	%	No.	%
Code desirable	84	58	167	63	90	39	341	53
No code wanted	56	38	85	32	112	50	253	40
Total	140	96	252	95	202	89	594	93
Not voting	6	4	14	5	26	11	46	7
Grand Total	146	100	266	100	228	100	640	100

Source: Data from *New England News Letter,* supplement, May 1935, p. 2.

A similar picture of small-business dissatisfaction with the codes emerges from the SSIC survey. No breakdowns of reactions of large and small firms are provided because the SSIC suggests that the industrial base it represents is overwhelmingly small firms, with 85 percent of the manufacturing plants in the South employing fifty workers or less. The Southern survey revealed that 34.2 percent of Southern manufacturers would have supported an extension of the NRA after June 1935 only with modifications, 43.4 percent would have let the program lapse, and 22.4 percent wanted it extended without modifications.[49] While twice as many firms opposed the extension of the NRA as supported its extension unmodified, about 57 percent favored some program like the NRA. At least some of those who favored modification wanted less government interference in business.[50]

The conclusion that center businesses benefited more from the codes than peripheral businesses would not be justified. A majority of small firms supported basically the same position that center firms in the BAC had taken with regard to the NRA—that the NRA should be continued, but only with modifications. Furthermore, many of the firms included in

49. SSIC, "What Should Be the Future of NRA," p. 4.
50. This was not information requested on the questionnaire mailed out, but more than 20 percent of those responding included comments to that effect unsolicited (ibid., p. 2).

the large-firm category of the New England Council report do not represent the oligarchical firms commonly understood to make up big business. The industry from which the second largest single number of big firms were drawn was the textile industry.[51] The textile market was characterized by bitter cutthroat competition among a large number of firms, none of which had developed any significant oligopolistic power. That the New England textile manufacturers would have supported an anticompetitive code is hardly surprising, because the New England textile industry was in decline, its marginal producers finding it increasingly difficult to compete with lower-cost Southern competitors.[52] It is perfectly consistent with the thesis being presented in this work that textile manufacturers supported the NRA.[53]

The most interesting data bearing on the revisionist thesis concerns the presumed NRA bias toward big business. The SSIC report on the attitudes of Southern manufacturers toward the NRA, without giving specific figures, did assert that many Southern manufacturers attributed their dissatisfactions with the codes to the machinations of an Eastern business elite: "A large portion objected to the domination of the Code Authorities by the large manufacturers of the North and East. They feel that the small manufacturer has no voice in the planning and administration of the codes. . . . This group has had no authoritative voice in the formulation or administration of the codes, for less than 10% of all code authority members are from the South."[54] Small New England firms, perhaps because they had more continuous interaction with large corporations and had less of the psychology of a peripheral region, were far less prone to blame their troubles on unfair competition. Some 79 percent of the 461 manufacturers who responded on this issue rejected the assertion that the codes tended to promote monopoly, and only twenty-two of the sixty-nine respondents who offered specific reasons that the codes would reinforce monopoly attributed it to big-business control of code administration.[55]

Complaints by peripheral businesses about the advantages big businesses had under the codes were often based on misperceptions. In interpreting their survey, the SSIC reported: "According to southern manufacturers, price-fixing is to the advantage of the large monopolies of the North and East and has worked to the advantage of this group in eliminating the

51. *New England News Letter*, Supplement, May 1935, p. 2.
52. Galambos, *Competition and Cooperation*, p. 285.
53. The number of textile firms in the category of large firms in the New England Council survey indicates that its tripartite firm size categories do not correspond to the distinction between peripheral and central firms developed in the previous chapter. The categories used in the New England Council survey could represent no more than subdivisions of peripheral businesses. Suggestively, the aggregate results for the New England survey are approximately the same as those for the Southern survey, which claims to be a survey of small business.
54. SSIC, "What Should Be the Future of NRA," p. 2.
55. *New England News Letter*, Supplement, May 1935, p. 4.

comparatively small manufacturer from competitive markets."[56] But the SSIC survey exaggerates the actual opposition of small manufacturers to price-fixing, for although the summary data they provide shows that only 22.7 percent of the respondents would favor outright price-fixing, 60.4 percent of the respondents favored fair trade practice provisions that progressives, such as Nye and Borah, had tended to identify with price-fixing.[57]

The SSIC report exemplifies a tendency in the consciousness of the small businessman. Price-fixing is often vilified as a device practiced by big business to take unfair advantage of the small firm, but provisions to prevent sales below costs are in the service of fair competition. The SSIC reports "overwhelming" majorities in favor of open price schedules and "government supervision to see that goods are not sold below costs." Yet only a handful of codes had price stabilization provisions that were put into practice and that went beyond those approved by the Southern manufacturers, and most of those were in highly competitive industries. The fear of big business was distorting the perception of peripheral businessmen regarding the operation of the codes, a bias that was intensified if the peripheral firms were in relatively isolated regions, remote from the mainstream of American commerce.

The third survey of business responses to the NRA was conducted by the Research and Planning Division of the NRA and was targeted explicitly at discovering the source of small-business complaints against the NRA.[58] The sample for this survey was selected by a preliminary analysis of the 5,710 letters of grievance from small firms that the NRA had received when the survey was begun.[59] The analysis had revealed complaints against forty-six codes, and more than half the complaints were directed at six codes: lumber, graphic arts, retail solid fuel, cotton garment, retail rubber tire and battery, and bituminous coal. Of the complaints studied in the preliminary analysis, "approximately 40 per cent were against code assessments; 12 per cent against price fixing; over 13 per cent against alleged discrimination by Code Authorities; and 10 per cent over wages and hours."[60]

56. SSIC, "What Should Be the Future of NRA," p. 3.

57. Ibid. John F. Sinclair, a member of the Darrow Commission, suggested that an analysis of small business complaints against NRA codes would reveal that "a large percentage of them, possibly 80 to 90 per cent, could be classified as coming from those who lack knowledge of the code and code procedures." John F. Sinclair to FDR, 14 April 1934, Richberg Papers, Box 45, File: Memo, etc., May 1934.

58. While an NRA survey might be suspect, the fact that the survey was carried out by the Research and Planning Division, which had been critical of the anticompetitive aspects of the NRA, gives the survey some credibility.

59. The results of the survey were based on visits to 328 firms of various kinds dispersed over twenty different states.

60. "The Status of Small Enterprises Under Auspices of the National Recovery Administration," Richberg Papers, Box 45, Memo, 22–25 May 1935, p. 2.

The preliminary analysis of small-business complaints to the NRA reveals several interesting facts concerning small business dissatisfaction with the NRA. The six codes that accounted for 50 percent of the complaints were in industries characterized by a high degree of competition rather than oligopoly, and they were codes that had more extensive anticompetitive devices than the average code.[61] Complaints against price-fixing and against discrimination by code authorities in these industries would therefore be complaints against the operation, and probably the relatively ineffective operation, of a peripheral firm cartel rather than against big business.[62] Moreover, 40 percent of all complaints concerned the issue of code assessments, not fair trade practices provisions. Financially strapped smaller firms could be expected to be unhappy about any additional costs (as they were about labor costs), even if the costs had been equitably distributed among firms of different sizes in an industry.

61. The peripheral character of bituminous coal is described in J. Johnson, p. 13. Dr. William Compton, secretary and manager of the National Lumber Manufacturers Association, described the lumber industry as "an industry or group of industries having tens of thousands of units, most of them small and competitively inconspicuous." See Wilson Compton, "What Went Wrong in Lumber Codes," *Nation's Business,* February 1935, p. 29. In the NRA the "graphic arts industry" referred to a collection of several more specialized industries. The graphic arts code was therefore a general code applicable to all and supplemented by additional code provisions applicable to each specific industry. Similarly, a general code authority was supplemented by thirteen more specific code authorities. While industry structure varied somewhat for each specific industry encompassed by the general code, none of the industries was significantly oligopolistic. The printing code covered 25,000 printing establishments, the photoengraving code covered 800 photoengraving establishments, and even the subcode for the most concentrated graphic arts industry—the book manufacturing industry—covered approximately 300 establishments. Lindsay Rogers, the deputy administrator in charge of the graphic arts code, commented that the approval of that code had brought "a hitherto sharply separated competitive industry under joint administrative control" (NRA Records, RG 9, Entry 267, Approved Code Histories: Graphic Arts Industries," Vol. I, pp. 25–27, 46; Vol. V, pp. 3–4). The cotton garment industry covered approximately 3,700 establishments, and its approved code history concluded that the attempt to enforce fair trade practices provisions to limit competition "was very unsuccessful" (NRA Records, RG 9, Entry 267, Approved Code Histories: Cotton Garment Industry, pp. 9, 46). The retail solid fuel industry covered 115,000 local establishments in "42 highly decentralized and almost autonomous geographical divisions." In its approved code history, F. A. Hecht, deputy administrator for the code, described the "inability of the general NRA Code Authority to administer the code for such an industry" and concluded that "considering the number of dealers involved," attempts to interfere with market pricing were not desirable (NRA Records, RG 9, Entry 267, Approved Code Histories: Retail Solid Fuel Industry, pp. i–iii, 2–3). Finally, the retail rubber tire and battery industry covered 154,273 establishments. Most of these establishments were filling stations, but these smaller businesses were in competition with large mail order houses, factory owned stores, and chain store supply houses. The code had extensive price control provisions in an industry in which large dealers enjoyed a significant cost advantage. This corroborates the NRA's assertion that "the purpose of the Administration was to provide temporary protection for thousands of small dealers who were being crowded out of business," for price-fixing prevented the large firms from exploiting their cost advantage (NRA Records, RG 9, Entry 267, Approved Code Histories: Retail Rubber Tire and Battery Trade, pp. 3, 10, 18–19).

62. Smaller businesses that objected to a cartel might nevertheless object to "big business" control of the code because to a firm employing less than ten employees a firm that employed 200 might appear large, even though from an economic standpoint the latter was only a medium-sized firm, and perhaps a small medium-sized firm at that.

The NRA had taken a number of steps to assure that smaller firms were protected from burdensome code assessments, and in industries with larger firms the latter sometimes bore a disproportionate percentage of the costs.[63] Thus the evidence from this preliminary data on the objections of small businesses to the NRA does not support the conclusion that small business was the victim of big-business machinations under the NRA.

The Research and Planning Division survey followed up on the initial analysis of small-business complaints to the NRA and concluded that between 75 percent and 85 percent of small enterprises were generally satisfied with their NRA codes and that only "a very small proportion indicated that certain provisions of their codes were discriminatory."[64] More-frequent criticisms were leveled at the discriminatory manner in which codes had been administered by code authorities, although only "a few critics insisted that the codes were written by big business and administered by representatives of big business." Complaints generally emphasized poor enforcement, code assessments, and violations of confidentiality of information sought by code authorities, more than the operation of codes of fair trade practices. In only one case, that of small printers, was it alleged that "price schedules were set too high and would eliminate small firms."[65] It was the unanimous judgment of the five Research and Planning Division investigators who conducted the survey that "the evil effects, alleged as due to code provisions, on small enterprises have been grossly magnified."[66]

63. See below, p. 218.
64. "The Status of Small Enterprises Under the Auspices of the National Recovery Administration," Richberg 45 Memo, 22–25 May 1935, p. 3. The significant differences between the New England Council survey and the NRA survey regarding basic small-business satisfaction with the codes probably has far less to do with political bias than with the constituencies being surveyed. The New England Council was surveying a predominantly manufacturing constituency, whereas the NRA survey was examining all small businesses, including small retailers, many of whom had codes that protected them from the competition of large chains and who would understandably have been more sympathetic to the NRA. Marc Rose, the editor of *Business Week,* also suggested that New England businessmen were probably more conservative than businessmen from the industrial heartland ("Address of Marc A. Rose . . . at the 36th Quarterly Meeting of the New England Council . . ." 21–22 November 1934, Roosevelt Papers, OF 172, No. 1, Business, July–October 1934).
65. This is the mechanism on which Hawley had focused as the means by which big business gained an advantageous position over small business during the NRA. The only example of this discovered by the Research and Planning Division occurred in a nonoligopolistic industry.
66. "The Status of Small Enterprises . . . ," p. 5. A preliminary *Business Week* survey of business under the NRA also supports the conclusion that small business did not fare badly under the program. This survey showed that in some industries small businesses located close to customers were springing up and taking sales away from larger firms. While some of the small businesses surveyed objected to NRA wage rates and to its failure to enforce codes, "the majority registered reactions favorable to the code program. One Western company, declaring '100%' for its industry code, said 'It has not hindered us as a small unit in a big industry.' A new competitor in tobacco manufacturing—which is easily dominated by large interests—believes NRA 'beneficial to small manufacturers' " (*Business Week,* 8 September 1934, pp. 24–25).

Industry Case Studies and the NRA

While the complex pattern of support and opposition to the NRA resists simple categorization, it may still be roughly accurate to suggest that the New Deal coalition was fashioned by aligning businessmen running peripheral firms with labor and farmers, albeit not without significant internal tensions within such a coalition, to challenge a conservative leadership that had been too deferential to the interests of center firms. However, systematic differences in attitudes toward the NRA between oligopolistic corporations, on the one hand, and peripheral firms, on the other, are to a considerable extent obscured by other more proximate and industry specific factors that were sometimes of greater importance in determining attitudes toward the NRA. The confounding causes for business dissatisfaction cannot be distinguished and systematically analyzed with the aggregate data available on business reactions to the NRA. This limitation dictates a research strategy based on industry case studies that permits the researcher to hold some of the confounding causes constant while examining the differences in the impact of the NRA on firms of different sizes within a single industry.

A number of excellent case studies of industries under the NRA already exist, and before we analyze the history of two critical industries under the NRA it is important to relate the findings of the existing case studies of industries that will not be analyzed to this study of the NRA. James P. Johnson's *Politics of Soft Coal* deals extensively with the bituminous coal industry under the NRA in his more comprehensive study of the bituminous coal industry from World War I through the New Deal. Similarly, Louis Galambos's study of the cotton textile industry in the early twentieth century devotes a great deal of attention to the NRA period. Both the bituminous coal and the cotton textile industries were highly competitive industries of peripheral firms. Confirming the hypothesis that peripheral firms were the fundamental business constituency of the NRA, there was strong support for the NRA in both industries.[67]

67. In suggesting that these works support the general thesis of this work, I refer primarily to their having demonstrated strong business support for the NRA in their respective industries. See J. Johnson, pp. 213–215, and Galambos, *Competition and Cooperation*, pp. 199–206, 275–279. I am not claiming that those authors would agree with the thesis being presented here, or that all the conclusions they drew from their case studies agree with this thesis. Indeed, Galambos believed that his conclusions were "for the most part" in accord with those of Hawley's revisionist study of the NRA (see Galambos, *Competition and Cooperation*, p. 279). But Galambos's conclusions did not always do justice to his empirical findings. A particularly interesting aspect of Galambos's study is the relationship of the cotton textile code to the Johnson & Johnson Company, one of the only vertically integrated corporations in the cotton textile industry. Johnson & Johnson was a leader of the faction within the cotton textile industry that opposed the introduction of production controls through the NRA code. Johnson & Johnson's subsequent unsuccessful efforts to dismantle the anticompetitive restrictions of the

A third extremely important case study must be examined in somewhat greater detail. Sidney Fine's superb analysis of the automobile industry during the NRA, *The Automobile Under the Blue Eagle,* is one of the few studies of a center firm industry during this period. Fine focused on the impact of the NRA on labor relations in the automobile industry because the automobile NRA code did not contain any provisions governing fair trade practices, a unique characteristic of the automobile code.[68] While Fine recognizes the importance of this fact for the evolution of labor policy in the automobile industry, he does not explore its significance for our understanding of business policy during the NRA.[69]

The automobile code dealt exclusively with labor matters—wages, hours, and collective bargaining—because the industry did not want a code of fair trade practices. The automobile industry had never been enthusiastic about the passage of the National Industrial Recovery Act and the NRA. Alfred P. Sloan, Jr., the president of General Motors, took strong exception to Section 7a and the threat to the open shop automobile industry that this posed, but he was no less concerned with the extension of government control over industry through the NRA, and he observed to Hugh Johnson that he "would rather be in the hands of the Labor Unions than . . . in the hands of the politicians." Herman L. Moekle, a member of the automobile committee that drafted the automobile code, noted there was "a strong sentiment in the committee that no code at all should be filed, if such a thing is possible," but that prudence compelled the industry to submit a code lest the federal government prescribe one for the industry.[70] The industry drafted the minimal code possible under NRA guidelines, a code basically concerned with wages and hours.

Henry Ford was even more adamant concerning these issues. He did not believe that the government could or should solve the economic problems posed by the depression, and he consistently sought to keep the automobile industry "as free as possible of controls." He refused to sign even the minimal code of labor practices drafted by his fellow automobile manufacturers for fear that he "would be giving away the control of his own business." When Josephus Daniels urged him to sign, he responded

---

textile code were opposed by the Cotton Textile Institute, which charged that Johnson & Johnson wanted to gut the code to drive smaller competitors out of business. This episode does not confirm Hawley's assertion that codes generally represented the interests of the larger center firms. Galambos, ibid., pp. 221–222, 252–255.

68. "It was unique among the major businesses of the nation in its lack of interest in the opportunity for cartelization that the N.I.R.A. provided" (Fine, p. 48).

69. Because the automobile industry did not want anything from the NRA, it was in a strong negotiating position with the government concerning labor provisions. So it is not surprising that Fine concluded that the NRA served big business. When his findings are placed in a broader perspective, they provide important evidence for the opposite conclusion. For a further discussion of Fine's conclusions, see Chapter 10.

70. Fine, pp. 46, 49, 56.

through his spokesman, William J. Cameron, "There can be no doubt . . . that proposals are being made in the name of recovery that have nothing to do with recovery, and that seriously affect the fundamental American idea. We doubt that it is necessary to scrap America in order to achieve recovery."[71]

Ford stuck to this convictions despite considerable economic risk to his firm. Although he did agree to abide by provisions of the automobile code, his refusal to sign the code prevented him from displaying the Blue Eagle on his products. Without the Blue Eagle, the government initially refused to purchase Ford cars, and there was considerable uncertainty about whether the public would buy them either. Hugh Johnson's appeals to individual consumers to boycott products that did not display the Blue Eagle had been relatively effective at the time Ford was refusing to place the emblem on his vehicles. Dismissing the concerns of other Ford executives, Ford defiantly proclaimed, "Hell, that Roosevelt buzzard! I wouldn't put it on the car." Under the NRA, he told his fellow automobile manufacturers, "every detail of our operation can be placed under control of a committee one-third of whom are politicians and one-third of whom are labor leaders."[72]

Ford's concerns were widely shared by his fellow automobile manufacturers, even if the lengths to which he would go to uphold his convictions were unusual. Leaders of the automobile industry came to play a prominent role in the American Liberty League in 1934 and 1935, and the industry was generally delighted when the Supreme Court finally struck the NRA down. The NRA experience had made the industry so leery of government regulation of the economy that when George Berry, who was appointed Coordinator for Industrial Cooperation by President Roosevelt on 26 September 1935, invited the industry to participate with labor and consumer representatives in a series of conferences on economic recovery later that year, the industry flatly refused. The Automobile Manufacturers Association was suspicious that the Berry conferences were "the first major move by the administration to sound out business sentiment on future industry-cooperation plans," and it anticipated that "some type of government 'supervision' would be necessary" because the administration was "skeptical about 'industry's ability to go it alone.'"[73]

71. Ibid., pp. 76–78.
72. Ibid., p. 78.
73. Ibid., p. 414. Trade associations in steel, petroleum, electrical manufacturing, and chemicals also rejected Berry's invitation to participate. When the conference convened without these industries being represented in December 1935, the majority of business delegates who did attend were hostile to Berry's attempt to revive an NRA-type program. As Hawley noted, "Only about three hundred attended the subsequent round-table meetings, and most of these were representatives of small businessmen in the less highly organized areas of the economy." Hawley, *The New Deal*, pp. 161–162.

The NRA appeared in such a negative light to automobile manufacturers because it had threatened the industry with unionization and government control and offered too few benefits to counterbalance these disadvantages. The industry simply did not need the NRA to promote cooperation between its oligopolistic firms. According to Fine, "Unlike so many other industries, the automobile industry, as we have seen, was not faced in 1933 with the problem of overproduction or of destructive price cutting, and the manufacturers, through the National Automobile Chamber of Commerce (NACC), had already standardized their trade practices to the extent they thought necessary."[74] If this perception of industry interest in maintaining a market free from government control were to hold true for other center firm industries as well, even if to a lesser extent than was true for the automobile industry, then the argument that the NRA benefited large businesses would have to be viewed with considerably greater skepticism.[75]

Even more light can be shed on the relationships between center and peripheral firms and government during the NRA by studying industries where large firms had developed but where oligopoly had not yet become established because peripheral-sized firms retained a sufficient share of the market to maintain competitive conditions. The most notable examples of this situation were in the retail industry, where chain stores were developing but independent retailers retained a significant share of the market, and in the oil industry, where major oil firms coexisted with a substantial number of independent producers and gasoline retailers. The existing historical research on the retail trades under the NRA generally supports the conclusion that the NRA protected the interests of peripheral firms. A number of codes in this sector protected independent distributors from the encroachment of the chain stores by eliminating or restricting the use of loss leaders (pricing a few items below costs to draw customers to a chain outlet) and quantity discounts.[76] The latter proved to be the most onerous

74. Fine, p. 48.

75. It is clear that these considerations were present, although not necessarily decisive, in other oligopolistic industries. For instance, Myron Taylor, chairman of U.S. Steel, called Roosevelt to "inquire whether the Government would be satisfied with a code containing only employment conditions and a general adherence to the Recovery Act, without trade practice features." Despite NRA approval of this option, the steel industry ultimately approved a strong code with extensive controls over fair trade practices. Taylor notes: "Apart from the opinion of this corporation [U.S. Steel] at that time, which was generally in favor of the simple code above outlined [i.e., just labor provisions], the industry felt a keen desire, as did some of our own executives, to try the cooperative experiment. In the face of this desire we joined with it" (Telephone message to the President from Myron Taylor, Roosevelt Papers, OF 342, No. 1, Steel, 1934–36). The tobacco manufacturing industry, another highly oligopolistic industry, also appeared more than willing to forgo the anticompetitive possibilities of an NRA code in order to avoid the labor provisions of the NRA. That industry procrastinated in presenting a code to the NRA until it was finally forced to do so. See William Green to FDR, 13 December 1934, Roosevelt Papers, OF 142, No. 1, AFL: 1933–36.

76. The local Retail Drug Code (RDC) authority of the Los Angeles metropolitan area wrote to

restriction because it limited the ability of the chains to translate their economies of scale into lower prices for consumers.

Peripheral retailers generally wanted NRA codes to be even more restrictive of competition than the NRA had allowed them to become. Drug retailers had managed to secure a particularly strong minimum-price provision in their code, and other retail groups had hopes that such provisions could be developed for their codes, a possibility that the larger chains vigorously resisted.[77] Hawley concedes that the retail trades are anomalous for a revisionist interpretation of the NRA: "Consequently, small distributors and their suppliers were particularly receptive to the type of reasoning that underlay the NRA codes.... In a number of respects, too, the distributive codes did reflect their point of view, particularly in the provisions for confining distribution to recognized channels, eliminating the buying advantages of large units, and prohibiting loss leaders."[78]

Furthermore, the NRA facilitated the organization of independent retailers and wholesalers and fostered an alliance between these two groups. In his study of retail and wholesale regulation, Joseph Palamountain, Jr., concluded: "Thus, although many codes broke down after some months, independents were given some relief from their disadvantage in buying prices and an appetite for more. In addition, many distributors derived valuable political and organizational experience from preparing and administering codes. By the end of the NRA some distributors were highly group conscious, well-organized, and had focused their attention on the problem of discounts."[79] This organizational legacy of the NRA was subsequently used to secure passage of the Robinson-Patman Act, the Miller-Tydings Amendment to the Sherman Act, and various state fair-trade laws that restricted competition in the distributive sector and limited the ability of the chains to expand their share of the retail market.

A second notable example of a code that dealt with direct conflict between large firms, on the one hand, and peripheral firms, on the other, was the petroleum industry code. Here the revisionist interpretation of the NRA appears to be on more solid ground. In his study of the oil industry in the 1920s and 1930s, Norman Nordhauser suggested that regulation

---

Marvin McIntyre, secretary to the president: "We are reconciled to the fact that the only certainty of hope or anticipation of recovery of the small merchant is the NRA and Code of Fair Trade Competition in the Drug Industry.... We are firm in our assumption that the chisellers and the gyp chain-store monopolists are the contributing factors in this drive to prevent N.R.A. and our Codes from being continued after June 16, 1935.... The Drug code ... restrains the vultures and chain stores from driving the small man out of business" (Lewis Clark [Secretary RDC, L.A. area] to McIntyre, 25 April 1935, Roosevelt Papers, OF 466, No. 3, NRA, May–June 1935).

77. *New York Times,* 13 May 1934; *Business Week,* 5 January 1935, p. 10.
78. Hawley, *The New Deal,* pp. 248–249.
79. Joseph C. Palamountain, Jr., *The Politics of Distribution* (Cambridge, Mass., 1955), p. 194.

during this era established "a network of formal and informal cooperative arrangements between the various segments of the industry and the state and federal governments" that "guaranteed effective stabilization of production."[80] The oil industry successfully used arguments for conservation to justify "stabilizing prices, limiting production and increasing profits." To Nordhauser the NRA exemplified this pattern of private capture of public authority, and this corporatist arrangement was *primarily* orchestrated by and served the interests of big business:

> In addition to pleasing well owners, higher prices for crude petroleum gave an important advantage to the larger refiners who utilized the most advanced technology in order to obtain higher yields of gasoline from a given quantity of oil. Control of production at the well struck at the small refiners whose plants required cheap crude oil as a basis for competing with the large cracking plants. Only the large corporations, those with access to the capital and patents necessary to build modern plants could run profitably on expensive crude oil.[81]

The case study of the oil industry provided in the following chapter will demonstrate why it is misleading to focus on the plight of small refiners and why from a more comprehensive perspective it is clear that peripheral businesses were the constituents of the NRA in this industry.

80. Nordhauser, p. 160.
81. Ibid., p. 162.

CHAPTER 7

The NRA and the
Oil Industry

The oil industry during the period of the NRA was a microcosm of the conflicting forces that determined the outcome of this national experiment in corporatism. The demand for stability and relief from cutthroat competition, the motive that purportedly propelled businessmen from a laissez-faire economy into the protective arms of government regulation, was intensified in the oil industry beyond the levels characteristic of most manufacturing industries. The oil market, already glutted by production from big fields in Texas, Oklahoma, and California, was further destabilized with the discovery of the enormous East Texas field in October 1930. The price of oil in East Texas dropped as low as five cents a barrel.[1] Whatever the long-range prognosis for diminishing supply and the need for conservation, the immediate problem of the market was overabundance. But unlike manufacturing industries, which could respond to a condition of excess supply by restricting production, the oil industry was unable to turn off the spigot.

The physical properties of underground oil, in combination with the legal system governing proprietary rights, subverted the self-regulating qualities of the petroleum market. Ownership of petroleum was conveyed under the "law of capture" by mixing one's labor with the natural resource in lifting it to the surface. However, the migratory character of underground oil compelled each of the joint owners of an underground pool to maximize individual production to prevent rival owners from capturing potential production. Thus, plummeting prices would not cause a contraction in production unless a near unanimous agreement among the joint owners of a pool was secured to prorate output. These voluntary agreements were almost impossible to conclude in practice, because many of the small owners viewed their investments as opportunities to get rich

1. *National Petroleum News*, 31 May 1933, p. 10; Nordhauser, p. 108.

175

quick and refused to take a long-term perspective on maximizing profits. Furthermore, antitrust laws prohibited such agreements.

Business responses to this situation varied according to the economic interests and fundamental beliefs of businessmen. The oil industry in the 1930s was dominated by approximately twenty vertically integrated firms— the majors—whose preeminence is attributable primarily to their sizable capital investments in refining and pipelines, stages of production where economies of scale were significant. Relative ease of entry and less-significant economies of scale in production and marketing, on the other hand, permitted a far less oligopolistic market structure. It is estimated that more than 50 percent of the market in production and 40 percent of the retail gasoline market was in the hands of independents in the period immediately preceding the NRA.[2] Even in refining, a number of smaller refiners using wasteful skimming techniques to extract gasoline from oil survived alongside the majors because the price of oil was so low.

A number of trade associations represented various industry interests. The "peak" association of the industry, the American Petroleum Institute (API), was the only association in which the majors all participated, but the API also included representatives of the independents. When the interests of the majors and the independents diverged, the API was often stalemated and forced to abstain from taking an active political role.[3] Under these circumstances, the majors generally acted quietly and informally, preferring to avoid the adverse publicity that generally accompanied attempts of an "oligarchy" to influence political outcomes. Where possible, the majors tacitly supported small groups of independents who voiced opinions similar to their own. The foremost organization representing the independents was the Independent Producers Association of America (IPA), under the leadership of Wirt Franklin. A smaller dissident group of independents, representing no more than 5 to 10 percent of the total U.S. production, formed the Independent Producers Association of America Opposed to Monopoly (IPA Opposed to Monopoly) during the early days of the New Deal.[4]

Contrary to the revisionist hypothesis, most of the majors sought to avoid *extensive federal* government controls over the oil industry. The majors were aware of the extent to which public opinion held business elites responsible for the depression and of the potential repercussions of the hostility toward major corporations. They feared federal regulation even more than the rigors of the competitive market because their interests

---

2. Nordhauser, pp. 56, 69; Myron Watkins, *Oil: Stabilization or Conservation* (New York, 1937), pp. 27–28.

3. It was noncommittal on the price-fixing provision of the NRA code because of internal dissension. See below.

4. Gerald Nash, *United States Oil Policy, 1890–1964* (Westport, Conn., 1968), p. 107; Nordhauser, pp. 102–103; *National Petroleum News*, 5 April 1933, p. 8.

were jeopardized by regulation under progressive New Dealers who were sympathetic to the interests of the smaller independents and labor. They were prepared to accept more uncertainty in the market as the price of autonomy because they were the firms best equipped to weather the economic costs of market instability.

The independents in the IPA were far more willing to exchange their freedom in an uncontrolled market for relative economic security under fairly extensive federal regulation. Unlike the majors, the independents could not generally afford to take a long-range view of their interests in preserving a free market. Furthermore, they were as confident that federal controls would be exercised to guarantee a "fair" minimum return on their investment as the majors were fearful that federal controls would eventually be used to stifle profits.

In stark contrast to the independents in the IPA, a smaller group of dissident independents in the IPA Opposed to Monopoly were even more radically committed to a laissez-faire domestic market than the majors, opposing state as well as federal controls. The IPA Opposed to Monopoly, led by John Elliot, argued that the price collapse in the oil market had been caused not by overproduction but by the deliberate manipulation of prices by oligopolistic producers who sought to drive out independents. To the extent that controls over the supply of oil were necessary, the IPA Opposed to Monopoly favored import barriers, a policy vigorously opposed by the majors who had extensive overseas holdings in oil. Beyond that, the IPA Opposed to Monopoly argued for stricter enforcement of antitrust statutes, action to divest the major producers of their pipeline affiliates, and suspending patent restrictions for the duration of the code.[5]

The crucial regulatory battles for the oil industry in the 1930s generally pitted the IPA against the majors, although the relatively small IPA Opposed to Monopoly at times played a crucial role in the struggle between these two groups. The conflict between the IPA and the majors focused on the choice between federal and state controls, not on the choice between a regulated industry and an unregulated industry. Given the prevailing market chaos, both the IPA and the majors acknowledged the need for some government controls. The IPA perceived state controls as an indispensable element in a more comprehensive package of market controls, which included federal regulation of prices through the NRA. The majors, on the other hand, viewed effective state controls as a sufficient means to effect long-term stability in the industry, without resort to more extensive controls.[6] Ironically, as antithetical as the goals of the

5. *National Petroleum News*, 5 April 1933, pp. 8–10. That they were distinguished from other independents on price-fixing is discussed in ibid., 30 August 1933, pp. 3–4.
6. *API Quarterly*, April 1933, pp. 2–11; *National Petroleum News*, 5 April 1933, pp. 7–8; ibid., 17 May 1933, p. 27; ibid., 28 November 1934, p. 7; ibid., 12 December 1934, pp. 15–16; ibid., 26 December 1934, p. 7.

majors and the goals of the IPA Opposed to Monopoly were, they found common ground in the opposition to federal control of the oil market. While the petroleum code under the NIRA contained concessions to each of these business factions, fundamentally the code was the culmination of the legislative program of the peripheral firms in the IPA.

Federalism and Industry Regulation

The constitutional and political limits on state and federal action illuminate the respective intentions of the majors and independents in supporting state or federal controls. According to reigning constitutional interpretation, federal control over interstate commerce did not extend to production, which remained within the sphere of state control.[7] This limitation on federal power guaranteed the states a role in any scheme of production allocation, and production allocation was an indispensable prerequisite for reestablishing market stability during this period. But while states had jurisdiction over their own oil wells, the regulation of interstate commerce was exclusively a federal concern, and the oil industry was primarily an industry engaged in interstate commerce. As long as the states were not preempted by federal legislation, they had some authority to regulate interstate commerce indirectly to secure the legitimate ends of state government, but the courts construed this power narrowly when state legislation impeded interstate commerce. As this doctrine of dual federalism had been developed by the Supreme Court during this period, many corporate activities had fallen into a no-man's-land between the respective responsibilities of the states and the federal government, and the majors attempted to preserve this constitutional status quo with minor modifications that would have allowed the minimal requisite government controls which even the majors conceded were necessary to stabilize the market.[8]

To the extent that government controls were necessary, the majors generally favored state regulation because it posed a less-severe threat to business autonomy. State prorationing of production certainly circumscribed an important area of managerial discretion for firms, but the firms retained considerable independence to chart their own course under state production controls. Furthermore, the majors could often effectively lobby against the imposition of undesirable state regulatory controls by threatening to move operations other than production wells to other states. Finally, the Supreme Court had been very aggressive in striking down state laws

---

7. *United States v. E. C. Knight Co.*, 156 U.S. 1 (1895).
8. Edward Corwin, *The Twilight of the Supreme Court* (New Haven, 1934).

that infringed on property rights.[9] State regulation of the oil industry must be subsumed under the general police powers of the state. While the police power is broadly defined as the power "to promote the public health, safety, morals and general welfare," in practice the Supreme Court imposed severe limits on the states through a broad interpretation of the due process clause of the Fourteenth Amendment, at least until 1937, when substantive due process went into eclipse as a judicial doctrine.[10]

Federal regulation of the oil industry, on the other hand, would have been based on the federal power to regulate interstate commerce, and even though the Supreme Court had more recently imposed important limitations on that power, there were precedents the Court could have cited that defined that power broadly and far fewer precedents relying on the due process clause of the Fifth Amendment to strike down federal regulation in defense of property rights.[11] Thus, the majors were more likely to secure limited regulation by favoring state control, while opposing federal control. To the extent that some coordination of the different regulatory programs of the individual states was necessary, the majors encouraged regional interstate compacts to address shared concerns.

The infringement on managerial prerogatives and on profits that the majors feared the most was from government price-fixing. Actually, during this period the price of crude oil was so low that price controls would have been used only to increase the price and benefit the industry. But the majors were aware of the long-range potential for price controls to diminish profits and were willing to forgo a short-term gain for a long-term interest in preserving managerial autonomy. Price-fixing was fundamentally a threat at the federal level, not at the state level. The Supreme Court had already struck down a Tennessee law fixing gasoline prices and differentials between wholesale and retail prices as a violation of the due process clause of the Fourteenth Amendment in *Williams v. Standard Oil Co.* in 1929,[12] whereas federal price-fixing under the Lever Act during World War I established presumptive federal authority to regulate prices during a severe domestic crisis.[13] Although the majors were concerned primarily with the threat posed by price-fixing, they were

9. Ibid., pp. 77–89.
10. Edward Corwin, *The Constitution and What It Means Today*, 13th ed., rev. by Harold W. Chase and Craig R. Ducat (Princeton, 1973), pp. 388–390.
11. See the Shreveport rate case, *Houston E.&W. Texas Ry. Co. v. United States*, 234 U.S. 342 (1914), for an expansive commerce clause case. See also Corwin, *The Twilight of the Supreme Court*, pp. 92–97, on substantive due process and federal regulation.
12. 278 U.S. 235 (1929). Concerning the majors' fight against Wisconsin's price-fixing order during the code, see *National Petroleum News*, 10 October 1934, pp. 11–17, and ibid., 24 October 1934, p. 15.
13. Alfred Kelly, Winfred A. Harbison, and Herman Bells, *The American Constitution*, 6th ed. (New York, 1983), pp. 448–453.

also deterred from advocating any form of federal production controls for fear that federal controls over production might eventually be broadened to include federal price controls.[14]

Many smaller producers could not afford the luxury of the long-term perspective adopted by the majors. Having gone into debt to finance their capital investment for production, they wanted to maximize their immediate returns to forestall bankruptcy.[15] To these independents, state controls alone appeared woefully inadequate, whereas federal controls did not pose the same threat they posed for the majors, because the New Dealers were committed to helping the small businessman. Thus the IPA demanded additional federal production controls to allocate production among the states and federal price controls through the NRA to fully stabilize the petroleum market and raise the price of crude oil to at least $1.11 a barrel.[16]

It is understandable that the independents would have been reluctant to rely primarily on state regulation of the oil industry. Prior to the New Deal, the states had been responsible for regulating the oil industry, and they had been unable to provide anything more than temporary relief to the hard-pressed independents. Texas and Oklahoma had enacted statutes governing wasteful practices in the industry at the turn of the twentieth century, and each had soon thereafter entrusted further regulatory responsibilities to independent commissions—the Texas Railroad Commission and the Oklahoma Corporation Commission respectively. The role of the commissions had expanded dramatically in the late 1920s and early 1930s, when the discovery of vast new oil fields had thrown the oil market into disarray and the commissions, with the support of the majors and a great majority of the independents, began issuing statewide proration orders restricting total production and allocating production quotas among individual producers.[17]

In 1931, successful federal district court challenges to these proration schemes by a few disgruntled independents had disallowed them, and in the ensuing market chaos the governors of both Texas and Oklahoma had been forced to declare martial law and send troops into the oil fields to enforce new emergency proration orders.[18] In both cases these actions led

14. *National Petroleum News,* 28 November 1934, pp. 7–8.

15. Wirt Franklin could not attend the Senate and House committee hearings on oil legislation in May and June 1933 because his own business was temporarily in the hands of receivers. Ibid., 7 June 1933, p. 11.

16. Nordhauser, pp. 136–137; *National Petroleum News,* 10 May 1933, p. 9; ibid., 31 May 1933, p. 11.

17. Robert E. Hardwicke, "Legal History of Conservation of Oil in Texas," in American Bar Association (ABA), *Legal History of Conservation of Oil and Gas* (Baltimore, 1938), pp. 217–229; Nash, *U.S. Oil Policy,* pp. 116, 124.

18. James P. Hart, "Oil, the Courts, and the Railroad Commission," *Southwestern Historical Quarterly* 44 (January 1941): 303–311; Nash, *U.S. Oil Policy,* pp. 117–118, 124–125.

to judicial censure, but they apparently enjoyed wide political support as emergency measures.[19] Despite judicial hostility, martial law was continued until late in 1932, when the Supreme Court finally reversed the original district court case that had overturned the Oklahoma proration statute and upheld the right of Oklahoma to limit production.[20] Judicial approval of a revised Texas proration statute followed in June 1933.[21]

Although state regulation had finally been vindicated in the courts, the problems encountered in institutionalizing state production controls for the oil industry in the early 1930s had discredited the claim that state regulation was sufficient to bring about market stability in the eyes of the independents. In contrast, the majors could afford to take the long-term view and saw these problems as temporary obstacles to a potentially effective program of state regulation, problems that had been fundamentally resolved by the beginning of 1933. Committed to at least giving state regulation a chance, they could hardly have concluded that state regulation was ineffective by the time the NRA was drafted, for the institutionalization of state controls in Oklahoma was completed only on 10 April 1933, and state controls in Texas did not win judicial approval until 25 June 1933.[22]

Had it not been for the problem of hot oil—oil produced illegally in violation of state proration statutes—the differences between the majors' advocacy of state regulation and the independents' advocacy of federal regulation would be clear and distinct. Hot oil, however, posed a problem that even the majors conceded required some role for the federal government.

The Demand for Federal Intervention

The completion of a legal framework for restricting production at the state level has proved to be a hollow victory, at least in the short run. Efforts to restrict production at well sites posed insurmountable problems of enforcement as long as a recalcitrant minority of well owners continued to evade the law. With more than 15,000 wells in East Texas alone, and with numerous deceptive techniques available to unscrupulous producers, a small army of enforcement officials would have been required to monitor every producer. Fortunately for the advocates of production control, a more realistic means of enforcement was available. The Achilles' heel of hot oil production was transporting the oil to distant markets, because

19. *E. Constantin et al. v. Lon Smith et al.*, F(2) 227 (E.D. Tex., 18 Feb. 1932). Appealed to the Supreme Court and the injunction enjoining declaration of martial law upheld in 287 U.S. 378 (1932); See Nordhauser, p. 86.
20. *Champlin Refining Co. v. Oklahoma Corp. Commission*, 286 U.S. 210 (1932).
21. ABA, pp. 241–245; *The Railroad Commission of Texas v. MacMillan et al.*, 287 U.S. 576 (1932); *Danciger Oil and Refining Co. v. Smith et al.*, 4 F. Supp. 234 (N.D. Tex., 25 June 1933).
22. Ibid.

transportation via railroads and ships—the dominant modes of shipment, —was particularly susceptible to government regulation. That regulation, however, could have been carried out only by the federal government, because it involved the regulation of interstate commerce.

For the independents, the fact that states could not effectively enforce their own proration statutes was just one more reason that state regulation should be supplemented with extensive federal regulation. The majors, on the other hand, sought a narrowly constrained federal role to correct the specific deficiencies of state regulation. The minimal requisite control sought by the majors included legislation that would have made it a federal crime to transport in interstate commerce oil produced in excess of state conservation statutes. Confining the federal role to support for the exercise of state police powers had historical precedents in federal restrictions on the interstate commerce of such items as lottery tickets, impure and falsely advertised foods, prostitutes, or liquor.[23] With the federal government acting only as a policeman for the state, the effectiveness of control could be increased without significant expansion of the scope of government regulation. As long as the state operated as an intermediary between the federal government and the industry, constitutional restrictions on state power established the limits of regulation. Thus, despite the majors' concession that the federal government did have a role to play in the regulation of hot oil, the broad differences between the preferred regulatory scheme of the independents and the preferred regulatory scheme of the majors remained.

If the regulatory controls preferred by the majors combined state production controls with a federal ban on hot oil, a control package that provided the minimum requisite stability while maximizing the autonomy of firms, their support for such a program was not consistent. The legislative history of the period reveals occasional support by the majors for more-extensive programs of federal control. Specifically, the majors supported the National Industrial Recovery Act in June 1933, eventuating in federal price and production controls, and they supported the Thomas-Disney Bill in the spring of 1934, which would have permanently institutionalized federal production controls.[24] In each case in which the majors deviated from supporting their preferred program of regulation, they did so as a compromise to avoid more-radical measures that threatened even greater controls over the industry. Support for the National Industrial Recovery Act was a timely maneuver to substitute the NIRA for the Marland-Capper Bill. Similarly, the majors' support for permanent federal production controls in the Thomas-Disney Bill was an effort to

23. Corwin, *The Constitution and What It Means Today*, p. 50.

24. *New York Times*, 23 May 1933; *National Petroleum News*, 31 May 1933, p. 7; ibid., 28 November 1934, pp. 3–4.

forestall the introduction into Congress of the Margold Bill, which would have established price controls and set retail and wholesale margins in both refining and marketing, as well as introducing federal production controls.

The NIRA

The support given by the majors for the enactment of the National Industrial Recovery Act has often been cited as evidence that the majors wanted federal regulation of their industry.[25] In retrospect, the NIRA led to federal production controls and would have permitted federal price controls. But these powers were not inherent in the NIRA. They were derived from the petroleum code, which was subsequently drafted under the NIRA to govern the industry. The only provisions relating specifically to the oil industry in the NIRA were those of Section 9. Sections 9a and 9b dealt with rate control for petroleum pipelines, including possible divestment proceedings against holding companies accused of monopolistic practices, and were clearly objectionable to the interests of the majors. Section 9c provided the minimal federal ban on hot oil, which the majors supported. The identification of provisions that were clearly objectionable to the majors in the NIRA supports the assertion that the majors saw the NIRA as the best compromise version they could hope for, rather than as an expression of their own preference for an extended regulatory state.[26]

Indeed, despite the ominous potential of Sections 9a and 9b, the majors saw the NIRA as a partial victory, because they had succeeded in bringing oil industry legislation within the rubric of general industrial recovery. Aligning themselves with other industries, the majors believed, would moderate regulatory controls.[27] Above all else, the majors feared being singled out as a problem industry, a designation that could become a prelude to public utility status and a justification for federal price-fixing. Wirt Franklin, acting on behalf of IPA independents, had helped draft the legislation that embodied the majors' fears. Introduced in both houses on 19 May 1933 by Congressman Ernest W. Marland and Senator Arthur Capper, this bill called for the secretary of the interior to allocate mandatory production quotas to the states and to the various pools within

25. The revisionists have incorrectly argued that the majors were as thoroughly disenchanted with state regulation as the independents were and therefore turned to comprehensive federal controls as the only viable alternative to market chaos. See Nash, *U.S. Oil Policy*, chaps. 6 and 7.

26. *National Petroleum News*, 26 April 1933, p. 18, indicates the majors' views on divestment. Warren C. Platt, editor of the *National Petroleum News*, urged acceptance of the NIRA as the best alternative available. See ibid., 31 May 1933, p. 7; see also *New York Times*, 23 May 1933, and *National Petroleum News*, 31 May 1933, p. 7.

27. *New York Times*, 27 May 1933; *National Petroleum News*, 17 May 1933, p. 27; ibid., 14 June 1933, p. 16.

a state on the basis of his determination of market demand, to limit imports and withdrawals from storage of petroleum and refined products, to determine equitable rates for transportation and storage, and to set minimum and maximum prices to prevent either unfair competition in the sale of petroleum or its products, or the exploitation of the public. Thus the majors' support for the NIRA, in light of the more radical Marland-Capper alternative, was consistent with their ultimate intention, always pursued in a flexible and pragmatic manner, to avoid federal controls.[28]

In the struggle over the Marland-Capper Bill, which was subsequently revised and introduced as an amendment to the NIRA, the success of the majors in resisting the extension of federal controls was at least partially derived from the strategic advantage that our political system bestows on any group resisting a new federal program. Roosevelt's desire for quick passage of a general recovery measure gave him little leverage against obstructionists, who preferred the disciplining power of unimpeded market forces to federal price and production controls. Yet if proponents of federal oil control were forced to compromise on specific amendments to the NIRA that would have explicitly provided for it, this proved to be a Pyrrhic victory for the majors when power shifted to the proponents of federal control after the NIRA was enacted. Because the NIRA provided the president with the power to impose a code if the industry could not come to an agreement, and because President Roosevelt favored more extensive controls, the independents were in the driver's seat when the petroleum code was drafted.[29] Now the pressure was on the majors to compromise their resistance to federal regulation, since autonomy within a federal program would be maximized if the industry presented a united front.

Taking advantage of the expanded scope for legitimate cooperation offered by the NIRA, on 16 June 1933 the industry gathered in Chicago to draft an industrial code. Despite the opposition of most of the majors, Wirt Franklin successfully marshaled the large majority of votes at the Chicago conference held by independents in favor of both production and price controls. The price-fixing clause, in particular, was the most hotly debated item on the agenda of the convention.[30]

Harry Sinclair, E. B. Resser of the Barnsdall Corporation, and Judge Amos Beaty of Phillips Petroleum were center firm leaders who for idiosyncratic reasons favored this clause; most of the other corporate leaders strongly disagreed. Judge C. B. Ames, chairman of the board of Texaco, warned that price-fixing was doomed to failure if supply was not

28. *National Petroleum News,* 19 April 1933, pp. 7–8.
29. The industry was aware that a failure to agree would maximize government control over the industry. See ibid., 14 June 1933, p. 11.
30. Ibid., 21 June 1933, pp. 7–12; *New York Times,* 24 June 1933.

brought into line with demand and that price-fixing was superfluous when such a balance existed. C. C. Herndon, vice-president of Skelly Oil Company, indicted the code for inviting the government to take charge of prices and profits and predicted that the industry would look back on the step with sorrow. R. G. A. van dear Woude, president of Shell Petroleum Corporation, described his experience in conducting business in the Netherlands, where price-fixing was an established fact. He asserted that government price-fixing was a benefit to the consumer at the expense of the producer because prices would be frozen at unprofitable levels by politicians subjected to public ire when prices increased.[31]

Price-fixing threatened to rigidify the market and strip the majors of important competitive advantages over smaller nonintegrated firms. Although the majors conceded that federal regulation was needed to stop the flow of hot oil, they believed that once production was limited the market would bring prices to an acceptable level. It was crucial that limitation of supply could be accomplished without creating a vast federal bureaucracy to monitor the activities of the oil industry. Indeed, it had been suggested that most of the federal responsibility for preventing the shipments of hot oil could be discharged through the Internal Revenue Service and preexisting state programs. Price-fixing, on the other hand, involved continuously sifting and monitoring huge amounts of information. Such a task would have required a specialized bureaucracy of the scope of the Interstate Commerce Commission (ICC), which fixed rates for the railroads. Whatever fond memories of cooperation between government and business during World War I still lingered, they were not memories of the price-fixing during this period.[32]

The arguments of the majors were of no avail against the rhetoric of the independents, who outvoted the majors at the Chicago conference and included a price-fixing provision in the proposed code. Wirt Franklin's rejoinder that he opposed "letting the powers that have fixed the prices in the past continue to fix them in the future" recast the issue for the independents.[33] The question "Should prices be fixed?" was displaced by the question "Who will fix prices: the majors or the government?" In that form the answer of the independents was clear. The majors lost at Chicago, but then continued to press for the elimination of the price-fixing clause.

On 26 June 1933, American Petroleum Institute representatives reported back to their board of directors on the proposed code, and a vigorous discussion concerning the implications of price-fixing by the federal government ensued. The API was aware of the dangers of disapproving

31. *National Petroleum News*, 21 June 1933, pp. 10–12.
32. Ibid., 31 May 1933, pp. 7–8.
33. Ibid., 21 June 1933, p. 10.

the proposed Chicago Code, for if that only set the stage for the president to impose a code, they might end up with even less entrepreneurial autonomy. Nevertheless, most of the majors were adamantly opposed to the proposed code. The API board resolved this dispute by approving the Chicago Code without denying the right of any member to oppose particular provisions at the upcoming federal hearings on the code. Gulf, Shell Union, Standard of Indiana, Standard Oil of New Jersey, The Texas Company (Texaco), Sun Oil, Atlantic Refining, Mid-Continent, Ohio Oil, Magnolia, and General Petroleum all approved the code with a reservation attached in opposition to the price-fixing clause.[34] Despite their opposition and the well-known reservations of General Hugh Johnson concerning price-fixing, the influence of the independents was sufficient to retain the controversial power in the final code.

The Privileged Position of the Independents

On 29 August 1933, Roosevelt named Harold Ickes, secretary of the interior, to administer the oil code. By this single administrative action he upset the carefully calculated legislative strategy of the majors prior to the passage of the NIRA, which had attempted to align the oil industry with other manufacturing industries under a general recovery measure. Now every other industry was subsumed under the National Recovery Administration, a new agency to be headed by Hugh Johnson, while the oil code was administered by the Interior Department. Ickes was a progressive Republican whose outspoken views of public regulation of business were more worrisome than the views of the more moderate Johnson.[35] The administrative isolation of the oil industry subjected it to the threat of far more extensive controls than any other industry, and Ickes exploited that isolation by holding the threat of conversion to a public utility over the heads of the majors.[36]

The institutional mechanism established to administer the code raised

34. *New York Times*, 18 June 1933; *Baltimore Sun*, 10 September 1933; Nordhauser, p. 119. The opposition of big business to price-fixing through the NRA was not confined to the petroleum industry. Charles Roos notes that a majority of the members of the Industrial Advisory Board, dominated by big business, were "opposed to price-fixing whether it was direct or through various schemes of prohibiting sales below cost." It is more plausible to assume that this general reluctance to engage in price-fixing through the NRA reflected business fears that prices would ultimately be set by government officials than to assume it reflected a commitment to a genuinely competitive market. See Roos, p. 70n.

35. One Ickes biographer, Linda Lear, characterized Ickes this way: "By 1933 he identified the leaders of big business and the owners of public utilities as villains, he could applaud as well Roosevelt's attacks on Wall Street and on commercial bankers" (Linda Lear, *Harold L. Ickes: The Aggressive Progressive, 1874–1933* [New York, 1981], p. 401).

36. *National Petroleum News*, 30 August 1933, pp. 3–4; René de Visme Williamson, *The Politics of Planning in the Oil Industry Under the Code* (New York, 1936), p. 30. The public

the most fundamental issues broached by the NRA. Poised between industrial self-government and federal bureaucratic control, administrative arrangements would determine the eventual locus of control. However willing the independents were to turn to federal relief from ruinous competition, even they were sensitive to the issue of outside control. Thus the Chicago proposal called for administration of the code by a National Emergency Committee of fifty-four oil men, equally divided between producers and refiners, on the one hand, and marketers, on the other. The power of the president remained the negative one of approval or disapproval of code provisions, including the right to suspend any provision that operated to the detriment of national recovery.[37]

This arrangement was not acceptable to the administration, and the structure that finally emerged duplicated the ambiguous public-private mixture of the NRA as a whole. The final code established a fifteen-member Planning and Coordination Committee (P&CC), primarily representing the industry but including three government representatives as well. All the members of the P&CC were to be appointed by President Roosevelt, but nominations for the industry representatives were to be solicited from the various groups within the industry. Officially, the P&CC acted only in an advisory capacity to the code administrator, a federal official.[38] The petroleum administrator would be aided by a federal agency, to be designated by the president, which had the power to investigate conditions in the industry and make an independent determination of reasonable market demand on which all production restrictions would be based. When Roosevelt selected Ickes to supervise the code, Ickes promptly established a Petroleum Administration Board (PAB) within the Department of the Interior to carry out these functions.[39] The struggle for power between the P&CC and the PAB shaped the later history of the petroleum code.

Ickes and Roosevelt were confronted by a divided industry when they sought nominations for the P&CC. The code called for twelve industry appointees and three government representatives, but each of the three factions in the industry put forward a slate of twelve nominees. Had President Roosevelt's primary concern been to achieve a balance among these factions, some nominees from each list would have been included in the final board. Instead, Roosevelt selected all his appointees from the IPA nominees of the Committee of 54, leaving most of the majors and

utility threat was later made explicit when Ickes addressed the annual API meetings on 12 November 1934. See *National Petroleum News*, 14 November 1934, p. 19; ibid., 21 November 1934, p. 17.

37. *National Petroleum News*, 21 June 1933, p. 25.

38. Article VII, Section 3 (see Mayers, p. 254). See also *National Petroleum News*, 30 August 1933, p. 4.

39. *API Quarterly*, October 1933, pp. 9–10.

dissident independents unrepresented on the final committee.[40] Thus, the limits of the government's commitment to industrial self-government was apparent from the very beginning. By excluding such prominent oil men as C. B. Ames of the Texas Company, C. E. Arnott of Socony Vacuum, W. H. Farish of Standard Oil of New Jersey, and J. Edgar Pew of Sun Oil Company, the P&CC came to rely more on its privileged relationship with government as the source of its authority than any other major industry's code authority.

The role of the federal bureaucracy as a catalyst for the organization of private interests was clearly displayed in the oil industry. The replacement of informal coordination of interests by a more formal organized mode of coordination was not a disinterested manifestation of a systemic organizational revolution; it had a direct impact on the interests that gained access to political decision makers. The independents, fragmented into a large number of regional and specialized associations, required formal organization to realize their potential political clout. When the NIRA forced these associations to agree on a common code and to establish an industry-wide committee to supervise the administration of the code, a corporatist arrangement between private interests and government actors emerged and overcame the organizational disadvantage of the dispersion of the independents. Such a corporatist arrangement was unnecessary for the majors, who could easily informally coordinate the political efforts of dominant firms.

Although the P&CC had institutionalized the alliance between progressive New Deal elites and the independents in the oil industry, the New Dealers were committed to retaining ultimate control over the oil code to assure that its implementation was compatible with the goals of the NRA. But the independents wanted industrial self-government dominated by the independents. The conflict latent in the ambiguously defined shared authority of the P&CC and the PAB surfaced soon after the code took effect and began to disrupt the honeymoon of business-government cooperation. By 12 October 1933 the tendency of the PAB to administrate without heed to the P&CC provoked Michael L. Benedum, one of the earliest and staunchest supporters of Roosevelt among oil men, to protest to the president:

> Ever since the first meeting of our Planning and Coordination Committee several weeks ago, there has been a persistent tendency on the part of the solicitors in the Interior Department to apparently interfere with the function

40. *National Petroleum News*, 23 August 1933, pp. 11–19; ibid., 7 September 1933, p. 12; Nordhauser, pp. 130–131. The P&CC did include Standard of California and Standard of Ohio, but none of the prominent anti-price-fixing group. Dissident independents were excluded because their laissez-faire views were antithetical to the spirit of the NRA, not because they were small producers.

of this Planning and Coordination Committee. This persistent interference in blocking and ignoring of the recommendation of your Committee have so discouraged the latter that we, Mr. Moffet and myself, find ourselves with the Committee, in the main, wondering if it is the desire of the Administration to support the Code and Rules approved by you and for which, as they thought, they were appointed to carry out. In other words, this Committee, composed of the most practical men of the highest intelligence and integrity in the Oil Industry, finds the vital parts of its recommendations, made after most careful work, completely ignored and disregarded by departmental attorneys, who know little or nothing about the Oil Industry, to the end that your program of recovery is actually jeopardized and the work of your Committee completely destroyed.[41]

When the matter was referred to him by the president, Ickes attempted to assuage Benedum's fears by defending the disinterested character of the bureaucrats who were "sincerely devoted to this administration." While their legalistic outlook and limited knowledge of the oil business might not seem efficient to the practical bent of men in the oil business, they prevented the administration from rushing into decisions that were not for the common good.[42]

The independence of the P&CC from the PAB and the Department of the Interior was asserted shortly thereafter, when the P&CC, contrary to the practice followed in September and October, began to give out press releases about its activities and recommendations without first clearing them with the secretary of the interior. Wirt Franklin defended this new practice, asserting, "We now find . . . and the conviction has been growing on us for some weeks, that such a course [i.e., clearing press releases with the Department of the Interior] is not conducive to the best results to be obtained in bringing that cooperation from the industry which is essential."[43] Citing the demand of the industry to be kept abreast of developments connected with the administration of the code, they informed Ickes that they could no longer honor his request that their reports be internal departmental documents. Ickes took strong exception to this action by the P&CC: "The almost inevitable result will be to confuse the public and cause it to believe that a conflict exists between your committee and the Oil Administrator."[44]

Having suggested that their direct access to the press would not make for "harmonious cooperation," Ickes objected particularly to their first press release. In this release the P&CC interpreted one of Ickes's orders, and while Ickes did not object to the specific interpretation, he reserved

41. Benedum to FDR, 12 October 1933, Ickes Papers, 1933, Box 217, Folder No. 3.
42. Ickes to Benedum, 23 October 1933, ibid.
43. Franklin to Ickes, 9 November 1933, ibid.
44. Ickes to Franklin, 11 November 1933, ibid.

the right to interpret his own orders and did not consider himself bound by any interpretation provided by the P&CC. He then added a crucial clarification regarding the status of industrial self-government under the NIRA:

> It cannot be said without substantial qualification that in the contemplation of the code, the oil industry is to be a self-governing industry. If this were true there would be no Oil Administrator or Federal Agency representing the Government, or if there were, they would be without power. In view of the very wide powers granted by the Oil Code to the President of the United States, and by him delegated to the Oil Administrator and the Department of the Interior, it cannot be seriously urged that the Oil Administrator is merely a figurehead. If the Oil Administrator has any power of authority under the code, that power and authority are in limitation of whatever power the Planning and Coordination Committee may have, and to the degree that such power exists outside of and not subject to the Planning and Coordination Committee, the oil industry is not in fact a self-governing industry.[45]

While Ickes asserted that he at all times sought to cooperate with the P&CC and sought its opinion before making any decisions, he noted that such opinions were recommendations that did not bind him: "Neither the Oil Administrator nor the Federal Agency is a subordinate of the Planning and Coordination Committee to whom orders can be issued." Ickes noted that his authority was as a direct representative of the president of the United States, with "wide powers delegated to him," and that he would faithfully perform the duties and obligations placed on him by the oil code.[46]

By early November the developing behind-the-scenes rift became public. Dissatisfaction with the code among some independent oil men opening new pools in Oklahoma led them to circumvent the procedure specified in the oil code of submitting their plans for future operations to the P&CC, and they submitted them directly to the PAB. This led the secretary of the PAB, Nathan Margold, to solicit the firms in the industry and inquire whether they preferred to deal directly with the federal government through the PAB or indirectly through the P&CC.[47]

Wirt Franklin, chairman of the P&CC, heard of Margold's request on 14 November 1933 from an editor of the *Oil and Gas Journal* while attending a meeting of the IPA in Tulsa, Oklahoma. Addressing the delegates, Franklin praised the progress toward stabilization made by government-industry cooperation, but indicated his opposition to government control. He forwarded Margold's request to the industry by casting the issue in

45. Ibid.
46. Ibid.
47. Franklin to Ickes, 15 November 1933, ibid.; *National Petroleum News*, 15 November 1933, p. 16.

terms of industrial self-government versus bureaucratic rule. Franklin went on to suggest that such majors as Standard Oil of New Jersey, whose opposition to price-fixing by the code authority was known, were behind the opposition among small producers to the authority of the P&CC. The 450 oil men attending the IPA banquet unanimously adopted a motion supporting the P&CC in its struggles with the PAB.[48]

Ickes responded to this challenge to his authority by reemphasizing the advisory status of the P&CC and asserting, "The conception of the code was that the President should be the final arbiter in oil matters."[49] Thus the hopes of the P&CC that the PAB would confine its activities to enforcing policies determined by the P&CC were quickly dashed.[50] While the authority of bureaucratic elites was certainly constrained by the interests of their small-business and labor constituencies, as is the case in the relationship of any elite to its social base, the dominant leadership role assumed by bureaucrats over small-business constituents enhanced their status beyond the level possible when big-business leaders acted as a counterweight to bureaucratic power.

Stabilization without Rationalization

The intention, if not always the effect, of administration under the oil code was to preserve the position and market share of small entrepreneurs by detailed controls that sought to mitigate competition and preserve individual competitors, sometimes even at the expense of economic efficiency and rationality. The federal stabilization of a chaotic market existed, at least in part, as an alternative rather than a supplement to the mode of stabilization sought by the majors is demonstrated most clearly by the controversy that erupted over vertical integration.

In the majors' program for stabilization of the retail stage of the petroleum industry, market discipline played an important role. It was precisely the harshness of the market that made independent retailers flock to the relative security of contractual arrangements with the majors. The majors sought a method of achieving vertical integration without investing exorbitant amounts of capital in the already overdeveloped market network. In 1929 they discovered a method of promoting exclusive dealings contracts that violated the spirit but not the letter of the Clayton Act. Lease and agency agreements, in which the refiner leases the service station from its owner and then reappoints the owner as the refiners' exclusive agent, spread like wildfire throughout the industry from 1929 to

---

48. *Tulsa World*, 14 November 1933, included in Ickes Papers, 1933, Box 217, Folder No. 3.
49. Ickes Press Release, 14 November 1933, ibid.
50. *National Petroleum News*, 25 October 1933, p. 12.

1932. By the latter year it was estimated that as much as 65 percent of the marketing capacity of the industry was under this form of agreement.[51]

Offering the independent retailer a fixed margin on his sales, and gasoline at a discounted rate, some small businessmen had eagerly traded their independence for the greater financial security of these arrangements. Others, compelled by economic necessity, resented being driven into such contracts. Those who resisted the inducements to submit to such arrangements resented the entry of the majors into the retail market and objected to the "unfair" discounts given to lease and agency outlets. The disposition of this hotly disputed practice deadlocked the Chicago Code conference, and Johnson resolved the conflict by freezing the status quo and relegating the final decision to the Federal Trade Commission (FTC).[52]

This status quo was extended for the next sixteen months when neither the FTC nor Ickes would commit to a final ruling, but that status quo was disruptive of the majors' plan for market stabilization. Control of 65 percent of marketing capacity would be of little value in mitigating competition as long as the other 35 percent remained fiercely competitive. When Ickes finally rendered a decision on 4 March 1935, he undoubtedly intended to phase out lease and agency agreements gradually without unduly disrupting the fragile recovery that was gaining momentum. Making permanent the temporary prohibition on lease and agency contracts, he also attacked the exclusive dealing incentives for such arrangements for both refiners and retailers.[53] The ruling never had a significant impact on the gasoline retail marketing structure because the NIRA was ruled unconstitutional shortly thereafter, but it exemplified the conflict between bureaucratic and big-business elites. Once the federal government, rather than the corporation, became the agency of stabilization, the superior political clout of the independents compensated for their weak market position.

The assertion that the interests of the majors were jeopardized by their NRA code would appear to be contradicted by developments that facilitated the cartelization of the gasoline market during the last months of the NRA. The program that permitted cartelization was a buying program initiated by the majors to purchase and store excess quantities of gasoline from smaller refiners to prevent it from demoralizing the market. In exchange for this, the smaller refiners agreed to not purchase hot oil and to abide by predetermined refining quotas. This program began operations in March 1935 and was continued through the end of 1936 before it was finally dissolved by an antitrust suit from the Justice Department.[54] It had

---

51. Watkins, p. 189.
52. *National Petroleum News*, 28 June 1933, pp. 11–17.
53. Watkins, pp. 188–191.
54. *United States v. Socony-Vacuum Oil Co.*, 310 U.S. 150 (1940).

been initiated with at least the tacit approval of Secretary Ickes.[55] What better proof that the NRA was a form of government sanctioned cartelization seeking to rationalize the market for the benefit of the majors?

Contrary to the images conjured up by the abstract notion of a cartel, the historical context from which the gasoline buying program emerged makes it clear that the buying program was not a preferred strategy of market rationalization on the part of the majors, but, at least initially, was forced on them to forestall an even more undesirable alternative—federal price-fixing. The buying program that began in 1935 was actually the successor to an unsuccessful buying program first established in the spring of 1934 with the approval of Ickes.[56] That program had collapsed in the fall of 1934 under joint pressure from the majors, who had found the program to be financially ruinous, and from the Justice Department's antitrust division.[57] The relationship of the NRA to the interests of the majors and the independents is particularly clear in the history of the first buying program.

The first buying program was begun in a period when federal effort to stem the flow of hot oil had not been successfully institutionalized. Although initial Interior Department efforts to monitor interstate shipments of oil had reduced railroad tank car shipments of illegal oil from an estimated 98,000 barrels a day to an estimated 36,000 barrels a day,[58] this success had proved short-lived as the courts hampered judicial enforcement, and recalcitrant refiners discovered ways to circumvent the controls that remained. The first buying program was implemented in April 1934, just after Judge Randolph Bryant, a Texas District Court judge, had ruled in *Panama Refining v. Ryan* that Section 9c of the NIRA was unconstitutional and had enjoined federal officials from inspecting East Texas refineries and wells.[59] While an appeals court reversed the district court ruling in May, the continuing cloud of unconstitutionality that hung over attempts to enforce the ban on hot oil hampered federal officials responsible for its enforcement. Indeed, the suspicion that the federal ban on hot oil was unconstitutional was confirmed when the Supreme Court upheld Bryant's reservations when it finally issued its ruling on the case on 7 January 1935.[60]

55. Nordhauser, p. 152; Nash, *U.S. Oil Policy,* pp. 152–153.

56. Nordhauser, p. 146.

57. Ibid., pp. 148–152; *National Petroleum News,* 21 November 1933, pp. 19–20.

58. Nordhauser, p. 115.

59. Ibid., pp. 144–148; *National Petroleum News,* 11 April 1933, pp. 7–11.

60. The *Panama Refining* decision foreshadowed the *Schechter Poultry* case overturning the NIRA itself. The Court held that Congress had failed to provide adequate standards the president could use to determine when to exercise his discretionary power to ban hot oil. Had it not been for an inadvertent deletion of a clause that declared the production of hot oil to be an unfair trade practice when the petroleum code was revised, the Court could have ruled on the constitutionality of the entire NIRA in this case. But the absence of such a provision in the petroleum code spared

These facts are extremely important in understanding the NRA-sponsored buying program. Cartels are generally ineffective without some controls over production, and attempts to corner a market by purchasing a commodity can be financially ruinous under conditions of runaway production. The majors were accepting substantial financial risks in launching their buying program when production had not yet been brought under control. The use of such a high-risk cartelization strategy must be explained. Because the majors had called for the industry conference that eventually led to the first buying program immediately after Secretary Ickes had announced on 16 October 1933 that the Interior Department would soon hold hearings to determine appropriate prices for petroleum products, and because the majors had vigorously fought inclusion of a price-fixing clause in the original petroleum code, it is reasonable to presume that the buying program was initiated to forestall the one contingency the majors feared above all else—government price-fixing.[61]

Ickes's announcement had caught the majors by surprise. Until this time, Ickes had given no indication that he was anxious to fix prices. In his initial acts as administrator he had declined to invoke price-setting powers given to him in the code, preferring to control supply through production quotas, limiting withdrawals from storage, and restricting imports. He stated to the press that he "saw no reason for invoking any powers under the code which it may not be necessary to exercise."[62] Later he indicated a clear perception of the size of the task if price-fixing were invoked: "We would have to have a great new building for the petroleum administration."[63] Ickes had only to look at the sizable administrative staff that the ICC required for determining rail rates to foresee the consequences of undertaking price-fixing in the petroleum industry. The internal dissension within the industry over this issue undoubtedly contributed to his caution, because any program without the support of most of the industry had the potential for becoming a bureaucratic nightmare.

Despite these reservations, Ickes responded to growing P&CC pressure to undertake further steps to stabilize the oil market. Unlike the majors, the IPA independents who controlled the P&CC were not reluctant to turn to price controls for immediate relief from distressed conditions. One of the first actions taken by the P&CC was its recommendation to Secretary Ickes that he promulgate a price-fixing order that would have pegged the price of mid-continent crude at $1.11 a barrel.[64] When production controls

---

the code from judicial review and permitted the justices to focus narrowly on the objectionable Section 9c.

61. *National Petroleum News*, 18 October 1933, p. 11; ibid., 22 November 1933, pp. 3–4.
62. Ibid., 6 September 1933, p. 8.
63. Ibid., 11 October 1933, p. 3.
64. Nordhauser, pp. 136–137.

then failed to prevent the periodic outbreak of gasoline price wars on the Pacific and Atlantic coasts, and when those price wars threatened to undermine existing production controls by creating a market for hot oil, Ickes decided to act.

Although there was uncertainty regarding the constitutional authority to regulate a local price war under the interstate commerce clause, Ickes, undaunted by the legal questions, promulgated a price schedule for the industry on 16 October. Controls were to become effective on 1 December after public hearings, begining 30 October, permitted objections to the proposed schedule to be entered.[65] When the Interior Department encountered difficulties in quickly gathering the relevant information to hold the hearings, the hearings were postponed until 20 November. A tentative price schedule, identical to the one submitted by the P&CC, established a basic price for crude oil of $1.11 a barrel and 6.5 cents a gallon for 60–64.9 octane gasoline, with guaranteed margins to jobbers and retailers.[66]

Anti-price-fixing forces in the industry quickly mobilized to oppose this action. While some of the opposition arose from concern about specific details in the proposed schedule, the majors were more concerned with the broader issues of free enterprise and government-regulated prices. They were already preparing to test any such order in court. By this time, however, even the P&CC had begun to fear that it was spawning a Frankenstein. When Ickes had announced price-fixing on 16 October, Nathan Margold, chairman of the PAB, also proposed a new administrative apparatus to set and enforce the prices. The size of this proposed new bureaucracy brought home even to the ardent advocates of federal intervention the potential dangers involved. Wirt Franklin, head of the IPA, wrote to Ickes concerning Margold's plans for expanding the PAB:

> We . . . write you again, this time emphasizing our opposition to the creation of a large governmental board, with nation-wide activities, for the purposes of the Petroleum Code.
>
> Whatever is necessary for enforcement, in conjunction with the industry's own efforts, should, of course, be provided, but we are certain that the industry will oppose any plan which may seem unduly expensive and paternalistic, and that the industry will not acquiesce in a special and additional tax to support such elaborate and far-reaching plans! . . . But the organization chart submitted by Mr. Margold and his questions about salaries and his estimate of an annual budget of $3,500,000 have filled us with alarm.[67]

65. *National Petroleum News*, 18 October 1933, p. 11.
66. Ibid., 22 November 1933, pp. 3–4.
67. Wirt Franklin to Ickes, 18 October 1933, Records of the Petroleum Administration Board, RG 232, Box 194; Nordhauser, p. 140.

But in the absence of any feasible alternative to government-imposed price controls, a realization of the dangers alone would probably not have been sufficient cause for the independents to forgo their plans.

The majors were aware that government-imposed price-fixing was imminent unless they could reconcile their differences with the independent-dominated P&CC and agree to an alternate plan. This led to new meetings between the majors and the independents on 14 November in New York City. While the majors and the P&CC differed in their estimation of the extent of bureaucratic control entailed by price-fixing, both realized that a divided industry could become a pretext for more government control. With both sides more willing to compromise, an agreement was hammered out just before the opening of the public price hearings on 20 November. The proposals were rushed to Ickes and arrived just as Margold called the public hearings to order. In light of these new developments, the hearings were postponed until 5 December, and implementation of the price schedule was postponed until 1 January.[68]

The plan finally agreed on by the majors and the independents involved a centralized buying pool that would purchase surplus supplies of crude, gasoline, and other petroleum products from independent producers and refiners. This buying pool would graduate the entry of petroleum products onto the market to avoid a price collapse. The plan was to have gone into effect after it was signed by the major oil companies and approved by Secretary Ickes and the P&CC. On 29 November, however, Senator McAdoo from California announced that he would push for a Senate investigation of the oil industry under the NRA. The majors, fearing that their efforts at stabilization would be perceived as exploitation of the consumer by an oil cartel, withdrew from the proposed agreement. But with no other alternatives to price-fixing, they were forced to reopen negotiations with the P&CC within a week. C. B. Ames of the Texas Company led a delegation to Washington for further consultations. Ickes, who was still reluctant to undertake government price-fixing, appeared favorably disposed to giving the industry another chance at voluntary self-regulation as long as the interests of the independents were being protected. As negotiations between industry factions bogged down, Ickes invited representatives of the majors and the P&CC to his office on 4 December. Issuing an ultimatum, he stated he would impose government price-fixing unless a voluntary plan was agreed on by 7 December. On that day the representatives of the industry emerged from the Department of the Interior with two new agreements that would spare the industry from government-imposed price-fixing.[69]

68. *National Petroleum News*, 6 December 1933, pp. 3–4.
69. Ibid.; ibid., 13 December 1933, pp. 11–13.

The first agreement established a gasoline equalization pool called the National Petroleum Agency to take surplus stocks of gasoline and crude oil off the market. The twenty-five subscribing companies committed $10 million to purchase distress gasoline from dealers who signed a standard market agreement. Refiners who signed such contracts bound themselves not to purchase any crude oil tainted with the suspicion of being hot oil. The program depended heavily on the success of federal efforts to enforce state proration laws, but it also reinforced such efforts by voluntary industry cooperation. With effectively enforced proration, nonsigners would be prevented from unduly expanding their market by their limited supplies. The independent refiners who signed were guaranteed a minimum supply of crude by the majors, who would contribute up to 1 percent of their own supply to independents if it became necessary. The pool squeezed the smaller, inefficient refiners who could survive only on cheap crude oil produced in excess of state conservation laws, but it promised relief to most of the other independents in the industry. It even secured a market position for smaller refiners who were willing and minimally efficient enough to play by the rules.[70]

The marketing agreement, to take effect only if 85 percent of the refining capacity of the country signed up, committed refiners to enforcing a program of resale price maintenance and fixed margins for all distributors of gasoline. Retailers and wholesalers who violated their contracts would be excluded from obtaining supplies from any party to the agreement. This agreement was to be administered by stabilization committees composed of two representatives of the majors and one from an independent integrated firm for each of the six regions into which the nation was divided. The pool would collapse if the glut of gasoline proved too great to absorb, so the objective to hold no more than 46 million barrels of gasoline stock by 1 July 1934 became the benchmark for continuing the pool after that date. If the desired effect of drying up the market for hot oil by guaranteeing refiners a reasonable return succeeded by 1 July, the board of directors of the pool was empowered to support higher crude oil prices than the present target of $1.00 a barrel. The independents still sought the eventual goal of $1.11 a barrel of 36–36.9 gravity mid-continent crude, with 60–64.9 octane gasoline prices pegged at 18.5 times the price of crude.[71]

Objections from the Justice Department quashed the plans for a National Petroleum Agency. During the life-span of the NRA, antitrust laws were enforced laxly, but they were never abandoned, and the Justice Department engaged Secretary Ickes in a running battle throughout the petroleum

70. Ibid., 6 December 1933, pp. 11–13.
71. Ibid.

code on the limits of permissible collusion. At more than one point the Justice Department prosecuted producers for participating in plans sanctioned by Ickes, endangering his efforts to stabilize the market.[72]

The demise of plans for a National Petroleum Agency at first shifted attention to a federal program of refinery production quotas to stabilize the chaotic gasoline market. The majors had sought to avoid extending federal controls over refining, but the failure to stabilize crude oil prices and to prevent the periodic outbreak of gasoline price wars undermined their efforts. While Ickes shared the majors' belief that production controls for crude oil were the fundamental remedy for the industry's problems, he had no compunction about extending controls over refiners. As early as 18 October 1933 he issued an order—one that clearly exceeded his power under the code—authorizing the P&CC to allocate production quotas to refiners. Once these allocations were approved by Ickes, refiners exceeding these quotas would be guilty of an unfair trade practice and liable for prosecution. Article IV of the code, which dealt with refining, only permitted the regulation of refining based on a ratio of inventories to sales, but Ickes expanded its scope to include production quotas. His interpretation was promulgated without any public hearings on the issue and apparently without consultation with the P&CC.[73] The P&CC declined to exercise this gratuitous power over refining until January 1934, when its attitude changed with the collapse of plans for a buying program. On 13 January 1934 the P&CC for the first time set production quotas for gasoline in each of the eight refining districts, but it still linked these quotas to securing the proper ratios of inventories to sales and sought voluntary cooperation to implement the program. When it became clear that these controls were not adequate to prevent the recurrence of gasoline price wars, the P&CC moved to amend Article IV and to provide legal grounds for enforcement of production quotas.[74]

In late March 1934 the P&CC began drafting a proposed revision of Article IV that would have empowered it to determine "quotas in commerce," a subterfuge for production quotas, for each refinery.[75] The P&CC plan called for the mandatory use of shipping certificates by refiners to entitle them to transport gasoline to marketers, with the P&CC retaining the power to issue these certificates. The majors countered with a proposal that relied predominantly on voluntary cooperation, with the powers available to the P&CC to be exercised only if necessary. Both

72. Nordhauser, p. 146.

73. *National Petroleum News*, 22 November 1933, p. 6.

74. Ibid., 30 May 1934, p. 10.

75. Because the Supreme Court was still adhering to the distinction advanced in *United States v. E. C. Knight Co.* between production and commerce, which denied federal jurisdiction over the former, the subterfuge of "quotas in commerce" was needed to circumvent constitutional objections to federal production controls. If one could regulate commerce in oil, one could regulate its production indirectly.

plans were submitted to the Petroleum Administration Board, which had called for hearings to consider amendments to the refining section of the code.[76]

Following the first hearing on 4 April, the PAB submitted its own plan for the control of refineries. Largely a compromise version of the two plans submitted by the industry, this plan differed from both by vesting more control in government officials. Specifically, the PAB would have been commissioned to set production quotas for motor fuel and to establish proper sales to inventory ratios in each refining district while leaving the P&CC to supervise individual refinery allocations. The PAB plan also included provisions for resuscitating a Gasoline Equalization Committee to supervise a gasoline purchase plan. This provision, replacing the recent agreement to form a National Petroleum Agency, approved the purchasing of distress gasoline from nonintegrated and semi-integrated firms.

The PAB plan confirmed the fears of the majors that the NRA was becoming a pretext for federal control of the industry, and the majors hastily scheduled meetings on 6 April and 7 April in New York City to consider the proposals. Aware that they would have to present a united front with the independents to resist the PAB plan successfully, a committee of 9 representatives of the independent refiners appointed by the Western Petroleum Refiners Association joined them on 9 April. Their basic purpose was to substitute the P&CC for the PAB as the authority responsible for establishing production quotas by districts, a proposal consistent with both the earlier industry plans. The new plan also substituted the P&CC for the proposed Gasoline Equalization Committee and empowered it, where necessary, to appoint district allocators, to review contested decisions, and to invoke quotas in commerce only in extreme cases rather than resort to mandatory shipping certificates.[77]

This final industry plan synthesized the previous plans of the majors and the P&CC without enlarging federal control. The majors conceded more sweeping powers to the P&CC than they had in their initial proposals, but in return they also won the right to representation on the P&CC. The industry plan called for an enlargement of the original committee of fifteen, three of whom were government representatives, by eleven new members, seven of whom were to represent the majors. Ultimately the majors gained only six new representatives, including W. C. Teagle of Standard Oil of New Jersey, C. B. Ames of the Texas Company, and E. G. Seubert of Standard Oil of Indiana.[78] If the majors remained leery that even these powers of self-government might be an excuse for eventual

76. *National Petroleum News*, 11 April 1934, pp. 7–8.
77. Ibid., p. 7.
78. Ibid., 18 April 1934, pp. 11–12; ibid., 25 April 1934, p. 17.

federal control, they accepted this risk as preferable to the federal controls proposed in the PAB plan. They were also all too aware of an oil control bill (the Margold Bill discussed below), being drafted at this time by the PAB for congressional action, which threatened even more extensive federal controls. The majors knew that discontent among hard-pressed smaller refiners caught between higher crude oil prices and gasoline price wars was fertile ground for demands for federal intervention, and they were willing to make concessions to these refiners' interests to avoid that outcome.

When the PAB resumed its hearings on extending controls over refineries, the independents rallied around the industry proposal in preference to that of the PAB. Jules Constatin, representing the Independent Refiners Association of East Texas, endorsed the plan: "Since we have been assured of an adequate supply of crude, markets for our products, and representation on committees to be appointed, we unqualifiedly submit to the plan and will recommend it to our associates in Texas."[79] These independents, while seeking more effective relief from market forces than that provided by the earlier voluntary proposals of the majors, had been unhappy with the ''czar-like'' powers conferred on district allocators and the requirements for shipping certificates for all gasoline entering interstate commerce in the PAB plan. That independents were well aware of the danger to the industry of drastic government controls was demonstrated at the April annual meetings of the Western Petroleum Refiners Association. At those meetings, speaker after speaker warned of the danger of excessive federal control over the industry. Profits would be jeopardized if the industry became regulated as a public utility. The independents embraced the new industry plan as a reaffirmation of the self-governing provisions of the original code, but with a buying program behind them to make them effective.[80]

Ickes considered the new industry plan for two weeks before he finally announced his approval on 24 April. As had been the case with the proposed National Petroleum Agency in the fall of 1933, Ickes was reluctant to impose a regulatory program on the industry when the independents and the majors could reconcile their differences and devise a plan that adequately safeguarded the interests of the independents. The PAB did retain the authority to fix national inventories of gasoline and a national production quota, a power that could have been used to protect consumers if industry attempts to stabilize their markets raised prices beyond the levels judged appropriate by the New Dealers, but the subdivisions of that quota were in the hands of the P&CC. Ickes would supervise the program and hear appeals from the P&CC. The success of

79. Ibid., 18 April 1934, p. 12.
80. Ibid., 11 April 1934, p. 20B.

this uneasy compromise would be contingent on crude oil stabilization, jeopardized by recent setbacks in the courts, and the forbearance of the antitrust division of the Justice Department.[81]

Beginning in late April, the majors paired themselves with smaller refiners and purchased their excess supplies of gasoline. As long as the smaller refiners refused to purchase hot oil and were willing to abide by the refinery quotas set by the P&CC, their "dancing partner" major could facilitate the orderly marketing of his production without depressing the price of gasoline. While the program succeeded in stabilizing gasoline prices over the summer of 1934, this stability was constantly endangered because hot oil continued to flow.[82] Throughout the summer of 1934, more than 100,000 barrels of hot oil found their way onto the market every month. Despite the appeals court reversal of the initial district court decision in *Panama Refining Co. v. Ryan,* which had handcuffed federal enforcement efforts, smaller refiners were able to circumvent controls and run hot oil while they sold their legally produced gasoline to the majors at inflated prices.

In October 1934 the majors were forced to suspend the buying program under the threats of ever-expanding illegal production, and gasoline prices promptly collapsed.[83] The majors' worst fears had been realized. They were left with large stocks of gasoline, for which they had paid the artificially high cartel price, in a market that was now collapsing.

Ickes responded swiftly to the collapse of the first buying program and the subsequent price wars that erupted in the gasoline market. The first buying program had foundered because the government had failed to stem the flow of hot oil onto the market, and to correct that problem Ickes resorted to a new method of hot oil enforcement. The new method required that legal tenders accompany shipments of oil to attest to their legal production, a requirement that made it easier to detect hot oil than when enforcement officials relied on post hoc monthly reports. A Federal Tender Board was created to supervise the tender system. This new method was immediately successful, but the improvement in the hot oil situation came too late to save the first buying program. Although the majors agreed to resume the buying program in early November with the hot oil situation now under control, the buying program was abandoned only one week later, when Ickes withdrew his approval for it under pressure from the Justice Department.[84]

With the renewed outbreak of gasoline price wars in November, C. E. Arnott, a vice-president of Socony Vacuum who had coordinated the administration of the marketing code, called for a meeting in early

81. Ibid., 25 April 1934, pp. 16–17.
82. Ibid., 30 May 1934, p. 8; Nordhauser, pp. 142–148.
83. Nordhauser, pp. 148–152; *National Petroleum News,* 21 November 1933, pp. 19–20.
84. Nordhauser, pp. 149–150; *National Petroleum News,* 24 October 1934, pp. 7–8.

December to deal with the situation. Attended by hundreds of members of the industry, its success laid the groundwork for a new buying program. Before this second buying program could get off the ground, however, a new obstacle had to be overcome. On 7 January 1935 the Supreme Court finally delivered its long-awaited decision in the *Panana Refining Co. v. Ryan* case and struck down Section 9c of the NIRA as an unconstitutionally vague delegation of power to the president of the United States. In the wake of this decision, the market was once again flooded with hot oil. In collaboration with Senators Thomas Gore and Tom Connally, Ickes responded quickly to this situation and reestablished control over production by rushing to the Congress a new bill that duplicated Section 9c except for the problematic delegation of power. The Connally Hot Oil Act passed within a month, and subsequent judicial approval finally established federal control over hot oil on a sound legal and practical basis.[85]

In the spring of 1935 the second buying program was finally initiated. This program helped raise the price of gasoline during 1935 and 1936 until it was successfully attacked by the Justice Department in *United States v. Socony Vacuum Oil Co.* Although Ickes had not explicitly legitimated the second buying program, neither had he discouraged it.[86] Committed to stabilizing the oil industry in order to protect the interests of the independents, he had allowed the oil industry to become cartelized. Despite his progressive suspicions of business, Ickes's attempts to realize the NRA's goal of fair competition had imperceptibly become a justification for promoting business cartels, because nothing less than a cartel could have saved many of the independents from bankruptcy.

The Thomas-Disney Bill

The majors' interest in the financially risky buying program had initially been stimulated by Secretary Ickes's plan for federal price-fixing for the oil industry. By the spring of 1934 the threat of price-fixing through the NRA had been compounded by the threat of production controls and price-fixing through additional legislation as well. The brief two-year authorization of the NIRA had encouraged efforts by independents to institutionalize market controls on a more permanent basis in any event, and the independents who favored federal control over production viewed the need for more permanent legislation as an opportunity to transfer more responsibility for production controls from the states to the federal government. The difficulties the NRA had encountered in stabilizing the oil market during its first months of operation, when the NRA

85. Nordhauser, pp. 154–155.
86. Ibid., p. 152.

shied away from federal price-fixing and production controls, only confirmed the judgment of these independents that more extensive federal controls were necessary. The restricted legislative mandates of some state regulatory agencies still allowed many producers to evade state regulations undetected or, when discovered, to hamstring controls by maneuvers in the courts. A persistent lack of cooperation between federal and state officials, each jealously defending their spheres of influence, gave further credence to the argument that additional federal controls were necessary. The P&CC, dominated by advocates of federal control, thus continued to push for new legislation to supplement the powers granted by the NIRA.[87]

By April 1934 there were at least two legislative efforts afoot. The first measure was a bill offered by Oklahoma Senator Elmer Thomas and Oklahoma Congressman Wesley Disney authorizing the secretary of the interior to set mandatory production quotas. The second measure, referred to as the Margold Bill because Nathan Margold of the Petroleum Administration Board had a hand in drafting it, went considerably beyond the Thomas-Disney Bill in extending federal control not only over production but over refining and marketing as well. Asserting that the oil industry was "affected with a national public interest," the Margold Bill empowered the PAB (1) to restrict the development of new facilities in wholesale or retail trade, (2) to set reasonable prices, differentials, and margins for petroleum and its products, and (3) to approve agreements by the industry to eliminate unfair competitive practices. The PAB was to be staffed by people with technical competence in oil matters but without any financial interests in the industry. The bill was a significant step away from the industrial self-government elements under the NRA. Finally, the Margold Bill prohibited judicial review of any consideration of facts unless new and additional evidence that indicated that the board's decision was unreasonable could be adduced. The Margold Bill was never actually introduced in Congress, but it played a critical role in the calculations of various conflicting industry groups.[88]

While there was no evidence that Roosevelt was behind the Margold Bill, the majors were sufficiently intimidated by its potential support to vote at the annual API meetings in May to support the Thomas-Disney Bill as a less extreme form of control.[89] Although the majors continued to put their faith in state production controls supplemented by a federal ban on hot oil, and they still feared that federal production controls would provide an entrée for federal price controls, they were forced to make concessions to secure the maximum feasible freedom from regulatory controls. The IPA independents, consistent with their previous support for

87. *National Petroleum News,* 17 October 1934, p. 11.
88. Ibid., 14 November 1934, p. 24Q; ibid., 28 November 1934, pp. 16A–16C.
89. Ibid., 28 November 1934, pp. 3–4.

federal regulation of production, supported the mandatory controls of the Thomas-Disney Bill on its merits rather than simply as a political ploy to forestall the Margold Bill.[90]

Despite the lukewarm support of the majors, the vigorous support of many independents, and several supporting letters and telephone calls by President Roosevelt, the Thomas-Disney Bill was not enacted that spring. Because this bill was opposed by a minority of East Texas producers, primarily the independents in the IPA Opposed to Monopoly, neither representative Morgan Sanders from East Texas nor Senator Connally from Texas wanted to take a stand on federal oil control during an election year. Pulling strings within the House and Senate, they persuaded Vice-President Garner, Senate Majority Leader Robinson, and Congressman Sam Rayburn, who chaired the House Interstate Commerce Committee, which was considering the Thomas-Disney Bill, to sidetrack it until after the upcoming election.[91]

In the fall of 1934, under the impact of collapsing gasoline prices as the first buying program was terminated, pressure again began to mount among independents for new federal legislation. In mid-December 1934 the Planning and Coordination Committee endorsed, by the close vote of 11 to 9, federal oil legislation along the lines of the Thomas-Disney Bill introduced the previous spring. But the threat of more drastic legislation like that proposed by the Margold Bill in the spring had abated, and most of the majors now resumed their opposition to mandatory federal production controls.[92] In place of this, the majors now rallied behind the idea of an interstate oil compact.

Even the federal regulation proposals of the P&CC showed some concern by the independents for the growth of bureaucratic power over the industry. The P&CC proposals modified the Thomas-Disney Bill by changing the makeup of the proposed PAB from a board of disinterested experts to a board of prominent industry leaders selected by the president of the United States from nominations made by trade associations within the industry. Furthermore, in the original Thomas-Disney Bill the authority to allocate "quotas in commerce" was vested in the secretary of the interior, although he could delegate this responsibility to the PAB. In the P&CC proposals, the authority to allocate was vested in a Federal Petroleum Board, which was chaired by the secretary of the interior but controlled by four industry representatives. The secretary's vote was decisive only when the board split evenly on an issue.[93]

---

90. Ibid., 23 May 1934, pp. 25–26; ibid., 14 November 1934, p. 24Q.

91. Ibid., 20 June 1934, pp. 7–8, 10.

92. The opposition of the majors accounts for the close vote of the P&CC, for by this point they had gained seats on the code authority. Ibid., 21 November 1934, pp. 11–12; ibid., 26 December 1934, p. 7.

93. Ibid., 17 October 1934, p. 12; ibid., 26 December 1934, p. 7.

Efforts to enact the Thomas-Disney Bill in any form were ultimately sidetracked when the majors succeeded in stabilizing the oil market through a second buying program without additional federal controls over production. As the market stabilized, independent support for more extensive federal regulation diminished, and support for the majors proposal for an interstate oil compact began to grow.[94] When such a compact was enacted later in 1935, it brought to completion the brief experiment with federal controls during the NRA and returned authority to the ultimate hands of the state.

The legislative history of the Thomas-Disney Bill actually demonstrates the consistency of the majors' approach to federal regulation of the oil industry. The majors were anxious to avoid federal production controls, and they supported the Thomas-Disney Bill only because it appeared necessary to forestall the far more radical threat posed by the Margold Bill. Despite the failure of state controls to restrain production without an effective federal ban on hot oil, the majors had faith that an approach to oil stabilization that relied primarily on the states could ultimately be efficacious. Unlike the independents, who demanded immediate stabilization, the majors had the patience to wait until an approach focusing on the states had been given an adequate chance because they had a greater capacity to weather the economic costs which the delays in institutionalizing that approach had imposed on producers.

Peripheral and Center Firms

Although the splitting-off of the oil code from the National Recovery Administration weakens the generality of any conclusions derived from a history of the oil code, the conflicts that emerged in the administration of this code do appear to be similar to the conflicts that dominated the NRA in other industries as well. The sharp divisions between independents and majors in the industry makes it a particularly revealing case for analyzing the constituencies the New Dealers intended to serve through the NRA, and the history of the code strongly supports the conclusion that the New Dealers favored the interests of peripheral firms over those of center firms. As will prove to be the case with the New Dealers and labor, however, their partiality toward peripheral firms did not mean that the New Dealers did not have their own agenda that could conflict with the interests of the independents. The conflicts between the PAB and the P&CC demonstrate that the New Dealers' progressive state was at least relatively autonomous

---

94. The independents at first supported the idea of an interstate compact in conjunction with federal controls, then they gradually dropped the demand for additional federal controls. Nash, *U.S. Oil Policy,* pp. 147–150; Nordhauser, pp. 161–162.

from even those interests groups with which it was aligned. Yet despite this administrative autonomy, the NRA facilitated the cartelization of the oil industry, just as it had facilitated cartelization in many of the other industries supervised by the Hugh Johnson's NRA. The Interior Department legitimated cartelization, not because it had been captured by the oil industry but because its own progressive goals—securing the well-being of the independents and transforming cutthroat competition into fair competition—were ultimately irreconcilable with the goals of preserving a competitive marketplace.

CHAPTER 8

The NRA and the
Steel Industry

The differences between the oil industry and the steel industry under the NRA were striking. The majors in the oil industry had been suspicious of the NRA from the very beginning, but by June 1935 even the independents had turned away from the program. Stabilization without extensive federal regulation had begun to appear to be a realistic alternative, and the independents had by then realized that New Dealers were not going to allow the independents to run a federal program. There were few regrets when the Supreme Court struck down the NRA. An editorial in the *Oil and Gas Journal*, one of the foremost trade journals for the industry, captured the mood of the industry:

> These personal qualities of audacity and dogged persistence [qualities being attributed to entrepreneurs] could not be found in official robots operating under a bureaucracy entangled in the red tape and routine of Washington.
> Happily the oil industry has been freed from that possibility. . . . For that was where we were drifting, to a numbered and fingerprinted status where the citizen would be submerged in the soviet. . . .
> The existing social order cannot be saved by discarding its fundamentals and substituting the theories of socialism. Government cannot regulate production, wages, and hours and stop there. To be consistent it must pass on to regulation of consumption, costs and profits, the whole gamut of nationalization, socialism or communism.
> There was the inherent danger in the Federal code system.[1]

One week before this editorial was published, the *New York Times* had run a front-page story covering the steel industry's reaction to the *Schechter* decision under the headline "Steel Chiefs Hope to Keep Code Alive." The story had described the steel industry's commitment to

1. *The Oil and Gas Journal*, "The Industry's Position," 6 June 1935, p. 22.

preserving the "beneficial features of the Steel Code" through voluntary cooperation among steel manufacturers. However, industry leaders had expressed fears that this form of private cooperation might be vulnerable to antitrust objections, and "the suggestion was made in some quarters that legislation be enacted promptly by Congress to sanction clearly such joint activities."[2]

What accounts for these extraordinary differences between the oil and the steel industries? Whereas the history of the oil industry under the NRA poses a severe challenge to revisionist interpretations of the NRA, the reactions of steel leaders to the demise of the NRA seems consistent with that interpretation. At least in some cases, big business could apparently do quite well under the NRA. Furthermore, critics of the NRA, with some justification, cited the steel code as an example of the way the NRA contributed to the cartelization of industry. If progressive New Deal elites were challenging the power of business elites in American society, and the NRA was trying to lay the foundations for a new economic order that could more effectively secure the public welfare and social justice, how can we explain the outcome of the NRA for the steel industry?

Steel before the Code

Prior to the depression, relationships between firms in the steel industry had both cooperative and competitive aspects. With large capital investments at stake and low marginal costs of production, the pressure to distribute overhead costs over a large volume of business provided powerful incentives to increase production, and this had often led firms to engage in fierce competitive battles to secure sales. But the capacity of the industry to stabilize its market through collective action was enhanced by the very factor that contributed to competition. The large investment needed to manufacture many types of steel posed a barrier to entry that was lacking in the production and marketing levels of the oil industry. This inhibition on new entrants facilitated the development of an oligopolistic market structure, which in turn simplified the negotiations to achieve collective agreements to mitigate "destructive" competition.[3]

The history of collective agreements among steel competitors extends back into the late nineteenth century. The first beam association was established by four structural steel manufacturers in the spring of 1880, one of the earliest national cartels.[4] While this cartel, and others that followed in its footsteps, successfully stabilized parts of the steel market

2. *New York Times,* 5 May 1935, p. 1.
3. Carroll R. Daugherty, Melvin G. de Chazeau, and Samuel S. Stratton, *The Economics of the Iron and Steel Industry,* 2 vols. (New York, 1937), 1:22, 554–558.
4. Ibid., p. 533.

for short periods of time, the industry structure as a whole remained competitive because some low-cost producers stood to gain more from expanding their market under competition than they would under stabilized market shares and artificial cartel prices. For the last three decades of the nineteenth century, the industry was dominated by the Carnegie Steel Company, and Carnegie was steadily increasing his share of the market based on the superior technical and managerial efficiency of his integrated production plants. Carnegie would agree to stabilize the market through some form of pooling arrangement when it suited his purposes, but his general marketing strategy was aggressive and price wars were not uncommon. It was not until the House of Morgan financed several consolidations among Carnegie's competitors in the late 1890s that the preconditions for more-lasting cooperation within the industry were established.[5]

The process of industrial concentration leapt forward in 1901 with the creation of the U.S. Steel Corporation. At its formation, the U.S. Steel Corporation combined 213 manufacturing and transportation companies, as well as 41 mines, 1,000 miles of railroad, and 112 ore vessels. The corporation controlled 43.2 percent of the nation's pig iron capacity and its share of the steel ingot production in 1901 was 66 percent.[6] Despite U.S. Steel's awesome size, however, it could not control the steel market based on monopoly power. Furthermore, its share of the market proceeded to drop gradually over the next twenty years, falling to 42 percent of the steel ingot market in 1925.[7] As such competitors as Bethlehem Steel and Republic Steel rose to challenge U.S. Steel's domination, price stabilization was possible only by mutual agreement among the largest corporations. But the requisite cooperation was generally forthcoming, and price stability was achieved by the 1920s with occasional exceptions.[8]

This stability did not depend on outright price-fixing by steel firms. In the 1907 panic, Judge Elbert Gary, chairman of the U.S. Steel Corporation, had instituted his famous "Gary dinners," where informal pressure was applied to firms to resist destabilizing price cuts, but ever since those dinners had been cited in the antitrust action against U.S. Steel initiated by President Taft, the corporation had been careful to avoid anything that might be construed as illegal collusion. Informal price leadership proved to be an acceptable alternative for highly standardized items because of the oligopolistic structure of the industry, but the possibility of hidden rebates on less-standardized orders continued to plague the industry.[9]

5. Melvin I. Urofsky, *Big Steel and the Wilson Administration* (Columbus, Ohio, 1969), pp. xxii–xxiii.
6. Ibid., pp. xxiii–xxix.
7. George J. Stigler, *The Organization of Industry* (Homewood, Ill., 1968), p. 108.
8. Daugherty et al., 1:541.
9. Maurice H. Robinson, "The Gary Dinner System: An Experiment in Cooperative Price Stabilization," *Southwestern Political and Social Science Quarterly* 7 (1926): 137–161; Urofsky, pp. 14–26, 35.

The lynchpin of the standardized pricing system was the Pittsburgh Plus basing point plan. In the 1860s and 1870s, steel producers generally quoted the price of steel as its price at the mill, a system known as f.o.b. mill base pricing. Under these conditions, steel cartels were generally unstable, because transportation costs were a major component of the delivered price of steel, and steel firms could always conceal a discount on steel prices through partial absorption of transportation costs by the manufacturer. To facilitate agreements among producers, steel manufacturers in the 1880s began using a basing point price system that included the cost of delivery in the listed price for steel, calculating the delivered price as the Pittsburgh base price plus rail transportation from Pittsburgh, regardless of the actual origin of the shipment or the actual mode of transportation. The basing point pricing system alone did not eliminate competition per se, since competitors remained free to set their own Pittsburgh base price, but price-fixing was facilitated insofar as transportation costs had been rendered uniform. Once the informal price leadership of U.S. Steel became an established practice in the industry, the conjunction of price leadership and a basing point system generally sufficed to keep competition within limits.[10]

The steel industry entered a new phase after 1921. The Pittsburgh Plus basing point system often guaranteed steel-producing centers other than Pittsburgh a higher price for their products through the addition of phantom freight charges, but it limited their ability to take competitive advantage of their proximity to major steel consumers and to expand their share of the market. As local markets grew in size, production centers other than Pittsburgh chafed under the old basing point restrictions and could not be forced into line by U.S. Steel. Chicago producers had broken away from the Pittsburgh Plus system from October 1911 to March 1912 and set up Chicago as an additional basing point, but the risks of all-out price competition had been sufficient to restore the Pittsburgh Plus system. By 1921, Chicago producers could no longer be denied and Chicago was recognized as a second basing point for steel bars, plates, and shapes.[11]

In 1924 the FTC further weakened Pittsburgh Plus by issuing a cease and desist order against it as an unlawful competitive restriction. The industry, already aware that Pittsburgh Plus did not correspond to the new economic realities of a more geographically dispersed steel industry, did not even contest the FTC decision in the courts. Instead they adopted a new multiple basing point plan and then gradually increased the number of basing points used in the system. By 1934 there were sixty-six basing points, although many basing points were restrictively used only for

10. Daugherty et al., 1:207, 533–544.
11. Ibid., pp. 204–206, 541.

particular steel products. Even under a multiple basing point system the industry was generally able to maintain stable and profitable prices.[12]

The depression, however, dealt a traumatic shock to stability in the steel industry. With idle capacity at unprecedented levels, the temptation to expand production by offering secret price concessions overwhelmed the previously effective informal restraints. This market chaos intensified steel manufacturers' interest in the revision of antitrust laws to permit more extensive forms of cooperation among competitors. But despite this interest in expanding private modes of market rationalization, at no point did the industry seek national economic planning and bureaucratic regulation of prices, production, or entry as an alternative to enhanced private controls.

Stabilization and the NRA

In confronting the threat of government regulation during the early New Deal, the steel magnates had one decisive advantage in comparison with the oligopolistic leaders of other industries like oil. Conflict between center and peripheral producers, which often served as an entering wedge for external regulation, was not a crucial factor in the steel industry. Even the peripheral producers had sufficient capital investments to identify their interests with those of the larger producers. Center firms could tolerate the peripheral firms, despite the relative success of the peripheral firms in encroaching on some of the markets of the giants, because the peripheral firms did not fundamentally threaten to destabilize the market. The controlled competitive environment established by the oligarchs served the interests of most of the firms in the industry. Cooperation between center and peripheral firms continued throughout the NRA years.[13]

A relatively unified industry could maximize its leverage to resist bureaucratic interference, and the code-making process in the steel industry reflected the presumption of the steel manufacturers that control would remain in their hands. One aspect of the steel code that tended to reinforce industry autonomy was the designation of the board of directors of the American Iron and Steel Institute (AISI) as the agency responsible for

12. Ibid., pp. 204–208, *The Iron Age,* 8 November 1934, p. 50.

13. Ronald Richberg noted that the Darrow Commission's critical invesigation of the steel industry could not substantiate its charge that the steel code oppressed small steel manufacturers. In fact, Richberg argued, "small enterprises within the industry have deluged the NRA with protests against changing the code and with arguments in favor of its continuing operation" (Donald Richberg, "Commentary of Majority Report of National Recovery Review Board," Richberg Papers, Box 46, File: Memo, etc., undated, p. 6. See also *Business Week,* 31 March 1934, p. 7. See also *Business Week,* 7 July 1934, p. 8). The leading trade journal for the industry, *The Iron Age,* generally portrayed the industry as presenting a united front to the government. It is unlikely that the trade journal was presenting a distorted view of the industry, for it did cover exceptional cases of producers disgruntled over the code. For instance, see *The Iron Age,* 11 April 1935, p. 39D. This is in striking contrast to petroleum industry trade association journals, which are filled with accounts of the struggle between the majors and the independents.

code administration. While this ambiguous public/private role for AISI was not unique, the NRA generally preferred a clear distinction between private trade associations and code authorities because established trade associations did not represent all the interests within an industry.[14] In the case of the steel industry, however, the NRA was forced to acknowledge that AISI adequately represented both large and small manufacturers.

Encouraged by Hugh Johnson to act quickly, the AISI completed an initial draft of the steel code and presented it to Johnson on 15 July 1933. Johnson promptly scheduled public hearings on the code, mediated the conflicts that emerged over the draft, and laid the final draft before Roosevelt for his signature on 19 August.[15] The speed with which the code sailed through the drafting process reflected the consensus among producers concerning an appropriate code. In many areas the code merely incorporated long-standing industry practices. The basing point system was formally legitimated, with some minor revisions that updated the basing points allowed for each of the standardized steel products, changes that were minor departures unlikely to cause any serious dislocations. But other trade practice provisions in the code went considerably beyond long-standing industry practices, and it was these provisions that made the steel code one of the strongest codes permitted by the NRA.[16]

The steel code provided for an ascending hierarchy of controls to stabilize the market, with the more-extensive controls acting as a backup system in the event of a failure of the less-extensive controls. The first tier of NRA stabilization devices facilitated agreement on base prices without actually fixing those prices. An open price system coupled with a ten-day waiting period provision was added to the pre-code basing point method of pricing. Because price cuts on basic steel products were frequently concealed in a manufacturer's offer to include extras without charge or to grant unwarranted discounts on ancillary aspects of the sale, openness and uniformity regarding discounts and extras was a precondition for successful stabilization. The proposed NRA code provided a standardized contractual form for determining such ancillary aspects of a sale as terms of

14. Lyon et al., pp. 205–209. In the oil industry, for instance, several trade associations spoke for specific constituencies in the industry. The NRA created a code authority—the Planning and Coordination Committee—without formal ties to any of the industry associations which continued to act as spokesmen for their members. In other cases, the creation of a code authority became the occasion for a reorganization of the trade association. This occurred in the trucking industry when two factions, represented by the Federated Truck Association of America and the American Highway Freight Association, submitted distinct proposals for a trucking code and the NRA insisted they reconcile their versions. Their negotiations led simultaneously to a compromise code proposal and to their amalgamation in the American Trucking Association (ATA), but even then the national code authority for the trucking industry remained distinct from the ATA because not all truckers were represented by the new association. See Meyer Fishbein, "The Trucking Industry and the National Recovery Administration," *Social Forces* 34 (October 1955): 172–173.

15. *The Iron Age*, 31 August 1933, p. 27f.

16. Ibid., 20 July 1933, p. 26M; Lyon et al., pp. 578–579.

credit, payment, and delivery. Consistent with the basing point system, the full cost of rail delivery was added to the base price, except on some coastal shipments, where lower ship transportation rates could be included. Free credit on purchases could be extended to customers, but only for thirty days after the date of shipment, or forty-five days on shipments from east of the Mississippi to the Pacific Coast.[17]

Other fair trade provisions disallowed certain forms of contract that could induce manufacturers to cut their base rate below a "reasonable cost" level in order to secure a particular sale. Long and exclusive contracts were eliminated by a rule limiting contracts to a three-month period, with an exception for consumers under contract to a third party at a fixed price. Shipments on consignment—in effect a form of discount, because the seller accepts the risks associated with a future sale of the commodity—were limited to steel pipe, where the practice had been long established. Most of these requirements were designed to prevent important consumers from using their buying power to circumvent an open price market with a uniform price for all.[18]

None of the above provisions explicitly established a cartel with direct control over either production or price, but the steel code did go beyond these open price provisions, which were common to most codes, to include two provisions for more-extensive controls. One provision limited the construction of new blast furnaces, open hearth, or Bessemer capacity on the part of established producers, unless approved by two-thirds of the board of directors of AISI. However, new producers would still be free to enter the market—as unlikely as this was, given the present market. In view of the excess capacity already present in the industry, the requirement did not appear unduly restrictive to any of the affected firms. A second and more radical provision empowered the AISI to roll back price cuts filed with the institute to an acceptable level where such price cuts were deemed unfair competition. The power to disallow unfair prices was granted to a number of code authorities, but the striking fact about the iron and steel code was the failure to specify some form of reasonable cost criteria to guide code authority discretion on this matter.[19]

As was the case for all codes of fair trade competition, once a code was ratified by the appropriate government and business officials the code became legally enforceable. It could be enforced against any member of the industry, regardless of their willingness to assent to the code or to join the American Iron and Steel Institute. Federal district courts were given jurisdiction to prevent and restrain violations, and district attorneys, under the supervision of the U.S. attorney general, were empowered "to institute proceedings in equity to prevent and restrain such violations."

17. Ibid.
18. Ibid.
19. Ibid.

Because violations were defined as unfair methods of competition, they were also proscribed under the terms of the Federal Trade Commission Act, which provided for a remedy through the power of injunction given to the FTC. Whether the NIRA was enforced through the FTC or through the attorney general, enforcement was deemed a government responsibility and code authorities had no role in enforcement beyond the initial stages of fact-finding, informing the violator of his legal responsibilities, and efforts to persuade him to comply voluntarily.[20]

In the case of the steel code, the NRA provisions for enforcement were supplemented by additional contractual penalties, a unique feature among codes. Members of the industry were encouraged to submit letters of assent in order to become members of the code. These letters bound the code member to fulfill the terms of the code or pay liquidated damages of $10 a ton on any product sold in violation of the code.[21] Fashioning a contractual enforcement mechanism that was applied by the code authority and that could ultimately be enforced by an appeal to civil courts had the advantage of retaining private control over the enforcement mechanism and thus controlling the inevitable discretionary elements in enforcement. The steel industry had been fully aware throughout the code drafting process that cooperation between business and government did not reflect a convergence of goals, and they tried to structure the administration of the code to maximize their future autonomy.

The success of the steel code, and therefore the relatively positive attitude of the steel industry toward the NRA, was to a considerable extent a consequence of the unique enforcement mechanism of the steel code. The AISI soon had letters of assent from firms representing 95 percent of the aggregate production of the industry, willingly subjecting themselves to liquidated damages if they violated the code.[22] The legal quagmire that eventually engulfed NRA enforcement efforts never undermined the steel code, and the steel code had one of the best compliance records in the NRA.[23] Using their newfound freedom from antitrust laws, the steel manufacturers created a powerful but essentially private and contractual arrangement for industrial stabilization. The steel code therefore came closer to approximating industrial self-government than any other major industry code.

It is crucial that industry satisfaction with the steel code did not reflect its success in capturing government authority and enlisting it in the service of private ends. Indeed, the industry was especially leery of involvement

20. Lyon et al., p. 262.

21. Article XI, Section 3, provides that, on approval, the code "shall constitute a binding contract by and among the members of the Code," and Article X, Section 2, provides for payment of liquidated damages to the treasurer of the Institute.

22. R. W. Shannon to J. J. Reinstein, 6 December 1934, NRA Records, Record Group (RG) 9, Entry 25, Consolidated Code Industry Files: Iron and Steel, Folder No. 5: Code Authority (C) Committees.

23. *The Iron Age*, 31 May 1934, p. 23.

with the NRA Division of Compliance. Government enforcement was used as a threat to persuade firms to join the code authority, yet once producers were induced to join, government enforcement could be circumvented by using contractual penalties as a substitute. The deputy administrator in charge of the steel code, R. W. Shannon, reported that the steel code authority was "not inclined to press charges of violations against members of the industry that are not members of the code."[24] When the NRA pressed the code authority to handle alleged cases of violation by nonmembers as a court of first reference in order to relieve the NRA Compliance Division of a crushing backlog of cases, the industry only reluctantly agreed to inform nonmembers of their responsibility to adhere to the code.

The extent to which the industry had relied exclusively on contractual arrangements was demonstrated by the response of the H. L. Brown Fence and Manufacturing Company to a letter from the executive secretary of the AISI informing the company that it was subject to the provisions of the steel code even though it had not agreed to become a member. "Naturally we were quite surprised to receive this letter since the Steel Code has been in effect for over a year and a half and we have been under the impression that, being a Code of Assent which means a mutual contractual arrangement between the assenting members, others who did not sign the usual form letter of assent, were not bound by the provisions of the code."[25] This response, dated 19 March 1935, only two months before the demise of the codes, clearly shows that the only form of government coercion the steel industry used to bring about industrial stabilization was the power to enforce contracts—a form of government coercion that even laissez-faire proponents conceded was legitimate because it enforced only voluntarily assumed obligations.

NRA officials had allowed the steel industry to draft a strong code because they were eager to codify the ten major U.S. industries quickly. This led them to gloss over some code provisions that were in retrospect likely to encourage behavior inconsistent with NRA goals. Johnson defended this policy, arguing that the first priority was to counteract the depression malaise by fostering the perception of a nation geared up for a cooperative leap forward and suggesting that the codes could be reexamined and revised later. The steel code, for instance, was approved only on a trial basis for ninety days, leaving the NRA free to renegotiate a more

24. Hays A. Morris to R. W. Shannon, 25 November 1933, NRA Records, RG 9, Entry 25, Consolidated Code Industry Files: Iron and Steel, Folder No. 10: Explanations. Morris was an attorney at Cravath, De Gersdorff, Swaine & Wood, responsible for drafting this particular section of the code.

25. Letter from H. L. Brown Fence and Manufacturing Co., Cincinnati, Ohio, 19 March 1935, NRA Records, RG 9, Entry 25, Consolidated Code Industry Files: Iron and Steel, Folder No. 11: General Work Sheets.

restricted code if abuses were prevalent.[26] For this reason, many of the struggles that illuminated the differences in goals between progressives and business elites emerged only after the NRA got off the ground.

Code Revisions

The revision process for the steel code highlighted the autonomy of the central NRA administration from the code authority. When the steel industry code first came up for review only ninety days after going into effect, the NRA was generally content to maintain the status quo because so little had been learned at this point about the effects of the code. But by the time the steel code came up for its second review, in late May 1934, the NRA had come under heavy public criticism for promoting monopoly, and the steel industry had been specifically cited for questionable practices by the Darrow Commission. Even though the NRA rejected Darrow's superficial analysis as a politically motivated attack, the NRA was determined to rationalize the steel code and bring it into line with the trend in NRA policies favoring greater competition.

The most significant power over prices contained in the original steel code was the provision in Section 5, Schedule E, which authorized the code authority to investigate and set aside an unfair price filed with it under the open price system. In its place the code authority could determine a fair minimum base price. This power had little effect on the operation of the code because it had never been exercised. Even its value as a threat to force price chiselers into line was severely limited by the knowledge that the decision to exercise the power had to have the prior authorization of the president of the United States. Nevertheless, the symbolic significance of such a provision was not lost on NRA officials, who were now as concerned with illicit collusion as with promoting stabilization. The NRA insisted that the clause be deleted from a revised code, and the industry complied.[27]

Other revisions struck at weaker but more heavily relied on provisions of the steel code, and these revisions provoked more opposition from the industry. Reinforcing the commitment to competitive pricing indicated by the deletion of provisions that supported a minimum price, the revised code also included provisions to inhibit informal price collusion. It became an unfair trade practice to use coercive means to induce a producer to withdraw or to change his base price. The ten-day waiting period between filing new prices and their taking effect was not eliminated across the board, but it was changed to permit any producer to meet

26. *The Iron Age*, 24 August 1933, pp. 34–35.
27. Ibid., 24 May 1934, p. 38E; ibid., 7 June 1934, pp. 27–29.

immediately a lower price quoted by a competitor.[28] Manufacturers were henceforth freed of the requirement to price their goods on a "cost of recovery" basis.

In some cases, steel code provisions were allowed to stand, but their exercise was subject to increased scrutiny. The administration of the code was revised to give the federal administrator broader power over the implementation of the code.[29] This was the case with the unique steel code provisions for contractual penalties as a method of enforcement. Although NRA officials had operated on the assumption that government enforcement was the fundamental mechanism to secure compliance, the problems the NRA had encountered in enforcing codes made them hesitant to dismantle the effective compliance mechanism of the steel code. They preferred to bring the steel code into conformity with NRA objectives through other revisions, in which case the effective compliance mechanism would have operated to further NRA goals. Nevertheless, the very effectiveness of the steel code enhanced opportunities for abuse, and the government warned the industry that the misuse of this power would result in a removal of NRA blessings on these contractual arrangements, and that would have rendered them subject to antitrust prosecution by the Justice Department and the Federal Trade Commission.[30]

The changes in the steel code were consistently favorable to more flexible and competitive pricing, but not all the changes were imposed on the industry from without. It was not uncommon for industries to discover that they had misperceived their own interests in drafting provisions that subsequently proved to have undesirable consequences, forcing the industry to renegotiate the code with the NRA. In the summer of 1933, steel producers confronted the problem of price-cutting induced by buyers who signed large long-term contracts in return for promises of future price cuts on the material contracted for. These contracts, an option only for those with significant buying power, had a tendency to undermine uniform prices to the disadvantage of producers and smaller consumers who could not obtain similar discounts. To prevent these contracts, the steel code restricted contracts to three months and prohibited price cuts on contracts that were to be filled in the next quarter. But in drafting this clause, steel producers failed to anticipate that buyers would be less willing to commit themselves to large contracts when price fluctuations promised a lower price for steel products in the future. The steel industry needed an immediate surge of orders, but their own code was discouraging buyers.

28. Ibid.
29. Article XI, Section 6, was amended to give the federal administrator the power to suspend or disapprove any action of the code authority that modified or granted an exemption from the provision of the code. See *The Iron Age,* 7 June 1934, p. 27.
30. Malcolm Sharp to R. W. Shannon, 28 May 1935, Richberg Papers, Box 46, Memo, 27–31 May 1935. See also *The Iron Age,* 14 March 1935, p. 48, for an example of the use of this threat.

In order to encourage buyers to place their orders immediately rather than speculate on future prices, the industry sought a modification of the code that would have permitted them to reduce prices on unfilled orders to their contractual customers if lower prices were subsequently filed. The code did add a less-rigid provision making it an unfair trade practice intentionally to secure orders with the promise to file new prices after the contract was signed, but the enforcement of that provision would clearly be more difficult.

Increased competition was not the only NRA goal in revising the steel code. The new code was also more favorable to labor. In the original code a provision calling for a maximum eight-hour working day had been contingent on achieving a production level of 60 percent of capacity, but in the revised code it went into effect immediately. Pieceworkers were also brought under the minimum rates of pay for hourly workers.[31]

As was generally the case with NRA codes, increased benefits to labor were usually most costly to peripheral firms. The NRA tried to compensate for this effect by assuring that other aspects of the codes of fair trade competition were responsive to the interests of peripheral firms and by assuring peripheral firms adequate representation on the code authorities administering the codes. These aspects of NRA policy were reflected in two changes in the NRA steel code. First, the method of apportioning expenses for code operations was changed to reduce the burden on peripheral firms. In the original code, assessments were made in proportion to voting power, whereas voting power was derived from a formula that gave weight to both size of firm and to the number of small enterprises. The voting power of a firm was determined by dividing the invoiced value of the products it delivered on domestic sales over the preceding year by $500,000, disregarding fractions. Because each member was guaranteed one vote, smaller firms were more heavily represented than under a strict volume-of-sale formula, but they paid for their greater representation by heavier assessments. Under the revised code, smaller firms were given expanded representation on the AISI board of directors and producers who filled less than $500,000 worth of invoiced orders were exempted from code assessments.[32] Thus, the voting and assessment formulas were both skewed in favor of the small firms.[33]

Even before these changes were introduced, there was evidence that the introduction of an NRA code of fair trade competition had tilted stabilizing arrangements in the steel industry in favor of the peripheral firms. On the whole, peripheral firms appear to have fared better financially during

---

31. *New York Times*, 26 August 1934; *The Iron Age*, 7 June 1934, p. 28.
32. *The Iron Age*, 31 May 1934, p. 23.
33. Ibid., 7 June 1934, p. 29.

the early days of the NRA than the larger firms. *The Iron Age*, the leading trade journal for the industry, surveyed 190 members of the iron and steel code and reported that the integrated companies (there were 57 of these, and they included most of the major steel producers) showed a net loss of approximately $12 million during the last half of 1933, the first months the iron and steel code was in effect, whereas the nonintegrated companies (there were 133 such firms) showed a net profit of $7 million during the same period.[34] These figures are not conclusive, because there were some fairly large nonintegrated companies and some fairly small integrated companies, but if it is true that smaller firms did better under the NRA, as the AISI claimed, this would have been a dramatic turnaround from the pre-code period, when the larger firms generally weathered the depression better than the smaller firms.[35] That smaller steel manufacturers did not suffer under the NRA was also demonstrated by the desire of small firms to continue the code when it came up for extension.[36]

No area of code revision was more pregnant with potential conse- quences than that concerning the basing point system. Critics of the basing point system objected to it on a number of grounds. Some were irate about phantom freight rates charged for shipment from imaginary points. Others complained that the basing point system involved calculating transporta- tion charges as the rail freight rate between points, regardless of the actual mode of transportation utilized. Because water transportation was consid- erably cheaper than rail, cities advantageously located on inland water- ways were deprived of their competitive advantage of location. The steel industry had altered their traditional arrangements by approving lower shipping rates to some coastal cities and recognizing some Gulf and Pacific ports as basing points in order to compete with foreign competitors who could also supply these cities, but the steel industry had particularly resisted the recognition of inland water routes.[37]

34. Ibid., p. 26.
35. Roos, pp. 412–413. Roos, however, argues that the steel code disadvantaged smaller producers even though his own data indicates that general economic factors probably account for the problems these companies faced far more than the disadvantages incurred under the code. Roos's concern for the fate of smaller producers under the steel code are based on the domination of the AISI by the large firms, which fact does not mean that the large firms were pursuing policies that disadvantaged small firms in the industry, and on a record of small firm complaints to the NRA concerning the steel code. The latter fact may or may not be significant, depending on the nature of the complaints—i.e., were they objections to the wages and hours provisions of the code, in which case they could be objections to the NRA's attempt to help labor, or were they objections to other fair trade practices provisions that advantaged big business directly? The NRA data that Roos cites does not provide any breakdowns concerning the nature of complaints and is therefore inconclusive. What is clear is that a record of peripheral business complaints alone does not indicate that a code disadvantaged peripheral businesses. The petroleum code also had a substantial record of small business complaints (Roos, pp. 411, 416), yet, as the preceding chapter demonstrated, it primarily served the interests of the independents.
36. *The Iron Age*, 24 May 1934, p. 38B.
37. Ibid., p. 28.

Most steel producers had a strong incentive to uphold some version of the current basing point system because they had located their plants to take advantage of the long-standing basing point rules. In general this meant locating closer to raw material sources than to markets. Increasing the number of basing points or allowing reduced inland water rates threatened to upset established patterns of trade and to shift incentives to locate plants advantageously for marketing purposes. Whatever the ultimate justification for the efficiency of such a measure, it would have reduced the value of contemporary investment by stimulating a movement toward geographical dispersion of productive capacity.[38]

Revision of the basing point system was not an issue that systematically divided large and small firms. Complaints against the basing point system came primarily from buyers, including the automobile giants, rather than from producers. The advantage conveyed to firms located at basing points worked to the benefit of large and small producers located there, and the great majority of small firms in the industry were located in those regions. The basing point system generally united large and small producers in a common struggle against new entrants who might exploit opportunities created by the rise of new markets for steel distant from producing centers.[39]

Despite the strong commitment of most in the steel industry to the basing point system, the NRA, prodded by the FTC and the Darrow Commission, had received enough complaints about the system to insist on its amendment. According to the new provision, shipments that took advantage of inland water routes or trucks were entitled to a deduction. The code authority was to approve standardized rates which were equitable and "necessary in order that competitive opportunity to producers and consumers shall be maintained." These rates were subject to review by the administrator. Permission to make deductions from the delivered price for alternative forms of transportation was expected to increase competition of prices in general.[40]

The most ominous change in the code from the point of view of the industry was the addition of a number of basing points. Yielding to FTC pressure, the NRA forced the industry to include such locations as Duluth, Minnesota, and several Gulf and Pacific coast centers as new basing points. Besides adding some new basing points, the amendments expanded the range of products available from some of the older basing points. The industry had remained firm on what was potentially the most disruptive change in the basing point system—inclusion of Detroit. If Pittsburgh- or Chicago-based plants were dislodged from the Detroit auto

38. Ibid., p. 38C This certainly was a threat hanging over the industry's head. See ibid., 27 December 1934, p. 33.

39. Ibid., 24 May 1934, p. 38C; Daugherty et al., 1:542–543.

40. *The Iron Age*, 7 June 1934, pp. 27–29; *Steel*, 6 June 1934, p. 12.

market by the creation of a Detroit basing point, which would have given Detroit steelmakers a decisive advantage in the Detroit market, the economic repercussions would have been severe.

The hesitation of the NRA to incur the wrath of the industry and to unsettle an already hard-pressed industry at this particular historical juncture did not reassure the industry. The steel code revisions constituted fair warning to the industry that further pressure to move toward mill based pricing could be expected. Indeed, the president approved the revised steel code only with reservations attached, indicating his future intentions regarding the industry:

> Conditions of economic emergency make necessary the retention in modified form of the multiple basing point system adopted in the original code and effective in the industry for many years. But revisions made in this code, increasing substantially the number of basing points, and modifications in practice under the code, while alleviating some of the inequities in the existing system, illustrate the desirability of working toward the end of having prices quoted on the basis of areas of production and the eventual establishment of basing points coincident with all such areas, as well as the elimination of artificial transportation charges in price quotations.[41]

Roosevelt went on to direct the FTC and the NRA to conduct a joint study of the basing point system and its effect on prices, and to report back to him within six months. This study was to provide a basis for recommendations for further revisions of the code when the code was extended one year hence.[42]

The distinctive approaches of the FTC and the NRA regarding codes of fair trade competition assured Roosevelt that a variety of proposals for reforming competitive practices would be considered in the final report. The FTC was the foremost institutional guardian of the antitrust legacy, and it had historically objected to many forms of industrial stabilization and specifically to the basing point system. The NRA, on the other hand, was based on the assumption that cooperation between businessmen, under government supervision, would contribute to the rationality of the market. The mutual suspicion these agencies had for one another proved to be too great for a cooperative study. Ignoring Roosevelt's instructions, each conducted its investigation independently of the other and issued its own report. The conclusions of each report reflected the distinctive perspectives of the agency that issued it. Yet despite the differences between the NRA and the FTC, the steel industry would not be able to draw solace from the position of either agency.[43]

41. *The Iron Age,* 7 June 1934, p. 30.
42. Ibid., pp. 27–29.
43. Ibid., 27 December 1934, pp. 32–33.

The FTC's hostility to the basing point system was long-standing. Having made clear its preference for f.o.b. mill based pricing back in 1924 when the FTC attacked Pittsburgh Plus pricing, it subsequently tolerated the industry's substitution of a multiple basing point system only for lack of evidence of its anticompetitive effects. The recently intensified concern of the FTC over anticompetitive practices fostered by the NRA left little doubt in the steelmakers' minds that the long-anticipated move against the multiple basing point system had arrived.[44]

The final FTC report presented few surprises. Characterizing the basing point system as a form of price-fixing, the FTC called for an end to presidential approval of the multiple basing point system. Once deprived of its NRA shield, the FTC could pursue an antitrust case through the courts. Even the FTC did not go as far as to suggest that there be a positive injunction on the industry to use f.o.b. mill base pricing, although it had made such a recommendation in the first FTC study of the steel industry under the code. Apparently impressed with the legal difficulties of mandating a pricing system in the face of industry opposition, the commission confined its proposal to attacking the existing multiple basing point system.[45]

The tensions between the NRA and the steel industry over the basing point system have been overshadowed by the more radical conflict between the steel industry and the FTC. Yet NRA skepticism toward the basing point system also posed a fundamental challenge to the stability of the industry. The NRA response to the FTC criticism's of the steel code in the spring of 1934 had not included a defense of the basing point system. According to Richberg, the NRA "has been critical from the beginning of the price provisions of the steel code, including the set-up of the basing point system." He dismissed the assertion that NRA approval of the code conveyed legitimacy to specific provisions. "The NRA has never taken the position that any particular multiple basing point system is economically sound as a method of price quoting or legally justified."[46]

The NRA report recommended an extension of modifications introduced when the steel code was renewed. The basing point system would be transformed into a group mill base system in which every locality producing 20,000 tons of steel a year or more automatically became a basing point for pricing steel. These automatic criteria for determining basing points would replace a provision that had required a two-thirds majority vote of the code authority for approval of new basing points, a provision that heavily favored the interests of established firms within the industry over new firms, which were more inclined to locate new facilities

44. Ibid., 8 November 1934, p. 49.
45. Ibid., 14 March 1935, pp. 50C–50D.
46. Ibid., 11 August 1934, p. 49; ibid., 24 May 1934, pp. 38D–38E.

near steel markets. Nineteen new group mill bases would have been immediately established, and the product lines offered from ten preexistent basing points would be expanded. Another suggested reform was designed to limit severely the addition of phantom transportation costs to price quotations. Under the system proposed by the NRA, a producer would be limited to absorbing transportation costs of $5 a ton on sales at other basing points. Prohibited from absorbing large transportation costs on distant sales, the manufacturer would have no justification for distributing transportation penalties over sales closer to home.[47]

These changes would have significantly modified the prevailing pricing mechanism of the industry. The group mill base system would have restructured economic incentives to favor local producers servicing local markets. Concessions to the goal of price stabilization were still admitted in the perpetuation of a districting system. Even under the new system of NRA pricing, prices would still represent a delivered price calculated by the addition of a base production district price to a transportation charge from the district basing point to the buyer. Taking cognizance of industry objections to f.o.b. mill base pricing, the NRA scheme permitted the standardization of pricing within a 50-mile district. Prices would be filed at that base by any firm for whom the transportation costs to that base were less than the comparable rate to any other base. But even though it was less radical than f.o.b. mill based pricing, it is clear that the extension of the multiple basing point system would have had serious commercial repercussions, especially because it threatened the Pittsburgh-based mills with a loss of their Detroit market. The NRA scheme was sufficiently radical to arouse the opposition of most producers.[48]

The NRA was declared unconstitutional before either the FTC or the NRA study of the basing point system could be brought to bear on code revisions for the steel industry. The industry still supported the NRA in the spring of 1935, despite the clear intention of NRA administrators to attack the existing basing point system, because its other option was even more unsavory. If the NRA was not extended, the industry would once again be subject to antitrust laws, and the oligopolistic structure of the industry made it a vulnerable target. Because the FTC study of the basing point system had proposed a wholesale attack on the basing point system, the industry had every reason to expect another FTC antitrust action as soon as the NRA was disbanded. The steel industry's choice was not between a regulated and an unregulated environment, but between two forms of regulation. NRA regulation appeared less ominous, not only because its proposals for reform of the basing point system were less radical than those of the FTC, but also because the industry would be able to negotiate

47. Ibid., 14 March 1935, p. 48.
48. Ibid.

with the NRA in the code revision process and might be able to soften the NRA position in exchange for industry cooperation.

Is Steel an Exception?

The overwhelming majority of business leaders were extremely concerned with the growing regimentation of the economy under the NRA as the state expanded its regulatory control over prices, production, and trade and labor practices. Despite this broad ideological consensus within the business community on the virtues of a free economy, however, business responses to the NRA varied considerably. Businesses facing the most immediate deprivations of managerial autonomy were generally the most vociferous opponents of the NRA because their short-term and long-term interests were congruent. Corporate leaders in industries like steel, on the other hand, found their short-term interests were served by the NRA even though they shared the general business community's perceptions of long-term interests. Industries like steel gave the NRA their conditional support.

The contrast between the oil and steel industries exemplifies the ways in which different industrial organizations shaped responses to the NRA. The oil industry and the iron and steel industry were at different stages of industrial development. The ease of entry in the oil industry left the majors facing a strongly competitive market in spite of their size. Their interest in extending their oligopolistic power over refining into production and marketing posed a direct threat to the independents. The steel industry, on the other hand, had achieved a sufficient level of concentration that a penumbra of peripheral firms did not present an impediment to collective agreement. As long as these peripheral firms did not present a threat to the pattern of price leadership prevailing in the industry, the larger firms would tolerate them. This benign tolerance of peripheral firms by the large, integrated firms in turn eased the fears of peripheral firms that the expansion of trade association power under the code would work to their disadvantage.

In both the oil industry and the steel industry a concern with external bureaucratic control was prominent, but center firms in each industry viewed their respective code authorities quite differently. The steel industry used the NRA to maximize industrial self-government through the AISI. Wide powers were sought for the steel code authority as a means of staving off unfriendly controls from higher bureaucratic levels. The industry feared that without broad powers the code might fail to stabilize the steel market and that an alternative stabilization scheme would then be imposed on the industry by government. Moreover, government could not exploit divisions within the steel industry, using them as a reason or pretext for intervention. The more confident industries were that discretion in the exercise of code powers would remain in their hands, the more willing they were to grant powers to begin with.

The confidence with which steel industry firms delegated powers to the Iron and Steel Code Authority differed from the caution displayed by producers in the oil industry. Because the oil industry controlled, and allegedly wasted, a natural resource, it was more intimately linked to the public interest. Constantly threatened with public utility status and bureaucratic price control, the majors were concerned from the beginning with limiting the powers of the code authority in order to limit the control of the federal bureaucracy. The distinction between powers and the agency to exercise them was less salient for the oil industry because the split between the majors and the independents made even the agencies representing industry views vulnerable to bureaucratic manipulation. The code authority was viewed by the majors as something of a Trojan horse of bureaucratic control, and the more extensive the powers it acquired, the greater its danger.

The steel industry presents the relatively anomalous case of an oligopolistic industry supporting the NRA, albeit with considerable reservations. Yet the steel industry did not support the NRA for the reasons that have been emphasized in traditional interpretations of the NRA. The steel industry did not use government to impose discipline on individualistic producers who refused to cooperate with fellow producers. Such a strategy appeared unrealistic to producers because government bureaucrats were not under their control, and once political authority was extended to encompass the prerogatives of management, the threat that they would use that authority to impose undesirable policies on business was too great. The steel industry liked the NRA, not because it extended the regulatory state but because it relaxed it. Lifting antitrust restrictions on such practices as open price systems and the standardization of extras allowed the industry to expand and strengthen its private control over the market. The legitimacy extended to the basing point system operated in the same manner. Most important of all, the NRA had allowed the industry to approximate industrial self-government to an unusual degree by developing its own contractual enforcement mechanism, a method that proved effective where NRA enforcement methods failed. Because the contractual enforcement mechanism was unique among NRA codes, the steel code is in this regard an idiosyncratic case.

Despite the exceptional character of the steel code, the same forces that were operative in the NRA as a whole are evident in the steel code as well. The severely depressed economic conditions of the industry, and the agreement between small and large producers concerning the needs of the industry, helped the industry to secure a particularly favorable code in the early days of the NRA. But the initial NRA emphasis on industrial self-government increasingly gave way to a more regulatory posture as it became evident that industries were using the NRA to cartelize. In the case of steel, this regulatory posture was evident in the increasing NRA criticism of the steel basing point system, a feature of the code that had been slated for drastic reform before the NRA was disbanded. Had it not been for the even more radical threat that an FTC antitrust suit would have posed to the industry were the NRA abandoned, it is questionable whether the industry would have continued to support the NRA after it began to threaten the basing point system.

Although some of the specific factors that account for the relatively positive response of the steel industry toward the NRA are idiosyncratic, the steel industry was not the only industry dominated by center firms that supported an extension of the NRA. Perhaps the other outstanding example was the oligopolistic copper industry, which was controlled by four large, vertically integrated firms.[49] In a brief discussion of the copper industry code, Charles Roos points out that the copper industry, like most natural resource industries, used conservation arguments to rationalize a proposed code that would have gone far to cartelize the copper industry. While the NRA did give some weight to these arguments, its Committee on Price Policy Provisions in Codes refused to sanction the proposed code, and protracted negotiations between the industry and the NRA had failed to produce an acceptable code by the spring of 1934. At this point, Hugh Johnson became impatient and intervened, pressuring his staff to come to an agreement with the industry. With the industry holding out for a favorable code, the staff was forced to make many concessions, in exchange for which they managed to get only some important concessions protecting the interests of smaller firms in the industry.[50]

While the outcome in this case was a code that served the interests of center firms, the factors operative in Roos's brief account of the approval of the copper code—an NRA staff assuming a regulatory stance vis-à-vis the copper industry, solicitude for small businesses in the industry, an administratively incompetent Hugh Johnson who was willing to concede too much to get the NRA off the ground (probably on the assumption that codes could always be revised afterward if they proved unacceptable to the administration)—are some of the same factors that were operative in the NRA generally, but with substantially different outcomes under different circumstances. An extended case study of the copper industry would be necessary to clarify the issues at stake, but provisionally it would appear that although the copper industry is, like the steel industry, an exception to the dominant pattern of an NRA benefiting peripheral industries, it is nevertheless not an exception that would necessarily lead us to question the validity of the broader thesis developed in this work.

49. On the importance of center firms in the copper industry, see Chandler, p. 362. For evidence of industry support for an extension of the NRA, see *Business Week*, 25 May 1934, p. 18.

50. Roos, pp. 354–358.

PART III

LABOR AND
THE NRA

CHAPTER 9

Labor Policy in

the NRA

In June 1933 the National Industrial Recovery Act was hailed by the president of the AFL, William Green, as the Magna Charta of organized labor.[1] John L. Lewis was just as laudatory of the NIRA: "From the standpoint of human welfare and economic freedom we are convinced that there has been no legal instrument comparable with it since President Lincoln's Emancipation Proclamation."[2] Besides the promise of higher wages and greater reemployment, the NIRA dramatically transformed the legal environment in which labor unions operated. Recognizing the need to strengthen unions to balance the organizational advantages of business, Roosevelt had readily agreed to include a collective bargaining provision in the recovery measure. Section 7a of the NIRA stated: "Employees shall have the right to organize and bargain collectively through representatives of their own choosing."[3] Yet, just as historians have questioned the reputation of Lincoln's Emancipation Proclamation as a crucial step in the abolition of slavery, so historians have questioned the extent to which the NRA fulfilled its progressive promise of securing freedom from employer coercion for the worker.

Inclusion of the right to organize unions within the freedom of association protected by state and federal bills of rights had occurred even before the Civil War, but prior to the NIRA the courts had recognized both the rights of workingmen to organize and promote their own interests, and the right of employers to unlimited discretion in hiring and firing.[4] In *Adair v. United States* and *Coppage v. Kansas,* the courts respectively struck down federal and state statutes restricting an employer's right to discharge union

1. Bellush, p. 27; Lewis L. Lorwin and Arthur Wubnig, *Labor Relations Boards* (Washington, D.C., 1935), pp. 47–49.
2. Schlesinger, *The Coming of the New Deal*, p. 139.
3. Roos, Appendix I, pp. 484–485.
4. *Commonwealth v. Hunt*, 4 Metc (Mass.) 111 (1842).

members as a violation of due process of law.[5] In 1917 the Supreme Court summarized the legal status quo of labor relations in *Hitchman Coal and Coke Company v. Mitchell:* "The employer is as free to make non-membership in a union a condition of employment as the workingman is free to join the union, and . . . this is a part of the constitutional rights of personal liberty and private property, not to be taken away by legislation, unless through some proper exercise of the paramount police power."[6]

Not until the NIRA did Congress provide the basis for limiting the employer's right to hire and fire in order to safeguard the employee's right to organize. Section 7a not only reasserted the previously acknowledged right of labor to organize, but added that labor "shall be free from the interference, restraint, or coercion of employers of labor, or their agents, in the designation of such representatives or in self-organization or in other concerted activities for the purpose of collective bargaining or other mutual aid or protection."[7] Because the power to hire and fire provided the employer with an instrument—indeed, the foremost instrument—of coercion over the organizational activities of his employees, the law was properly interpreted to forbid discharge for engaging in union activities. Equally under interdiction were yellow-dog contracts, which demanded as a precondition of employment that the employee relinquish the right to join a union.

The unions stood to gain not only from the enhanced freedom of workers to organize and bargain collectively, but also from the relaxation of antitrust laws. While antitrust statutes were primarily directed at corporations, the courts had interpreted the laws in such a way as to hamper union activities as well. The NRA held out the possibility of an expansion in the scope of legitimate union activities through judicial tolerance for such previously forbidden practices as secondary boycotts, interference with contractual relations, or refusing to work on nonunion goods.[8]

But employers were not about to acquiesce passively in the unionization of the American work force. Before the NRA, many employers had argued that the opportunity for the worker to quit and offer his labor elsewhere provided reasonable and sufficient protection to the worker's interest, and they inferred that their employees were satisfied with their employment conditions because they chose to continue working for their firms. New Dealers, such as Donald Richberg, had refused to give any credence to such arguments: "Of what value were constitutional guaranties of liberty to citizens denied an opportunity to earn a living? Of what value were the protections of law and order to those who had no property and no means

5. *Adair v. United States*, 208 U.S. 161 (1908); *Coppage v. Kansas*, 236 U.S. 1 (1915); Schlesinger, *The Coming of the New Deal*, p. 136.
6. 245 U.S. 229 (1917).
7. Roos, Appendix I, pp. 484–485.
8. Emmett B. McNatt, "Organized Labor and the Recovery Act," *Michigan Law Review* 32 (1934): 782–783.

of livelihood to be protected? It was becoming apparent to millions of long-suffering men and women that a government must do more than merely preserve an existing order; that it must do more than merely sanction whatever economic system happened to develop, because the political freedom and security of a people depend upon their economic freedom and security."[9] New Dealers insisted that the abstract legal rights of individuals could not protect real choices unless those choices were legitimated and upheld by the power of organization, for in a world inhabited by powerful business corporations, the rights of farmers, small businessmen, and workers would be secured only through counterorganization. After the 1932 elections, business appeals to an ideology of individualism and freedom of contract had little political appeal beyond the business community, and politically astute business leaders began to search for alternative means to defend business interests.

Forced to abandon their preferred mode of dealing individually with employees, many employers tried to preempt independent unions by initiating company unions or employee representation plans.[10] These "organizations" often operated under constitutions that severely limited their autonomy. Organizational expenses were generally paid by company funds, and there were no provisions for a strike fund. While they satisfied a need for a nonconflictual channel of communication between management and labor to resolve issues of mutual concern, company unions without any provisions for strike funds hindered workers' efforts to exercise their most effective weapon against employers over the important issues where their interests diverged.

Section 7a had politicized industrial relations by establishing the right of workers to organize and bargain collectively free of any coercion on the part of employers. But recognition of the right to bargain collectively did not specify how the representation of workers could be determined, nor did the guarantee against interference or coercion in self-organization specify what constituted interference or coercion. The ambiguous Section 7a potentially held great promise for the organization of the working class, but the interpretation of the statute would determine the extent to which labor was presented with genuine new opportunities to enhance its organizational strength, and the administrators of the NRA would exercise considerable discretion in implementing its provisions.[11] In the struggle between business and labor, government held the controlling hand.

9. *Congressional Record*, 74th Cong., 1st sess., 1935, 79:1286.

10. Some 400 manufacturing and mining companies out of 627 surveyed by the National Industrial Conference Board in November 1933 had established company unions under the NRA. See I. Bernstein, *The New Deal Collective Bargaining Policy*, p. 57. The growth of company union membership was even more dramatic than the growth of AFL membership. It is estimated that it grew from 1.3 million at the end of 1932 to between 2.5 and 3.0 million at the end of 1934. See Lyon et al., pp. 523–524.

11. Schlesinger, *The Coming of the New Deal*, p. 137.

Labor Policy: The Early Period

Hugh Johnson, sympathetic to labor's interests but inexperienced in labor relations, had turned to Donald Richberg during the drafting of the NIRA. Richberg was a prominent labor lawyer who had defended railway unions throughout the 1920s against federal injunctions limiting the unions' freedom to strike and the efforts of railroads to dismantle their powerful organizations and substitute company unions. His contribution to this effort included his role in drafting the Railway Labor Act of 1926 and the Norris-LaGuardia Act of 1932, the two greatest legislative victories of labor during the years preceding the New Deal.[12]

Richberg was strongly committed to the advancement of the trade union movement: "If we believe in democratic principles we must find means for the organization and representation of every large economic interest in the community in the shaping of economic and political programs. Yet two vast groups of our working population, farmers and wage earners, have not been adequately organized for either collective thinking or collective action, although as individuals they have been for decades practically helpless to control their living and working conditions."[13] Once the NRA was established, he assumed an important role as the general counsel of the program. In view of his solidly pro-labor reputation, his prominence in the NRA was an indication that Johnson and Roosevelt saw the advancement of labor's interests as one of the primary goals of the program.

Neither Johnson nor Richberg accepted the arguments of employers that locally based company unions adequately protected the interests of workers while avoiding the mutual hostility and strife that AFL-style international unions and industry-wide collective bargaining promoted. Nor could they accept the employers' gloss on industrial history of amicable relations before outside troublemakers stirred up conflict. Speaking to a national meeting of code authorities in March 1934, Johnson admitted that company unions were within the letter of the law if freely chosen. But Johnson asserted that "99 times out of 100, you and I know this is not the case." "If a labor unit confined to a single company is absolutely free of suggestion, influence, favor, or domination by the management as to form, method, or membership, and in such freedom has been set up or selected by a group of employees, I believe not only that it is authorized by the Recovery Act, but also that any attempt by any government board or official to interfere with it is wholly unlawful. But I also must in frankness say that I have grave doubt that there are very many of such

12. Freidel, p. 415; Schlesinger, *The Coming of the New Deal*, p. 136; Irving Bernstein, *The Lean Years* (Boston, 1972), pp. 216, 396–397, 403, 410, 414; Bellush, pp. 12, 32.
13. Richberg, *The Rainbow*, p. 53.

unions in existence.''[14] Johnson felt legally bound to protect all legitimate self-organization on the part of workers, but his tolerance did not extend to every subterfuge employers resorted to in order to circumvent Section 7a.

Johnson was perfectly aware that most company unions were not independent of management domination and that subtle forms of pressure (and at times not-so-subtle pressure) were exerted by management to herd employees into company unions, but he was also aware that the AFL did not enjoy the confidence of many workers. Nevertheless, Johnson argued, even if management did not dominate and co-opt a company union, such unions would not have the requisite organizational strength to advance the interests of labor. As long as competitive market forces constrained individual firms, wages were determined by market forces rather than humanitarian considerations. Bargaining at the company level ''will not give to either management or labor the full benefits of the Recovery Act, because they relieve neither the management of a particular company nor the labor of a particular company from the competition of cut prices of any other company (with or without a company union) which decides to enter the competitive lists on the basis of reduced wages and increased hours.''[15] Only bargaining at the industry-wide level could uniformly impose equitable wage settlements above those resulting from cutthroat competition.

Although Johnson wished to see society organized along corporatist lines, with each economic interest organized and represented in institutions designed to facilitate collective bargaining, he did not assume that the NRA granted him carte blanche to impose his organizational predilections on society. As a public official, Johnson believed that his discretion as an administrator should be circumscribed by the statutory basis of his authority. Ambiguous phrases that guaranteed that employees ''shall be free from the interference, restraint or coercion of employers'' were broadly construed by Johnson to protect union members, because he believed such an interpretation was consistent with the act. But Johnson found no similar justification for transforming the NRA from an agency protecting the rights of employees to organize to an agency compelling unionization: ''It is not the function of government or organize labor. The whole intent of the Act was to leave organization and representation to the men themselves, unhampered and uninfluenced by any outside source.'' Indeed, had Johnson felt duty bound to promote union organization, his preference for vertical or industrial unions would have roused the ire not only of antiunion employers but also of the AFL, with its predominantly craft union structure.[16]

14. H. Johnson, p. 342.
15. Ibid.
16. ''It will be recalled by those who have followed NRA that from *the very outset* I expressed the opinion that the ideal form of labor organization is a vertical union on the model of the United Mine Workers'' (ibid., pp. 317, 345).

Not authorized to compel unionism, he nevertheless believed that the public protection of the freedom to organize would ultimately further the goal of independent unionism. If employer coercion was broadly construed in interpreting the NRA, the NRA would pose a significant blow to company unions, and Johnson did construe employer coercion to include the employer's most frequently used weapon of intimidation—discharging employees for their union activities.[17] Admonishing business to "submit to law," Johnson expressed his preference for dealing with "Bill Green, John Lewis, Ed McGrady, Mike MacDonough, George Berry and a host of others I could name, than with any Frankenstein that you may build up under the guise of a company union."[18] Similarly, Richberg insisted that the interests of the workers would never be adequately represented until unions were "free from any control by representatives of the competing economic interests of ownership and management."[19] Johnson's efforts to create the prerequisites of a truly voluntary system of interest groups became known as voluntarism.

Richberg, like Johnson, remained firmly wedded to the principle of voluntarism. Expressing "a strong belief in the value of an organization extending beyond the influence of a single employer," he nevertheless drew back from imposing that on workers. "But if a group of workers desire to organize in some apparently foolish or weak way, if they do not (in the opinion of more experienced persons) see their own interests clearly, I do not believe in the value of forceful education either by an employer or a labor leader."[20]

Johnson's commitment to voluntarism brought him into conflict with the closed shop organizational propensity of the AFL when he concluded that while union contracts limiting the freedom of association of workers, such as those providing for a closed shop, were not necessarily banned by Section 7a, neither were they encouraged. Balancing his reservations against the closed shop with his reservations against the open shop preferred by most employers, Johnson announced on 23 August 1933, "The words 'open shop' and 'closed shop' are not used in the law and cannot be written into the law." The legitimacy of such arrangements would depend on their compatibility with the principle of free choice among employees to select their own representatives. Two weeks later Johnson, in accord with the logic of his voluntarist position, went further, questioning the compatibility of the closed shop with the right to organize and bargain collectively: "If an employer should make a contract with a particular organization to employ only members of that organization, especially if that organization did not have 100 percent membership

17. NRA Release 625, 4 September 1933, p. 7.
18. Schlesinger, *The Coming of the New Deal*, p. 150.
19. *Congressional Record*, 74th Cong., 1st sess., 1935, 79:1292.
20. Richberg, *The Rainbow*, pp. 55–56.

among his employees, that would in effect be a contract to interfere with his workers' freedom of choice of their representatives as with their right to bargain individually and would amount to employer coercion on these matters which is contrary to the law."[21] Yet despite these differences in Johnson's outlook and that of the AFL, both could overlook this difference while cooperating to liberate the working class from employer coercion regarding self-organization during the first few months of the NRA.

The voluntary organization of labor under the NRA was not completely paralleled by a voluntary organization of employers. Because employers held the formal power to determine minimum wages and set maximum hours, which the NRA sought to regulate, an asymmetrical emphasis on employer organization reflected the character of the NRA regulatory task. The organization of employers was a prerequisite to the enforcement of the NRA. Trade associations played a critical role in investigating alleged violations of fair trade practices and persuading employers to comply with the codes. "But while the law specifically requires NRA to *promote the organization of industry* it does not direct it to promote the organization of labor but, on the other hand, looks to the absolute freedom of labor in selecting its own form of organization."[22] Nevertheless, to the extent that the NRA differentially promoted the organization of employers, it also differentially imposed responsibilities on those organizations. The task of the NRA was to confine the organizational benefits conveyed on business to those consistent with the broader purposes sought by government.

Despite the formal-legal role assumed by code authorities during the NRA, Johnson did not impose compulsory membership in trade associations even on employers.[23] The protection of their self-interest under legally binding codes generally proved to be adequate motivation to entice firms to join associations. "What our few critics overlook is that we have not had one Code *that has not been voluntarily presented and concurred in by an overwhelming majority of the industry and nearly the whole of American industry is now here with Codes.*"[24] While occasionally using the threat that a code could be forced on an industry that failed to adopt one voluntarily, the NRA expended great effort in negotiations with industry to arrive at a mutually acceptable arrangement.

The institutional implications of the NRA's commitment to voluntarism did not emerge immediately after the NRA was launched. During the initial period of code drafting, other issues superseded it. With a few exceptions, business had refused to include labor on the code authorities that were to participate in code drafting and code administration, and they had prepared proposed codes, including labor provisions concerning

21. NRA Release 625, p. 6.
22. H. Johnson, p. 317.
23. Ibid., p. 237.
24. NRA Release 625, p. 8. Emphasis in the original.

minimum wages and maximum hours, without any input from organized labor.[25] The NRA was forced to institutionalize labor participation in the NRA through alternative means. Johnson turned to the Labor Advisory Board, a board created by Roosevelt when the NRA was set up to advise him on labor matters, and he insisted that all proposed codes be submitted to this board for review. Public meetings to air differences over proposed codes were scheduled, and the NRA insisted that organized labor be represented in these meetings. William Green subsequently admitted that "the codes finally adopted for each industry did represent to a degree the give and take of collective bargaining between representatives of labor and management" even though "labor was given no direct participation in the formulation of minimum wage and maximum hour standards."[26]

Code administration posed distinct problems. When disputes arose concerning the more routine administration of hours and wages provisions, they could often be handled by informal negotiations between code authorities, the NRA, and the Labor Advisory Board. But the administration of Section 7a, which had been included in every code, posed difficulties of a different order. Johnson knew that business-dominated code authorities were incapable of judging these labor disputes even-handedly, and they were clearly unacceptable to organized labor as an arbitration agency, so he refused to grant code authorities jurisdiction over any disputes concerning labor's right to organize and bargain collectively. On 5 August, Johnson responded to a joint initiative of the NRA's Labor Advisory Board and Industrial Advisory Board and created the National Labor Board (NLB) as an administrative mechanism for resolving such labor issues.[27]

The NLB was to have equal representation of labor and management, with an impartial chairman to resolve deadlocks. Solicitous of the working man, Johnson not only chose prominent AFL leaders (rather than company union leaders) to represent labor, but also selected such noted business liberals as Gerald Swope, Walter Teagle, and Edward Filene to represent business on the NLB. These businessmen, all of whom were somewhat sympathetic to the "legitimate" demands of organized labor, hardly represented a cross-section of business opinion. Employers noted for their commitment to the open shop—the predominant opinion in the business community at the time—were excluded. Finally, Johnson named Senator Wagner, who already had a reputation as a leading spokesman for labor interests, as the "impartial" chairman of the NLB. Just as the NRA allowed code authorities sympathetic to business interests to act as a primary forum of dispute resolution regarding trade practice matters, so

25. Some 26 of the 775 approved basic and supplemental codes in operation allowed labor representation on the code authority. See Lyon et al., p. 459.
26. Ibid., pp. 42–43, 105, 120–123, 427–430; Green, p. 141.
27. Schlesinger, *The Coming of the New Deal*, p. 146.

the NRA initially permitted the NLB, which was decidedly sympathetic to labor, to act as the court of first resort in any labor dispute involving Section 7a.[28]

In the fall of 1933 the NLB began simultaneously to act as a mediator in labor disputes (it settled 88 percent of its cases in its first three months of operation without resort to legal coercion[29]) and to delineate a "common law" for the resolution of management-labor disputes. Both employers and unions claimed the sanction of the NIRA in promoting their respective employee organizations, and within a month after the passage of the NIRA a wave of strikes over union recognition threatened the recovery and reemployment goal of the NRA.[30] Clarifying the ambiguously defined rights of Section 7a would be one of the first challenges of the NLB and the NRA.

Confronting hosiery manufacturers in Reading, Pennsylvania, who claimed to speak for their workers, the NLB offered a settlement based on what came to be known as the Reading Formula. According to the Reading Formula, a government-supervised election was the only acceptable method of determining employee representation. It was assumed by both the NLB and the NRA that these elections would select a single organization, to be determined by the principle of majority rule, to represent exclusively all the workers for that electoral unit.[31] Later this principle would become the main source of controversy in early New Deal labor policy. In this first NLB-supervised election, the American Federation of Full-fashioned Hosiery Workers won a majority in thirty-seven mills, and nonunion representatives carried seven mills. Last-ditch resistance by thirty-six of the employers who refused to sign written agreements with the union was subsequently also struck down by the NLB, and collective bargaining was legitimated.[32]

The most dramatic success of the NRA and the NLB in advancing labor rights in the face of stiff employer resistance occurred in the dispute between the United Mine Workers (UMW) and the steel companies over working conditions in "captured mines," mines owned by steel companies that sold their coal exclusively to their parent company. The powerful UMW, led by John L. Lewis, had played a crucial role in the development

28. Lorwin and Wubnig's account of the establishment of the NLB attributes responsibility for the choice of personnel solely to Roosevelt, but Frances Perkins makes it clear that Johnson played a crucial role as well. See Lorwin and Wubnig, pp. 87–95; Frances Perkins, *The Roosevelt I Knew* (New York, 1964), p. 237.

29. James Gross, *The Making of the National Labor Relations Board, 1933–1937*, vol. 1 (Albany, N.Y., 1974), p. 21.

30. Lorwin and Wubnig, pp. 88–91; Schlesinger, *The Coming of the New Deal*, p. 402; H. Johnson, pp. 319, 323, 344.

31. After the Reading decision, the NRA cooperated with the NLB in attempting to enforce it. See Schlesinger, *The Coming of the New Deal*, pp. 147–149; Irving Bernstein, *Turbulent Years* (Boston, 1970), pp. 174–176; Lorwin and Wubnig, pp. 96–107.

32. I. Bernstein, *Turbulent Years*, pp. 174–175.

of the coal code and had greatly strengthened its position as an agent for collective bargaining through the code, even securing a provision for the checkoff of union dues. The steel industry, which had been vigorously resisting unionization of its steel works, refused to be bound by the coal code, arguing that their vertically integrated mines did not sell on the open market and were therefore in a different category from other coal mines, and it refused to negotiate with the UMW.[33] The UMW, inspired in part by NRA administrator Edward McGrady's promise that "the President guarantees that there will be an end to company unions— that the Coal Code will bar them," struck to secure conditions for coal miners in captured mines that were comparable to those for miners in other coal mines.[34]

Initial negotiations between Roosevelt, the NRA, the UMW, and the steel companies culminated in an agreement on 21 September to "comply with the maximum hours of labor and minimum rates of pay which are or shall be prescribed, or pursuant to the Coal Code for the district in which such mine is located, so long as the Coal Code shall remain in effect."[35] UMW leaders acquiesced in the ageement because Roosevelt had insisted that it included an acceptance of the labor provisions in Section 7a and Hugh Johnson had told UMW Vice-President Philip Murray that the checkoff of union dues was one of the terms that employers in the captive mines had agreed to respect. Despite the assurances of the UMW leadership that the union had now won the de facto right to a voice in wage settlements in the captive mines through the commitment of steel companies to match coal industry settlements, the rank and file refused to ratify the agreement without formal union recognition.[36]

The steel companies had a significantly different perception of the September agreement. They had been told by Donald Richberg that the union dues checkoff was not included among the working conditions that steel employers would be agreeing to respect.[37] After Roosevelt wrote U.S. Steel Chairman Myron Taylor to inform him that the checkoff was definitely included, Richberg conceded that he had misunderstood this

33. The lengths to which steel employers carried their hostility to the AFL was demonstrated by an episode involving Secretary of Labor Perkins. The presidents of six steel companies, including U.S. Steel and Bethlehem, had come to discuss a proposal for a steel code with Perkins. Sensitive to labor's interests, Perkins had asked William Green, president of the AFL, also to attend the meeting and speak for the unorganized steelworkers. When the steel employers were unexpectedly confronted with Green in Perkins's office, they refused even to be introduced to him, fearful that their actions might be interpreted as a recognition of organized labor. See Schlesinger, *The Coming of the New Deal*, pp. 142–143.

34. J. Johnson, p. 156.

35. Memorandum concerning Captive Mine Labor Controversy, 6 August 1937, Richberg Papers, Box 47, FDR's Public Papers, 1937.

36. J. Johnson, p. 174.

37. T. M. Girdler (Chairman of Republic Steel Corp.) et al. to FDR, 6 October 1933, Roosevelt Papers, OF 175, No. 1, Coal, October 1933, p. 4; J. Johnson, p. 174.

provision.[38] As these conflicting perceptions were clarified, agreement once again faded away. Roosevelt was forced to intervene a second time as he called the heads of the steel companies to the White House on 6 October. This conference was followed by a statement from Roosevelt that the captive mines were within the jurisdiction of the coal code and that the workers were free to select representatives for collective bargaining. Any unresolved questions between the UMW and the captive-mine operators would be arbitrated by Roosevelt along the lines of the settlement in the commercial mines.[39] Roosevelt persuaded those mine workers still out on strike to return to work on the strength of the promise by captive-mine owners that they would enter into negotiations with the representatives of the workers in good faith.

As tension between the owners and the miners persisted, Roosevelt prodded the negotiators toward an agreement. Finally, on 30 October, Roosevelt issued a press release that summarized respective informal agreements between the president and the UMW and the president and the mine owners to adhere to an agreement "at least as favorable" as that in effect in the Appalachian region under the coal code.[40] Employers granted the checkoff and were willing to submit outstanding differences concerning union recognition to the NLB for a binding decision within ten days if no agreement were forthcoming. The NLB assumed jurisdiction over the captive-mines dispute in early November and immediately ordered an election to resolve the question of representation. These elections gave the UMW a majority in twenty mines and independent representatives a majority in the other nine, although the union carried only seven of the sixteen camps in the important Frick mines owned by U.S. Steel. Because the majority rule question had not yet been raised as an issue, the representatives of the majority were accepted as authorized bargaining agents for the entire mine.[41]

Despite the elections, the issue of union recognition continued to be a stumbling block. The captive-mine operators still refused to negotiate with the UMW. Defending their position before the NLB, they insisted that the president's October press releases had misrepresented their agreements with him. Arguing that the NLB election had selected individual representatives for the workers, who happened to have an institutional affiliation, they insisted the agreement should be between the companies and the individual representatives of "the majority voting." Furthermore, nominations in such elections should have been confined to those who serve on local pit grievance committees in the mines they represent, a

---

38. FDR to Myron Taylor, 4 October 1933, Roosevelt Papers, OF 175, No. 1, Coal, October 1933.
39. J. Johnson, pp. 174–175; I. Bernstein, *Turbulent Years*, p. 58.
40. J. Johnson, pp. 174–176; I. Bernstein, *Turbulent Years*, pp. 59–60.
41. J. Johnson, pp. 174–176.

policy that would have barred most UMW officials from participation.[42]

After conducting hearings on the lingering captive-mines dispute in early January, the NLB released its decision on 19 January 1934. The board provided a face-saving compromise for the Frick Company that granted labor all the substantive rights of Section 7a, the right to the checkoff in mines where a majority of employees voted for it, and denying the employers' claim that only local men could represent a district. But the NLB did not grant the UMW the symbolic victory of formal recognition, allowing the contracts to be signed by "John L. Lewis et al." in their individual capacities as union officers.[43] Employers could not yet bring themselves to acknowledge the UMW, but collective bargaining had been achieved de facto. The NRA and the NLB cooperated to bring about one of the most impressive labor victories under the NRA.

The UMW had demonstrated that the NRA could benefit the working man. Lewis was an astute leader who was perfectly capable of calling the UMW out on strike when circumstances required, but who was equally willing to bargain and make concessions when it was in the interests of the UMW. Lewis had been willing to trust Roosevelt and Johnson, and he restrained more radical rank-and-file elements in the UMW while embarking on the moderate path of negotiation. He could do so because negotiations under government supervision provided a context in which many labor demands could be met. Government provided seemingly neutral third-party negotiators who provided face-saving formulas that permitted business to surrender considerable power to unions without a mutually destructive contest of force. During the lifetime of the NRA, Lewis remained one of its staunchest defenders, viewing it as an adequate framework for transforming industrial relations.[44]

As long as the issue of dispute between business and labor remained the right to a government-supervised election, this provided a common denominator for cooperation between the NLB and the NRA, and recalcitrant employers found the forces of government solidly aligned against them. Both agencies agreed that employees had to be free of employer coercion in choosing their own form of labor representation, and government-supervised elections were recognized as an appropriate mechanism for determining which organization had the loyalty of workers. Cooperation among the agencies was essential, because the most expeditious enforcement device available to the NLB—the removal of the Blue Eagle from a firm that violated an NLB order—was a prerogative of the NRA.[45]

42. Ibid.
43. Ibid.
44. Schlesinger, *The Coming of the New Deal*, p. 166.
45. The NLB could also have turned to the Justice Department to bring a court case, but this was a lengthy and uncertain process, especially with a predominantly conservative judiciary. See Lyon et at., 483–487.

Although differences among these agencies were apparent even in the fall of 1933, they generally revealed differences in personal style and tactics rather than different fundamental goals. Even later, after more significant policy differences emerged, a common denominator of sympathy for labor occasionally allowed the NRA and the NLB to put aside differences for the sake of advancing labor's interests.[46]

Angered by the advances made by AFL affiliates under the NRA, employers bitterly resisted NRA and NLB enforcement of Section 7a. Both the Weir Steel Company and the Budd Automobile Company became causes célèbre for employers when they refused to allow NLB-supervised elections in their plants. The Weir case arose when the unresolved labor dispute in the captive mines spilled over into the steel industry's operations as well. On 2 October more than 13,000 employees of the Weirton Steel Company had joined a "holiday" movement demanding recognition of their chapter of the Amalgamated Association of Iron, Steel, and Tin Workers as an agent for collective bargaining. Picketers at Weirton had been joined by striking coal miners from the surrounding county and they had jointly resisted the efforts of Johnson and the UMW leadership to end the strike with the promise of government action in support of their demand for recognition.[47] Ernest Weir, chairman of the board at Weirton, was refusing to acknowledge the jurisdiction of the NLB over this matter, but he did agree to appear informally before the NLB.[48]

Discussion between Weir and the NLB appeared to have paid off when on 16 October an agreement was signed which adhered to the Reading Formula in providing for an NLB-supervised election in the second week of December to determine the agent of collective bargaining for the Weirton workers. The NLB was to determine the procedure and methods for this election and to be the court of last resort for any disputes over the terms of the agreement. The strike was to be terminated immediately, and all striking workers were entitled to return to work without discrimination against union members. Although Weir signed the agreement, the fragility of the truce was apparent from his simultaneous disavowal either that the NLB had jurisdiction over the dispute or that he would ever negotiate with a union.[49]

Weir promptly embarked on a campaign to defeat the Amalgamated in the upcoming election, even resorting to scarcely veiled coercion by showing the Weirton workers letters from such major steel customers as

46. For instance, the Walsh National Industrial Recovery Bill, a watered-down version of the Wagner Act discussed later in this chapter, was introduced in the Senate in May 1934 and won the near-unanimous approval of New Dealers. See I. Bernstein, *The New Deal Collective Bargaining Policy*, pp. 74–75.

47. *New York Times*, 4 October 1933.

48. Ibid., 2 October 1933; I. Bernstein, *Turbulent Years*, p. 177.

49. *New York Times*, 17 October 1933; I. Bernstein, *Turbulent Years*, p. 177.

Ford, Chevrolet, and the American Can Corporation warning that a union victory would encourage them to take their business elsewhere, letters that Weir had solicited from employers sympathetic to his cause. Despite these precautions, Weir's control of the election was threatened when the NLB announced during the first week in December that the rules to govern the upcoming elections would set aside the primary election scheduled for 11 December and substitute nominations by petition. Using a minimal threshold of ten signatures to nominate, the NLB procedure would have permitted ninety-eight nominees to compete in a general election rather than the forty-nine expected from the plan formulated by the company union at Weirton. The new nomination procedure would probably have guaranteed the Amalgamated greater representation.[50]

Weir had no intention of recognizing an AFL union in his plant. He charged the NLB with abrogating the truce of 16 October despite the explicit provision for NLB determination of election rules, and he announced that without NLB supervision he would hold the primary as originally planned on 11 December. The Amalgamated encouraged its men to boycott the primary, but under employer pressure approximately 9,000 men cast their ballots out of an eligible pool of 11,000 voters. Weir claimed that the 80 percent vote was a repudiation of the AFL, and he quickly became a symbol of employer resistance to what was coming to be perceived by many employers as government-imposed unionization.[51]

Once again, both the NRA and the NLB rallied to support the workers before this clear violation of Section 7a. Just before Weir held his questionable primary, Johnson telegraphed him that a company-dominated vote could result in the loss of the Blue Eagle: "In my opinion you are about to commit a deliberate violation of federal laws, and . . . if you do so, I shall request the Attorney General to proceed against you immediately."[52] After conferring with Senator Wagner, Johnson agreed to defer NRA proceedings against Weir to remove his Blue Eagle, while Wagner took the case to the Justice Department for criminal prosecution. But Johnson continued to exert public pressure on Weir by denouncing this company-dominated election as a violation of the Recovery Act and of the steeel code. "Anybody with any industrial experience knows when an election is held under the supervision of the foremen the men will vote with their eyes on the Boss."[53]

The Weir case demonstrated the authenticity of the NRA's commitment to the protection of the rights of labor. Unwilling to allow employers to co-opt labor through controlled elections that supplied workers with

50. *New York Times*, 16 November 1933.
51. Ibid., 13 December 1933; I. Bernstein, *Turbulent Years*, p. 178.
52. Lorwin and Wubnig, p. 104.
53. *New York Times*, 16 December 1933.

innocuous choices between preselected alternatives, the NRA insisted that consent was established through an impartially supervised election in which the AFL could play a role. Cooperation between the NRA and the NLB was at a high point. When the resistance of Weir revealed the tenuous legal authority of the NLB to conduct elections—for the presidential order establishing the NLB had authorized it only to protect labor's rights during the code drafting process when industries were governed by the President's Reemployment Agreement (PRA), but had not given it any responsibilities after the code was approved—the NRA supported Roosevelt when he strengthened the NLB by Executive Order 6511, issued on 16 December 1933. This order supplemented the NLB's jurisdiction over labor disputes arising from the PRA with those arising from approved NRA codes as well.[54]

The Split between the NRA and the NLB

By the beginning of 1934, roughly six months after the passage of the NIRA, organized labor had considerable grounds for optimism. Most of Johnson's pronouncements interpreting Section 7a of the NIRA were directed toward employer resistance to the new definition of workers' rights. Johnson chastised those who would endanger "this great cooperation to maintain some stubborn point" and suggested that the "plain meaning" of Section 7a was to guarantee freedom of association to workers, thus protecting employees against objectionable forms of employer coercion.[55] Dramatic union membership gains had already been recorded, and the government was breaking down employer control over labor by politicizing industrial relations and providing an impartial electoral mechanism for determining worker consent. A newfound labor militance was spurring unions to try to recapture ground lost over the previous decade, and a high proportion of industrial conflicts involved demands for the rights recognized in Section 7a.[56] Employers had been denied their most potent legal weapon for suppressing labor dissatisfaction—the right to fire workers who promoted unionization. The NRA had done a great deal to liberate workers and establish a climate in which they could directly challenge the interests of their employers.

Employers, on the other hand, were on the defensive. Some rallied behind Weir and supported outright defiance of the NRA. Others, while they shared Weir's hostility to the AFL, counseled moderation and

---

54. Lorwin and Wubnig, p. 106; Schlesinger, *The Coming of the New Deal*, pp. 148–149; I. Bernstein, *The New Deal Collective Bargaining Policy*, p. 59.

55. NRA Release 463, 23 August 1933.

56. Close to 50 percent of the strikes during this period were disputes over union recognition, the issue addressed by Section 7a of the NIRA, whereas only 19 percent of strikes in 1932 were over union recognition (U.S. Bureau of the Census, *Historical Statistics*, 1:97–98).

resisted the strongly confrontational approach of Weir at this point in hopes of working out an accommodation with the administration. These moderates gradually formulated an alternative to the NLB's majority-rule position, which had more plausibility than the hypocritical assertion that labor was satisfied with their current status combined with a refusal to allow labor to express its own opinion in a supervised election. It had become apparent that unions were winning a significant proportion of NLB elections, but that significant minorities of workers still identified more strongly with the company than with the union. Employers questioned the right of the majority of employees who voted for an AFL union to speak for such minorities. Employers advocated some form of "collective bargaining pluralism," which granted some representation to all the groups that found support among the employees within the relevant bargaining unit.

The NLB flatly rejected collective bargaining pluralism. The NLB was not formally confronted with a case involving the conflicting claims of majority rule and proportional representation until early 1934, when it handed down its *Denver Tramway* decision in favor of majority rule.[57] But long before then, Senator Wagner was persuaded that schemes of proportional representation were unworkable in practice and served only to weaken legitimate trade unions. The NLB steadfastly adhered to the majority-rule Reading Formula and sought to strengthen its mandate from Roosevelt for implementing this rule. Obliging Wagner, the president issued Executive Order 6580 on 1 February authorizing the board to conduct elections for the selection of employee representatives when requested by a "substantial number" of employees, and he directed the board to report to the NRA administrator for appropriate disciplinary action any employer who refused to "recognize or to deal" with these representatives. According to the executive order, the elections were to be conducted on the principle of majority rule.[58] The NLB systematically refused to treat the problem of union coercion of workers on the same plane with employers' coercion of workers.

The case for collective bargaining pluralism found a more receptive audience in the NRA. Collective bargaining pluralism was in fact more in the spirit of the voluntary organization of interests encouraged by Johnson than the AFL's preference for majority-rule elections. In situations where the primary loyalty of some workers, however misbegotten, remained with the firm rather than with the union, the NRA believed it had no right to compel them to join the AFL.[59] Section 7a protected the right of

57. National Labor Board, *Decisions of the National Labor Board* (Washington D.C., 1934), "The Denver Tramway Corporation and the Amalgamated Association of Street and Electric Railway Employers of America, Division 1001," 1:64.
58. Lorwin and Wubnig, pp. 106–111.
59. Even the NLB had allowed company unions to compete in NLB-supervised elections and

individual workers to organize and bargain in whatever manner they chose, Johnson argued, and majority rule and exclusive representation would deprive some workers of that right.[60] However, it was not until Roosevelt issued Executive Order 6580, favoring majority rule, that the NRA publicly began to disagree with the NLB over the interpretation of Section 7a. On 3 February, Johnson and Richberg released an interpretation of Executive Order 6580 that described its intent as providing an electoral mechanism for the majority to designate their representatives but leaving minorities free to bargain separately with employers. They went on to deny that the president's order discredited all company unions as by nature subservient to employer interests. As long as a company union was freely chosen by the employees, and labor elections were demonstrating that significant minorities of workers, and occasionally majorities, chose to be represented in this manner, the logic of voluntarism dictated that company unions should play a role in collective bargaining.[61] Despite bitter denunciations from labor leaders, who resisted the NRA when it applied to unions the same voluntaristic logic used to limit employer coercion against unions, the NRA steadfastly defended collective bargaining pluralism throughout the remaining lifetime of the NRA.

The balance of power between the NRA and the NLB would be determined by Franklin Roosevelt, and the subsequent history of the early New Deal suggests that Roosevelt's primary commitment was to the NRA. The most plausible interpretation of Executive Order 6580 is that Roosevelt had not yet grasped the issue at stake between proportional representation and majority rule. This is hardly surprising because neither the NLB nor the NRA had articulated this issue in the fall of 1933. Even employers had failed to see the significance of the issue during this period.[62] The initial conflicts over Section 7a, which aligned the NRA with the NLB, concerned the right to an impartial election. Majority rule was assumed by both the NLB and the NRA. It was only later that the secondary issue of minority rights and representation emerged. The

conceded that when a majority of the workers in an election supported the company union it was the legitimate representative of those employees.

60. Johnson thus claimed that his voluntarist policy "was the law I had sworn to execute." Although this claim is usually dismissed because the NIRA was more ambiguous than Johnson claimed, and Johnson's interpretation of the law would therefore appear to have reflected his normative predispositions, Johnson may have genuinely believed that this was his legal mandate. He did subsequently argue in his autobiographical account of the NRA that he "did not regard a majority and a minority union in the same shop as practicable" and that he believed it expedient that "the law should be amended," and he went on to implicitly support the Wagner Act. See H. Johnson, pp. 293–294 and Chapter 4, footnote 12, above.

61. The NLB held 183 labor elections. Some 69.4 percent of all the workers polled in those elections cast their ballots for independent trade unions, and 28.5 percent cast their ballots for employee representation plans (in the remaining cases no representative was chosen). See Lyon et al., p. 472; Lorwin and Wubnig, p. 110; Schlesinger, *The Coming of the New Deal*, p. 149.

62. Fine, p. 190.

division of the NRA and NLB over the latter issue was still inchoate when Roosevelt strengthened the NLB by Executive Order 6580 in order to deal with cases like that of Weirton.

Two considerations serve to reinforce this hypothesis. First, Roosevelt never repudiated the NRA interpretation of his order, even though it undermined the principle of majority rule. Second, Executive Order 6580 is the only occasion during the NRA period on which Roosevelt unambiguously supported majority rule. While Roosevelt allowed the NLB, and later the NLRB, to proceed on a majority-rule interpretation, every major Roosevelt initiative to resolve industrial disputes during this period strengthened the hand of those favoring proportional representation.

The conflict between the NRA and the NLB interpretation of Section 7a came to a head when the government intervened to prevent a threatened strike in the automobile industry. The AFL, having made modest inroads in organizing this mass-production industry, called for a strike during the 1934 spring period of seasonal expansion in automobile production. On 14 March the United Automobile Workers Union (UAWU) presented a series of demands to the auto companies, among which were the demand for an NLB-supervised election and official recognition for the UAWU in any plant in which it secured a majority. Hearings before the NLB broke down when William Knudsen, executive vice-president of the General Motors Corporation, declared that General Motors would not agree to an NLB election or recognize the AFL, although it was willing to hold discussions with the representatives of any group of employees if these representatives would disclose the employees for whom they spoke. The unions would never have agreed to such a demand, for fear of exposing their members to retaliation by hostile employers.[63]

The deadlock before the NLB brought Johnson into the dispute as Roosevelt's personal representative. On 25 March both parties agreed to a settlement that had more in common with Johnson's interpretation of Section 7a than with the NLB doctrine of majority rule.[64] The president appended to the agreement a restatement of the meaning of Section 7a that recognized the right of employees to organize "into a group *or groups*" and choose representatives. "The government makes it clear that it favors no particular union or particular form of employee organization or representation. The government's only duty is to secure absolute and uninfluenced freedom of choice without coercion, restraint, or intimidation from any source."[65] Employers were required to bargain with representatives of these groups and were not to discriminate against any employee on the grounds of labor union affiliation. The automobile settlement fulfilled

---

63. Ibid., pp. 215, 219.
64. Labor agreed to the settlement because they were too weak to extract a solution they would have viewed as more favorable.
65. Lorwin and Wubnig, p. 356.

Johnson's commitment to voluntarism by establishing an institutional mechanism to permit colllective bargaining with more than one union. Labor would be represented on a works council on which representation would be prorated according to the total membership of each group.[66]

The automobile settlement was not strictly a victory for the employers, although it later came to be perceived that way. The terms of the automobile settlement demanded that the employers recognize the AFL union as the legitimate representative of the employees who were its members. Granting this recognition was not in accord with the initial preferences of employers. Prior to the automobile settlement the employers had conducted their own employee representation plan elections, which allowed workers to select individual representatives but excluded any other *organization* from participation in collective bargaining. Many employers had fought bitter battles against granting any sort of recognition to the AFL, as a representative of either a majority or a minority of its workers. Recognition accorded legitimacy, and the employers were generally opposed to allowing the AFL any foothold in their plants. Employers were forced to cede ground on this issue.[67] The AFL, however, believed that the automobile settlement would not fundamentally threaten employer interests. As long as employee loyalty was divided between a company union and the AFL, it seemed unlikely that the AFL would develop the organizational strength to challenge employer domination.

Despite these AFL reservations, Roosevelt viewed this settlement as more than just a compromise between conflicting interests. He saw in the concept of a works council the institutional reconciliation of a progressive sympathy for the organization of the working man with progressive suspicion of all forms of private coercion, either by unions or by corporations:

> In the settlement just accomplished two outstandings [*sic*] advances have been achieved. In the first place, we have set forth a basis on which, for the first time in any large industry, a more comprehensive, a more adequate, and a more equitable system of industrial relations may be built than ever before. It is my hope that this system may develop into a kind of works council in industry in which all groups of employees, whatever may be their choice of organization or form of representation, may participate in joint conferences with their employers; and I am assured by the industry that such is also their goal and wish.[68]

66. Fine, p. 223.

67. The employers had also been forced to accept an independent labor board, divorced from the automobile code authority, which would adjudicate disputes over job tenure and discrimination against union members, and they had accepted a well-defined rule governing layoffs and rehirings that placed greater emphasis on seniority and family status than on "individual skills and efficient service." The latter concession virtually undermined the merit clause the automobile industry had demanded when drafting its code. Ibid., pp. 221–225. See the following chapter for a discussion of the automobile merit clause.

68. Lorwin and Wubnig, p. 357.

Roosevelt hoped that proportional representation on a works council would provide the unity necessary for collective bargaining while adequately protecting minorities unrepresented under the majority rule election favored by the NLB.

The automobile settlement proved to be a decisive blow to the prestige of the NLB. Once it became apparent that an appeal to the president might overturn NLB policy, employers felt free to ignore its decisions. Abandoning the NLB as a vehicle for labor's advancement, Senator Wagner began to place his hopes on the passage of a Labor Disputes Bill, which he had introduced into Congress to provide a legislative mandate for the administrative policies developed by the NLB. The Wagner Labor Disputes bill, a prefiguration of the later Wagner Act, would have reaffirmed the right of workers to organize and bargain collectively and defined as unfair labor practices such employer actions as an employer's interference with this right, an attempt to establish a company union, or a refusal to bargain with representatives of his employees. Selection of employee representation was to be determined by an NLB-supervised election, but the bill did not specifically require majority rule, probably because majority rule had been crucial for combating company unions that were disallowed by this bill in any case. The NLB's powers of enforcement would have been enhanced by allowing it to issue cease and desist orders against unfair labor practices.[69]

Even political leaders sympathetic to the intent of the bill found substantial grounds for criticism. The sweeping application of the bill to intrastate as well as interstate commerce raised doubts as to its constitutionality. Hearings on the Wagner Labor Disputes Bill in March and April of 1934 produced predictable responses from labor and business. Business bitterly attacked the bill, and labor, by this point disenchanted with Johnson and the NRA, both because of Johnson's role in the automobile settlement and because of the snail's pace of litigation in the Weirton case (which had received a setback in federal court in May 1934), rallied behind Wagner's bill. With congressmen under pressure to adjourn and prepare for the 1934 congressional elections, the fight looming over the Wagner Labor Disputes Bill under ordinary circumstances would have suggested postponement until the next session of Congress. But 1934 was already well on its way to becoming an unprecedented year of labor unrest, primarily over the issue of union recognition. With a steel strike threatened for 16 June, the pressure was intense to reconcile some of the divergent perspectives on labor legislation and reach a compromise that could deal with at least those labor problems on the immediate horizon.[70]

The approaching steel strike posed a particularly significant threat to the

69. I. Bernstein, *The New Deal Collective Bargaining Policy*, pp. 60–64.
70. Ibid., pp. 66–72.

government's program for recovery. Given the frustration of auto workers with the decisions of the Automobile Labor Board, it was widely assumed that a steel strike could provoke sympathetic strikes in other durable goods industries, with the potential of becoming the first nationwide general strike.[71] Roosevelt had acted to diffuse the coming confrontation when he approved the revised steel code on 30 May 1934, appending to the executive order approving the code a guarantee to provide government-supervised elections.[72] But while such assurances had previously been sufficient to defer the threat of a strike, in the aftermath of the automobile settlement a vague promise of elections did not go far enough.

Because Congress could not simply abdicate its responsibility to act, the chairman of the Senate Committee on Education and Labor, Senator Walsh, began to search for a compromise that could pass Congress before the summer adjournment. Walsh's National Industrial Adjustment Bill would have restricted the coverage of the act to interstate business, removed the duty of employers to bargain, permitted employers to initiate company unions but not dominate them or contribute financial support to them, reduced the list of unfair labor practices, and placed the NLB within the jurisdiction of the Department of Labor. This bill still prohibited employers from interfering with the self-organization of employees and permitted the NLB to determine employees' representation by an impartial election (neither majority rule nor proportional representation was specified).[73] The Walsh Bill then became the rallying point for progessive forces, with support coming from the president, the Department of Labor, the NRA, and Senator Wagner. Once again progressives proved that in spite of their differences on the labor question, they could unite behind moderate measures that curbed the most offensive abuses of employee rights.

The major obstacle to legislative action solidifying labor's rights to organize and bargain collectively was the irreconcilable opposition of business. The employers' antagonism toward the Wagner Labor Disputes Bill had not been assuaged by Walsh's revised National Industrial Adjustment Bill.[74] Employers were convinced that even this toned-down version would still permit the AFL to impose a closed shop on industry. The NAM and the Chamber of Commerce both denounced the bill, and they rallied conservative Republican opposition to its passage that session. Business generally favored an obstructionist strategy on the assumption that Roosevelt would lose support in the 1934 congressional elections and that radical legislation would enjoy even less support during the next Congress.[75]

71. *The Nation*, 30 May 1934, p. 612.
72. Lorwin and Wubnig, p. 333.
73. I. Bernstein, *The New Deal Collective Bargaining Policy*, pp. 72–79.
74. *The Iron Age*, 31 May 1934, p. 28; "A Statement of the Steel Industry's Position on the Revised Wagner Bill," NRA Records, RG 9, Entry 25, Consolidated Code Industry Files: Iron and Steel, File 16: Labor-Collective Bargaining, S–Z; Fine, p. 228.
75. I. Bernstein, *The New Deal Collective Bargaining Policy*, p. 75; Fine, p. 228.

Although sympathetic to business concerns, conservative Republicans were aware that, despite their power to delay the act, ultimately the Democrats had the votes to pass the National Industrial Adjustment Bill if Roosevelt played an active leadership role and Congress was willing to extend the current session. The Republicans pragmatically played on the Democrats' desire to adjourn to win as many concessions as possible without risking the backlash that a totally obstructionist position might have provoked.[76] Roosevelt was amenable to a temporary compromise that granted the government sufficient power to deal with the impending crisis in industrial relations while postponing a final determination of the issues at stake. On 15 June 1934 a resolution suggested by Roosevelt was introduced in each house after consultations and agreement with Republican leaders. This resolution, enacted on 16 June as Public Resolution No. 44 (P.R. 44) and signed by Roosevelt on 19 June, provided legislative authority to "insure the right of employees to organize and to select their representatives for the purpose of collective bargaining as provided in Section 7a of the Industrial Recovery Act."[77]

The most important contribution of P.R. 44 to advancing the right of labor to organize and bargain collectively was that it provided legislative authority for a new National Labor Relations Board (NLRB) to replace the NLB. Whereas the NLB had relied on the legally questionable authority of its enabling executive order, now the president had legislative authorization to establish a board or boards to investigate conflicts concerning Section 7a and, when it was in the public interest to do so, to order elections to determine "by what person or persons or *organization*" labor would be represented. While the reference to "organization" rather than "organizations" might appear to favor majority rule instead of proportional representation, the legislative history of P.R. 44 makes it clear that Congress expected Roosevelt to insist on proportional representation and that the resolution did not preclude this.[78] Conservatives had attempted to water down the electoral guarantees of P.R. 44 by removing from the clause the word "organization," but Roosevelt had insisted that the word be restored.[79] The NLRB, and other more industry-specific labor boards that might also be created, would be empowered to subpoena witnesses and documents such as payroll lists in order to fulfill its responsibilities. The NLB had been hamstrung by the lack of this power.

The NLRB would also have more effective means for enforcing its orders than the NLB. When the NLB concluded that an employer was violating Section 7a, it was forced to turn the case over to the NRA for appropriate action, which might include removal of an employer's Blue

---

76. I. Bernstein, *The New Deal Collective Bargaining Policy*, pp. 78–79.
77. Ibid., p. 78.
78. *The Iron Age*, 21 June 1934, pp. 39–40. Emphasis added.
79. I. Bernstein, *The New Deal Collective Bargaining Policy*, p. 79.

Eagle or criminal prosecution by the Justice Department. Neither remedy had been particularly effective during the previous year. The removal of a Blue Eagle did not necessarily deter employers, and criminal prosecution of an employer was a time-consuming and unwieldy enforcement mechanism. Under P.R. 44, NLRB orders would be enforced in the same manner as the orders of the Federal Trade Commission, and the agency could appeal directly to the courts to issue mandatory injunctions to enforce its election orders, the violation of which would entail contempt penalties.[80]

Public Resolution 44 fell short of both the Labor Disputes Act and the National Industrial Adjustment Bill in important ways. This resolution was essentially the part of the Wagner Labor Disputes Act that dealt with provisions for elections, but without further specification of unfair labor practices or a prohibition on company unions. Of course, since the statutory basis for the NLRB included the NIRA as well as P.R. 44, the board could continue to proscribe practices that interfered with Section 7a rights. The boards were granted wide discretion to prescribe supplemental rules and regulations to give effect to their judgments both with regard to investigations of disputes and in conducting elections.[81] More fundamental, however, P.R. 44 did not resolve the conflict between majority rule and proportional representation, because it left the matter to the discretion of the labor board.[82]

Not all of the New Deal coalition was immediately persuaded by Roosevelt's appeal for postponement of consideration of the issues raised by the Wagner Bill. Senator LaFollette insisted on offering amendments that would have incorporated most of the features of the Wagner Bill into the Senate version of P.R. 44. It required an appeal from Wagner to restrain LaFollette from forcing the issue and possibly damaging the prospects for Wagner's bill in the next session of Congress.[83] Senator Walsh, whose National Industrial Adjustment Bill had gone considerably beyond P.R. 44 in protecting labor's right to organize and bargain collectively, argued that this resolution would not guarantee free elections because elections would never be free as long as employers could exercise economic pressure against employees. Nevertheless, he conceded, the resolution was "of considerable benefit" insofar as it permitted the Labor Board to determine which of two groups—generally a company union or an AFL affiliate—represented workers. Elections were a necessary if not sufficient mechanism for the expression of free choice.[84] Senator Huey Long concurred:

80. Ibid., p. 78.
81. Ibid.
82. Ibid., p. 79; Gross, p. 73.
83. I. Bernstein, *The New Deal Collective Bargaining Policy*, p. 80.
84. National Labor Relations Board, *Legislative History of the Nat'l Labor Relations Act* (Washington, D.C., 1949), pp. 1187–1192.

While probably I would write the joint resolution a great deal more in favor of labor than my colleagues would, I see in this joint resolution one thing—a guarantee by which fairly and honorably, without exposing themselves to peril, laboring men may actually express their wish to be free from company unions, and to be organized under a leadership that is not subject to company influence. That seems to me, if carried out, to be a guarantee that they may honestly and freely express themselves, without peril, in favor of a fair organization to represent them. That much seems to be quite a forward step to the laboring people.[85]

Wagner's judgment carried great weight among progressives because of his role on the NLB. His assurance that P.R. 44, despite its limitations, would be helpful to labor was important in rallying support for the measure. According to Wagner,

The Congress and the country during the past year have united in passing and applying the most varied and sweeping changes in our economic life that have ever occurred in so short a time. Perhaps it may be a good thing to allow these reforms to encounter an additional period of trial and error, so that the processes of education and understanding may catch up with the social program that has been inaugurated. That is the judgment of the President with regard to the labor-disputes bill, and I am prepared to go along with him. No one is in a better position than he to weigh the program in its entirety, and no one is more determined than he that we are but commencing a new deal that will in proper time be pushed forward to its ultimate conclusion.[86]

Because the battle lines between employers and unions had been drawn over the issue of elections, and the most conspicuous failure of the NLB was its inability to compel them, P.R. 44 would protect labor by opening this avenue for legal recognition to the AFL. As such it would "meet the most serious and immediate difficulty" while postponing a definitive solution.[87]

The AFL was certainly disappointed by P.R. 44 after their hopes for passage of the Wagner Labor Disputes Bill had been raised. William Green stated labor's official position: "Labor firmly believed that the enactment of the Wagner Disputes Act was necessary if the working people of the Nation were to be accorded the enjoyment of the right to organize and bargain collectively as provided for in Section 7(a). . . . The submission of a compromise Wagner bill is a keen disappointment to Labor. . . . Labor can neither approve nor endorse the so-called compromise Wagner bill."[88] Nevertheless, there were sober leaders in the labor

---

85. Ibid., p. 1193.
86. Ibid., p. 1183.
87. Ibid.
88. *Amalgamated Journal*, 21 June 1934, quoted in I. Bernstein, *New Deal Collective Bargaining Policy*, p. 81.

movement who saw P.R. 44 as an advancement of labor's cause. According to Charlton Ogburn, general counsel of the AFL, "The President's substitute is an advantage to us and . . . we have much more to gain than to lose under it."[89] Ogburn believed that the vague mandate of the NLRB would be interpreted to labor's benefit by progressive administrators. Others in the AFL must have concurred with this judgment, for despite the AFL's refusal to publicly support P.R. 44, they did not oppose it once it became apparent that the Wagner Bill would face rough sledding without Roosevelt's backing.

P.R. 44 has often been dismissed as a betrayal of labor's interest, a conclusion that taints Roosevelt's progressive credentials.[90] Critics of Roosevelt's labor policy have invariably cited a statement of the vice-president in charge of industrial relations of U.S. Steel to discredit the compromise measure: "I view the passage of the joint resolution with equanimity. It means that temporary measures that cannot last more than a year will be substituted for the permanent legislation proposed. . . . I do not believe there will ever be given as good a chance for the passage of the Wagner Act as exists now, and the trade is a mighty good compromise. I have read carefully the joint resolution, and my personal opinion is that it is not going to bother us very much."[91]

The perspicacity of this officer can be retrospectively called into question by the eventual enactment of the Wagner Bill, but his judgment was not even representative of the opinions of his business contemporaries. Generally, business was not happy with the measure, and Henry Harriman, president of the U.S. Chamber of Commerce and a "corporate liberal," came closer to capturing this mood: "The pending joint resolution is in my judgment a most dangerous measure. The board, or boards, appointed by the President may prescribe any rules and regulations which they deem necessary or desirable in carrying out the provisions of the resolution. . . . Under this broad language, the board could prescribe as a rule and regulation any and every labor practice suggested or prohibited in the original labor disputes bill, and even go further. The sky would be the limit, depending on the temper of the board."[92] The temporary character of the measure did not prevent it from becoming a decisive precedent for future action, a concern that business frequently mentioned regarding the NRA itself.

In particular, employers in the steel industry viewed this measure as a political maneuver by the AFL that snatched political victory from the

---

89. Ogburn to Green, 16 June 1934, Shishkin Papers, quoted in I. Bernstein, *The New Deal Collective Bargaining Policy*, p. 81n.

90. Bellush, pp. 112–113.

91. Quoted in I. Bernstein, *The New Deal Collective Bargaining Policy*, p. 81.

92. *New York Times*, 15 June 1934. For other indications that business was unhappy with P.R. 44, see *Business Week*, 23 June 1934, p. 10; *The Iron Age*, 21 June 1934, p. 40.

jaws of workplace defeat. The employers in that industry had braced for a threatened steel strike, confident that such a precipitous action would break the back of the nascent steel union. The employers knew that despite the dramatic growth of the Amalgamated Association of Iron, Steel, and Tin Workers, many workers were still deeply suspicious of it. Furthermore, employers had fortified their factories, hired security men, and had few back orders to fill. They had every reason to believe that a major steel strike would have been as disastrous for the steel union as their ill-fated 1919 strike had been. Even the AFL had been fearful that the union would lose.[93] AFL president Green had counseled the steel workers at their annual convention to postpone their impending strike in view of their organizational weakness.[94] Having secured promises from Roosevelt that a National Steel Labor Relations Board (NSLRB) would be established to resolve the dispute as soon as P.R. 44 was enacted (P.R. 44 established the authority for this board), Green could persuasively argue that workers had a better opportunity to further their cause by awaiting additional government action rather than striking precipitously. The union postponed its strike.[95] P.R. 44 had provided a face-saving way for the union to back down from its rash threats while still winning a significant part of its demands.

P.R. 44 exemplified the triumph of moderation and represented the high point of Roosevelt's industrial statesmanship in the steel industry. Both labor and business were forced to cede ground. Each side had reason to be dissatisfied with the result, but moderates in each camp realized that other alternatives that were far less appealing had been avoided. In this case, however, simple moderation proved insufficient. P.R. 44 had temporarily eased tensions in the steel industry, but its success in doing so would last only as long as the administration could avoid clarification of P.R. 44 ambiguities. P.R. 44 had not resolved many of the underlying issues that divided the NRA and the NLB, now reconstituted as the NLRB. When the NLRB adopted NLB precedents and supported majority rule, business and labor once again resumed their intense conflict. Tensions between the NLRB and the NRA began to mount as well.

Voluntarism in Retreat?

By the summer of 1934 it had begun to appear as if President Roosevelt was abandoning his commitment to collective bargaining pluralism and veering toward majority rule and exclusive representation. Although P.R.

93. I. Bernstein, *Turbulent Years*, pp. 198–199; *The Iron Age*, 21 June 1934, pp. 39–40, 70; ibid., 7 June 1934, p. 42a.
94. Bellush, p. 111.
95. Lorwin and Wubnig, p. 335; *New York Times*, 16 June 1934.

44 had not specified whether labor elections would be conducted on the basis of majority rule or proportional representation, the NLB majority-rule precedent favored the adoption of the former, and Roosevelt did not attempt to steer the NLRB away from accepting that precedent.[96] On 30 August 1934 the NLRB adopted the majority-rule position in the Houde Engineering Company case. When Francis Biddle became chairman of the NLRB in mid-November of the same year, conversations with labor department officials gave him reason to believe that Roosevelt supported the Houde decision.[97] Furthermore, Roosevelt allowed the NLRB to expand its authority over labor disputes.[98] The NLRB aspirations to become the final court of appeal for controversial policy decisions above all the special labor boards being established on an industry by industry basis to defuse tensions in those industries were on the verge of being fulfilled.

But just when it seemed that the administration was shifting its position in favor of the NLRB and its majority-rule position, the wings of the NLRB were clipped. A case involving discrimination against a union member in the newspaper business erupted into a jurisdictional battle between the NRA and the NLRB in the fall of 1934, and Roosevelt sided with the NRA in January 1935. Although Roosevelt sugar-coated his decision, telling the NLRB that there were only a few areas where it could not assert jurisdiction, the decision had thwarted NLRB aspirations to become the Supreme Court of industrial relations.[99] Moreover, even before he had rendered this decision, Roosevelt had demonstrated his continuing support for NRA voluntarism when he attempted to mediate the growing tensions between labor and management in the steel industry in October.

On 1 October 1934, Roosevelt appealed to both labor and industry generally to observe a temporary truce in the battle over labor recognition. Roosevelt's plea for moderation won the acclaim of the National Association of Manufacturers and the AFL, but each side proceeded to interpret the appeal consistent with their own interests. The NAM urged the president to uphold the status quo in labor relations for the duration of the depression. Industries conducted on an open shop basis would remain free of unions. William Green urged an AFL convention to bow to Roosevelt's request, but he defined the status quo to include the common law on industrial relations emerging from labor board decisions. A viable truce was conditional on employers obeying this law. Neither side appeared ready to give ground to the other.[100]

96. Gross, p. 76.
97. Ibid., p. 100.
98. Lyon et al., pp. 449, 477.
99. Gross, pp. 109–121.
100. *New York Times*, 2 and 3 October 1934.

Taking the initiative in the steel industry, the NSLRB drafted a new compromise collective bargaining plan that called for employer recognition and collective bargaining with unions, but only as the representative of union members, a plan bearing a strong resemblance to the automobile settlement of the previous spring except that it was proposed as a temporary measure. On 4 December 1934 the Carnegie Steel Company, still awaiting the outcome of an NSLRB case in which the Amalgamated sought a majority-rule election, submitted a proposal along the lines suggested by the NSLRB to the Amalgamated. With the understanding that this proposal had the assent of the other companies in the American Iron and Steel Institute, Carnegie agreed to receive and negotiate with any organization "as representatives of those employees whom they represent, irrespective of their number." In return, the Amalgamated was to hold in abeyance any petitions for elections "without waiving its position on the question of majority rule following elections or in any wise assenting to the principle of minority representation or proportional representation."[101]

Roosevelt was convinced that this proposal represented a genuine effort to compromise on the part of employers. Arranging a conference, on 18 December Roosevelt met with leaders of the steel employers and the Amalgamated to help them reach an accord.[102] But labor refused to budge from its original position. Green repeated the argument that collective bargaining based on majority rule was the only practical formula that put labor and management on equal terms. Such an arrangement was "a matter of simple justice and fair dealing," which "represents democracy in industry." Compromise with company unions was impossible because any compromise would undermine labor's united front: "There could be no basis of accommodation upon which the representatives of company unions and of free, independent American Federation of Labor Unions could stand. One organization of workers would be pitted against another; that would mean the workers would be divided into hostile camps while the management of the steel industry would be united in a single collective bargaining agency. This would mean weakness for the workers but strength for the management of the steel industry."[103]

Green went on to point out that proportional representation would give a foothold for communist labor organizations, whereas the advantage of majority rule was that a minority like the communists would be excluded from collective bargaining. The alternative he presented was an either/or

101. "Counter Proposal Worker Out as a Result of Conference in New York," 12 April 1934, NRA Records, RG 9, Entry 396, National Steel Labor Relations Board, General Files, File: Carnegie Steel Co., Duquesne Plant; Memo, 21 December 1934, Roosevelt Papers, OF 342, No. 1, Steel, 1934–36.

102. *New York Times*, 19 December 1934.

103. William Green to Stacey, 4 January 1935, NRA Records, RG 9, Entry 396, National Steel Labor Relations Board, General Files, File: Carnegie Steel Co., Duquesne Plant.

choice between company unions and free and democratic unions. "There could be *no* stability under such a plan of procedure. It would mean chaos and confusion. *All* the elements of practicability and constructive procedure which tend to make collective bargaining a *complete* success would be *entirely lacking*. Through such a plan the steel corporations *would completely control* the economic power of its employees."[104]

Green's intransigence concerning proportional representation thwarted Roosevelt's attempt to fashion a comprehensive truce between business and labor, and Roosevelt once again resumed a hands-off policy, biding his time until a more propitious moment for achieving an agreement arose. Allowing the NRA, the NLRB, and the various specialized labor boards to pursue independent policies, Roosevelt tolerated both the proportional-representation position of the NRA and the majority-rule position of the NLRB. The latter was tactically useful because it established a more radical alternative to Roosevelt's preferred voluntarist solution and Roosevelt could use it to cajole businessmen into granting the concessions necessary to assure the success of voluntarism. But tolerance for the majority-rule position never evolved into active support during the lifetime of the NRA. At the crucial junctures where Roosevelt intervened in the class struggle between labor and business during the early New Deal—the automobile settlement, the replacement of the Wagner Labor Disputes Bill by P.R. 44, and the attempt to mediate a truce in the steel industry in December 1934—Roosevelt had either explicitly supported proportional representation or had at least refused to support the majority-rule position. For that reason, by January 1935 some union leaders were calling for an open break with Roosevelt and the NRA.[105]

The Failure of NRA Labor Policy

NRA labor policy failed to achieve the goals the NRA had established. The NRA had attempted to institutionalize a new cooperative relationship between business and labor based on collective bargaining. Instead, it had intensified class conflict. The failure of the NRA to provide a new cooperative framework for labor and business is evident in the data regarding industrial strikes during this period. In 1932, the year before the NRA began, there were 829 strikes and lockouts, accounting for the loss of 6,462,973 man-days of work. In 1933 those figures rose to 1,562 strikes and lockouts, accounting for the loss of 14,818,846 man-days of work, and in 1934 the figures peaked at 1,637 strikes and lockouts, accounting for the loss of 18,666,000 man-days of work.[106] Similarly, the

104. Ibid. Emphasis added.
105. *New York Times*, 3 February 1935; Schlesinger, *The Coming of the New Deal*, p. 401.
106. Roos, p. 210.

total number of workers involved in strikes for union recognition went from 73,000 in 1932 to 288,000 in 1935.[107]

Whether the NRA merely failed to contain the rising tide of worker militance rooted in distressed economic conditions, or whether the NRA actually stoked the fires of labor conflict is not clear, although there are powerful reasons for believing the latter was the case. One can confidently dismiss the assertion of employers that the New Dealers had disturbed the harmonious labor relations that prevailed prior to the New Deal, but worker dissatisfaction would not necessarily have culminated in increased labor militance without New Deal intervention in labor relations. During downturns in economic cycles, the bargaining position of organized labor is weakened by the large number of unemployed who could take the place of striking workers. Membership usually falls off as workers are reluctant or unable to contribute union dues. Under these circumstances, labor militancy is unlikely unless political factors intervene.[108] Certainly it would be plausible to attribute the intense labor militancy of the NRA period to a perception of growing labor strength in the political arena.

Within the contours of basic NRA policy, Roosevelt and the NRA administrators had done everything in their power to restrain labor militance so that it would not undermine the goals of the NRA. They had favored voluntarism because they hoped it would provide a moderate meeting ground for labor and business, and they had attempted to strengthen the authority of moderates within the labor and business community by giving them prominent roles in the NRA and by negotiating with them when conflicts arose. But these attempts to promote moderation could not stem the growing polarization between labor and business. The politicization of the business-labor relationship through the NRA held out the promise that government intervention would no longer be ad hoc intervention for the sake of mediation, but authoritative adjudication on the issue of union recognition. At least initially confident that the New Deal was sympathetic to their cause, workers had been emboldened to risk everything to uphold their politically defined "rights." Restraints based on realistic calculation of business and union strength were jettisoned when the workers could hope for government intervention. The NRA had unintentionally generated unrealistic labor expectations that government would immediately overcome their economic and social subordination to business, and that fueled workplace militance even if the NRA was not exclusively responsible for it.

Labor militance and business intransigence with regard to union recognition sealed the fate of NRA labor policy just as business cartelization had undermined the NRA's fair trade practices policy. Widespread strikes

---

107. Mancur Olson, Jr., *The Logic of Collective Action* (Cambridge, Mass., 1965), p. 80.
108. Ibid., pp. 77–79.

were retarding economic recovery just as artificially inflated prices were retarding economic recovery. Both the NRA's business policy and its labor policy had presupposed the development of a new social ethic, and in each case interest groups had remained true to their nature by pursuing their economic self-interest. The failure to propagate a new social ethic had led to the failure of the program, because without an ethical revolution the government simply could not impose a corporatist solution on business and labor. Such an attempt would have required massive regimentation, an outcome that neither government, business, or labor wanted.[109]

However, to focus on the societal corporatist aspirations of the NRA as the source of problems in the NRA's labor policy is at this point premature. As was the case with NRA business policy, that focus on the goals of the program, rather than the means that were used to realize those goals, would be justified only if it could be demonstrated that the failure of NRA labor policy did not *fundamentally* arise from the manner in which it was administered. Did weak administrative leadership or the corporatist inclusion of private interests (particularly business interests) undermine NRA labor policy?

In contrast to the development of fair trade practices policy, Hugh Johnson's weaknesses as an administrator did not appear to play a significant role in the unraveling of NRA labor policy. While his lack of tact and diplomatic skills did at times alienate labor leaders and make it more difficult to negotiate agreements, Roosevelt took a far more active hand in the evolution of NRA labor policy than he had in the evolution of NRA business policy. Labor's unwillingness to cooperate with the NRA was rooted in its rejection of the NRA's voluntarist policy, a policy with which Roosevelt concurred. It had little to do with Johnson's personal style. Roosevelt, with his considerable political and administrative skills, could not make a success of NRA labor policy any more than Johnson could.

Examining the possibility that NRA labor policy failed because the NRA had included private interests in the NRA administrative apparatus will require a far more extended analysis. Critics of administrative corporatism have argued that such arrangements allow powerful private interests to co-opt public authority and use it to secure private ends. These arrangements are presumed to work to the benefit of the best-organized

109. Prior to the NRA, labor had been strongly committed to the voluntarist self-help policy of Samuel Gompers (not to be confused with NRA voluntarism), rejecting extensive government intrusion into industrial relations. While this policy was moderated during the New Deal, the AFL remained as suspicious of government regimentation as industry did. William Green asserted, "we believe that if self-government is not developed in industry it will be necessary to extend political control into this sphere and that such political control will inevitably be of an arbitrary nature" (Green to FDR, 11 February 1935, Roosevelt Papers, OF 142, No. 1, AFL, 1933–35). Naturally, Green was committed to industrial self-government in which labor was a full and equal partner.

CHAPTER 10

Pluralist Theory and the NRA: The Case of Labor

The pluralist characterization of the early New Deal Roosevelt as a broker-politician, a leader who aggregated and mediated conflicting interest group demands, is initially quite plausible.[1] Unlike strict political moralists or idealists, Franklin Roosevelt never seemed to flinch at the compromises necessary to sustain his power. Early in his administration, he refused to support national legislation that would have made the lynching of blacks in the South a federal crime,[2] defending his action as necessary because he could not afford to alienate the Southern votes he needed for his economic program. Later he solidified his control over the Democratic party by coming to terms with the urban bosses, the traditional nemesis of progressive politicians.[3] When Roosevelt's realism concerning political power is combined with his experimental approach to economic policy—an approach that demonstrated an extraordinary flexibility regarding the means to economic recovery—it is easy to form the impression that Roosevelt is a political broker. Flexibility and realism regarding the means to economic recovery is assumed to imply flexibility (i.e., lack of principles) and realism regarding the ends of politics as well.

James MacGregor Burns's *Roosevelt: The Lion and the Fox* provides an example of critical pluralist historiography in its interpretation of the NRA. Burns describes the NRA as a brokered state, the institutional analogue of the brokered politician's style of leadership. Businessmen had sought a relaxation of antitrust statutes in order to facilitate industrial self-government, and the NRA appeared to be a response to this demand. Labor had been accommodated by the inclusion of Section 7a, guaranteeing

---

1. Throughout this chapter the term "pluralism" is used to refer to the pluralist theory developed by such political scientists as David Truman and Robert Dahl during the 1950s, and to historiography that is fundamentally grounded in that theoretical framework.
2. Leuchtenburg, *FDR and the New Deal*, p. 186.
3. Burns, *Roosevelt: The Lion and the Fox*, pp. 64–65, 364.

the right to organize and bargain collectively. For Burns the NRA is little more than the resultant of a vector of interest group forces, devoid of any independent progressive commitment to reform. Burns's application of pluralist theory to the NRA can be characterized as critical because it purports to demonstrate how pluralist interest group bargaining can go awry in contexts where some groups, such as big business, are disproportionately powerful.[4]

One problem with this interpretation is that Roosevelt did not conceive of his role as that of a political broker. In 1934, Roosevelt reminded bankers: "The old fallacious notion of the bankers on one side and the Government on the other side as being more or less equal and independent units has passed away. Government by the necessity of things must be the leader, must be the judge of the conflicting interests of all groups in the community, including bankers."[5] Roosevelt had been angered at the audacity of bankers, who began their 1934 American Bankers Association convention with assertions that the president and the bankers were independently but equally authorized to represent the public good. In private Roosevelt told Tugwell: "Imagine referring to a representative of the American Bankers Association and the President of the United States as equals: And imagine what national policy would be like if, instead of requiring such groups to conform to the public interest, they were free to bargain about what they would or would not consent to accept. Outrageous!"[6]

Roosevelt's rejection of the political broker role vis-à-vis business interests was paralleled by a rejection of the political broker role vis-à-vis labor interests, as he demonstrated by his selection of Frances Perkins as secretary of labor. The Departments of Agriculture, Labor, and Commerce have traditionally had very close relationships with agricultural groups, labor unions, and trade associations respectively. Not only had the AFL played an important role in the formation of the Department of Labor in 1913, but every secretary of labor since its formation had been a union leader. This tradition had been upheld even by the conservative presidents of the 1920s, although Hoover had dared to name William Doak, a leader in the Brotherhood of Railroad Trainmen, which was not affiliated with the AFL, over the opposition of the AFL.

Anticipating a continuation of this clientele relationship from a president so friendly to labor, the AFL soon after Roosevelt's election lined up behind Dan Tobin, president of the Teamsters, as their nominee for secretary of labor. Tobin's credentials for the position were impeccable: he was a strong Democrat, a Roosevelt backer who served on the Democratic Labor Committee during the 1932 campaign, and a prominent labor

4. Ibid., pp. 191–202.
5. Leuchtenburg, *FDR and the New Deal*, p. 89; Roosevelt, *Public Papers*, 3:436.
6. Leuchtenburg, *FDR and the New Deal*, p. 90; Tugwell, *The Democratic Roosevelt*, p. 381.

leader. When rumors began to circulate that Frances Perkins, the industrial commissioner in New York while Franklin Roosevelt was governor, might get the nod, Perkins wrote to Roosevelt, "One straight from the ranks of some group of organized workers should be appointed to reestablish firmly the principle that *labor is in the President's councils.*"[7]

Ignoring these arguments, Roosevelt acted on his own opinions concerning qualifications for the job. As sympathetic as Roosevelt was to the cause of organized labor, he trusted the dispassionate judgment of progressive experts over that of an interest group advocate. Roosevelt chose Frances Perkins for her distinguished progressive reputation and for her personal loyalty to him. Although Roosevelt's desire to appoint the first woman to a cabinet position also played a role in the decision, this exemplified Roosevelt's progressivism rather than a concession to interest group politics, because the appointment did not signify a commitment to give benefits to women as a special interest group. Organized labor was furious at Roosevelt's choice. While they could not deny that Perkins was qualified and had long been a friend of labor, her appointment reflected Roosevelt's intention to use the department to carry out his policies, and the AFL realized that their policy-making role in the new administration could be peripheral.[8]

The political broker can be usefully contrasted with the statesman. The statesman goes beyond the minimal broker role of harmonizing group interests in his attention to a comprehensive image of the destiny or ideals of the state. Thus the statesman has an autonomous impact on the intersecting interest group forces as he promotes his image of the common good, a good that the statesman believes subsumes the partial goals of each conflicting group. A statesman may defend groups that are comparatively weak, so that his policies will not simply reflect the balance of interest group forces. Furthermore, a statesman will be at least as concerned with the objective interests of groups, interests that the groups themselves may not perceive, as with the interests that the groups are actively pursuing. While the statesman will be prudent in the implementation of state purposes, taking due account of the limits on the realization of state goals imposed by the power of groups either not sharing, or only partially sharing, such goals, the statesman does not respond to situations on a strictly ad hoc basis. He has long-term goals that are a guiding star for his actions, providing a thread of continuity from one situation to the next.

Roosevelt may or may not have been a statesman in the highest sense of that term, but he was certainly much closer to the statesman than he was to the political broker. To a certain extent, statesmanship is a matter of the

---

7. I. Bernstein, *Turbulent Years,* p. 9.
8. Ibid., pp. 10–11.

times as well as the person, and during the New Deal the times were propitious for political statesmanship. Decisive action was called for, and people turned first to President Roosevelt for relief. Brokerage politics as usual would not do in these circumstances, and if Roosevelt had not provided leadership, others would have seized the opportunity to fill the void. Furthermore, the sense of crisis freed Roosevelt from many of the political constraints that limit possibilities for statesmanship during other eras. Public opinion could be mobilized on behalf of the president's program. Public opinion did not dictate any particular path of action; it generally followed the president's lead.

Roosevelt entered the presidency with a clear, principled commitment to progressive reform, a commitment that had been fashioned and tested over a long political career. Imitating the career path of his family mentor, Theodore Roosevelt, Franklin Roosevelt had gained his first experience of Washington as assistant secretary of the Navy in Woodrow Wilson's administration.[9] Later, rising to national political prominence as governor of New York during the early depression years, he upheld his progressive reputation by his support of minimum-wage legislation, relief programs, and conservation.[10] Finally, as president, Roosevelt enacted the reform measures of the New Deal. These continuities in Roosevelt's progressive commitments cannot be reconciled with an interpretation of him as merely a power broker.

In contrast to the political broker who shores up the status quo and tries to avoid conflict that might jeopardize it, Roosevelt was committed to reform for the sake of social justice, and he did not shy away from the political conflict that such reforms might entail.[11] Convinced that the increasing concentration of wealth and corporate control over the economy

9. Burns, *Roosevelt: The Lion and the Fox*, pp. 50–66.
10. James Sunquist, *Dynamics of the Party System* (Washington, D.C., 1973), p. 194.
11. The New Deal origins of the welfare state attest to Roosevelt's commitment to social justice. Critics of the New Deal often suggest that Roosevelt's new social security system was "regressive" and that Roosevelt was therefore not genuinely committed to social justice. The social security system compelled workers to contribute to their own retirement funds instead of placing the costs exclusively on employers, and it made social security benefits at least partially proportionate to the income levels of the recipient prior to retirement. However insufficient this system may appear from an idealized egalitarian viewpoint, it was a distinct advance toward social justice in comparison with what preceded it. Before social security, workers generally had to save for their own retirement without any help from employers. At most, one could condemn the New Deal for its modest conception of social justice rather than for a lack of any such conception, and even that judgment fails to recognize that a more redistributive social security system could be built on the foundations of the New Deal system once Roosevelt had established the basic principle of a safety net. Roosevelt prudently secured those foundations by building a system that did not depart so radically from traditional American values that it would have been vulnerable to a conservative counterattack once he left office. To condemn Roosevelt for this, critics would have to demonstrate that a more redistributive system was politically feasible at the time and would have been no less vulnerable to conservative attempts to restore the status quo ante. What is troubling about the New Deal is not the depth of Roosevelt's commitment to social justice, but the manner in which social justice was "reconciled" with other fundamental values in

were "steering a steady course toward economic oligarchy, if we are not there already," Roosevelt insisted that new forms of regulatory control and a more equitable distribution of wealth were essential if democracy was to survive. "I believe the human race can and will attain social justice through social action."[12] Roosevelt's quest for social justice was clearly evident in New Deal reforms that led to the creation of a welfare state, but that quest had corporatist overtones as well.

It is true that Roosevelt was never firmly wedded to a particular theory of economic recovery, but certainly an ideal typical statesman would not assume an office like the presidency with a rigidly fixed agenda. One mark of his statesmanship would be his capacity to learn on the job, to adapt to changing circumstances without thereby sacrificing his ultimate purposes. Roosevelt's New Deal exemplified these characteristics. The New Deal retained a steady commitment to progressive purposes, even though its history is replete with false starts and vestigial branches that withered as New Deal progressivism took on historical concreteness. Roosevelt's shifts in economic policy (from a tight to a loose monetary policy and from a balanced budget to deficit spending) did not indicate vacillation about fundamental principles, because with regard to such touchstone progressive beliefs as the denial of laissez-faire and the need for state intervention to secure greater social justice, Roosevelt was always consistent. He was flexible regarding means, but not regarding ends.

The image of the brokered state captures an important prudential dimension to Roosevelt's New Deal, but it fails to display that prudence in the service of any higher goals. This failing has been particularly egregious when it comes to the NRA. The claim that the NRA institutionalized a brokered state has gained unjustified credence from the juxtaposition of benefits to labor and to business in the NRA. According to this interpretation, the NRA was an incoherent mixture of interest group demands because labor and business acquiesced in parts of the program sympathetic to the other as a quid pro quo for their own gains. Labor accepted the cartelization of industry in exchange for the right to organize unions, and business accepted the higher costs of code hour and wage requirements in return for the promise of higher prices. Pluralists would agree with Ellis Hawley when he argued:

> Within the confines of a single measure, then, the formulators of the National Industrial Recovery Act had appealed to the hopes of a number of conflicting pressure groups. Included were the hopes of labor for mass organization and collective bargaining, the hopes of businessmen for price and production controls. . . . Overlying these more selfish economic purposes

---

the American political system. In the case of the NRA, economic inefficiency and political regimentation were tolerated for the sake of securing social justice.

12. Roosevelt, *The Public Papers*, 1:771–780.

were a *veneer* of ideals and conflicting ideologies, conflicting beliefs as to what the act would do and the ultimate form that the business system should take.[13]

To the extent the progressive ideas are important in such an interpretation, it is only insofar as they rationalize the more fundamental economic interests that underlie them.

This portrait of the NRA is not totally erroneous. The NRA did involve concessions to both business and labor interests, because the voluntary cooperation of both groups was essential for the success of the program. The relaxation of antitrust laws was intended to compensate business for the higher labor costs it would bear under the NRA. Yet the incoherence of the NRA can be exaggerated. While separate provisions dealt with the problems of business and labor, this act was not an example of pork barrel legislation because the benefits distributed by the NRA to each group were not discrete goods. The NRA was a *plan* for national recovery in which the increased purchasing power generated by benefits to labor were intended to rebound to the benefit of industry by increasing sales and profits. The mitigation of competition for industry likewise was intended to rebound to the benefit of labor, because intense competition invariably put downward pressure on wages and lengthened hours as employers sought to cut costs to meet the competition. Insofar as the NRA can be represented as an integrated approach to recovery, it can be seen as a manifestation of the relatively coherent progressive goals of the New Deal political elite.

Organized labor, recognizing the linkage between fair trade practices and minimum wage and maximum hours provisions, supported a broad scope for industrial codes. A minimal code dealing solely with wages and hours could have formally exempted wages from the pressure of cost reduction, but voluntary adherence to the codes would have been uncertain unless competitive pressures were eased generally. In industries with a long history of cutthroat competition, such as bituminous coal, labor went as far as to assist the industry actively in the drafting and enforcement of codes to protect their own wages.[14]

Not only did the NRA have more internal cohesion than the model of the brokered state would anticipate, but also the distribution of benefits to labor and business hardly reflected their respective organizational strengths. Inclusion of Section 7a in the NIRA had advanced the interests of labor and threatened business interests. Yet the AFL was in no condition in 1933 to have staged such a coup. Membership in labor unions had plunged during the 1920s and early 1930s, and unions had been further weakened by the attenuation of the strike threat during the depression

13. Hawley, *The New Deal*, p. 33. Emphasis added.
14. J. Johnson, pp. 153, 162–163, 196.

when high unemployment meant that scab labor was readily available to break strikes.[15] Given these circumstances, it is implausible to believe that organized labor imposed Section 7a on Roosevelt. The discrepancy between interest group strengths and interest groups benefits in the NIRA clearly suggests that the NIRA was not the mere aggregation of interest group demands but a program that fashioned interest group demands to serve progressive purposes.

Granting that labor lacked the organizational strength to compel Roosevelt to defer to its lobbying efforts as an interest group, perhaps its political clout as a potentially hostile electorate was decisive in compelling Roosevelt to include Section 7a. In the most plausible version of this scenario, Congress, being more immediately accountable to public opinion, should have registered constituency dissatisfaction and pushed Roosevelt to the left, at least regarding the labor provisions of the NRA. James MacGregor Burns argued, "Roosevelt's main job in 1933 and 1934 was not to prod Congress into action, but to ride the congressional whirlwind by disarming the extremists," and Burns believed that "Congress had the effect of pushing Roosevelt a bit further toward the left."[16] Bernard Bellush explicitly accounts for the origins of Section 7a of the NIRA in such a manner. "Despite his disinterest in collective bargaining, Roosevelt endorsed the general consensus for such legislation, feeling that it would insure him the support of labor and be an excellent start for a successful omnibus approach."[17]

Among the circumstances that condition the exercise of political leadership in the modern world, pressure from the left (or right) is an omnipresent factor. However, the explanatory power of this fact in accounting for concrete historical outcomes varies appreciably according to the relevant configurations of political power. That Roosevelt in some sense promoted the NRA in part to forestall more radical measures cannot be denied, but it is also not very revelatory. The real question is whether Roosevelt was able to channel the pressure from the left into support for his own progressive program, or whether he was compelled to acquiesce in a program that violated his own commitments in deference to the power of other actors.

Central to Bellush's explanation of Roosevelt's support of Section 7a of the NIRA is the fact that Roosevelt did not introduce the NRA until May 1933, after his hand was forced by Senate approval of Black's thirty-hour bill.[18] Can we therefore conclude that the NRA, including Section 7a, was not indigenous to the New Deal, but rather was a provision forced on

15. I. Bernstein, *The Lean Years*, pp. 83–90.
16. Burns, *Roosevelt: The Lion and the Fox*, pp. 175, 185.
17. Bellush, p. 13.
18. See above, Chapter 3.

Roosevelt by groups outside his administration? Certainly the Black Bill precipitated action on Roosevelt's part, but it hardly forced him politically to the left. The sequence of events surrounding Black's bill only suggests that Roosevelt acted sooner than he might have without the bill, not that he acted differently from the way he would have in the absence of external pressure. In fact, the first proposals for the NRA were being laid on Roosevelt's desk on Inauguration Day, well before he was surprised by his reversal on the Black Bill in the Senate.[19]

Furthermore, Roosevelt had the power to squash the Black Bill without compromising his own political agenda. His control over the House was firmer than his control over the Senate, and Speaker of the House Rainey had already announced that he would "put over Mr. Roosevelt's program."[20] Roosevelt could also count on a deferential rules committee, which would take its cues on the Black Bill from Roosevelt. Representative Rayburn, chairman of the Rules Committee and an ally of Roosevelt, had already announced that the House would take up the Black Bill only if Roosevelt made it a part of his program.[21] Finally, Roosevelt could have simply vetoed the bill with little fear of a congressional override.

Roosevelt's freedom to fashion a recovery measure largely suitable to his own taste would not face a significant challenge until the mid-1930s, when the opposition to him could coalesce. For the time being, normally obstreperous congressmen referred to Roosevelt as the Moses who would lead them out of the depression and in most cases gave him a blank check. When Roosevelt finally introduced the NIRA, Representative Rayburn facilitated its movement through the House by granting it a drastically restrictive rule with the following words: "It is very true that under this bill—and I shall not attempt to discuss its merits—the President of the United States is made a dictator over industry for the time being, but it is a benign dictatorship. . . . For my part, I am proud to trust him and proud to follow him."[22]

Roosevelt was in the driver's seat when it came to the legislative process. The political forces to the right of him were too weak to obstruct his "must" legislation, and representatives more radical than Roosevelt had generally been easily foiled in their attempts to force him further to the left. Under these circumstances it is implausible to assume the NRA, including Section 7a, was not freely embraced by Roosevelt. The centrality of the NRA to Roosevelt's New Deal, the enthusiasm with which he

19. Roos, p. 36.
20. Burns, "Congress and . . . Economic Policy," p. 3; E. Pendleton Herring, "First Session of the 73rd Congress," *American Political Science Review* 27 (1934): 65–83.
21. Burns, "Congress and . . . Economic Policy," pp. 13–18, 45; I. Bernstein, *Turbulent Years*, p. 27.
22. Burns, "Congress and . . . Economic Policy," p. 45; *Congressional Record*, 73d Cong., 1st sess., 1933, 77:4188.

supported it, and its consistency with the progressive ideals he had espoused earlier in the 1932 campaign justify attributing the responsibility for the program to Roosevelt. Congressmen, interest group leaders, and the general electorate were reacting to his proposals at this point, not determining them.

The brokered state model is problematic not only because Roosevelt was not a broker politician and because the legislative process leading up to the passage of the NIRA was not dominated by interest group politics,[23] but also because the structure of the NRA itself reflected an intention that cannot be easily accommodated within an interest group framework. The NRA had been structured to provide central bureaucratic supervision of the activities of code authorities, and despite hopes that it would basically be a program of industrial self-government, it had never allowed business to control the program. As demonstrated in Part II of this work, the administrative history of the NRA codes of fair trade practices is largely the history of struggles between the state, which proved to be an autonomous actor pursuing progressive goals, and business groups, who were attempting to use the program to further their own interests. The progressive goals of NRA administrators included a commitment to aid peripheral firms in business and to restrain the power of center firms. Because the hypothesis that the NRA exemplified the brokered state would predict that a well-organized constituency like the big-business center firms would do quite well under the NRA and that poorly organized peripheral firms would not fare nearly as well, the conclusions of Part II challenge not only the revisionist interpretation dealt with in Chapter 5, but also the brokered state hypothesis. The question that remains is whether the brokered state hypothesis is any more successful at explaining labor policy during the NRA.

The Progressive State and the Unions

Just as the brokered state model initially seemed to provide a plausible account of Roosevelt's experimental approach to economic recovery, so the same model initially seems persuasive with regard to NRA labor policy, and particularly with the administrative development of that policy. The most important labor policy decision made by NRA administrators— the decision to promote a voluntarist policy of organizational pluralism— was supported by big business, the most powerful and well-organized group, and condemned by the weaker AFL.

At the same time, the brokered state model provides an explanation for facts that would appear anomalous in an explanaton that focused strictly

23. See above, Chapter 3.

on the hegemony of the capitalist class. The pluralistic perspective that lies behind the brokered state conception acknowledges that some groups are better organized than others, but this does not mean that any one group is simply hegemonic. Some unions are well organized. In some contexts, labor proves to be more strategically astute than business. Some labor successes are to be expected.[24] Thus, within the brokered state perspective one might be able to explain why the same Roosevelt who at one moment advocates labor union voluntarism is the next moment granting the AFL more legitimacy than company unions by selecting only AFL representatives to sit on NRA labor advisory boards.[25] These vacillations in labor policy could be explained in the brokered state conception as localized responses to the demands of whichever groups proved most powerful in a specific situation.

As the precending chapter demonstrated, however, the most striking fact about NRA labor policy is that it did not simply shift from situation to situation in response to variations in interest group strength. The universal application of Section 7a to all industries, regardless of the specific configuration of power between business and labor, and the continuity of Roosevelt's commitment to voluntarism throughout the NRA, regardless of temporal and situational shifts of power between business and labor, both attest to the conclusion that Roosevelt's labor policy was principled.

Of course, the policy did show some sensitivity to the need for adaptation to specific historical context. When the automobile industry threatened to reject the NRA altogether unless Section 7a was modified by a "merit clause" that qualified the industry's acknowledgment of labor's right to organize free from coercion with an assertion of an employer's right to hire and fire based on its discretionary judgment of the efficiency of a worker, Roosevelt approved the amendment. Even though the merit clause "interpreted" Section 7a in a way that potentially weakened its effectiveness because an employer could use inefficiency as a pretext for firing those who joined unions, Roosevelt was forced to make this concession because he had so little leverage over the automobile industry.[26] But unlike the political broker, who is unfettered by principles in his search for an expedient compromise, Roosevelt's approval of the automobile merit clause was the action of a principled person making an exception on prudential grounds. Thus Roosevelt personally intervened in the code making process immediately after the automobile merit clause was permitted to forbid inclusion of such interpretations in any other code.[27]

24. Burns, *Roosevelt: The Lion and the Fox*, pp. 192–193, 197–198.
25. Lorwin and Wubnig, pp. 57, 282–283.
26. Fine, p. 48.
27. FDR to Hugh Johnson, 19 October 1933, Roosevelt Papers, OF 407, No. 1, Labor, 1933–34.

While the brokered state model can accommodate occasional and modest concessions to labor's interest during the NRA, it could not explain a systematically pro-labor policy. Initial appearances to the contrary notwithstanding, NRA labor policy was systematically pro-labor. The very existence of Section 7a attests that the NRA was not a perpetuation of the status quo of business hegemony. Under any reasonable interpretation, Section 7a would provide an impetus for labor organization. Hugh Johnson's voluntarist interpretation of Section 7a was no more a ratification of the status quo in industrial relations than the NLB majority-rule position. Many industries had conducted industrial relations according to practices that did not conform to any possible interpretation of Section 7a, and to these industries the New Deal signified unsettling change. The politicization of labor relations through the guarantee of a government-supervised election provided a focus for conflict rather than serving to diffuse it. It was hardly a coincidence that 1934 was one of the most strike-prone years in U.S. labor history.[28]

The NIRA had redefined the rights of workers to include the right to organize and bargain collectively without employer interference, a dramatic legal victory for organized labor. Though the abstract clarity of legal definition fades into a somewhat more ambiguous picture once legal rights are viewed in relation to material interests within a specific historical context, this discrepancy between legal right and substantive realization would not justify discarding legal advances as an ideological screen concealing a real politics based on economic interests. The discrepancy indicated only that the new legal protections guaranteed by Section 7a did not automatically translate into benefits. In many industries, unions failed to capitalize on new opportunities; in others they were prevented from doing so. Legal advances were a necessary but not sufficient condition for a strong and independent union movement.[29] Nevertheless, the new set of legal rights created a propitious climate in which union advances could be more readily achieved.

The most astute leaders in organized labor moved quickly to exploit the opportunity presented by Section 7a, rallying workers to the union banner with the claim "The President wants you to unionize" or "The United States Government has said LABOR MUST ORGANIZE."[30] Total union membership increased by approximately 900,000 during the NRA years, reversing a fairly steady decline since the early 1920s.[31] But this statistic

28. U.S. Bureau of the Census, *Historical Statistics*, 1:97–98.

29. Noting that a sympathetic political administration was no substitute for organization and self-help at the local level, the United Mine Workers journal preached to its workers that "the bill will only be helpful to those who help themselves." See Schlesinger, *The Coming of the New Deal*, p. 139.

30. Ibid., p. 139.

31. U.S. Bureau of the Census, *Historical Statistics*, 1:97–98. If non-dues-paying members are included, the union growth in this period may have been closer to 2 million. See Lyon et al., p. 492.

alone does not convey a sense of the revitalization of the labor movement that occurred during the NRA, for much of the growth was concentrated in particular industries and during short periods of time. In August 1932 there were 307 federal and local unions affiliated with the AFL. In July and August 1933, immediately after the passage of the NIRA, 340 new charters to federal and local unions were issued. In the following year 1,196 more charters were issued.[32] The United Mine Workers had dwindled from a membership of more than 400,000 in 1920 to fewer than 100,000 in 1933, but within five months after the passage of the NIRA it had resumed its former strength. Other unions that aggressively organized also profited. The International Ladies Garment Workers Union trebled its membership under the leadership of David Dubinsky. The Amalgamated Clothing Workers, whose fate had been more benign than other unions in the late 1920s and early 1930s, still increased its membership by 20 percent.[33]

The most significant developments, however, were in the mass production industries without a history of successful vertical unionism, where the rising tide of interest in unionism by unskilled workers threatened to swamp such staid skilled crafts unions as the Amalgamated Association of Iron, Steel, and Tin Workers. In mid-1933 the Amalgamated had 3,000 dues-paying members. Two months after it started its union drive under the NRA, it counted 125 new lodges and more than 60,000 union pledges for membership.[34] The membership of the United Textile Workers of America (UTWA) grew from a few thousand to nearly a quarter million during the NRA.[35]

The case of workers in the automobile industry is particularly interesting. Prior to the NRA, the automobile industry had had a well-entrenched open shop policy, and the AFL had had little success in organizing its workers. The weak automobile unions had been unable to win significant concessions from the industry when the automobile code was formulated, and the NRA had been unable to counteract the imbalance of power that prevailed in the industry because automobile manufacturers had no interest in using the NRA to promote fair trade practices in the industry, giving New Dealers little leverage to extract concessions from the industry on labor issues.[36] With its merit clause, the automobile code was more unfavorable to union organization than the code of any other mass-production industry.

Automobile workers were burdened with other disadvantages during the NRA. The NRA administrator of the automobile code, Robert W. Lea,

32. Lyon et al., p. 495.
33. Schlesinger, *The Coming of the New Deal*, pp. 140, 142.
34. *The Nation*, 4 July 1933, pp. 9–10.
35. Kenneth S. Davis, *FDR: The New Deal Years*, p. 405.
36. Fine, p. 48.

was characterized by an aide to the Labor Advisory Board as someone inclined "to weep copious tears on behalf of the industrialists." Finally, the weakness of automobile labor unions had forced the AFL to accept proportional representation and collective bargaining pluralism in the automobile settlement of the spring of 1934, a concession that workers in other industries rejected. Sidney Fine observed in his extended study of the automobile code: "It is little wonder that a contemporary observer described the automobile code as 'as rotten an egg as was ever hatched by the Blue Eagle' and that a U.A.W. president at a later time referred to it as 'the No. 1 scandal . . . of the N.R.A.' from the point of view of organized labor."[37]

Fine goes on to conclude that the history of the automobile code demonstrates in an "exaggerated fashion" a more general truth about the NRA as a whole, "that despite the talk of the partnership of government, industry, and labor in the implementation of the N.I.R.A., organized labor, where it did not have the power to challenge organized industry, was at best a limited partner." Fine believes that conclusions based on the automobile code can be generalized because Roosevelt had devoted a great deal of attention to the automobile code, and automobile labor policy, a policy that Fine characterizes as having consistently "leaned in the direction of management," reflected his fundamental commitments.[38]

Yet Fine also notes that some labor leaders came to have a more sympathetic view of the NRA in retrospect. A former president of an AFL local at the Cleveland Fisher Body plant conceded, "I do not think there was any real urge for unionism until the law [the NIRA] made it possible or made it look like it was going to be possible to have a union without a lot of discharges and so forth." William Green also noted that UAW federal labor unions were established "under the inspiration of the National Recovery Act and as a result of it." Yet another union official stated that the changes that occurred under the NRA and the automobile code were "almost more than I ever expected to see happen in my lifetime."[39] Even Fine himself, despite his characterization of NRA labor policy as sympathetic to management, concluded that the NRA did have a profound long-term impact on labor relations in the automobile industry. As a result of the NRA, automobile labor practices "were never again to return to the conditions that had prevailed before June 16, 1933."[40] And if this was true in the automobile industry, where labor was more severely disadvantaged than in any other NRA code, it is likely that labor advances in other industries were even more striking.

37. Ibid., pp. 57, 428.
38. Ibid., pp. 427–428.
39. Ibid., p. 429.
40. Because automobile unions became powerful and well-organized in the late 1930s and early 1940s, Fine is clearly implying that the NRA made an important contribution to this final outcome. See ibid., p. 429.

The general growth of labor power during the NRA is strong evidence that the NRA advanced the interests of labor. Organized labor often grew in spite of its own organizational ineptitude and in spite of the serious problems that the craft-based AFL faced in addressing the organizational needs of unskilled workers in mass-production industries. It grew because through the NRA the federal government had adopted a new and more positive approach toward labor unions, and many labor unions were able to exploit that. As labor became more confident that government would protect its interests and rights, labor began to emphasize tactics that would compel government to intervene in labor disputes. Only secondarily did strikes become contests of strength between workers and employers; they were far more useful as means to focus government attention on the plight of workers in a particular industry.[41]

Labor benefited not only from Section 7a, which stimulated unions to renew organizational efforts, but by the extension of the regulatory arm of the government over wages and hours. Perviously docile workers became infused with a new sense of assertiveness in such demands. The United Textile Workers of America, under the leadership of the aging Thomas McMahan, was not prepared for the significant gains the NRA opened up. Repeated failures to organize new workers, particularly in the South, had sapped the vitality of the union. When Secretary of Labor Perkins sought out the union leader to get his views on a code for the industry, he had given the matter little thought. Perkins reports their exchange as follows:

> "We have always struggled," he said, "to get the eight-hour day, so I thought I would say, if you want me to appear at the public hearing on the code, that we want the eight-hour day [McMahan is assuming a six-day work week here]." "This code stipulates a forty-hour week," I said. "Don't for pity's sake talk about forty-eight-hour demands. Haven't you been reading the paper? The forty-hour week is to be recommended by the Department of Labor and the employers' group. Surely labor can't be behind on that."
>
> With a startled expression he said, "All right, if you say so, Miss Perkins."[42]

Here the government is not acting as an intermediary to resolve previously articulated interests, but stimulating the expression of private interests in order to further the politically determined goals of the administration. The administration was generally committed to a forty-hour work week, with sufficient flexibility to accommodate variations by type of industry and type of worker that were relevant to maintaining cost-effective production. Similarly, the government was committed to

41. Fine, p. 214; Lyon et al., pp. 501, 521–522.
42. Perkins, p. 224.

increasing the share of the national income that found its way into the hands of workers. In cases where workers were unorganized or poorly organized, the government often took on an advocacy posture vis-à-vis business and secured higher wages or shorter hours than would have been the case without their intervention.[43]

The brokered state hypothesis is contradicted by this evidence that the NRA was fundamentally sympathetic to organized labor, just as it was contradicted by evidence that NRA labor policy was coherent and principled. Yet problematically the core of this principled commitment was voluntarism, the very position that labor castigated as a probusiness stance. Is it possible to reconcile the tension between these two distinct lines of argument?

Despite labor's denunciations of the NRA and its voluntarist labor policy, it is by no means clear that voluntarism was intrinsically inhospitable to the development of powerful and independent labor unions. One of the greatest victories in the battle to organize the steel industry, coming only a year and a half after the demise of the NRA, provided recognition for the Steel Workers Organizing Committee (SWOC) on substantially the same voluntarist terms that the AFL vehemently rejected during the NRA. On 28 February 1937 the U.S. Steel Corporation, represented by Myron Taylor, and the Congress of Industrial Organizations (CIO), represented by John L. Lewis, agreed to a statement of principles governing steel labor relations. U.S. Steel conceded:

The Company recognizes the right of its employees to bargain collectively through representatives freely chosen by them without dictation, coercion or intimidation in any form or from any source. It will negotiate and contract with the representatives of any group of its employees so chosen and with any organization *as the representative of its members*, subject to the recognition of the principle that the right to work is not dependent on membership or nonmembership in any organization and *subject to the right of every employee freely to bargain in such manner and through such representatives, if any, as he chooses.*[44]

---

43. The cotton textile code provides a good example of this pattern. The cotton textile manufacturers proposed a minimum-wage scale of $8 a week in the South and $9 a week in the North. Although textile unions were very weak and had little hope of single-handedly compelling employers to offer more, Johnson defended their interests. Giving the manufacturers' "a rude shock," he insisted that wages be raised substantially, and although Johnson ultimately settled for less than he had hoped for, he at least forced the manufacturers to consent to minimum wages of $10 and $11 a week in the South and the North respectively. See Galambos, *Competition and Cooperation*, pp. 207, 210. The steel industry provides another example of a similar government role. See Perkins, pp. 213–225; Mayers, *The Handbook of NRA Laws, Regulations, and Codes*, pp. 130–131; *The Iron Age*, 3 August 1933, pp. 44–46; ibid., 24 August 1933, pp. 35–36.

44. William Hogan, *Economic History of the Iron and Steel Industry in the United States*, 3 vols. (Lexington, Mass., 1971), 3:1173. Emphasis added.

The following week a preliminary contract between the Carnegie-Illinois Steel Corporation and the SWOC was announced. It provided for the freedom of employees to select their own agent for collective bargaining without discrimination. In accordance with the statement of principles, the company recognized "the union as the collective bargaining agency for those employees of the Corporation who are members of the union." Differing from William Green and the AFL, John L. Lewis understood the value of union recognition by employers even when this fell short of recognition as an exclusive bargaining agent. By 10 April the SWOC had negotiated contracts with fifty-one steel companies, and by 1 May 280,000 workers were employed under SWOC contracts.[45]

The wisdom of Lewis's realism in accepting the form of partial recognition that Green and the AFL had rejected during the NRA was demonstrated by his success in using that settlement, which Green asserted would lead to the demise of independent unionism, as the basis for rapid union growth. Green's intransigence regarding the issue of labor union voluntarism may have been based on the expectation that a hard line AFL attitude would eventually compel the state to accede to labor's majority-rule position. Lewis operated in a different political environment. While the New Deal was just as sympathetic to organized labor in 1937 as it had been during the NRA years, its wings had been clipped by adverse Supreme Court decisions. Furthermore, the tension between the AFL and the CIO made the government leery of intervening when that intervention might be interpreted as taking sides.

At first glance it is surprising that Lewis was more conciliatory after the passage of the Wagner Act than Green had been before it. The Wagner Act was more favorable to the CIO's aspirations to become the unified voice of labor in industries like steel than the NRA had been to similar AFL aspirations, and the Wagner Act's affirmation of majority rule as the basis of an exclusive bargaining relationship made compromises, such as the one Lewis accepted in the steel industry, appear unnecessary. In fact, the widely shared anticipation that the Supreme Court would overturn the Wagner Act justified Lewis's reliance on the indigenous organizational capacity of workers rather than an imposed political solution.[46]

Majority rule and the right of exclusive bargaining representation were eventually imposed on the industry after the Wagner Act was upheld in April 1937. The NLRB gradually extended these requirements over the steel industry throughout 1938 and 1939. Whereas 60 percent of the 486 contracts signed before the end of 1937 had been for "members only," only 14 percent of the 317 contracts signed during 1939 were restricted to "members only." Yet the dramatic growth in union membership occurred

45. Ibid., pp. 1174, 1177.
46. Gross, p. 149.

before the NLRB began to implement the provisions of the Wagner Act. By the end of 1937 the unions had already received pledges from 526,000 workers, compared to which the advances under the rule of exclusive bargaining were marginal.[47] Independent unions could and did prosper in competition with company unions without the operation of a majority-rule principle as long as employers accepted the right of unions to organize without employer interference, and the guarantee of this right was never subject to negotiation or compromise under the NRA.

Although the NRA's voluntarist labor policy may not be as inherently hostile to the development of labor unions as the AFL presumed, it certainly was not as conducive to the development of powerful labor unions as the NLB's majority rule-exclusive bargaining policy. That the NRA would have supported a labor policy that was less than optimal for the growth of AFL unions still demands explanation. Can the divergence between the demands of the AFL and the policy of the NRA be explained in a manner consistent with the assumption that progressive elites were hostile to oligarchic power and committed to the achievement of social justice for the working man?

Many of the paradoxes of New Deal labor policy reflect the general dilemma of moderate reformers who unleash the forces of reform with one hand and seek to moderate their expression with the other. Given the significant contribution to labor militancy already implicit in Section 7a, the creation of the NRA and the NLB, and the general politicization of industrial relations, it is not surprising that some New Dealers also felt compelled to restrain excessive labor militance so that economic recovery would not be jeopardized by class conflict. Leo Wolman, chairman of the Automobile Labor Board, exemplified this tendency in New Deal thinking. Wolman believed that industrial relations could not be changed overnight by legislative fiat and that if recovery was not to be sacrificed to achieve reform it was necessary to introduce reforms gradually. "You have to edge it in. They [the employers] have to get accustomed to it."[48] Labor reform pushed too quickly would alienate the business community and undermine the cooperation essential for economic recovery and for the establishment of a new economic order, whereas moderate reform held the possibility of winning begrudging acquiescence from business. The art of reform is to know how much one can do, and how quickly.

To progressives like Hugh Johnson and Donald Richberg, NRA voluntarism appeared to represent a happy medium between the open shop option preferred by most businessmen and the AFL aspiration to become the exclusive representative for labor interests. NRA voluntarism would provide a climate more conducive to labor organization than had existed in

47. Hogan, p. 1178.
48. Fine, p. 232.

the pre-NRA era, yet it would allow a more gradual transition to a new industrial relations order. Furthermore, voluntarism would avoid thrusting too much responsibility onto the AFL too quickly, allowing it time to mature into a responsible spokesman for labor interests. The goal of the NRA was not simply to organize labor, for the NRA could succeed only if labor and business exercised self-restraint once they were organized. Thus NRA progressives fostered "responsible" unions, and they expected unions "to observe the same ethical and moral responsibilities" that they expected business to observe.[49] As Roosevelt bluntly wrote to William Green:

> Long and active association, both with A.F. of L. unions and unions outside the A.F. of L., has given me a sincere respect for the achievements of organized labor and a hope that it may develop its leadership so as gradually to assume greater responsibilities. But however great may be the desire which friends of the labor movement have to see it extend its usefulness, I do not see how informed and thoughtful persons could wish to see it suddenly take on so large an order as would be involved in trying to incorporate immediate unionization within the scope of the National Recovery Administration. Frankly, with all due respect to yourself and other good men in the labor movement, I do not believe that its leadership is as yet equal to so vast an undertaking.[50]

Just as the NRA had not proved to be a carte blanche for business cartelization, even when it favored peripheral business, similarly it offered only moderate encouragement to unionization.

While the progressives did not equate unions with cartels—they repudiated Supreme Court decisions that rendered unions subject to antitrust laws—unions were still viewed somewhat skeptically as centers of private power.[51] The NRA envisioned a new and positive role for trade associations and trade unions, but these secondary associations would facilitate the realization of the ends of the state only if the state supervised their activities and disciplined the factious interests that also found expression in these groups. The constraints that the state placed on unions were intended to further the realization of progressive goals, not to weaken unions vis-à-vis business.

The NRA's voluntarist labor policy can be understood once the interests of the working man are distinguished from the interests of unions. The fulfillment of the idea of democracy was the progressive project, and democracy was more highly developed in the state, with its formal

---

49. Ibid., p. 224.

50. FDR to William Green, 24 July 1933, NRA Records, RG 9, Entry 25, Consolidated Code Industry Files: Iron and Steel, File No. 11: General, A–H. This letter was in the NRA files unsigned, so it is not clear whether it was actually sent.

51. Kurt Braun, *The Right to Organize and Its Limits* (Washington, D.C., 1950), pp. 33–36.

mechanisms of democratic accountability, than it was in secondary associations. Hence, the progressives emphasized the state more than unions as a vehicle for promoting the interests of labor, at least in the short run. Unions were expected to play an important role in the NRA in defending the interests of workers and preventing exploitation by the business class, but it was a secondary and complementary role to that of the state. At a time when labor unions could not legitimately claim to speak for more than a minority of the total working force, an abdication of state power in favor of unions would have violated progressive principles.[52]

Ideally the NRA embodied a division of labor between the state and unions. The state established minimum wages and maximum hours in each industry, mitigating the forms of cutthroat competition that deprived workers of a living wage in a relentless effort to cut costs. Once the state had secured the prerequisites of a humane capitalism, the unions could maintain proper wage differentials and working conditions through collective bargaining.[53] Despite this notion of complementary functions, progressives could not assume a smoothly operating division of power and responsibility. Conflict was to be expected, but the conflict between the state and unions was not a derivative form of the conflict between employers and unions. Instead it is analogous to the conflict between progressive reformers and labor unions over a federal social security program. Prior to the New Deal, unions resisted state intervention in the field of social security because the assumption of such responsibilities by the state would have stripped unions of an important function and hence an incentive for joining the union.[54] Not only could control over social security be an incentive for unionization, but the discretion inherent in such control gives the union an important instrument of social control over dissidents. Social control over dissidents is in turn a prerequisite for unified action against their common enemy, the employer. Yet even though the development of the welfare state and its social security programs deprived unions of a potential weapon in their fight against employers, few would suggest that progressive support for a federal social security program was motivated by a desire to undercut labor unions in their struggle with employers. As the depression had clearly demonstrated, labor unions could not even meet the needs of their own retired workers, much less the needs of nonunion Americans.

Similarly, conflict between the progressive state and the unions over voluntarism in part reflected tensions between the broader vision of social justice that progressive political elites held and the narrower pursuit of

52. See I. Bernstein, *Turbulent Years*, p. 10.
53. H. Johnson, p. 341.
54. David Greenstone, *Labor in American Politics* (New York, 1970), pp. 25–26; Elizabeth Brandeis, "Organized Labor and Protective Labor Legislation," in *Labor and the New Deal*, ed. Milton Derber and Edwin Young (Madison, Wisc., 1957), p. 230.

class interests by labor union elites. Unions understandably perceived proportional representation as hostile to labor's interest because joint participation on a works council accorded company unions, as long as they were freely chosen, the same legitimacy as AFL unions. Even this limited legitimation of company unions (limited because it ruled out all company unions not freely chosen) was intolerable to the AFL. Divisions within the ranks of labor provided management with an opportunity to play one faction of labor off against another. Locked in battle with the employer-promoted company unions, and AFL deemed it essential to their survival to eradicate what they perceived to be forms of pseudo-representation. Not only did unions seek to eliminate employer coercion, but they also wanted to prohibit employers from trying to organize company unions on the basis of such positive inducements as preferential financial aid. They demanded powerful unions to counterbalance the power of employers, and they were to some extent justifiably skeptical that the state could handcuff the employers' ability to interfere with the self-organization of employees. As long as labor leaders believed that their organization was fundamentally threatened by business, they were unlikely to concern themselves with the rights of their own minorities.[55]

Progressive political leaders were far more optimistic about the power of the state. If they were less willing to grant unions an organizational carte blanche, it was in part because the state had now assumed responsibility for permitting employees to organize and bargain collectively. Union coercion could only have been justified to meet employer coercion, but the progressives were attempting to strip business of its powers to coerce labor and to reserve powers of coercion exclusively for the state. Progressive elites had generally insisted that weaker groups within the business community, like small businesses, be protected from dominant elements in business, and they were no less solicitous of minorities within labor. Because the loyalty of workers was in fact divided between company unions and the AFL, as attested to by NLB-supervised elections, forcing unwilling workers into the AFL was inconsistent with progressive ideals.

Progressive political elites decisively shaped NRA labor policy in accord with their own reform agenda. Once the autonomy of the progressive state is recognized, industrial relations during the New Deal takes on new meaning. The NRA's voluntarism no longer appears to be a probusiness position; it is an expression of a pervasive progressive suspicion of private groups as presently constituted. Of course, business seized on voluntarism to advance strategically their own interests, just as labor exploited tensions

---

55. Labor's desire to establish the closed shop has been widely noted, as has its frequent lack of sensitivity to minorities, who then cannot establish their own organizations. See J. Q. Wilson, *Political Organizations*, pp. 119–120; Olson, pp. 69–70.

between the state and business when it was to their advantage. But the congruence between state policies to restrict union power and business policies to restrict union power is not the expression of fundamental shared goals. The same reasons that justified legal restrictions on unions also applied to legal restrictions on business.

The historical record of labor relations during the NRA points to the contingency of the consensus between big business and New Dealers regarding proportional representation as an appropriate rule governing labor elections. Initially the New Deal's insistence that Section 7a rights be recognized threw employers and government into conflict. When employers became aware of the futility of their effort to perpetuate their advantage in individualized bargaining between management and each employee through such subterfuges as the inclusion of open shop provisions and merit clauses in the NRA codes, then employers turned to employee representation plans as a defensive strategy to limit the damage of Section 7a.[56] As long as employers tried to perpetuate management control through coercion over workers, they came into conflict with the New Deal. But once employers began to exploit the loyalty of some workers to co-opt an independent labor movement in a competition based on consent, they could limit the advances of organized labor by an appeal to progressive ideals, the same progressive ideals that were turned against the interests of business on other occasions. The NRA voluntarist labor policy evoked bitter opposition from the AFL, but it was principled and progressive despite that. The brokered state hypothesis cannot account for either of these attributes.

Beyond the NRA: The Wagner Act

No discussion of NRA labor policy would be complete without an explanation of Roosevelt's decision to support the Wagner Act. Within two weeks after the demise of the NRA, Roosevelt had put the Wagner Act—which repudiated NRA voluntarism by affirming the principle of majority rule for labor elections and prohibiting company unions—on his must list of legislation. With the passage of the Wagner Act on 5 July 1935, the AFL had secured its foremost political goal. The Wagner Act alone would probably have sufficed to unite business elites in opposition to the New Deal, but when Roosevelt added insult to injury by proposing a variety of other regulatory measures that were highly unpopular with business in the ''second one hundred days'' of the summer of 1935, indelible battlelines were drawn between the New Deal and the business

56. Lyon et al., pp. 523–526.

elite.[57] Do the "second one hundred days" provide additional evidence of the inadequacies of the brokered state description of the NRA?

To understand the problems that the "second one hundred days"—and particularly the Wagner Act, as the most dramatic about-face of the policy realignment of this period—pose for the brokered state description of the early New Deal, it is necessary to reflect generally on some aspects of pluralist theory. One difference between the pluralists and the revisionists is that the former admit that the New Deal and the Wagner Act led to fundamental changes in the character of American politics. Labor became a powerful political actor after the Wagner Act. Initially, it may appear as if pluralist theory is particularly well suited to describe the transformation of the American polity. Pluralism describes a fluid political world of constantly shifting coalitions and a political elite of nonideological mediators. In the early New Deal, big business was an element of the dominant coalition. By 1935, economic conditions were changing and new policy issues were emerging, providing opportunities for a new coalition to emerge. Big business was excluded from the new coalition, and labor was included. Franklin Roosevelt was able to change horses midstream precisely because he was a broker politician, a man who took his bearings from the configuration of political forces rather than from unchanging principles.

The inadequacies of any such attempt to provide a comprehensive pluralist theory of the New Deal were evident to pluralist theorists, such as David Truman, as well as to political scientists, like James MacGregor Burns, who applied the pluralist model to the early New Deal. Coalition politics in pluralism referred to coalition building within a highly fragmented world of narrowly based interest groups. The "second one hundred days" initiated a period of class conflict, not of group conflict. Labor in the 1930s was not just another group to be accommodated, and its incorporation into the American polity entailed fundamental changes. Those changes are best described as changes in the "rules of the game" rather than as incremental changes produced by a coalition shift within established "rules of the game." David Truman acknowledged that the New Deal "was something very close to a revolution."[58] "It [the New

57. Roosevelt renewed his attack on the power trust with his Public Utilities Holding Company Act, which included a "death sentence" provision permitting the SEC to dissolve any utility holding company it deemed contrary to the public interest after 1 January 1940. The Banking Act of 1935 increased the power of the federal government over the Federal Reserve System and diminished the power of private bankers by centralizing control over regional banks in a newly named board of governors. Finally, in the summer of 1935 Roosevelt proposed to Congress a "soak the rich" tax measure that would increase taxes on inheritances and gifts and establish new graduated income tax on "very great individual net incomes" and corporate income. See Louis M. Kohlmeier, Jr., *The Regulators* (New York, 1969), pp. 236–237; Schnitzer, pp. 93–96; Victor Goldberg, "Banking Reform in the 1930s," in *Regulatory Change in an Atmosphere of Crisis,* ed. Gary M. Walton (New York, 1979), pp. 79–90; Leuchtenburg, *FDR and the New Deal,* pp. 150, 152.

58. Truman, *The Governmental Process,* p. xlvii.

Deal] was a revolution not only in the sense that certain groups secured a place at the political table from which they had previously been barred but also in the sense that the American people tacitly accepted certain propositions about an industrialized society that ten years earlier would have been rejected by all but an insignificant faction of the population."[59] However well suited pluralist theory is to describe the political system that emerged from the New Deal, it did not purport to be a theory that could describe the political upheavals of the New Deal itself.

Burns tacitly acknowledges the limits of pluralist theory as a description of the New Deal by applying the term "brokered state" only to the early New Deal and the NRA. Pluralist theory can describe the early New Deal because, according to Burns, the political upheaval that occurred during the New Deal did not really begin until the "second one hundred days." After the summer of 1935, Roosevelt the political broker increasingly gave way to Roosevelt the political leader. "The shift [the shift to the left in the "second one hundred days"] put him in the role of leader of a great though teeming and amorphous coalition of center and liberal groups; it left him, in short, as a party chief. From mid-1935 to about the end of 1938 Roosevelt deserted his role as broker among all groups and assumed the role of a party leader commanding his Grand Coalition of the center and the left."[60] Burns qualifies this theory of the two New Deals in a number of ways. He argues that Roosevelt stumbled leftward in a somewhat ad hoc fashion without fully embracing his new role. His leadership during the second New Deal was uneven, vacillating between the brilliance of his legislative leadership during the "second one hundred days" and his inept attempts to pack the Supreme Court and purge the Democratic party. To some extent, his failures in the second New Deal were rooted in his lingering attachment to the brokered leadership style of the first New Deal. But these qualifications only blunt the force of the distinction between the two New Deals, they do not undermine it.

If the pluralist description of the early New Deal as a brokered state is apt, it must be possible to provide a plausible account of the transition to the politics of the second New Deal, which even the pluralists acknowledge cannot be described except secondarily as a period of pluralist politics. The pluralist description of Roosevelt as a political broker in the early New Deal asserted that Roosevelt was particularly responsive to well-organized private interests like big business. Why would Roosevelt suddenly abandon his powerful business constituency and advocate measures universally resisted by employers? Only as a last resort does a politician abandon old allies. Even if Roosevelt were merely a political opportunist who was not held to his original constituency by any ideologi-

59. Ibid.
60. Burns, *Roosevelt: The Lion and the Fox*, pp. 375–376.

cal attachments, it would require dramatic transformations in the political world to initiate such a risky political gamble. The law of inertia applies to political actors as well as to falling objects, and in the absence of new political forces, steady commitment to previously successful coalitions is to be anticipated. Furthermore, to extend the analogy, a deviation from a predicted political path can be explained only by a force commensurate with the size of the deviation. The political upheaval that surrounded the transition from the first to the second New Deal should have been of revolutionary proportions if their constituencies were as different as pluralists like Burns assert they were.

Furthermore, the precipitant for the change would have had to occur within a fairly limited time span if the Wagner Act is indicative of Roosevelt's political shift. At the beginning of May 1935, Roosevelt was still cool to the idea of the Wagner Act—as he had been the previous spring, when Wagner first introduced it.[61] Yet by the beginning of June he swung his full support to it. Two events in May might explain Roosevelt's shift, and the explanation of that shift depends on which event is seen as critical. On 2 May the U.S. Chamber of Commerce at its annual convention publicly declared war on the New Deal, and later that month, on 27 May 1935, the Supreme Court handed down the *Schechter* decision, declaring the NRA unconstitutional.[62] Burns asserts that the *Schechter* decision was actually handed down after Roosevelt had decided to support the Wagner Act and that it therefore cannot account for this critical decision. The split between the Chamber of Commerce and Roosevelt, on the other hand, was at least symbolically critical in Burns's view, for he asserts, "The main reason for the new posture [i.e., the "second one hundred days"] was the cumulative impact of the attacks from the right."[63]

But the historical record would not seem to justify attributing such importance to Roosevelt's split with the Chamber of Commerce. If the business constituency had been important to Roosevelt, one would have expected strong efforts to avoid a breach and conciliatory gestures at least initially after the break occurred. Yet Roosevelt refused even to send a presidential greeting to the Chamber of Commerce in 1935 (he had addressed the annual meeting of the Chamber in 1933, and had sent a presidential greeting in 1934), an action that suggested that his disenchantment with the business community had preceded the explicit Chamber attack by some time and therefore does not account for his change of heart concerning the Wagner Act in early June. Furthermore, when the U.S. Chamber of Commerce attacked the New Deal, Roosevelt responded by

61. Ibid., p. 219; Gross, p. 141.
62. Leuchtenburg, *FDR and the New Deal*, pp. 147–148.
63. Burns, *Roosevelt: The Lion and the Fox*, pp. 219, 225.

condemning the failure of the Chamber to see "the human side" of the unemployment problem rather than attempting to heal the breach with the business community. He went on to describe the Chamber as an association that did not truly represent businessmen and that had "never yet initiated and pressed one single item of social betterment."[64]

Moreover, why would business repudiate Roosevelt if he were furthering their interests? Burns offers two explanations for this "paradox"— businessmen were reacting to a decline in status, and they were wedded to a rigid laissez-faire ideology.[65] Neither explanation suffices.[66] In the early New Deal, the status of businessmen would generally have been enhanced by New Deal solicitude for their interests, and the opportunity to participate in the corporatist NRA potentially opened new avenues for acquiring status. Similarly, Burns's suggestion that a rigid business ideology led businessmen to reject the early New Deal even though it served their interests unjustifiably divorces business interests from business ideology. Nor can it account for the dissatisfaction with the early New Deal by corporate liberals who were not committed to a rigid laissez-faire ideology. Finally, while laissez-faire ideology was an important factor in explaining business hostility to the NRA in May 1935, those who were hostile to the NRA on ideological grounds were in many cases hostile to the NRA long before this. The American Liberty League, which came to represent the antagonism of the business community to the New Deal, had been formed in August 1934, at the height of the "friendly" NRA. If business was reacting to the NRA on ideological grounds well before the summer of 1935, then an important prerequisite for pluralist politics—groups that pursue narrowly based economic interests—was absent. And if Roosevelt backed the NRA for some time despite strong ideological opposition from some important elements in business, can we describe the NRA as a manifestation of the brokered state?

There is one additional problem with Burns's explanation of Roosevelt's decision to support the Wagner Act. Burns fails to differentiate this decision from the decisions to support other programs that composed the legislative agenda of the second "one hundred days." If Roosevelt had in fact shifted to the left in the summer of 1935, it would be reasonable to expect that the decision to support the Wagner Act was linked to the decision to support the Public Utilities Holding Company Act or the Banking Act of 1935. Yet the Public Utilities Holding Company Act was drafted in January 1935 at Roosevelt's request, almost four months prior to the break with the Chamber of Commerce and at a time when Roosevelt was still resisting the Wagner Act. Similarly, the Banking Act had been

64. Leuchtenburg, *FDR and the New Deal*, p. 147; Schlesinger, *The Politics of Upheaval*, p. 273.

65. Burns, *Roosevelt: The Lion and the Fox*, pp. 205, 239–240.

66. See above, Chapter 5.

drafted and introduced into Congress with Roosevelt's approval in February 1935.

Roosevelt's legislative agenda for 1935 was hardly calculated to placate business, and any argument that portrays Roosevelt as passively reacting to a shift in business opinion during the summer of 1935 fails to acknowledge the extent to which any shifts in opinion that occurred were caused by the policies of the New Deal. A better understanding of the significance of the events of the summer of 1935 is possible if we recognize that Roosevelt was far more upset by the *Schechter* decision than the split with the Chamber of Commerce. He referred to the *Schechter* decision as "one of the most important decisions ever rendered in this country" and severely castigated it. The *Schechter* decision, in conjunction with other Supreme Court decisions that obstructed the New Deal, so angered Roosevelt that he later undertook one of the riskiest and most costly political maneuvers of his presidency—the court-packing scheme.

Burns had dismissed the suggestion that Roosevelt was forced to turn to the Wagner Act after the Supreme Court overturned the NRA because he believed Roosevelt "came out for the bill [the Wagner Act]" on 24 May 1935, three days before the Supreme Court's *Schechter* decision. Actually Roosevelt's commitment to the Wagner Act was still quite vague on 24 May. Roosevelt appears to have concluded by mid-May that he would have to make some concessions to strong congressional sentiment for additional labor legislation, and he allowed Congress to proceed with its consideration of the Wagner Act without either endorsing it or opposing it. After the bill passed the Senate and had won the approval of the House Committee on Labor he scheduled a meeting on 24 May with Senator Wagner, Frances Perkins, Donald Richberg, Assistant Attorney General Harold Stephens, William Green, Sidney Hillman, and John L. Lewis. A debate between Richberg and Wagner ensued, and Roosevelt "made it clear that he wanted the Wagner Bill *in some form*" (emphasis added). Roosevelt did not seriously commit himself to the passage of the Wagner Act in the form it had passed the Senate until 13 June, two weeks after the *Schechter* decision.[67]

The crisis in the New Deal provoked by the Supreme Court casts the shift to the "left" in the summer of 1935 in a different perspective, one that acknowledges that a shift occurred but characterizes the shift in a manner consistent with Roosevelt's progressive character during the early New Deal. Prior to *Schechter,* Roosevelt assumed an active role for the state in rationalizing labor relations. As long as the state assumed

67. Burns, *Roosevelt: The Lion and the Fox,* p. 219; Schlesinger, *The Coming of the New Deal,* pp. 405–406; I. Bernstein, *The New Deal Collective Bargaining Policy,* pp. 118–119; Gross, pp. 142–144; Bellush, p. 179.

responsibility for the protection of labor's rights and set a floor on minimum wages and maximum hours, labor unions played an auxiliary role in the protection of the working man. The *Schechter* decision struck down the keystone in that edifice. The state was the indispensable instrument of man's liberation from oligarchical power, and as long as the state was handcuffed by what Roosevelt perceived as a "horse and buggy" interpretation of the Constitution, the optimistic vision of a new society was incapable of realization.

Once the state's capacity to protect labor was hobbled by judicial conservatism, Roosevelt was forced to turn to a less-desirable alternative. Strengthening labor unions via the Wagner Act was a distinctly second choice for Roosevelt because labor unions were centers of private power. The progressive ethos demanded the subordination of private power to public authority, a standard that was impartially applied to labor as well as business when the progressive impulse was dominant. The Wagner Act strengthened the private power of unions to counterbalance the organizational power of business, but without reference to the subordination of private power to public authority. In specifying unfair labor practices by employers but remaining silent on unfair labor practices by unions the Wagner Act assumed a class bias that was uncharacteristic of the progressive orientation.[68] Unions found themselves accepted into the American polity with clearly defined rights and vaguely defined responsibilities. But New Dealers felt compelled to adopt the Wagner Bill approach for fear that attempts to restrain unfair union practices would be perverted by the courts into an instrument for undermining unions altogether.[69] Unable to bring to fruition a vision of society that transcended competition between private groups, Roosevelt had been forced to equalize the bargaining power among groups. Ironically, the true constituents of the New Deal were revealed more clearly in the period of disillusionment for progressive elites than in their initial program for reform.

While it would be correct to argue that business opposition to the New Deal reached new heights after the second one hundred days, this does not imply that the first New Deal was viewed with favor by big business. Many in the big-business group found the Securities and Exchange Act and the Tennessee Valley Authority offensive.[70] Many were appalled by such measures as the renunciation of the gold standard and the monetarization of silver.[71] These measures alone would suggest more continuity between the first and second New Deals than Burns's two New Deals theory could accommodate. When these considerations are combined with the interpretation of the NRA provided in this work, it becomes implausible to

68. I. Bernstein, *The New Deal Collective Bargaining Policy,* p. 95.
69. Ibid.; Gross, p. 141.
70. Schlesinger, *The Coming of the New Deal,* pp. 325–326, 444.
71. Ibid., pp. 200–203.

characterize the shift from the early New Deal to the later New Deal as a break with big business or a rupture with the right.

The first New Deal is the radical New Deal. It was during the first New Deal that the state acted forcefully to subordinate private power, not simply by regulating private organizations but by more ambitiously attempting to bring about an organizational and ethical revolution that would transform trade associations and trade unions into institutions serving public rather than private interests. Regarding the aspirations entertained for the state, the second New Deal is restrained in comparison. The *Schechter* decision played a crucial role in the transition. Although Roosevelt's optimism—his high hopes that the New Deal could subordinate self-interest to a new ethics of social responsibility—foundered on the harsh realities of interest group conflict during the NRA, as well as on the limits on state activity imposed by the Supreme court in the *Schechter* decision, Roosevelt had not recognized the futility of the NRA by June 1935 because he still sought to extend the NRA when it came up for renewal. It was the *Schechter* decision that closed the door on that option.

The Autonomy of the Progressive State

The NRA's essentially voluntarist labor policy was vigorously opposed by organized labor, but labor unions nevertheless gained more from the NRA than they lost. The politicization of the struggle for union recognition during the NRA had opened a new era in labor relations. In the old laissez-faire order, employer associations had proved more than a match for unions, especially in the mass-production industries. But once labor rights were redefined by the New Deal, and its administrative agencies assumed the responsibility to guarantee the new rights, the balance of power between labor and business began to shift more in favor of the former. The AFL ultimately recognized this, for despite their occasional heated threats to break with the New Deal and the NRA, they supported the extension of the NRA in 1935.[72] Businessmen were no less aware of that fact, and labor advances during the NRA were an important reason many businessmen opposed an extension of the NRA in 1935 unless it was radically reformed.[73]

The most revealing characteristic of early New Deal labor policy is not that labor was broadly speaking the constituency benefiting from the policy, but that progressive political elites were actively shaping policy to fulfill their own ideologically defined purposes rather than passively responding to interest group demands. Those progressive purposes entailed

72. AFL to FDR, Roosevelt Papers, OF 466, No. 10, NRA Codes, Misc., May 1935.
73. William Wilson, "Chamber of Commerce," p. 99.

both the encouragement of labor union organization so that unions could assume their rightful place in a new corporatist economic order and the restraining of labor unions as centers of private power that might use their organizational strength to pursue private interests, an ambivalence that characterized progressive responses to trade associations as well. The latter goal generated considerable tension between New Dealers and organized labor, just as powerful tensions have often surfaced between unions and Social Democratic political elites when Social Democrats have governed Western European liberal democracies.[74] That similar but even more radical tensions were visible in the relationship of the progressive state to business is powerful evidence that the tensions between the early New Deal state and labor unions did not indicate progressive hostility to the interests of workers.

These conclusions challenge the brokered state conception of the early New Deal and Lowi's related hypothesis that the NRA's corporatist structure permitted private groups to co-opt public authority in the service of private ends. NRA labor policy did fail to achieve its end—the creation of a cooperative relationship between business and labor based on collective bargaining—but it did not fail because administrative corporatism was an inappropriate means for achieving that end. NRA labor policy failed for the same reason that NRA business policy failed. It had attempted too much. The NRA was an attempt to fashion a societal corporatist social peace treaty of the sort that have softened labor conflict in a number of Western European countries. It was an attempt to replace conflict rooted in self-interest with cooperation and self-sacrifice rooted in a new social ethics. That self-sacrifice would have been forthcoming only if the NRA had been viewed as the moral equivalent of war, yet despite Johnson's best efforts to sell the NRA on those grounds, the NRA had soon lapsed into bitter struggles between labor and business as they jockeyed for a relatively advantageous position beneath the rhetoric of self-restraint. Unlike the war, the depression had not been perceived as a sufficient national danger for groups to lay aside their particular and conflicting interests on behalf of an overarching national purpose. The moral prerequisites for a societal corporatist peace treaty simply did not exist.

74. These tensions are even more characteristic of contemporary Marxist regimes. Marxists have gone even further than progressive political elites in substituting the state for unions as the organization ostensibly suited to advance working-class interests, for they have attempted to repress labor unions altogether. Clearly the conflicts between labor unions and Marxist states have not signified the responsiveness of those states to capitalist interests.

Conclusion: Juridical
Democracy Reconsidered

In January 1935 the Supreme Court dealt its first blow to the NRA in *Panama Refining Co. v. Ryan*,[1] a decision that declared Section 9c of Title I of the NIRA to be an unconstitutional delegation of congressional power. But because Section 9c concerned only the oil industry, the rest of the NRA was not immediately jeopardized, and Donald Richberg remained optimistic that the NRA would weather future constitutional tests. He was soon proved wrong. On 27 May 1935 the Supreme Court unanimously struck down the National Industrial Recovery Act in *United States v. Schechter Poultry Corporation*.

Richberg had hoped that the case that ultimately tested the constitutionality of the NRA would involve a major national industry clearly engaged in interstate commerce, but his legal strategy for assuring this faltered, and the case that first reached the Supreme Court was a case against the Schechter brothers, owners of a small poultry business that slaughtered and sold chickens in Brooklyn. In October 1934 the Schechter brothers had been convicted in federal district court for eighteen violations of the live poultry code.[2] Reversing on appeal, the Supreme Court rejected the government's attempt to impose legal sanctions to enforce the poultry code because the NIRA was determined to have unconstitutionally regulated intrastate as well as interstate commerce and to have relied on an excessively vague delegation of congressional authority to the executive. In the wake of the Supreme Court decision, congressional efforts to extend the NIRA beyond its initial two-year trial collapsed, despite Roosevelt's continuing support for the program.

Henceforth, altering the character of the Supreme Court became a top Roosevelt priority. Although his efforts to pack the Court with more liberal

---

1. 293 U.S. 388 (1935).
2. Because one violation concerned a fair trade practice provision governing the sale of unfit and uninspected poultry, the case was soon dubbed "the sick chickens case."

justices would be rebuffed by Congress, Roosevelt's interpretation of the Constitution eventually triumphed on the Court and among legal circles. The *Schechter* decision became a legal anachronism. Since 1935, courts have consistently upheld delegations even when they were not accompanied by clear standards to guide the discretion of administrators responsible for the act.[3] Similarly, the restriction of federal powers over commerce to interstate commerce were increasingly ignored. It was not until the appearance of Theodore Lowi's *End of Liberalism* in 1969 that political scientists began to seriously reconsider the conventional wisdom that *Schechter* was simply the last hurrah of laissez-faire conservatism, at least with regard to the decision's invocation of the nondelegation doctrine.

Lowi's explicit antagonists in *The End of Liberalism* were those who repudiated the rule of law and defended discretionary administration. Lowi attributes such a defense of discretionary rule to the pluralists, but he could have more persuasively directed his criticisms toward the pragmatists and the progressives. These reformers' disenchantment with the rule of law, their conviction that the rule of law was largely a myth that had protected and concealed the growing power of an oligarchical elite, encouraged them to ignore its restraints for the sake of achieving a more democratic and humane state. Rather than reform the rigid and conservative legal tradition that had emerged from the late nineteenth century, to a considerable extent they abandoned it. Repudiating these aspects of earlier reform movements, Lowi appeals for a return to the rule of law.

Juridical democracy, however, is not simply a critique of the New Deal's brand of discretionary administration. It also implicitly challenges the views of the American framers and of those who have elaborated their understanding of the rule of law. It is this latter challenge, even though it is not explicit in Lowi's work, which is ultimately of greater theoretical and practical interest. It is of greater theoretical interest because classical American liberalism was based on a more profound understanding of politics than was pragmatism. It is of greater practical interest because the unbounded faith in science and experts that inspired pragmatists and New Dealers alike has largely been discredited in the contemporary period, and the most important political discussions since the 1970s have disputed the meaning of the rule of law, not its possibility or its value.[4] That Lowi's conclusions regarding the rule of law differ from those of the dominant American legal tradition does not demonstrate that Lowi is wrong, but it does allow us to see the issues Lowi has raised in a more comprehensive perspective.

3. The courts did haul the nondelegation doctrine out of mothballs in *Indus. Union Dep't AFL-CIO v. American Petroleum Institute*, 448 U.S. 607 (1980), so the doctrine is not quite defunct.

4. There is, however, a new "critical legal studies" school of thought, which is not as enamored of scientific expertise as the original "legal realist" school was but which carries on the legal realists' attack on legal formalism. For a representative sampling of this school, see David Kairys, ed., *The Politics of Law: A Progressive Critique* (New York, 1982).

Lowi and the American Legal Tradition

Lowi identifies the rule of law with governance through general rules, and he contrasts the legitimacy of this form of rule with the illegitimacy of unprincipled ad hoc bargaining based on particularistic interests. As indispensable as rules are in legitimizing authority and protecting rights in Lowi's framework, however, mere formalism is insufficient. Formalism must be combined with democracy if it is to have the specific properties that Lowi esteems.

> Juridical democracy is, however, two words; and each helps define the other. While the juridical stresses form and the real impact of form, democracy stresses particular forms and particular contents. Taken by itself, the juridical principle appears to be comfortable with, say, segregation as well as integration laws, as long as the laws possess legal integrity. But within the context of democracy, especially if one lived by the juridical principle, it would simply not be possible to support segregation in any form, because a democracy cannot abide two systems of law, two criteria for the provision of governmental services—in brief, unequal protection of the laws. On a host of issues, therefore, juridical democracy has very clear and profound substantive implications; it is not merely a procedural matter.[5]

The nondelegation doctrine is the core of Lowi's juridical democracy because it is the crucial bridge between formalism and democracy, compelling Congress to provide clear standards with its delegations (which at least approximates governance through rules), while at the same time assuring that it is Congress, a democratic body, that makes the rules.

Although Lowi's attempt to revive the *Schechter* decision's restrictive nondelegation principle for the sake of limiting discretion in administration appears to be a conservative appeal for a return to a sound precedent, this characterization of Lowi's project fails to do justice to the fact that *Schechter* is a relative anomaly in constitutional law. Before the *Panama* and *Schechter* decisions regarding the NRA, the courts had never struck down a federal law on nondelegation grounds.[6] Although the *Schechter* decision's insistence that delegations must be accompanied by clear standards relied on two precedents that upheld delegations (*Butterfield v. Stranahan*[7] and *J. W. Hampton, Jr. & Co. v. United States*),[8] it was a clear departure from the most important nineteenth-century case dealing with delegation of powers, *Wayman v. Southard*.[9]

---

5. Lowi, *End of Liberalism*, p. 299.
6. Kenneth Culp Davis, *Administrative Law Text*, p. 26.
7. 192 U.S. 470 (1903).
8. 276 U.S. 394 (1928).
9. 10 Wheat. 1 (1825).

Wayman v. Southard tested the constitutionality of the Federal Process Act of 1792. This decision is especially significant because it was written by Chief Justice Marshall, a man whose skill as an interpreter of the Constitution has rarely, if ever, been rivaled. The Federal Process Act had delegated to the federal judiciary the power to override state procedures with regard to the manner of enforcing judgments and writs of execution when "the said [federal] courts respectively shall, in their discretion, deem expedient."[10] In exercising that discretion, federal judges in Kentucky rejected accepted procedures in that state by refusing to honor notes from the Bank of the Commonwealth of Kentucky for the repayment of debts upheld by federal court judgments, insisting that the debts be repayed in gold or silver. Kentucky appealed the decision of these federal judges to the Supreme Court, insisting that state procedures were binding on federal judges in Kentucky.

Marshall's decision upheld the Federal Process Act, but initially it appeared to sanction only a limited power of Congress to delegate. Rejecting the idea that Congress could delegate "powers which are strictly and exclusively legislative," Marshall characterized a legitimate delegation as one in which Congress, having made general provisions regarding a certain subject, left to others the responsibility for "filling in the details." But Marshall then goes on to suggest that the line distinguishing powers that are strictly legislative from those that can be delegated is indistinct, and as he further delineates what he has in mind by "filling in the details," he makes it clear that this can encompass objects as general as "that course of administering justice . . . which consisted . . . with the spirit of the Constitution, and with what might safely be considered as the permanent policy, as well as interest, of the states themselves."[11] The cautious words that Marshall used to formulate his decision were thus belied by his own application of his doctrine, and his decision would in fact permit very extensive delegations of congressional power.[12]

The power of Marshall's reasoning in *Wayman v. Southard* is strongly supported by the historical record of the American founding period. The framers did not explicitly address the issue posed by the nondelegation

10. 3 Annals 1388, 1389 (1792), quoted in Sotirios Barber, *The Constitution and the Delegation of Congressional Power* (Chicago, 1975), p. 64.

11. Ibid., pp. 63–72.

12. For these insights I am indebted to Barber's discussion of *Wayman v. Southard* in his *Constitution and the Delegation of Congressional Power.* His compelling defense of the nondelegation doctrine does not reinforce Lowi's thesis. Barber argues that the central question in nondelegation cases should not be whether there are standards accompanying the delegation, an overly restrictive doctrine, but whether Congress has made a choice among salient policy alternatives or is using the delegation as a means for making a choice in the near future. By this criteria, even the NIRA would have passed constitutional muster, because it authorized the NRA for only two years, at which point Congress would have had the opportunity to clarify its choice. Barber's version of the nondelegation doctrine, unlike Lowi's, is not linked to the assertion that law can be identified with rules.

doctrine in the constitutional convention, but the practices of the first Congress, whose decisions are generally weighty considerations in constitutional law because so many of the framers of the Constitution participated in its deliberations and because it was as concerned with constitutional issues as with policy issues in its decisions, would support an expansive interpretation of the nondelegation doctrine. The first Congress did not supply standards to superintendents who were authorized to license "any proper person" to trade or engage in other forms of intercourse with the Indian tribes, nor did it limit in any way the discretion of the president in prescribing rules and regulations to govern the same superintendents. It was equally expansive in its delegation to the courts of the power "to make and establish all necessary rules for the orderly conducting of business in the said courts," limiting them only with the admonition that such rules should not be "repugnant to the laws of the United States."[13] If neither the first Congress, Washington, nor his cabinet found these delegations objectionable, there are strong grounds for believing that *Wayman v. Southard* was correctly decided and that the reasoning in *Schechter* fundamentally misconstrued the character of American constitutionalism.

Lowi's defense of *Schechter,* however, cannot be explained as a failure to interpret the Constitution properly. In fact, *The End of Liberalism* is devoid of constitutional exegesis, and *Schechter* is not praised because it is good constitutional law but because it democratizes legal formalism. The paucity of references to the U.S. Constitution in a book that constantly refers to the rule of law may seem surprising, because the Constitution is frequently considered one of the most ambitious attempts to subordinate arbitrary power to the rule of law, but it is no oversight on Lowi's part. Lowi implicitly denigrates the Constitution by portraying it as the product of laissez-faire liberalism, which he characterizes as an ersatz public philosophy antithetical to the rule of law. As a strong nationalist, Lowi finds the framers' Constitution no less objectionable because he believes it divided sovereignty between the federal government and the state governments, thereby undermining the capacity of the federal government to govern.[14] Rhetorically, Lowi's appeal to *Schechter* beckons us to return from modern aberrations to the true constitutional path, but beyond rhetoric there is nothing traditional about Lowi's argument. His rule of law is a radical alternative to American constitutionalism.

Although the nondelegation doctrine is the cornerstone of Lowi's attempt to reduce discretion in government, it is not the only element in his reform package. Lowi concedes that even if the *Schechter* rule was "applied in good faith" it "could never eliminate all the vagueness in legislative enactments and could never eliminate the need for delegation of

13. Kenneth Culp Davis, *Administrative Law Text*, pp. 34–35.
14. Lowi, *End of Liberalism*, pp. 272–273.

power to administrative agencies." Lowi recommends "two ways to compensate for that slippage and to bring these necessarily vague legislative formulations back to a much closer approximation of the juridical principle": administrative formality and codification. Lowi then equates administrative formality with a much heavier reliance on formal rulemaking procedures. Both these recommendations reflect Lowi's identification of law with rules, and this identification is as radical a departure from the common law foundation of American law as his stringent interpretation of the nondelegation doctrine is from constitutional law.[15]

The history of the absorption and transformation of the English common law in our legal systems is far too complex a topic to deal with adequately in this discussion. Nevertheless, a brief reference to that history suffices to indicate the extent to which Lowi's juridical democracy is a repudiation of the dominant legal tradition of the early American republic. The fate of American common law in this period was inextricably intertwined with party politics, for Jeffersonians and Federalists generally had distinct positions concerning the role that common law should play in the American regime. Jeffersonians, suspicious of the common law because it was mired in feudal anachronisms and because its flexibility granted too much scope for judicial discretion, generally refused to recognize any legal jurisdiction resting solely on a common law basis and insisted that written constitutions and duly enacted statutes were the only basis for the legitimate exercise of authority. This view was challenged by Federalists who generally asserted that the Constitution had incorporated the common law tradition within our laws. Admiring the flexibility of the common law, and believing that its feudal anachronisms could be eliminated through moderate reforms, the Federalists were confident that the common law could be reconciled with the principles of republican government.[16]

The struggle over the status of the common law within the American legal tradition culminated in the 1820s and 1830s, when the Jeffersonians mounted a powerful movement to codify state laws. The codification movement hoped to simplify the laws, to make them comprehensible to the ordinary citizen, and to curb the influence of a predominantly Federalist judiciary by limiting their discretion. This attempt to restrain judicial discretion through legislatively formulated rules, which bears a strong resemblance to Lowi's attempt to limit administrative discretion through legislatively formulated rules, was resisted by some of America's most prominent jurists.[17] To preserve the common law and its highly valued

15. Ibid., pp. 302–303.
16. McDowell, pp. 55–69.
17. Ibid. The affinity between the codification movement and Lowi's juridical democracy are unmistakable because Lowi himself promotes codification of our laws as a means of realizing the rule of law. See Lowi, *End of Liberalism*, pp. 305–309.

flexibility from the challenge of the codifiers, these jurists began to publish legal treatises demonstrating that the common law was a rational system of precedents based on underlying principles that could fully serve America's legal needs. John Milton Goodnow's *Historical Sketches of the Principles and Maxims of American Jurisprudence,* Chancellor Kent's *Commentaries on American Law,* and Joseph Story's *Commentaries on Bailments, Commentaries on the Constitution of the United States,* and *Commentaries on Equity Jurisprudence* all helped to revitalize the common law and stem the tide of codification. Through their efforts a rigid, rule-bound understanding of the rule of law was rejected in the formative era of the American legal tradition.

Closer to the twentieth century, however, the initial victories of the common law were to some extent overshadowed by the inability of the common law to provide an adequate legal framework for a modern industrial society. Statutory law has increasingly replaced common law. Nevertheless, this greater reliance on statutory law has not signaled the demise of common law techniques, for common law techniques have been appropriated by administrators in the "age of statutes." As Lowi repeatedly reminds us, many of the statutes that are the basis for the modern regulatory state are vague, general statutes that leave a great deal of discretion to administrators. The policies that actually govern society have to a large extent been developed by administrators through case-by-case adjudication with a reasonable degree of deference to administrative precedents. This administrative method, introduced by Thomas Cooley, the first chairman of the first federal independent regulatory commission, the Interstate Commerce Commission (ICC), has perpetuated the initial victories of common law proponents over codifiers. Thus even in the twentieth century the dominant American legal tradition has continued to reject Lowi's assertion that the rule of law is narrowly identified with governance through general rules.

The rejection of both premises of Lowi's juridical democracy—the assertion that legitimacy is premised on governance through rules and the nondelegation doctrine—by the American framers and founders of American jurisprudence did not indicate a lack of concern with the potential abuses of discretionary authority. Neither can the commitment to the rule of law of Thomas Cooley, one of the founders of the modern administrative state, be doubted. No less than Lowi, these men would have been skeptical of the claims of the New Dealers that a scientific elite held democratically accountable could be safely entrusted with unchecked discretionary authority. But unlike Lowi, they believed that discretion was intrinsic to governance and that the threat posed to the rule of law by discretion could be successfully addressed by upholding the Constitution or the common law, as the case may be—forms of law whose restraints on authority were far less onerous than those of juridical democracy.

Lowi and American Political Institutions

The contrast between juridical democracy and the founding principles of the American regime are particularly clear when the institutional implications of juridical democracy are highlighted. Lowi's faith in law entailed a faith in the quintessential lawmaking institution—Congress. His restrictive nondelegation doctrine necessarily implies a dramatic shift of power from the presidency to the Congress as well as a shift of power from the bureaucracy to Congress, for the powerful presidency that has emerged in the era since the New Deal has acquired many of its enhanced powers through broad delegations of congressional power. Lowi elaborated this implication of his argument for a restrictive nondelegation principle in his latest work, *The Personal President*, and attempted to substantiate the argument by demonstrating that modern presidents not only have failed to use their powers to restrain the growing power of organizational elites but also have actually aided and abetted the development of a corporatist system that serves the interests of those elites because such a system also enhances presidential power.[18]

Congressional government, Lowi argues, would shatter the corporatist mold. Lowi assumes that Congress is the only body in which the diverse interests of the nation can all be represented, and he believes that when the congressional process is structured as a rulemaking process (by excluding discretionary grants of power) the clash of interests will tend to produce rules serving the public interest. Even though Lowi does not assume that every rule Congress legislates will be in the public interest, he does believe that, as long as Congress sticks to rulemaking, the rules inconsistent with the public good will generate demands for reconsideration, and on successive iterations the rules will come to approximate those that ideally serve the public good. Lowi does not simply deny the judgment widely shared by contemporary political scientists that Congress is the institution most responsive to particularistic interests, but his assertion that Congress would be transformed by a systematic application of the nondelegation doctrine suggests that the problems with Congress are less intractable than many political scientists have supposed.

Lowi's faith in Congress, or at least in a Congress that does not delegate powers, is a sharp departure from the view of the framers of the Constitution. As *The Federalist Papers* makes clear, the American framers were more suspicious of Congress than of any other branch of government.

> But in a representative republic where the executive magistracy is carefully limited, both in the extent and the duration of its power; and where the legislative power is exercised by an assembly, which is inspired by supposed

18. Theodore J. Lowi, *The Personal President* (Ithaca, N.Y., 1985).

influence over the people with an intrepid confidence in its own strength; which is sufficiently numerous to feel all the passions which actuate a multitude, yet not so numerous as to be incapable of pursuing the objects of its passions by means which reason prescribes; it is against the enterprising ambition of this department that the people ought to indulge *all* their jealousy and exhaust *all* their passions.[19]

It was for this reason that the framers searched for constitutional arrangements that would shore up the executive and judicial branches, not only to protect these branches against legislative usurpations but also to enhance the capacity of government to secure individual rights and the common good.

In the framers' judgment the weaknesses of Congress were largely endemic, for its weaknesses sprang from the same source as its strengths. Congress was the body closest to the people and most responsive to public opinion. This assured a democratically accountable government, but it also subjected government to the whims, passions, and factious interests that shaped public opinion. Limiting Congress' freedom to delegate, and compelling it to act only through specific rules, would do little to mitigate this problem, for congressionally enacted rules themselves could serve factious interests. Thus when Madison discusses the problem of faction in Federalist Paper No. 10, he distinguishes the judicial context, where liberals had long acknowledged the power of general rules to reduce injustice, from the legislative context, where the groups that will participate in a democratic rulemaking process will be passing on rules that differentially affect their own interests and those of other groups, and it can be expected that groups will favor rules partial to their interests.[20] Not only will the fact that Congress acts through a specific rule do little to curb the problem of faction in this context, but there is no presumption in Madison's analysis that rules animated by faction will necessarily be subject to periodic review or that a process of successively revising rules as they are found to be defective is any more likely to approximate the public interest.

If the framers were less sanguine than Lowi concerning the potential of Congress as an institution, they were more sanguine than Lowi concerning the potential of the executive branch. The constitutional convention had considered and explicitly rejected the idea of a weak, ministerial executive who would serve as no more than an errand boy of Congress.[21] Persuaded that a strong and independent executive was not only compatible with the idea of republican government but also indispensable to any government's success, the framers focused on institutional arrangements that would

19. *Federalist Papers*, p. 309. Emphasis added.
20. Ibid., pp. 79–80.
21. Charles Thatch, *The Creation of the Presidency, 1775–1789* (Baltimore, 1969), pp. 89–90.

provide powerful incentives for the executive to exercise his powers for the public good. Most of the powers that the Constitution granted to the president—including the power to direct the armed forces as the commander-in-chief, the power to mitigate the severity of laws by granting pardons, the power to nominate individuals to fill the most important posts of government, and the power to call special sessions of Congress when circumstances merited it—were discretionary powers. Surely a Constitution that granted discretion to the executive in such matters did not require that discretion in the administration of laws be eliminated insofar as possible and that the function of the executive be narrowly conceived of as one of routinely applying rules supplied by Congress.

The faith of the American framers in the presidency rested to a considerable extent on the belief that the president would be more independent of the whims of public opinion and the influence of faction than the Congress. An indirect mode of selection through the electoral college and a longer term of office than that of members of the House of Representatives—which the framers assumed would be the dominant voice in Congress—were chosen to insulate the president from the influence of faction. As a national leader, the president was better situated to resist the influence of faction than congressmen, who would be accountable to more-limited constituencies, for an enlarged constituency diminishes the influence of special interests. Finally, because the presidency was the preeminent political office in the nation, the framers believed that "there will be a constant probability of seeing the station filled by characters preeminent for ability and virtue," and this moral elevation would allow the president to resist the corruption of factious interests to a greater extent than could be expected of congressmen.[22]

The American framers had rejected a sharp dichotomy of a government of laws or a government of men, a dichotomy that Lowi still accepts, in favor of a government that combined both—a government based on the separation of powers. While their enterprise is still a source of controversy today, as it was in their time, it is interesting to note that their defense of an energetic executive exercising extensive discretionary powers is consistent with well-established contemporary conclusions regarding the respective institutional capacities of Congress and the president, whereas the institutional implications of Lowi's juridical democracy fly in the face of those conclusions. The views of Thomas Cronin, a student of the presidency who has been critical of many of the modern developments in that institution and who therefore can hardly be accused of being biased toward presidential power, are particularly noteworthy. Cronin expresses a widely shared judgment when he asserts, "Nearly all representatives and most senators tend to look after local interests first and national interests

22. *Federalist Papers*, pp. 77–84, 411–415.

second [because] their chief incentives dictate that they first serve the immediate interests of powerful groups in their home district.'' His desire to provide more effective checks on abuses of presidential power in the wake of Watergate and the Vietnam War notwithstanding, Cronin concluded, "National security and international economic requirements all move in the direction of increasing presidential responsibilities. Congressional regeneration is clearly needed; but no one, not even the most partisan congressionalist, entertains the notion of a return to Congressional government." An attempt to return to congressional government, Cronin clearly implies, would be inconsistent with rational and effective governance.[23]

Post–New Deal Congresses have voluntarily relinquished the powers that Lowi would have them exercise, in part because they have concluded that other institutions can exercise those powers more effectively and no doubt in part because they prefer to avoid the political heat that congressional decision making would entail. Even when Congress chose to reassert itself, as it did in the early 1970s in response to the Vietnam War and to Watergate, it has shown little desire and even less capacity to thoroughly subordinate the presidency, a requirement for establishing juridical democracy. And if the courts have thus far rejected Lowi's appeal for a return to a restrictive nondelegation doctrine, is it not because they correctly understand that if Congress refuses to rule then the courts cannot compel it to do so?

Lowi departs from the American framers in another way, which also is at variance with widely accepted conclusions in contemporary political science. In Federalist Paper No. 10, Madison realistically argued that in a liberal state with many interest groups the governing process, including the administrative process, is necessarily suffused with interest group politics. "The regulation of these various and interfering interests forms the principal task of modern legislation and involves the spirit of party and faction in the necessary and ordinary operations of government."[24] Administrators charged with the responsibility for making important government decisions will necessarily have to possess the skills of a politician, a capacity to find politically viable compromises that can reconcile conflicting interests.

Lowi, on the other hand, insists on a radical distinction between administration and politics when he criticizes discretionary administration because "broad discretion makes a politician out of a bureaucrat." In juridical democracy, administration becomes the legalistic application of general rules to particular cases. The role of the administrator is assimilated to the role of the judge. Consistent with this attempt to confine politics to Congress, Lowi argues for a return "to the ideal of the neutral civil

23. Thomas Cronin, *The State of the Presidency* (Boston, 1975), pp. 3, 307.
24. *Federalist Papers*, p. 79.

servant." Just as contemporary institutional political science has rejected the ideal of congressional government and acknowledged the virtues of a strong and independent presidency, so the modern study of administration had rejected a radical distinction between politics and administration as unrealistic because an earlier progressive attempt to draw a similarly radical distinction, based on a faith in the neutrality of scientific experts rather than on the neutrality of law, had proved theoretically untenable and practically unworkable.[25]

Lowi's challenge to the American political and legal tradition, however, cannot be met by an analysis narrowly focused on institutions. The framers had defended the Constitution as an institutional framework based on a broad political analysis that asserted, primarily in Federalist Paper No. 10, the virtues of pluralist politics, and it is that thesis which Lowi fundamentally questions through his analysis of American administrative corporatism. How satisfactory is Lowi's analysis of administrative corporatism in light of this study of the NRA? Does the development of administrative corporatism undermine the conclusions of Federalist Paper No. 10, and do we therefore need new institutional arrangements for coping with interest group politics in its new guise?

Lowi and the NRA

In Federalist No. 10, Madison argued that the foremost virtue of the national government which the proposed Constitution would create was its capacity "to break and control the violence of faction," where faction was defined as any group "united and actuated by some common impulse of passion, or of interest, adverse to the rights of other citizens, or to the permanent and aggregate interests of the community."[26] In considering the problem of faction, Madison addressed the issues of fundamental concern to Lowi. Two aspects of Madison's analysis of faction highlight the fundamental differences between their respective approaches to the problem of faction.

Madison was primarily concerned with the problem of majority faction. He was convinced that the republican government that the Constitution would establish was a sufficient safeguard against minority or oligarchical faction because a majority could "defeat its sinister views by regular vote." Oligarchical factions could still pose a threat (they could "clog the administration" or "convulse the society"), but they could not advance their designs "under the forms of the Constitution." Second, the American framers concluded that the most effective remedy for the problem of

25. Lowi, *End of Liberalism*, p. 304.
26. *Federalist Papers*, pp. 77–78.

majority faction was simply to provide for an enlarged republic with a great multiplicity of factions so that no single faction, or even group of factions, could easily dominate government. "Extend the sphere and you take in a greater variety of parties and interests; you make it less probable that a majority of the whole will have a common motive to invade the rights of other citizens; or if such a common motive exists, it will be more difficult for all who feel it to discover their own strength and to act in unison with each other." Madison does not deny that majority factions can form in an enlarged republic, but such a faction would be less probable to form because it would have to be an unstable coalition of diverse groups that would soon be pulled apart by the centrifugal forces of group self-interest.[27]

Lowi's analysis of the problem of faction challenges both these assertions in Federalist Paper No. 10. On the one hand, Lowi, invoking Robert Michels's "iron law of oligarchy" to describe the rise of an organizational elite over the past hundred years, argues that an oligarchical faction is the fundamental threat to individual rights and to the public good. Lowi's oligarchical faction cannot narrowly be identified with business elites, but it is clear that the faction Lowi has in mind would have been categorized as a minority faction in the argument in Federalist Paper No. 10. This faction exerts its control over government primarily through the administrative process, not, as a majority faction would, through the electoral process. For that reason, Lowi is seeking to restore democratic accountability and majority rule, whereas the American framers were seeking to temper the excesses of majority rule.[28] On the other hand, Lowi argues that interest group politics in our enlarged republic have produced a stable system of factional rule. According to Lowi, organizational elites have a shared interest in preserving a stable environment to facilitate organizational maintenance and to secure their own positions, and they have successfully shaped their environment to conform to their needs. New and emergent groups are effectively locked out of the system.

This study of the NRA supports the analysis of faction provided in Federalist Paper No. 10 and challenges Lowi's assertion that the organizational revolution which has bureaucratized interest groups has fundamentally altered the political problem posed by factions. We have demonstrated that the NRA is best understood as a democratic and progressive attempt to restructure the economy and to secure social justice for the working man and for businessmen in periphery firms. Despite the immense gap between the intentions of the progressive New Dealers who conceived and administered the NRA and the consequences of the program, the NRA on the whole did aid its intended constituencies, albeit in a qualified sense.

27. Ibid., pp. 80, 83.
28. David Schaefer, "Theodore Lowi and the Administrative State" (Paper presented at the 1986 Annual Meeting of the American Political Science Association, Washington, D.C., September, 1986).

Labor did better than any other group under the NRA. Finally having achieved federal recognition of the right of labor to organize and bargain collectively, labor unions underwent a revitalization. Reversing a decade of steady attrition in membership, labor unions added 900,000 new workers to their rolls within two years.[29] Unions in particularly advantageous positions under the NRA made even more spectacular gains, sometimes doubling or tripling their membership.[30] The abolition of child labor, long a goal of progressives and labor unions, finally became national policy. Wages were increased in most industries, and the maximum hours that workers could be compelled to work were decreased. Michael Weinstein estimates that the NRA was responsible for as much as a 26 percent annual increase in wages, which more than offset a 14 percent annual increase in prices during the same period. Once the NRA was overturned, labor lost its comparative advantage, suffering a 14 percent annual decrease in wages while prices declined at a rate of only 7 percent annually. Furthermore, at least in the case of some aspects of the labor picture it may have been the weakest workers who benefited the most. Weinstein has argued that the NRA reduced the differentials in average earnings between skilled and unskilled workers, between workers in low-pay and high-pay industries, and between men and women. The reduced differentials were most striking for hourly earnings, but they were significant even for weekly wages, where the influence of a relative increase in hourly wages was offset by greater reductions in the number of hours worked by disadvantaged workers. Finally, a Brookings Institution study estimated that the maximum-hours provisions of the NRA added approximately 2 million workers to the payrolls—a 6 or 7 percent increase assuming the same general level of economic activity as prevailed prior to the NRA.[31]

The NRA's record with regard to periphery firms is more ambiguous because there was a substantial gap between the intentions of the program and its actual effects, but the conclusion that the NRA provided advantages to these businesses, particularly in their competition with oligopolistic center firms, has been well substantiated in this study. Industries with peripheral firms tended to benefit the most from the acceleration in the "organizational revolution" sparked by the NRA because they were the least well organized to begin with. To the extent that the NRA fostered cartels, peripheral firms generally benefited from these because they tended to be the least-efficient producers, and artificially high prices

29. U.S. Bureau of the Census, *Historical Statistics,* pp. 97–98.
30. Schlesinger, *The Coming of the New Deal,* pp. 140–142.
31. M. Weinstein, pp. 29–30, 106. The latter qualification is critical. More fundamental, the NRA retarded economic recovery and therefore limited progress toward full employment. However, this qualification is more important for assessing the wisdom of progressivism than it is for determining whether the NRA was a genuinely progressive program.

allowed them to stay in business despite their higher costs. Peripheral firms gained these advantages because NRA officials insisted that the interests of these firms be represented and respected in both code-making the code administration.

Just as the NRA promoted the interests of labor and peripheral firms, so, conversely, did business elites in center firms generally find their interests threatened by the NRA. Increased government regulation was limiting their ability to exploit competitive advantages and was viewed as a potentially serious threat to profits, particularly if price-fixing became institutionalized. It was also enhancing the power of labor unions at a time when center firms were generally hostile to unions.

On the whole, these relationships between the NRA and economic classes were reflected in the pattern of support for and opposition to the extension of the NRA. Business elites from center firms were divided in their responses to the NRA—with corporate liberals trying to work with the New Dealers in order to moderate them, and conservatives moving into outright opposition through groups like the American Liberty League— but big business was united in its determination to preserve the market from heavy-handed New Deal regulators. An NRA-type program would have been acceptable to most of these elites, but only if it genuinely permitted industrial self-government.[32] Only under relatively idiosyncratic conditions, such as those prevailing in the steel code, were center firms fairly sympathetic to the existing NRA, and even that sympathy was heavily qualified. Peripheral firms, primarily in the textile, coal, and retail sectors, along with the AFL, provided the backbone of support for extension even without fundamental reforms.

This simple pattern is confounded, however, by a number of other factors. In some peripheral industries the codes proved unenforceable, either because the code the industry drafted proved too ambitious or because the industry lacked the organizational infrastructure to monitor compliance. Other peripheral firms found the advantages of a code of fair trade practices more than outweighed by the disadvantages of paying increased wages for fewer hours to labor. Some peripheral firms objected to the NRA because they believed the NRA was controlled by big business, although in many cases, as we have argued, that belief was unwarranted. Organized labor's support was only lukewarm because it hoped to secure most of the advantages that it had under the NRA with fewer of the disadvantages through the anticipated passage of the Wagner Act.

Despite the complexity introduced by these considerations, they do not

---

32. Hawley, *The New Deal*, p. 157; "Resolution adopted by the Executive Committee of the Business Advisory and Planning Committee," 13 March 1935, Roosevelt Papers, OF 3Q, Box 9, Folder 1933–35.

refute the basic conclusion of this study that the NRA was a progressive program. That the corporatist NRA, which was authorized by a sweeping, vague delegation of congressional power, would have primarily aided labor and peripheral businesses challenges Lowi's assertion that discretionary administration and administrative corporatism are inherently instruments favoring an oligarchical status quo, even when oligarchy is understood broadly as a class of established organizational elites rather than narrowly as a wealthy elite. Few eras in U.S. history have been as disruptive of the status quo as the New Deal, and the NRA is the quintessential New Deal program. The NRA contributed to the destruction of big business's organizational hegemony, for its legacy was an organizational revolution in which the organizationally disadvantaged had become organized, permanently altering the character of American politics.

The progressivism of the NRA does not, however, mean that the NRA should not be analyzed in terms of factionalism. If we accept Madison's definition of "faction" as any group pursuing goals adverse to "the permanent and aggregate interests of the community," it would be no exaggeration to suggest the program degenerated into an orgy of factionalism. Big business refused to recognize the legitimate aspirations of labor unions, small business demanded cartels to protect their interests, and organized labor placed its interests in promoting collective bargaining above the national interest in economic recovery when it intransigently rejected the modest reforms Roosevelt proposed, repeatedly went out on strike to secure union recognition, and supported cartelization when it furthered labor's interests. Every serious scholar who has examined the NRA has concluded that the program was contrary to "the permanent and aggregate interests of the community," and that judgment stands even after it is conceded that the NRA aided peripheral businesses and labor.

Economists have provided the most cogent case for considering the NRA in light of factional politics. They have unanimously condemned the NRA for stifling competition and retarding economic recovery. That was the conclusion of Brookings economists in the 1930s, some of whom had participated in the administration of the act, and that conclusion has been reaffirmed and strengthened by a more recent study by Michael Weinstein.[33] Weinstein estimated that "the codes eliminated a potential 8 percent average annual increase in real output (and a 15 percent reduction in the number of individuals who were unemployed during the NRA period)" and that "NIRA-induced diminution of real wealth (due to the inflationary consequences) was responsible for a 6–11 percent reduction in annual GNP during the two years of the NIRA codes."[34] Even if one credits the NRA with having snapped the psychology of despair and the crisis of

33. Lyon et al., pp. 871–880; M. Weinstein, pp. 146–147.
34. M. Weinstein, pp. 30–31.

confidence that paralyzed the American economy in the early days of the New Deal, that effect was dwarfed over the two-year period by the adverse economic consequences of this program. Moreover, the NRA led us further down the road to economic regimentation than any peacetime program in American history. Only the moderation of New Deal elites prevented the program from degenerating into a wholesale attack on individual economic rights.

The progressive animus of the NRA simply makes it clear that the NRA is the product of majoritarian factional politics. The examples of majoritarian factional politics provided in Federalist Paper No. 10 included "a rage for paper money, for an abolition of debts, for an equal division of property."[35] What these examples have in common is that they would be legislative projects initiated by the representatives of the economically disadvantaged that would tend to undermine the system of credit and property rights that underlies the market economy envisioned by the framers.[36] The NRA was initiated by progressive elites who sought to establish a new economic order that would better protect the interests of peripheral businesses and labor, but their vision of a comprehensive social peace treaty between labor and business (and farmers through the Agricultrual Adjustment Act) was unrealistic and quickly became a vehicle for the expression of factional self-interest. In practice, the NRA tended to undermine a market economy by stifling competition and entrepreneurship through a regimented system of codes of fair trade competition. As is often the case with majoritarian factional schemes, a program motivated by a resentment of the wealth and power of the economically advantaged rebounds to the detriment of the economically disadvantaged as well.

The history of the NRA not only confirms the fears of the American framers that majoritarian factions would pose a serious threat to rights and to "the permanent and aggregate interests of the community," it also testifies to the virtues of an enlarged republic in diffusing that threat. To secure an electoral majority, New Dealers had to appeal broadly to farmers, to peripheral businessmen, and to labor. Conflicts between these broad "groups," however, made it difficult to sustain a program like the NRA. Peripheral businessmen resented paying increased wages. Labor objected to business cartelization when prices increased and ate away the increased purchasing power they had won through higher wages. Farmers objected to higher prices for industrial goods, and recognized that higher wages would contribute to higher prices. These conflicts were compounded by conflicts between competing interests within each of these broad groups. Sectoral and regional conflicts, conflicts

35. *Federalist Papers*, p. 84.
36. On the commitment of the American framers to a capitalist economy see Marc Plattner, "American Democracy and the Acquisitive Spirit," in *How Capitalistic Is the Constitution?* ed. Robert A. Goldwin and William A. Schambra (Washington D.C., 1982).

between craft and industrial workers, conflicts between small and medium-sized businesses—all further destabilized the NRA. The NRA would almost certainly have collapsed or evolved into a significantly different program even if the Supreme Court had not declared it unconstitutional. The idealistic progressive corporatist vision was not viable in a large and heterogeneous polity like that of the United States, but neither was there much danger that a program that came to serve factional interests would become permanently institutionalized in such a republic.[37]

Legal Formalism and the Administrative State

Lowi's concerns with discretionary administration, however, were not confined to its presumed oligarchical consequences. Discretionary administration and its attendant administrative corporatism are also objected to on the grounds that they fragment the administrative process and undermine the sovereignty of the state. Planning is replaced with ad hoc bargaining, and the state is rendered incapable of securing the public good. Thus the administrative process would not be adequately reformed merely by democratizing interest group liberalism so that all groups could participate in its pork barrel politics, a strategy for reform that Lowi analogizes to universalizing the practice of fixing parking tickets. The administrative inefficiency of the NRA appears to provide greater support for the thesis that discretionary administration and administrative corporatism are inconsistent with good government.

The NRA was a public policy failure, but that failure cannot be attributed to discretionary administration and administrative corporatism. Discretionary administration, Lowi would assert, is captured administration. Its influence on public policy will reflect the balances and compromises struck by powerful special interests. Such a description hardly does justice to the role of top administrators (including Franklin Roosevelt as chief administrator) in the NRA. As we have seen, ideology and the institutional interests of the state played a more important role in determining the behavior of those administrators than special interest demands, and the ideology they shared was generally not an ideology congenial to big business interests, the best-organized class of the period. Furthermore, and ironically, the aspect of the NRA that has been criticized most heavily, the anticompetitive character of codes of fair trade competition, derived from a rulemaking process rather than a more discretionary adjudicatory process. The negotiations that led to the codes of fair trade competition

---

37. For a similar conclusion regarding the New Deal based on an analysis of New Deal political thought, see William A. Schambra, "The Roots of the American Public Philosophy," *The Public Interest*, no. 67 (1983): 36–48.

embodied the very practice of bargaining over rules that Lowi praises, and the NRA's rulemaking process included reasonable procedural safeguards to assure broad representation for concerned parties.

It was NRA administrators (including the president in his administrative role) who restricted the use of price-fixing clauses in codes of fair trade competition from the beginning, who insisted on revisions encouraging more competition in codes that were being abused, who excluded merit clauses qualifying the impact of Section 7a, who chose to administer the oil code through the Interior Department rather than through the NRA, and who chipped away at the basing point system in the steel industry. In each of these cases the opposition of powerful economic interests did not fundamentally deter the administration from pursuing an autonomous policy that furthered the goals of the New Deal. To single out such decisions as evidence of the public-spiritedness of administrators when the program as a whole clearly benefited private interests at the expense of the public may appear disingenuous. But it is in these kinds of decisions that administrative discretion was genuinely operative. The fact that the NRA permitted a significant degree of cartelization of the American economy was less a consequence of decisions made in administering the act than it was a consequence of decisions made in enacting the legislation in the first place.

It was the president in his legislative role and Congress that accepted the fallacious economic reasoning which suggested that artificially raising prices could fuel the recovery rather than follow it.[38] Similarly, it was the president and Congress that entrusted administrators with the impossible task of defining fair competition. In a political context where faith in the market had been shattered by the depression and where producer groups were adamant in their demands for protection and relief, and president and the Congress proved all too willing to enact inefficient, anticompetitive policies. Besides the NRA, the New Deal gave us the Guffey coal acts, the Robinson-Patman Act, and the Agricultural Adjustment Act, all of which had significantly diminished competition in different sectors of the economy and in some cases through provisions that allowed far less scope for administrative discretion.

The fact that the anticompetitive character of the NRA was to a large extent determined by the legislative process does not imply that the administration of the act was beyond reproach. While a number of factors contributed to the administrative morass that eventually overwhelmed the NRA, none was as serious as the repeated failure to evaluate realistically the administrative feasibility of its decisions. The most striking examples of this were the decisions to expand the NRA to encompass all sectors of the economy as soon as possible and to allow businessmen to draft codes

38. Lyon et al., pp. 8–14, 756–775, 871–877.

for narrowly defined industries.[39] These decisions made the NRA responsible for supervising the drafting and administration of more than 500 codes in a very short period of time, a task beyond the abilities of the NRA.

A great deal of the responsibility for the administrative weaknesses of the NRA can clearly be attributed to Hugh Johnson. Roosevelt had chosen to ignore the warning of Bernard Baruch, Johnson's superior on the War Industries Board, that Johnson was a good number-two man but was not a wise choice to head the NRA.[40] In retrospect, Baruch's reservations concerning Johnson proved to be well founded. Johnson could be dynamic and vigorous, and he was quite successful at drumming up public support for the NRA in the short run, but he lacked the patience, judgment, and detachment that the job demanded over the long run. As the problems confronting the NRA grew, Johnson increasingly found an escape in alcoholism, and the NRA foundered without effective leadership.

The problems posed by Johnson's weaknesses were greatly magnified primarily because of a pervasive lack of administrative sophistication in the NRA as a whole. Roosevelt had rejected the option of entrusting the NRA to an established government agency like the FTC, which had considerable experience at least in the area of unfair trade practices, in favor of creating a new agency. Roosevelt preferred a new agency because he feared a conservative bias predominated in many of the established agencies. At the time the NRA was being established, Roosevelt was still struggling to recast the FTC in a more progressive mold. Throughout the summer of 1933, he was requesting the resignation of Commissioner Humphrey, one of Hoover's most vociferous conservative appointees and an influential commissioner.[41] Creating a new agency to administer a new program like the NRA enhanced the likelihood that the program would not be undermined by uncooperative bureaucrats sabotaging its implementation, but that benefit must be weighed against the inefficiencies associated with a new and inexperienced agency. The problem was further compounded by Roosevelt's decision to exempt the NRA from civil service laws, a decision that allowed him to staff the NRA with officials loyal to the Democratic party's program but that subjected the recruitment process to patronage pressures, pressures that have retarded the development of efficient administration in many other areas of government.[42]

The decision to create a new agency to implement a new regulatory program was not exceptional in the early New Deal. Indeed, it was the

39. Schlesinger, *The Coming of the New Deal*, p. 176.
40. Burns, *Roosevelt: The Lion and the Fox*, p. 191.
41. Humphrey refused to resign, and Roosevelt fired him in the fall of 1933, an action that the Supreme Court ultimately rejected as unconstitutional in the landmark *Humphrey's Executor v. United States*, 295 U.S. 602 (1935.)
42. Lyon et al., pp. 8, 41–42.

dominant administrative strategy of this era. A host of new agencies—the Works Progress Administration, the Public Works Administration, the Securities and Exchange Commission, and the Civilian Conservation Corps, to list only a few—sprung up at this time. And although this strategy succeeded in creating agencies committed to their programs, at times carrying out their responsibilities with almost missionary zeal, it also frequently created agencies like the NRA, which lacked the administrative sophistication to address the problems it would confront. Roosevelt's distrust of the bureaucracy, which was at least in part well founded, had made it extraordinarily difficult to develop well-administered programs. Nevertheless, the fact that many of the same problems that plagued the codes administered under the NRA also plagued the oil code administered under the Department of Interior, which had the administrative experience the NRA lacked, would strongly suggest that administrative inefficiency did no more than exacerbate the problems that were intrinsic to its ambitious societal corporatist goals.

Even the administrative weaknesses that did plague the NRA were not rooted fundamentally in the discretion it accorded administrators or in its administrative corporatist structure. The deregulation of the airline industry during the late 1970s provides a good example of why it is inappropriate to target administrative discretion in attempting to eliminate captured administration. The Civil Aeronautics Board (CAB), unlike the NRA, was a government agency that had become too deferential to the interests of a well-organized industry. Yet the destruction of the cozy relationship between the agency and the industry was produced primarily by interrelated shifts in CAB and presidential policy. In implementing a new policy, the CAB and the president used the discretion they had under the New Deal statute that authorized the CAB to initiate a policy more responsive to consumer interests. Indeed, in a broader study of deregulation in three industries, Martha Derthick and Paul Quirk concluded, "The broad, flexible grants of statutory authority enjoyed by the commissions emboldened reform-oriented chairmen to fundamentally reverse long-standing practices."[43] Discretion can work to the benefit of weakly organized interests such as consumers.

The same is true of administrative corporatism. Thomas McCraw, in a recent article on the formative years of the Securities and Exchange Commission (SEC), has demonstrated how that agency, which also had broad discretion to pursue its goals, used an administrative corporatist strategy to secure stock market reform. Rather than build up an extensive network of federal agents to monitor compliance with SEC requirements,

43. Martha Derthick and Paul J. Quirk, *The Politics of Deregulation* (Washington D.C., 1985), pp. 242–244. For the importance of a reform-oriented chairman in the reform of the CAB, see McCraw, *Prophets of Regulation*, chap. 7.

the SEC, like the NRA, relied to a considerable extent on private groups to police their own industry. But in the case of the SEC the administrative corporatist strategy was so successful (i.e., substantially increased protection for the interests of disorganized stockholders) that the SEC has repeatedly been praised as "the strongest Commission in the Government."[44] Similarly, Theda Skocpol and Kenneth Finegold have recently argued that the Agricultural Adjustment Act was much more successfully administered than the NRA, despite an administrative corporatist structure linking Department of Agriculture officials to farm groups.[45] The success of administrative corporatist strategies in these two programs suggests that

44. Thomas McCraw, "With Consent of the Governed: SEC's Formative Years," *Journal of Policy Analysis and Management* 1, no. 3 (1982): 347, 352–354.

45. Theda Skocpol and Kenneth Finegold, "State Capacity and Economic Intervention in the Early New Deal," *Political Science Quarterly* 97 (1982). Skocpol and Finegold argued that the NRA failed because it was entrusted to an ad hoc agency exempted from civil service laws, whereas the AAA succeeded because it was entrusted to the better-established Department of Agriculture. Skocpol and Finegold accepted many of the traditional arguments about the NRA that are questioned in these pages. Their assertion that the NRA failed because it was administratively inefficient and because businessmen therefore became disenchanted with it is particularly vulnerable to criticism. The NRA lost the support of many in the business community because they were concerned with the growing power of the Washington bureaucracy. Had the NRA been administered exclusively by professional civil servants instead of by an amalgam of experts and businessmen, these fears would have been intensified even if the NRA had been more efficiently administered in a narrow, technical sense of the term. Administrative efficiency in a broader sense might well have suffered if the NRA received even less cooperation from the business community.

The conclusion of Skocpol and Finegold that the administrative weakness of the NRA is rooted in the ad hoc character of the agency is partly supported by this argument, but there are in our respective conclusions important differences that should be made explicit. In Skocpol and Finegold's argument, state capacity is closely identified with the development and institutionalization of a professional civil service. This argument does not do justice to the weighty reasons Roosevelt had for not entrusting the NRA to the established bureaucracy, and it does not attribute sufficient importance to the reorganization of the Department of Agriculture carried out by Henry Wallace and Rexford Tugwell, a reorganization that critically supplemented professionalism because it infused the bureaucracy with a more progressive spirit. If the Department of Agriculture successfully administered the AAA because it was a government agency with an established, proficient civil service, as Skocpol and Finegold suggest, how can one reconcile this finding with the traditional conclusion of most political scientists that the Department of Agruculture has been one of the best examples of a captured government agency because it has so often placed the interests of farmers above broader national interests?

The problem with the Skocpol and Finegold interpretation is its tendency to equate state capacity with the development of a professional civil service. Certainly no modern state could function efficiently without a professional civil service. However, the routinization of tasks in established bureaucracies makes it difficult for them to respond to extraordinary problems, and under these circumstances the greater flexibility of ad hoc agencies may be a virtue. Traditionally, the War Industries Board was held up as an outstanding example of what ad hoc agencies could accomplish under difficult times, although more recently that view has been questioned. In any case, it is at least clear that flexibility is as essential to state capacity as institutionalized expertise, and that there are trade-offs between these two prerequisites of effective governance. Below we shall argue that the creation of professional civil service would have to be accompanied by the creation of a Senior Executive Service if state capacity more broadly understood were to be enhanced. See also Schlesinger, *The Crisis of the Old Order*, p. 473; William F. Willoughby, *Government Organization in War-Time and After* (New York, 1919); Robert D. Cuff, *The War Industries Board: Business-Government Relations During World War I* (Baltimore, 1973).

we must turn to factors other than administrative corporatism to understand the weaknesses of the NRA and of the American regulatory state in general.

Lowi's analysis of administrative corporatism and its relationship to discretionary administration does not provide a suitable framework for understanding the NRA, even though the NRA was chosen as an almost paradigmatic case of the phenomena Lowi seeks to illuminate. Although Lowi's thesis that a decline in the rule of law facilitated the emergence of corporatism is partially justified, that thesis takes on a radically new meaning when the NRA is examined more closely. The origins of the NRA lay in the progressive tradition, a tradition that had grown increasingly skeptical of the rule of law and increasingly interested in developing nonlegal modes of conflict resolution. This progressive distrust of law and the legal system, when combined with a powerful distrust of markets in the wake of the depression, systematically skewed the policy orientation of New Dealers, encouraging them to adopt radical measures like the NRA in conjunction with more narrowly targeted and ultimately defensible reform measures like stock market and banking regulation. If the New Dealers had been less enamored of their corporatist dream of a new era of social cooperation, if they had acknowledged the intractable realities of individual and interest group competition and had unambiguously committed themselves to the task of providing a more rational legal order to regulate that competition, the nation would have been spared the painful NRA experience. An appeal for a return to the rule of law in this context provides a healthy antidote to progressive utopianism.

Nevertheless, the institutional imperatives of this justifiable appeal to the rule of law are not those of juridical democracy. The NRA failed because it attempted to institute societal corporatism in a large and economically diverse nation whose traditions were antithetical to its communal aspirations. Yet juridical democracy is an attempt to prevent discretionary administration and administrative corporatism, not just societal corporatism. This remedy is too extreme, because it prohibits discretionary administration and administrative corporatism even in the many contexts in which they occur divorced from any grandiose attempt to institutionalize societal corporatism. Because discretionary administration and administrative corporatism can be useful policy instruments when they are not conjoined to societal corporatist aspirations, juridical democracy would hamper rather than facilitate effective governance.

Administrative Reforms

If global assaults on administrative discretion and administrative corporatism are unjustified, are there other reforms that would have held greater promise for improving the administration of the NRA and that might yet lead to improvements in the efficiency of the administrative state? Even New Dealers were dissatisfied with the administrative record of the NRA and other early New Deal programs. Thus later in his administration, when it became clear to Roosevelt that the New Deal's reform and recovery goals were being jeopardized by a lack of coordination among the new agencies he created, Roosevelt turned to a new administrative strategy.[46] This strategy, proposed by the Brownlow Commission, was embodied in the Administrative Reform Bill of 1938. That proposed legislation would have considerably enhanced the power of the president to control the bureaucracy by creating an expanded presidential staff loyal to his program and by bringing the independent regulatory commissions more directly under his supervision. This second administrative strategy was an improvement on his first, for if a president could control the established bureaucracy, he would not have to create new agencies to run new programs.

It was many years before Roosevelt's second administrative strategy was substantially institutionalized. The Administrative Reform Bill of 1938 was defeated because Congress had grown increasingly skeptical of Roosevelt's efforts to centralize power in his own hands, and it was only gradually, through a series of reforms, that presidents acquired most of the powers and resources it proposed. In 1939 an executive order created the Office of the President and provided more staff assistance for the president.[47] The responsiveness of independent regulatory commissions to presidential agendas was enhanced in the 1950s and 1960s by reforms that allowed the president to appoint their chairmen and then centralized power within the commissions in the hands of the chairmen.[48] Regular departments of government were brought under presidential control by the development of secondary and tertiary levels of presidential appointees in the departments who could aid the secretaries of departments in securing compliance with the president's agenda.[49]

The extent to which these reforms had realized the vision of the president as chief administrator were made dramatically visible by the early 1980s, for Ronald Reagan successfully used them to impose a radical change in priorities on bureaucrats who had powerful incentives, both ideological and material, to oppose him but who lacked the power to do so. However, the Reagan presidency demonstrates not only the successful institutionalization of the Brownlow Commission's recommendations, but also their limitations. The fact that Reagan used his appointment powers

46. See Barry Karl, *Executive Reorganization and Reform in the New Deal* (Chicago, 1963) for a general discussion of Roosevelt's second administrative strategy.

47. Ibid., pp. 256–258.

48. Derthick and Quirk, p. 64.

49. Richard Pious, *The American Presidency* (New York, 1979), pp. 217–220.

primarily to infuse the bureaucracy with ideologically committed but
sometimes administratively incompetent officials shows that the reforms of
the last fifty years have been more successful in ensuring accountability to
the president than in assuring administrative efficiency.

A potentially more balanced approach to administrative reform would
emphasize a prominent role for the Senior Executive Service (SES), an
elite corps of civil servants created by the Civil Service Reform Act of
1978.[50] The creation of an SES was the realization of a recommendation
made by Former President Hoover as chairman of a prominent commission studying administrative reorganization in the mid-1950s. Of the 314
proposals for administrative reform made by this Hoover commission,
Hoover singled out the recommendation for setting up a senior civil
service as the single most important proposal.[51] A Senior Executive
Service would transform the character of the highest ranks of the civil
service by designating a new grade of top civil servants who can be
promoted and transferred at the discretion of the president, breaking down
the rigid rules regarding promotion and job assignment that have traditionally
safeguarded civil service employees from politically motivated interference. The SES would provide an avenue for ambitious civil servants to
assume top policy making positions from which they might otherwise
have been excluded, and the opportunity to acquire greater honor, power,
and income from the higher positions that would be opened up could more
than compensate the ambitious for the risks of demotion and transfer that
accompany promotion to the SES.

This reform is no less desirable from the perspective of the president
because it gives him the opportunity to select the senior civil servants who
are most sympathetic to his programs to head them. Furthermore, it
creates a class of administratively experienced bureaucrats who nevertheless have powerful career incentives to serve the president, because their
advancement at the highest levels will depend on presidential favor. If
presidents can manipulate the incentives of at least upper-level bureaucrats
more effectively than they can under civil service rules, it would not be as
necessary for presidents to turn to "outsiders" to staff the agencies critical
to their political agendas.

50. It is regrettable that the promise of the 1978 Civil Service Reform Act has even now not
been realized. In the early days of his administration, Reagan generally sidestepped the Senior
Executive Service and entrusted administrative responsibility in political appointees who had
passed the ideological litmus test. Congress has complied in the weakening of the SES by cutting
back funds for executive bonuses, leading many who joined the SES feeling betrayed because
they had sacrificed civil service security in part for the opportunity to compete for higher
financial rewards. The demoralization this produced in the SES encouraged more than 2,300 of
its members to quit in the first three years of the Reagan presidency. According the Charles
Goodsell, "By mid-1984, 45 percent of the executives who had joined the SES when it was
formed in 1979 had left the government" (Charles T. Goodsell, *The Case for Bureaucracy*, 2d
ed., [Chatham, N.J., 1985], pp. 173–174).
51. Neil MacNeil and Harold W. Metz, *The Hoover Report: 1953–1955* (New York, 1956), p. 29.

If there had been an effective Senior Executive Service when Franklin Roosevelt took office, the most serious administrative flaws of the NRA, not to mention many other programs, might well have been avoided. Under these circumstances Roosevelt would not have confronted the dilemma of whether to establish a totally new NRA agency staffed by party and progressive loyalists or whether to turn the program over to an established agency like the FTC. Roosevelt may well have chosen the lesser of two evils in creating a new NRA agency, but this strategy was unsuccessful in the case of the NRA, just as approximately forty years later a similar strategy conceived by Richard Nixon to circumvent the regular departments and run the government through the White House staff was to prove unsuccessful.[52]

The creation of a Senior Executive Service is as defensible on constitutional grounds as it is on policy grounds, for it fulfills the institutional aspirations of the framers. In *The Federalist Papers*, Hamilton had argued that administration in its "precise signification" falls "peculiarly within the province of the executive department." A staunch defender of a strong presidency, Hamilton believed that a prerequisite for effective governance was presidential control over the administrative apparatus of the state. "The persons, therefore, to whose immediate management these different matters are committed ought to be considered as the assistants or deputies of the Chief Magistrate, and on this account they ought to derive their offices from his appointment, at least from his nomination, and ought to be subject to his superintendence." Having carefully constructed the office of the president to assure insofar as possible that the president would exercise his powers for the sake of the common good, Hamilton was not reluctant to entrust the president with significant powers. Presidential control of the bureaucracy would unify and energize the executive branch, and "energy in the executive is a leading character in the definition of good government."[53]

Hamilton had insisted on the accountability of administrators to the president even though he recognized that this entailed a significant risk: "To reverse and undo what has been done by a predecessor is very often considered by a successor as the best proof he can give of his own capacity and desert. . . . These considerations, and the influence of personal confidences and attachments, would be likely to every new President to promote a change of men to fill the subordinate stations; and these causes together could not fail to occasion a disgraceful and ruinous mutability in the administration of the government."[54] For Hamilton these risks were manageable because presidential reeligibility minimized them, permitting

52. Richard P. Nathan, *The Administrative Presidency* (New York, 1983).
53. *Federalist Papers*, pp. 423, 435–436.
54. Ibid., p. 436.

good executives to serve multiple terms. It was Hamilton's hope that we would change presidents relatively infrequently.

The development of the two-term tradition for presidents (which became a formal constitutional requirement with the Twenty-second Amendment), compounded more recently by the electoral difficulties incumbent presidents have encountered in seeking reelection, have thwarted Hamilton's hopes for stability in the executive office. Furthermore, the framers' expectations that the president would be insulated from the demands of factious groups if selected by the Electoral College proved unrealistic. Under these circumstances, institutional innovations are called for. The creation of a Senior Executive Service provides an alternative means for securing both energy and stability in administration, thereby fulfilling Hamilton's institutional aspirations.

Reformers and Liberal Democracy

Our liberal democratic regime has tendencies that destabilize it unless checked and moderated. Some of the most significant of these tendencies become manifest in reform movements that arise periodically and challenge our constitutional framework. The abuses that inspire these reform movements are often real. Capitalism is the economic foundation for our liberal democratic system, and the humanization of capitalism is a never-ending political task. Development of appropriate regulatory controls for capitalism often lags behind changes in the economic world. When this occurs, the self-interestedness that capitalism unleashes is not harnessed, and liberalism can degenerate into a simple rationalization for greed. But when these historical lags generate exaggerated fears of oligarchical power, and these fears in turn lead to democratizing reforms that are inconsistent with the spirit of the Constitution, then liberal democracy is weakened, not strengthened.

The early New Deal was such a period. Reacting against the excesses of laissez-faire capitalism, New Dealers sought to achieve economic democracy and social justice through the corporatist NRA. The cooperative vision that inspired the NRA, with its associated hostility to capitalism and the pursuit of economic self-interest, were antithetical to the spirit of the Constitution. Fortunately, the failure of the NRA at least partially chastened New Dealers, forcing them to shelve their dreams of a new political economy and to focus more realistically on piecemeal reforms that could better accommodate the self-interest of labor and peripheral businesses and better secure the welfare of the American citizenry. As a result, the enduring legacy of the New Deal was not the NRA but a more expansive regulatory and welfare state, and that was generally consistent with the spirit of the Constitution.

During the 1960s and 1970s another reform movement arose that challenged capitalism and our constitutional framework. Relying on criticisms of the American political system provided by Theodore Lowi and others, reformers in this movement, with considerably less justification than the New Dealers, also argued that oligarchy posed a fundamental threat to American democracy. They demanded and secured extensive political reforms to meet this threat. But in some cases it has already become clear that the reformers mistook democratic form for democratic substance. The outstanding example of this is the McGovern-Fraser reforms of the Democratic party. These reforms led to a rapid increase in the number of primaries used by the Democratic party (and indirectly the Republican party) to determine their nominee for president. The "undemocratic" rule of party bosses was seemingly replaced by direct popular control over party nominations. In retrospect, however, the decline of the Democratic party and the increasing importance of a media-based manipulatory politics of image can both be traced, at least in part, to these reforms. The first presidential nominee of the Democratic party selected under the new rules was enthusiastically supported by a new class of amateur activists, but he proved so unpopular with such traditional Democratic constituencies as labor that many longtime Democratic voters went Republican in the 1972 presidential elections. The new "more democratic" procedures had in fact produced a candidate who was less representative of Democrats than candidates chosen under the old procedures.[55]

There are strong grounds for believing that a similar dynamics has been operative with regard to the reforms of the administrative process in the 1960s and 1970s. These reforms have ostensibly made the administrative process more open, more accountable, and more participatory, but they have also made it more formalistic and rule-oriented. Institutionally, the importance of legal formalism in this reform era has been most notable in the prominent role that courts have come to play in the political process, for an emphasis on legal formalism invites judicial review of the administrative process to determine whether due process has been observed. In theory, legal formalism has been a means to realize democratic ends, but in practice legal formalism has taken on a life of its own. The new administrative process has actually enhanced the power of a rising class of "public interest" activists who have been extraordinarily successful in manipulating the new procedures to further their own political agenda.[56]

55. James Ceasar, *Reforming the Reforms: A Critical Analysis of the Presidential Selection Process* (Cambridge, Mass., 1982); Austin Ranney, *Curing the Mischiefs of Faction* (Berkeley and Los Angeles, 1975).
56. Irving Kristol, *Two Cheers for Capitalism* (New York, 1978), pp. 23–28, 40–45. In a similar vein, McCann argues that reformers in this era turned to the courts, winning short-run victories, but failed to develop a popular constituency for their agenda. See Michael W. McCann, *Taking Reform Seriously: Perspectives on Public Interest Liberalism* (Ithaca, N.Y., 1986).

This emphasis on legal formalism in the 1960s and 1970s reflects a radical shift in reform mentality from the antiformalism of the New Deal. While reformers during both reform eras sincerely affirmed democratic values and claimed to speak for the people, the authenticity of the claims of the reformers of the 1960s and 1970s was dubious at best. The political agenda of those latter reformers often clashed with the political agenda of elected representatives, and it is the elected representatives who had a far more legitimate claim to represent the people than the self-appointed spokesmen of public interest groups. For that reason, these groups often resorted to the courts to win victories they could not have hoped to have achieved in the political arena. By contrast, no one can sensibly doubt that the New Dealers had majority support for their reform program.

The modern public interest reformers' preference for legal formalism was hardly surprising, for legal formalism has always been attractive to minorities who seek to control the political process. Thus, during the New Deal it was business elites and political representatives sympathetic to their interests who were most strongly committed to legal formalism. Legal formality was a means for straightjacketing the administrative process and preventing democratically elected leaders from pursuing policies that business opposed. It also facilitated judicial intervention at a time when the courts were sympathetic to business interests. Finally, formal procedures worked to the advantage of well-organized business elites who had the sophistication and legal expertise to exploit those procedures. The exploitation of legal formalism by the new activists of the 1960s and 1970s is no less objectionable than its earlier use by big business, but it is more insidious because it is concealed beneath a democratic rhetoric.

This is not to suggest that reformers in the 1960s and 1970s were deliberately duplicitous in promoting their "democratizing" reforms. Indeed, the central paradox of this latest era of reform is that reformers genuinely committed to democracy have introduced reforms that have made our political system less authentically democratic. This paradox is not altogether new to American politics. During the American founding the Antifederalists unjustly accused the Federalists of an attempt to foist an undemocratic Constitution on an unsuspecting nation. The Antifederalists were particularly critical of the provisions establishing the House of Representatives. They argued that two-year terms for representatives were too long (they preferred one-year terms) to assure democratic accountability and that the Constitution's initial provision for only sixty-five representatives meant that the House would be too small to represent the diverse interests of the nation adequately. Responding to the latter complaint, Hamilton argued: "The people can never err more than in supposing that by multiplying their representatives beyond a certain limit they strengthen the barrier against the government of a few. Experience will forever admonish them that, on the contrary, after securing a sufficient number for the purposes of safety, of local information and of diffusive sympathy with the whole society, they will counteract their own views by every addition to their representatives. *The countenance of the government may become more democratic, but the soul that animates it will be more oligarchic.*"[57] Hamilton's rejoinder to the Antifederalists is equally applicable to the reformers of the 1960s and 1970s.

Reformers of the 1960s and 1970s were misguided when they concluded that pluralist politics and administrative corporatism simply masked oligarchical rule and therefore sought to establish a formalist democracy, just as the early New Dealers were misguided when they concluded that democratic formalisms simply masked oligarchical rule and therefore sought to establish a corporatist economic democracy. In both cases the errors arose from the most fundamental of all democratic prejudices— excessive fear of oligarchy and excessive confidence in democratization as the path to good government. If reform is to strengthen liberal democracy, we must return to those earlier liberal thinkers who still understood the strengths and weaknesses of democracy, and we must learn to chart a moderate course between the charybdis of antiformalist democracy and the scylla of formalist democracy. The constitutional vision that established this nation remains the most effective guide for intelligent reform and the most effective antidote to the excesses of twentieth-century reform movements.

57. *Federalist Papers*, pp. 360–361. Emphasis added.

Bibliography

Government Records

Record Group (RG) 9. Records of the National Recovery Administration. National Archives, Washington, D.C.

Record Group 232. Records of the Federal Oil Conservation Board and of the Petroleum Administration Board. Washington National Records Center, Suitland, Maryland.

Manuscript Collections

Harold L. Ickes Papers. Library of Congress. Washington, D.C.

Donald Richberg Papers. Library of Congress. Washington, D.C.

Franklin Delano Roosevelt Papers. F.D.R. Library. Hyde Park, New York.

Government Documents

Congressional Record. 71–73d Congresses. 1933–1935. Washington, D.C.

Senate Committee on Finance. *Investigation of National Recovery Administration.* Hearings pursuant to S.Res. 79. 74th Cong. 1st sess. 1935. Washington, D.C.: Government Printing Office, 1935.

National Labor Board. *Decisions of the National Labor Board.* Washington, D.C.: Government Printing Office, 1934.

Newspapers and Periodicals

Business Week. 1933–1935.

The Iron Age. 1933–1935.

National Petroleum News. 1933–1935.

New York Times. 1933–1935.

Oil and Gas Journal. 1933–1935.

Ackerman, Bruce A., and William T. Hassler. *Clean Coal / Dirty Air.* New Haven: Yale University Press, 1981.

American Bar Association. *Legal History of Gas and Oil.* Chicago: American Bar Association, 1938.

Aristotle. *Art of Rhetoric.* Translated by J. H. Freese. Cambridge, Mass.: Loeb Classical Library, 1926.

Barber, Sotirios A. *The Constitution and the Delegation of Congressional Power.* Chicago: University of Chicago Press, 1975.

Bellush, Bernard. *The Failure of the NRA.* New York: Norton, 1975.

Bentley, Arthur. *Makers, Users, and Masters.* Edited by Sidney Ratner. Syracuse, N.Y.: Syracuse University Press, 1969.

Bernstein, Barton J. "The Conservative Achievements of Liberal Reform." In *Towards a New Past: Dissenting Essays in American History,* ed. Barton J. Bernstein. New York: Vintage Books, 1968.

Bernstein, Irving. *The Lean Years.* Boston: Houghton Mifflin, 1972.

――――. *The New Deal Collective Bargaining Policy.* Berkeley and Los Angeles: University of California Press, 1950.

――――. *Turbulent Years.* Boston: Houghton Mifflin, 1970.

Bernstein, Marver. *Regulating Business by Independent Commission.* Princeton: Princeton University Press, 1955.

Bingham, Joseph. "My Philosophy of Law." In *My Philosophy of Law: Credos of Sixteen American Scholars,* ed. Julius Rosenthal Foundation. Boston: Boston Book Co., 1941.

Brand, Donald R. "Reformers of the Sixties and Seventies: Modern Anti-Federalists?" In *Remaking American Politics,* ed. Richard Harris and Sidney Milkis. Boulder, Colo.: Westview Press, forthcoming.

――――. "Three Generations of Pluralism: Continuity and Change." *Political Science Reviewer* 15 (1985): 109–141.

Brandeis, Elizabeth. "Organized Labor and Protective Labor Legislation." In *Labor and the New Deal,* ed. Milton Derber and Edwin Young. Madison: University of Wisconsin Press, 1957.

Braun, Kurt. *The Right to Organize and Its Limits.* Washington, D.C.: The Brookings Institution, 1950.

Burch, Philip H., Jr. "The NAM as an Interest Group." *Politics and Society* 4 (1974): 97–130.

Burner, David. *Herbert Hoover: A Public Life.* New York: Alfred A. Knopf, 1979.

Burns, James MacGregor. "Congress and the Formation of Economic Policies." Ph.D. diss., Harvard University, 1947.

――――. *Roosevelt: The Lion and The Fox.* New York: Harcourt, Brace & World, 1956.

Cardozo, Benjamin. *The Nature of the Judicial Process.* New Haven: Yale University Press, 1921.

Ceasar, James. *Reforming the Reforms: A Critical Analysis of the Presidential Selection Process.* Cambridge, Mass.: Ballinger, 1982.

Chandler, Alfred D. *The Visible Hand.* Cambridge, Mass.: Belknap Press, 1977.

Childs, Marquis. "They Hate Roosevelt." In *The New Deal: The Critical Issues,* ed. Otis L. Graham, Jr. Boston: Little, Brown, 1971.

Cleveland, Alfred S. "NAM: Spokesman for Industry?" *Harvard Business Review* 26 (1948): 353–371.

Collins, Robert. "Positive Business Responses to the New Deal: The Roots of the Committee for Economic Development, 1933–1942." *Business History Review* 52 (1978): 369–391.

Corwin, Edward S. *The Constitution and What It Means Today.* Revised by Harold W. Chase and Craig R. Ducat. 13th ed. Princeton: Princeton University Press, 1973.

———. *The Twilight of the Supreme Court.* New Haven: Yale University Press, 1934.

Croly, Herbert. "The Future of the State." *The New Republic,* 15 September 1917, pp. 179–183.

———. *Progressive Democracy.* New York: Macmillan, 1915.

———. *The Promise of American Life.* New York: Macmillan, 1918.

Cronin, Thomas. *The State of the Presidency.* Boston: Little, Brown, 1975.

Cronon, David E. *Labor and the New Deal.* Chicago: Rand McNally, 1963.

Cuff, Robert D. *The War Industries Board: Business-Government Relations During World War I.* Baltimore: Johns Hopkins University Press, 1973.

Daugherty, Carroll, R.; Melvin G. de Chazeau, and Samuel S. Straton. *The Economics of the Iron and Steel Industry.* 2 vols. New York: McGraw-Hill, 1937.

Davis, Kenneth Culp. *Administrative Law Text.* 3d ed. St. Paul: West, 1972.

———. *Discretionary Justice: A Preliminary Inquiry.* Urbana: University of Illinois Press, 1971.

Davis, Kenneth S. *FDR: The New Deal Years, 1933–1937.* New York: Random House, 1986.

———. *FDR: The New York Years, 1928–1933.* New York: Random House, 1985.

Derthick, Martha, and Paul J. Quirk. *The Politics of Deregulation.* Washington, D.C.: The Brookings Institution, 1985.

Dewey, John. *Experience and Nature.* New York: Norton, 1929.

———. "Logical Method and Law." *Cornell Law Quarterly* 10 (1924): 17–27.

———. *The Public and Its Problems.* Denver: Alan Swallow, 1927.

———. *Reconstruction in Philosophy.* Boston: Beacon Press, 1948.

Dicey, A. V. *Introduction to the Study of the Law of the Constitution.* New York: Macmillan, 1885.

Diggins, John P. *Mussolini and Fascism: The View from America.* Princeton: Princeton University Press, 1972.

Dodd, Lawrence C., and Richard L. Schott. *Congress and the Administrative State.* New York: Wiley, 1979.

Douglas, William O. "Stare Decisis." In *Essays in Jurisprudence from the Columbia Law Review.* New York: Columbia University Press, 1963.

Dworkin, Ronald. *Taking Rights Seriously.* Cambridge, Mass.: Harvard University Press, 1978.

Elliot, William Y. *The Pragmatic Revolt in Politics.* New York: Macmillan, 1928.

Faulkner, Robert K. *The Jurisprudence of John Marshall.* Princeton: Princeton University Press, 1968.

Fine, Sidney. *The Automobile under the Blue Eagle: Labor, Management, and the Automobile Manufacturing Code.* Ann Arbor: University of Michigan Press, 1963.

Fishbein, Meyer. "The Trucking Industry and the National Recovery Administration." *Social Forces* 34 (October 1955): 171–179.

Forcey, Charles. *The Crossroads of Liberalism: Croly, Weyl, Lippmann, and the Progressive Era, 1900–1925*. London: Oxford University Press, 1961.

Frank, Jerome. *Courts on Trial*. Princeton: Princeton University Press, 1949.

———. *Law and the Modern Mind*. Gloucester, Mass.: Peter Smith, 1970.

Freidel, Frank. *FDR: Launching the New Deal*. Boston: Little, Brown, 1973.

Fusfeld, Daniel R. *The Economic Thought of Franklin D. Roosevelt and the Origins of the New Deal*. New York: AMS Press, 1970.

Gable, Richard W. "NAM: Influential Lobby or Kiss of Death?" *Journal of Politics* 15 (1953): 254–273.

Galambos, Louis. *Competition and Cooperation*. Baltimore: Johns Hopkins University Press, 1966.

———. "The Emerging Organizational Synthesis in Modern American History." In *Men and Organizations: The American Economy in the Twentieth Century*, ed. Edwin J. Perkins. New York: G. P. Putnam's Sons, 1977.

Gilmore, Grant. "Legal Realism: Its Cause and Cure." *Yale Law Journal* 70 (1961): 1037–1048.

Goldberg, Victor. "Banking Reform in the 1930s." In *Regulatory Change in an Atmosphere of Crisis*, ed. Gary M. Walton. New York: Academic Press, 1979.

Goldman, Eric F. *Rendezvous with Destiny: A History of Modern American Reform*. New York: Vintage Books, 1956.

Goodsell, Charles T. *The Case for Bureaucracy: A Public Administration Polemic*. 2d ed. Chatham, N.J.: Chatham House, 1985.

Green, William. *Labor and Democracy*. Princeton: Princeton University Press, 1939.

Greenstone, J. David. *Labor in American Politics*. New York: Vintage Books, 1970.

Gross, James A. *The Making of the National Labor Relations Board, 1933–1937*. Vol. 1. Albany: State University of New York Press, 1974.

Hamilton, Alexander; James Madison; and John Jay. *The Federalist Papers*. Reprint. New York: Mentor Books, 1961.

Harbaugh, William H. *The Writings of Theodore Roosevelt*. New York: Bobbs-Merrill, 1967.

Hardwicke, Robert E. "Legal History of Conservation of Oil in Texas." In American Bar Association, *Legal History of Conservation of Oil and Gas*. Baltimore: American Bar Association, 1938.

Hart, James P. "Oil, the Courts, and the Railroad Commission." *Southwestern Historical Quarterly* 44 (January 1941): 303–311.

Hawley, Ellis W. "Herbert Hoover, The Commerce Secretariat, and the Vision of an 'Associative State,' 1921–1928." In *Men and Organizations*, ed. Edward J. Perkins. New York: G. P. Putnam's Sons, 1977.

———. *The New Deal and the Problem of Monopoly: A Study in Economic Ambivalence*. Princeton: Princeton University Press, 1969.

Herring, Pendleton, E. "First Session of the 73rd Congress." *American Political Science Review* 27 (1934): 65–83.

Himmelberg, Robert F. *The Origins of the National Recovery Administration*. New York: Fordham University Press, 1976.

Hofstadter, Richard. *The Age of Reform: From Bryan to F.D.R.* New York: Vintage Books, 1955.

————. *The Progressive Historians.* New York: Vintage Books, 1968.

————. *Social Darwinism in American Thought.* Boston: Beacon Press, 1971.

Hogan, William. *Economic History of the Iron and Steel Industry in the United States.* 3 vols. Lexington, Mass.: Lexington Books, 1971.

Holmes, Oliver Wendell, Jr. *Collected Legal Papers.* New York: Peter Smith, 1952.

————. *The Mind and Faith of Justice Holmes.* Ed. Max Lerner. New York: Modern Library, 1954.

Holt, James. "The New Deal and the American Anti-Statist Tradition." In *The New Deal: The National Level,* ed. John Braeman, Robert H. Bremner, and David Brody. Columbus: Ohio State University Press, 1975.

Hoover, Herbert C. *The Challenge to Liberty.* New York: Schribner's, 1934.

Horowitz, Donald. *The Courts and Social Policy.* Washington, D.C.: The Brookings Institution, 1977.

Irons, Peter. *The New Deal Lawyers.* Princeton: Princeton University Press, 1982.

Jacobsohn, Gary J. *Pragmatism, Statesmanship, and the Supreme Court.* Ithaca, N.Y.: Cornell University Press, 1977.

————. *The Supreme Court and the Decline of Constitutional Aspiration.* Totowa, N.J.: Rowman & Littlefield, 1986.

Johnson, Hugh S. *The Blue Eagle from Egg to Earth.* New York: Greenwood Press, 1968.

Johnson, James P. *The Politics of Soft Coal: The Bituminous Industry from World War I Through the New Deal.* Urbana: University of Illinois Press, 1979.

Kagan, Robert. *Regulatory Justice.* New York: Russell Sage Foundation, 1978.

Kairys, David, ed. *The Politics of Law: A Progressive Critique.* New York: Pantheon Books, 1982.

Karl, Barry. *Executive Reorganization and Reform in the New Deal.* Chicago: University of Chicago Press, 1963.

Kelly, Alfred; Winfred A. Harbison, and Herman Bells. *The American Constitution.* 6th ed. New York: Norton, 1983.

Kloppenberg, James. *Uncertain Victory.* Oxford: Oxford University Press, 1986.

Kohlmeier, Louis M., Jr. *The Regulators.* New York: Harper & Row, 1969.

Kolko, Gabriel. *The Triumph of Conservatism: A Reinterpretation of American History, 1900–1916.* Chicago: Quadrangle Books, 1963.

Kristol, Irving. *Two Cheers for Capitalism.* New York: Mentor, 1978.

Lasch, Christopher. "Donald Richberg and the Idea of a National Interest." Master's thesis, Columbia University, 1955.

Lear, Linda. *Harold L. Ickes: The Aggressive Progressive, 1874–1933.* New York: Garland, 1981.

Leuchtenburg, William E. *Franklin D. Roosevelt and the New Deal.* New York: Harper & Row, 1963.

————. "The New Deal and the Analogue of War." In *Change and Continuity in Twentieth-Century America,* ed. John Braeman, Robert H. Bremner, and David Brody. New York: Harper & Row, 1964.

Lorwin, Lewis L., and Arthur Wubnig. *Labor Relations Boards.* Washington, D.C.: The Brookings Institution, 1935.

Loth, David. *Swope of G.E.* New York: Simon & Schuster, 1958.

Lowi, Theodore, J. *The End of Liberalism.* 2d ed. New York: Norton, 1979.

————. *The Personal President: Power Invested, Promise Unfulfilled.* Ithaca, N.Y.: Cornell University Press, 1985.

———. *The Politics of Disorder.* New York: Basic Books, 1971.

Lustig, R. Jeffrey. *Corporate Liberalism: The Origins of Modern American Political Theory, 1890–1920.* Berkeley and Los Angeles: University of California Press, 1982.

Lyon, Leverett S.; Paul T. Homan; Lewis L. Lorwin; George Terborgh; Charles L. Dearing; and Leon C. Marshall. *The National Recovery Administration.* Washington, D.C.: The Brookings Institution, 1935.

McCann, Michael W. *Taking Reform Seriously: Perspectives on Public Interest Liberalism.* Ithaca, N.Y.: Cornell University Press, 1986.

McConnell, Grant. *Private Power and American Democracy.* New York: Vintage Books, 1966.

McCraw, Thomas. *Prophets of Regulation.* Cambridge, Mass.: Belknap Press. 1984.

———. "Rethinking the Trust Question." In *Regulation in Perspective,* ed. Thomas McCraw. Cambridge, Mass.: Harvard University Press, 1981.

———. "With Consent of the Governed: SEC's Formative Years." *Journal of Policy Analysis and Management* 1 (1982): 346–370.

McDowell, Gary L. *Equity and the Constitution: The Supreme Court, Equitable Relief, and Public Policy.* Chicago: University of Chicago Press, 1982.

McNatt, Emmett B. "Organized Labor and the Recovery Act." *Michigan Law Review* 32 (1934): 780–810.

MacNeil, Neil, and Harold W. Metz. *The Hoover Report, 1953–1955.* New York: Macmillan, 1956.

McQuaid, Kim. "Competition, Cartelization, and the Corporate Ethic." *American Journal of Economics and Sociology* 36 (1977): 417–428.

Marcus, Alfred. "Environmental Protection Agency." In *The Politics of Regulation,* ed. James Q. Wilson. New York: Basic Books, 1980.

Martin, Benjamin, and Everett Kassalow, eds. *Labor Relations in Advance Industrial Societies: Issues and Problems.* Washington, D.C.: Carnegie Endowment for International Peace, 1980.

Mashaw, Jerry L. *Due Process in the Administrative State.* New Haven: Yale University Press, 1985.

Mayers, Lewis, ed. *The Handbook of NRA Laws, Regulations, and Codes.* Washington, D.C.: Federal Codes, 1933.

Melnick, R. Shep. *Regulation and the Courts.* Washington D.C.: The Brookings Institution, 1983.

Milkis, Sidney. "Franklin D. Roosevelt and the Transcendence of Partisan Politics." *Political Science Quarterly* 100 (1985): 479–504.

Moley, Raymond. *After Seven Years.* New York: Harper & Row, 1939.

———. *The First New Deal.* New York: Harcourt, Brace & World, 1966.

Nash, Gerald D. "Experiments in Industrial Mobilization: W.I.B. and N.R.A." *Mid-America* 45 (1963): 157–174.

———. "Franklin D. Roosevelt and Labor: The World War I Origins of Early New Deal Policy." *Labor History* 1 (1960): 39–52.

———. *United States Oil Policy, 1890–1964.* Westport, Conn.: Greenwood Press, 1968.

Nathan, Richard P. *The Administrative Presidency.* New York: John Wiley, 1983.

Nordhauser, Norman. *The Quest for Stability: Domestic Oil Regulation, 1917–1935.* New York: Garland, 1979.

Ohl, John Kennedy. *Hugh S. Johnson and the New Deal*. Dekalb: Northern Illinois University Press, 1985.

Olson Jr., Mancur. *The Logic of Collective Action*. Cambridge, Mass.: Harvard University Press, 1965.

Palamountain, Joseph C., Jr. *The Politics of Distribution*. Cambridge, Mass.: Harvard University Press, 1955.

Patterson, James T. *Congressional Conservatism and the New Deal*. Lexington: University of Kentucky Press, 1967.

Perkins, Frances. *The Roosevelt I Knew*. New York: Harper & Row, 1964.

Pious, Richard. *The American Presidency*. New York: Basic Books, 1979.

Plattner, Marc F. "American Democracy and the Acquisitive Spirit." In *How Capitalistic Is the Constitution?* ed. Richard A. Goldwin and William A Schambra. Washington D.C.: American Enterprise Institute, 1982.

Pohlman, H. L. *Justice Oliver Wendell Holmes and Utilitarian Jurisprudence*. Cambridge, Mass.: Harvard University Press, 1984.

Pound, Roscoe. *An Introduction to the Philosophy of Law*. New Haven: Yale University Press, 1954.

———. "Mechanical Jurisprudence." *Columbia Law Review* 8 (1908): 605–623.

———. *The Spirit of the Common Law*. Boston: Marshall Jones, 1921.

Prothro, James. *The Dollar Decade: Business Ideas in the 1920s*. Baton Rouge: Louisiana State University Press, 1954.

Purcell, Edward A., Jr. *The Crisis of Democratic Theory: Scientific Naturalism and the Problem of Value*. Lexington: University Press of Kentucky, 1973.

Rabkin, Jeremy. "Bureaucratic Idealism and Executive Power: A Perspective on *The Federalist*'s View of Public Administration." In *Saving the Revolution: The Federalist Papers and the American Founding*, ed. Charles R. Kesler. New York: Free Press, 1987.

Radosh, Ronald, "The Myth of the New Deal." In *A New History of Leviathan*, ed. Ronald Radosh and Murray N. Rothbard. New York: E. P. Dutton, 1972.

Radosh, Ronald, and Murray N. Rothbard. *A New History of Leviathan*. New York: E. P. Dutton, 1972.

Ranney, Austin. *Curing the Mischiefs of Faction*. Berkeley and Los Angeles: University of California Press, 1975.

Rawls, John. *A Theory of Justice*. Cambridge, Mass.: Harvard University Press, 1971.

Richberg, Donald. "Democratization of Industry." *The New Republic*, 12 May 1917, pp. 49–51.

———. *The Rainbow*. Garden City, N.Y.: Doubleday, Doran, 1936.

———. *Tents of the Mighty*. New York: Willett, Clark & Colby, 1930.

Robinson, Maurice H. "The Gary Dinner System: An Experiment in Cooperative Price Stabilization." *Southwestern Political and Social Science Quarterly* 7 (1926): 137–161.

Roos, Charles F. *NRA Economic Planning*. New York: Da Capo Press, 1971.

Roosevelt, Franklin D. *Looking Forward*. London: William Heinemann, 1933.

———. *On Our Way*. New York: John Day, 1934.

———. *The Public Papers and Addresses of Franklin D. Roosevelt*. Edited by Samuel Rosenman. 13 vols. New York: Random House, 1938.

Rudolph, Frederick. "The American Liberty League, 1934–1940." *American Historical Review* 56 (1950): 19–33.

Rumble, Wilfrid E., Jr. *American Legal Realism*. Ithaca, N.Y.: Cornell University Press, 1968.

Salisbury, Robert H. "Why No Corporatism in America?" In *Trends Toward Corporatist Intermediation*, ed. Philippe Schmitter and Gerhard Lehmbruch. Beverly Hills, Calif.: Sage Publications, 1979.

Scalia, Antonin. "Back to Basics: Making Law Without Making Rules." *Regulation*, July–August 1981, pp. 25–28.

Schaefer, David. "Theodore Lowi and the Administrative State." Paper presented at the 1986 Annual Meeting of the American Political Science Association, Washington D.C., September 1986.

Schambra, William A. "The Roots of the American Public Philosophy." *The Public Interest*, no. 67 (1982): 36–48.

Schlesinger, Arthur M., Jr. *The Age of Jackson*. Boston: Little, Brown, 1946.

———. *The Age of Roosevelt: The Coming of the New Deal*. Boston: Houghton Mifflin, 1959.

———. *The Age of Roosevelt: The Crisis of the Old Order, 1919–1933*. Boston: Houghton Mifflin, 1957.

———. *The Age of Roosevelt: The Politics of Upheaval*. Boston: Houghton Mifflin, 1960.

Schmitter, Philippe C. "Still the Century of Corporatism?" In *Trends Toward Corporatist Intermediation*, ed. Philippe Schmitter and Gerhard Lehmbruch. Beverly Hills, Calif.: Sage Publications, 1979.

Schnitzer, Martin. *Contemporary Government and Business Relations*. Boston: Houghton Mifflin, 1983.

Schuck, Peter H. "Litigation, Bargaining, and Regulation." *Regulation*, July–August 1979, pp. 26–34.

Seltzer, Alan. "Woodrow Wilson as 'Corporate-Liberal': Toward a Reconsideration of Left Revisionist Historiography." *Western Political Quarterly* 30 (1977): 183–212.

Siegel, Fred. "Is Archie Bunker Fit to Rule? or, How Immanuel Kant Became One of the Founding Fathers." *Telos* 69 (1986): 9–29.

Silver, Thomas B. *Coolidge and the Historians*. Durham, N.C.: Carolina Academic Press, 1982.

Skocpol, Theda. "Political Responses to Capitalist Crisis: Neo-Marxist Theories of the State and the Case of the New Deal." *Politics and Society* 10 (1980): 155–201.

Skocpol, Theda, and Kenneth Finegold. "State Capacity and Economic Intervention in the Early New Deal." *Political Science Quarterly* 97 (1982): 255–278.

Skowronek, Stephen. *Building a New American State: The Expansion of National Administrative Capacities, 1877–1920*. Cambridge, Eng.: Cambridge University Press, 1982.

Stigler, George J. *The Organization of Industry*. Homewood, Ill.: Irwin, 1968.

Stone, Alan. *Economic Regulation and the Public Interest: The Federal Trade Commission in Theory and Practice*. Ithaca, N.Y.: Cornell University Press, 1977.

Story, Joseph. *Commentaries on Equity Jurisprudence*. 3d ed. 2 vols. Boston: Little, Brown, 1842.

Strout, Cushing. *The Pragmatic Revolt in American History: Carl Becker and Charles Beard*. Ithaca, N.Y.: Cornell University Press, 1958.

Summers, Robert Samuel. *Instrumentalism and American Legal Theory*. Ithaca, N.Y.: Cornell University Press, 1982.

Sunquist, James. *Dynamics of the Party System.* Washington, D.C.: The Brookings Institution, 1973.

Swope, Gerald. *The Swope Plan.* New York: Business Bourse, 1931.

Taggart, Herbert. "Minimum Prices Under the NRA." *Michigan Business Studies,* vol. 3, no 2. Ann Arbor: University of Michigan Press, 1936.

Thatch, Charles. *The Creation of the Presidency, 1775–1789.* Baltimore: Johns Hopkins University Press, 1969.

Truman, David. *The Governmental Process.* 2d ed. New York: Alfred A. Knopf, 1971.

Tugwell, Rexford G. *The Democratic Roosevelt: A Biography of Franklin D. Roosevelt.* Baltimore: Penguin Books, 1957.

———. *The Industrial Discipline and the Governmental Arts.* New York: Arno Press, 1977.

———. *In Search of Roosevelt.* Cambridge, Mass.: Harvard University Press, 1972.

U.S. Bureau of the Census. *Historical Statistics of the United States: Colonial Times to 1957.* Washington, D.C.: Government Printing Office, 1960.

Urofsky, Melvin I. *Big Steel and the Wilson Administration.* Columbus: Ohio State University Press, 1969.

Vadney, Thomas E. *The Wayward Liberal: A Political Biography of Donald Richberg.* Lexington: University Press of Kentucky, 1970.

Van Hise, Charles R. *Concentration and Control: A Solution of the Trust Problem in the United States.* New York: Arno Press, 1973.

Verkuil, Paul. "The Emerging Concept of Administrative Procedure." *Columbia Law Review* 78 (1978): 258–329.

Warwick, Paul. *The French Popular Front: A Legislative Analysis.* Chicago: University of Chicago Press, 1977.

Watkins, Myron. *Oil: Stabilization or Conservation.* New York: Harper & Brothers, 1937.

Weinstein, James. *The Corporate Ideal in the Liberal State, 1900–1918.* Boston: Beacon Press, 1969.

Weinstein, Michael M. *Recovery and Redistribution Under the NIRA.* Amsterdam: North-Holland, 1980.

West, William F. *Administrative Rulemaking: Politics and Processes.* Westport, Conn.: Greenwood Press, 1985.

White, Morton. *Social Thought in America: The Revolt Against Formalism.* Boston: Beacon Press, 1957.

Wiebe, Robert H. *The Search for Order, 1877–1920.* New York: Hill & Wang, 1967.

Williamson, René de Visme. *The Politics of Planning in the Oil Industry Under the Code.* New York: Harper & Brothers, 1936.

Willoughby, William F. *Government Organization in War-Time and After.* New York: Appleton-Century, 1919.

Wilson, James Q. *Political Organizations.* New York: Basic Books, 1973.

Wilson, William. "How the Chamber of Commerce Viewed the NRA: A Re-examination." *Mid-America* 44 (1962): 95–108.

Wilson, Woodrow. *A Crossroads of Freedom: The 1912 Campaign Speeches of Woodrow Wilson.* Edited by John Wells Davidson. New Haven: Yale University Press, 1956.

Woll, Peter. *American Bureaucracy.* 2d ed. New York: Norton, 1977.

Index

Nondelegation doctrine, 2, 4, 292
Nordhauser, Norman, 173–174
Norris-LaGuardia Act of 1932, 232
Nye, Senator, 157

Ogburn, Charlton, 253
Oil and Gas Journal, 207
Oil industry, 173–174
  antitrust actions against, 197–198, 202
  cartelization of, 120, 192–202, 206
  codes of fair trade, 184–191
  conclusions about, 224, 225
  cutthroat competition in, 175
  federal intervention, necessity of, 181–183
  federal oil legislation, 202–205
  Gasoline Equalization Committee, 199
  hot (illegally produced) oil, 181–182, 185,
    193, 201–202
  independent regulatory commissions, 180
  Interior Department as supervisor for, 120,
    186, 189–190, 191, 193, 195
  lease and agency agreements, 191–192
  marketing agreement, 197
  market structure, 176
  martial law for, 180–181
  National Petroleum Agency (gasoline
    equalizing pool), 197–198
  NIRA, support for, 182–184
  NRA's demise, response to, 207
  overabundance problems, 175
  price-fixing issue, 179, 184–186, 194–197
  production quotas for refiners, 198–201
  self-regulation problems, 175–176
  state v. federal controls, 176–181, 182
  trade associations, 176
  vertical integration controversy, 191–192
Oliphant, Herman, 37, 46
Open price systems, 110–112, 150
Organizational revolution historiography, 71–73

Palamountain, Joseph, Jr., 173
Panama Refining Company v. Ryan, 193, 201,
  202, 290
Parrington, Vernon, 16
Patten, Simon, 77
Peak associations, 19, 21, 131
Peek, George, 99, 122
Peirce, Charles Sanders, 17
Peripheral businesses:
  cartelization by, 108
  center firms, complaints about, 165–168
  codes of fair trade, attitude toward
    enforcement of, 155–156, 162–168
  cooperation among, 156
  credit crunch, 153, 154
  definition of, 146
  dissatisfaction with NRA policies, 149,
    153–157, 159, 166–168
  labor interests, conflict with, 154
  NRA, surveys of attitudes toward, 162–168
  NRA policies helpful to, 157–158, 159,
    172–174, 218–219

NRA policies injurious to, 153–155
NRA's record on, 152, 303–304
open price systems, use of, 150
revisionist perspective on, 152–153,
  157–158, 173
of steel industry, 211, 218–219
support for NRA policies, 147–148,
  151–152, 159
trade association movement and, 150–151
Tugwell's views on, 78
types of, 147
Perkins, Frances, 86, 262–263, 274, 286
Personal President, The (Lowi), 297
Petroleum Administration Board (PAB), 187,
  188–189, 190, 195, 199, 203, 204
Pew, J. Howard, 145
Pinchot, Gifford, 62
Planning and Coordination Committee
  (P&CC), 187–191, 194, 195, 196,
  198, 203, 204
Pluralist historiography:
  brokered-state interpretation of NRA, 23–24,
    26–27, 261–269
  brokered-state interpretation of NRA labor
    policy, 269–281
  classical liberal economics and, 6
  corporatism, perspective on, 6, 13, 16–17
  first and second New Deals, interpretation
    of, 282–288
  Lowi's criticisms of, 10–11, 16
  pluralist theory, development of, 5
  Roosevelt, broker-politician characterization
    of, 261, 262–265, 283–284
  Roosevelt's break with business, 284–286
  Roosevelt's support for Section 7a of NIRA,
    266–269
Political reforms of the 1970s, 317
Politics of Soft Coal (Johnson), 169
Pound, Roscoe, 16, 34, 35, 36, 46, 48–50
Power trust, 126
Pragmatic jurisprudence, 33–34
  a priori principles, beliefs on, 43
  common law, response to, 44–45
  empirical approach to the law, 38–39
  flexibility in judicial interpretation, 41–44,
    45
  legal realism, 37–38, 39–40, 41
  making and applying law, skepticism of
    distinction between, 47–49
  mechanical jurisprudence, opposition to,
    34–36, 38–39
  natural rights jurisprudence, comparison
    with, 41–43
  precedent skepticism, 44–45
  rationality, emphasis on, 39
  rule of law undermined by, 44
  rule skepticism, 39–40
  "rules of thumb," 40
  separation of powers and, 47–49
  social sciences, guidance from, 46–47
  sociological jurisprudence, 34–36, 48

Library of Congress Cataloging-in-Publication Date

Brand, Donald Robert, 1948–
   Corporatism and the rule of law.

   Bibliography: p.
   Includes index.
   1. United States. National Recovery Administration.   2. Trade regulation—United States.
   3. Rule of law—United States.   4. Corporate state.   I. Title.
KF6011.B73   1988   353.0083   88-7167
ISBN 0-8014-2169-1 (alk. paper)
ISBN 0-8014-9495-8 (pbk.: alk. paper)